The Children o

An Awakening

Order this book online at www.trafford.com
or email orders@trafford.com

Most Trafford titles are also available at major online book retailers.

Note for Librarians: A cataloguing record for this book is available from Library
and Archives Canada at www.collectionscanada.ca/amicus/index-e.html

Printed in Victoria, BC, Canada.

ISBN: 9781-4269-1046-3

*Our mission is to efficiently provide the world's finest, most comprehensive
book publishing service, enabling every author to experience success.
To find out how to publish your book, your way, and have it available
worldwide, visit us online at www.trafford.com*

Trafford rev. 8/14/09

TrafFord www.trafford.com
PUBLISHING®

North America & international
toll-free: 1 888 232 4444 (USA & Canada)
phone: 250 383 6864 ♦ fax: 250 383 6804 ♦ email: info@trafford.com

The Children of Light

~~~~ BOOK ONE ~~~~

An Awakening

By

Heather Krenk

Edited by: Tara Truss

To the future.

May it be light.

Illuminated by those willing to stand.

Willing to lead.

Preface

My daughter slammed the book, which had engaged her attention for the previous thirty minutes, shut with an explosive sigh.

"What's wrong?" I asked, surprised by the outburst.

"It was just getting good," she lamented, "but then they started to…"

I understood immediately. How many times had this happened to my oldest daughter? She checked out books from our local library, or from the school library, only to return the novels early. Unread.

So many of the books written expressly for children today insult their intelligence. Interspersed with vulgarity, immorality and gratuitous violence, they pull and tear at the fabric which, for so many centuries, has hemmed up our society.

What is to happen when those seams are irreparably torn apart? Where are the innocence and freedom our children once enjoyed?

And so, the writing of this book began…
And turned into a journey.

CONTENTS

Every person on earth has been given gifts.
Talents.
These gifts vary in substance and intensity.
All are here to develop these talents; to use these gifts for a common purpose.
Because they worked diligently, some honed their skills to incredible levels.
Their gifts have followed them here.
Here is where they will be tried.
Here is where they will be tested.
Here is where some of them will rise...
and here is where some of them will fall.

Πάντες ὑμεῖς υἱοὶ φωτός ἐστε καὶ υἱοὶ ἡμέρας. Οὐκ ἐσμὲν νυκτὸς οὐδὲ σκότους.

Ye are all the children of light, and the children of the day:
we are not of the night, nor of darkness.
1 Thessalonians 5:5

Chapter One
Decision Day

October 11, 2009
Shanghai, China

"Nautas, this has already been decided." Branch dropped his head, weary of the fight. It had come to this. He knew precisely what would occur and had been anticipating it for months. But as the experience unfolded, disappointment and sadness threatened to overwhelm him.

"So you say," Nautas spat, his face stone-like. And his eyes. Those eyes that had once been youthful and kind. Those eyes that had listened to half a life-time of secrets and dreams were now filled with resentment and hatred.

"No," began Branch slowly, shaking his head, "so say an overwhelming majority." The frustration he was feeling, emotions he struggled desperately to control, peeked through his words.

Nautas smiled wickedly. Anger, yes, that was good. "I don't care about numbers," began the dark man, turning quickly to face the crowd. "This is not about numbers." His words were harsh and thundered loudly enough for all in the cavernous room to hear. "This—IS—ABOUT—POWER!"

A portion of the audience erupted into applause and began shouting their consent.

"POWER!"

"POWER!"

"POWER!"

Their voices echoed through the massive, domed room in cadence. The air vibrated with a deafening roar. Yes! His army! Nautas slowly raised sweeping arms for silence, savoring the theatrics. As the crowd quieted the dark man turned to face the table of leaders heading up the room. "You see," he began menacingly, "*we* don't understand why you would *sacrifice* us." His challenging visage prompted several people to divert their eyes. Nautas directed his attention toward their leader. "Why would you lose your soldiers, <u>and for what?</u>"

The man to whom Nautas aimed his comments met his gaze, undaunted. The betrayal, the treachery, how could he do this? Branch's soul was suffused with sadness. "Keep trying," he prodded himself, "your brother is still in there and needs you, keep trying."

The leader of the academy pushed back a heavy metal chair from the table, rising deliberately. Light brown shoulder length hair, prematurely streaked with gray, seemed slightly unkempt as if the man had not slept in days. Tired and haggard, his appearance betrayed his thirty two years. The turmoil of the past several weeks had taken a terrible toll. Branch wore khaki pants and a soft-tan turtle neck sweater. This contrasted sharply with Nautas's black suit and traveling cloak. Branch was not a particularly handsome man, but kind eyes immediately revealed the type of person he was; patient, understanding, full of humility. As he stood, the room fell into reverential silence, the air electrified as his gaze shifted from one side of the auditorium to the other. This was a man to be reckoned with. This was a man of quiet power, not a thundering tyrant.

Turning to the right, Branch rounded a stretching wooden table, and planted himself next to Nautas. Both men appraised each other. Nautas filled with hatred and envy, Branch with disappointment and sadness. The men peered into each others eyes.

"It doesn't matter," Nautas said.

"It does matter my brother," Branch replied, their conversation low and private. "Come." It was an invitation, not a command. Spoken softly, with love.

"Why of course little brother," replied Nautas spitefully as the room began spinning around them. In a burst of light, their surroundings flashed out of sight.

A thousand childhood memories. A thousand shared secrets. A thousand days of play, and nights of laughter and innocence.

The dark man doubled over slightly in pain. "No. No more," he tore himself away. "It doesn't matter. That is over."

Branch again dropped his head, breathing deeply. "This is your final decision?"

Branch's gaze was still focused on the floor, his question caught Nautas by surprise. The vengeful man smiled haughtily, "you knew I wouldn't change my mind. Why did you even try?"

Nautas's expression changed abruptly from contempt to impatience, and Branch braced himself for the oft proposed request. He did not have to wait long.

"You know I'll remain, know I'll support you." Nautas's voice raised an octave as he fervently attempted to sell his designs, convince his brother of the gross error being made. He grasped Branch by the arm and stared, pleading into his eyes. "*You know that*. It's merely your methods which must change. *You* make the decisions. *You* steer the academy. Just allow me to lead them. Give me a little leeway, that is all I've ever requested. You speak of understanding, of higher ideals, and yet you will not budge. Will not even give an inch. You speak of encouraging thought and input, and yet *my* pleas are ignored."

The proposition was tempting; it always had been. It would prevent the division about to occur. But could he live with himself if he allowed Nautas to... What his brother was capable of, if given power and authority, tore at Branch. When had it happened? When had Nautas become a monster?

He could not waiver. "You know the answer, I have already given it. I can not accept trickery, repression, bribery, slavery, greed, force, murder. That is what you pawn Nautas."

He needed to end this. Needed to salvage as many as possible. Drawing out the fight was of no use. Branch raised his head quickly, locked eyes with the dark man sharing the spotlight, and shook his head. "I would do almost anything to prevent this fracture, but I can not, will not..." A vicious smile spread across Nautas's face as Branch spoke, and the younger man broke off. "Do not pretend Nautas. Not with me. I have always seen your arguments for what they are; a smoke screen camouflaging ulterior motives."

Branch motioned toward the crowd, raising his voice for all to hear. "They must be able to choose, decide for themselves." He was still pleading, still entreating his opponent to join him, to stop this chasm before it grew too large. But in his heart he knew what the reply would be before it was spoken. Although painfully aware of what was coming, the words, once uttered, drove themselves into his being like a jagged dagger.

"Then you have DESTROYED THEM!" Nautas roared, turning from Branch quickly as he flipped the corner of his cloak around himself.

"No," began Branch, holding his stance. "It is not *I* who will harm them…" The words were strong, yet sad and forlorn. As if this harm of which the men were speaking was already known to him. As if he had already witnessed it.

"YOU WILL," countered Nautas, cutting over him, and turning to face his opponent again. "By denying them a strong leader. By allowing them to fumble in the dark instead of leading them! By playing by the rules," The last four words were sputtered in a mocking sing-song intended to degrade. "Instead of getting the job done!"

"I deny them nothing," replied Branch firmly, focusing his gaze on the crowd. Branch tipped his head back as if gathering strength. "You would have them ruled with an iron fist," he stated simply, as if to record the facts of this case. As if to ensure the line was drawn and each person who made their decision would make it knowingly. Would make it well informed. "You would engage in every questionable practice imaginable."

Nautas smiled. The decision would be made this day! He had been waiting so long! "YES!" The exhilaration in the dark man's voice was palpable. "We can accomplish more than any of us can imagine!" Many from the crowd were on their feet, voicing their opinions, mesmerized by what was occurring at the front of the room. Others wore looks of fear and uncertainty as the tumult built.

"NO!" thundered Branch and the crowd fell into strained silence. All of Nautas's followers sank to their seats immediately, cowed by the leader of those who opposed them.

The euphoria which filled Nautas just moments before melted away, resentment from its loss exploding in his mind. Why did they relent? They are weak! They are WEAK!

Some of Branch's supporters who were still standing looked unsure. But a number stood tall, their eyes fixed on Branch, their faces impassioned. They stood defiantly in support of their leader. Defiantly. Branch smiled sadly; they were loosing so many. But his supporters… they were strong.

Those who sided with Nautas began murmuring, casting disparaging glances at those still on their feet in support of Branch. Several sank into their chairs, intimidated. Those goading them snickered and jeered in reply.

"I will not have a conscribed army. I will not support evil," finished Branch.

Nautas laughed wickedly. The disappointment he felt with his followers, his hatred for those who opposed him, his resentment at being belittled by his little brother, all of his dark emotions took form in the noise which emanated from his mouth. "But I will," he spat.

"Your methods are beyond heinous…"

Branch's indictment stung the dark man, and before Branch finished his sentence, Nautas interrupted, "I get the job done!"

"That doesn't matter!" Branch quickly retorted. "It is *how* that job is accomplished."

"YOU!" accused Nautas, rounding on Branch and swinging an arm around to point an accusing finger at the man thwarting his aspirations, "are unwilling to push forward to reach your goal. That is weakness!" The dark man punctuated each of his last three words, by pumping his fist into the air for effect.

"What you propose," countered Branch, "is not strength... it is tyranny."

"It is for the good of the whole," refuted the dark man with a dismissive wave. "You can not dispute that," he challenged loudly.

"I *can* and *will* dispute that if it strips *anyone* of their freedom. *Anyone*."

Nautas winced at the words. He hated them. Hated what they stood for. Hated what they embodied. Hated their supporters. Hated where they would lead. "Freedom," he spat in disgust as if the word left a rancid taste in his mouth, "invariably leads to DESTRUCTION." The final word was screamed red-faced at the crowd. His supporters once again rose to their feet, agitated into action. "It is a proven fact," he finished, turning toward his brother. Poking him in the chest with an index finger, he repeated through clenched teeth, "a proven fact." Nautas breathed heavily, nostrils flaring in anger. Unable to remain still, he fed on the frenzy of emotions barely contained in the vast room. "Allow them to govern themselves, and they govern themselves into oblivion. Just look around the world! The proof supporting my accusations is in action all around us! You want to keep them safe? Take away their ability to decide. If they can not make decisions, they can not falter."

Branch again drew a deep breath, shaking his head. Half truths. That is what his opponent was pawning. How could anyone fall for his lies? "Nautas..." He paused, glancing at his older brother. Although his whole being would have rather done something else, anything else, he knew pressing on was the only viable option.

Branch's attention was drawn into the crowd, his gaze resting upon a beautiful Asian woman standing several rows into the mob. Petite yet strong, her long, black hair cascaded over a bright red and gold waist coat. She appeared to be confused, torn.

"*Anna?*" He reached out to her, entering her thoughts, but met resistance. Which side would she choose? Waiting tentatively several moments, she reluctantly admitted him. "*You're confused,*" he began softly, wanting her to make the decision on her own. She shuttered. "*It's alright,*" he thought soothingly, "*you will do what is right... I believe in you.*" The words seared her conscious. Not wanting to cause any more pain, he withdrew and turned his attention back to the throng of people in front of him.

"Your proposal has already been denied, and yet you continue to rebel. What is your intent?" Branch demanded authoritatively.

Nautas took a surprised step back and appraised his brother condescendingly. He strutted slowly up to Branch and leaned close, whispering in his ear. "You stole the academy from me."

"Nautas, everyone voted."

The dark man continued, deaf to the contradiction. "So now, I will steal your best sillemlem, and then... I will destroy them," he said passionately, pulling back a bit to watch Branch's expression. Hoping to see anger. Fear. Resentment. Sorrow. To his disappointment, his brother's expression did not change, so the dark man pressed on, irritated. "*And* I will hurt you; payment for usurping my authority." No response. Nautas's blood boiled at this lack of retaliation. "But first, I will raise an army to fight against everything you stand for."

Branch was tired. Of the argument. Of the betrayal. Of the treachery. It needed to end. The mass of people in the room were fixed upon the two men, waiting.

"My only intent," began Nautas, now speaking to the crowd, "is to place those who are powerful in positions of authority." His supporters voiced their consent. "My only intent," he continued fervidly, "is to garner the funds necessary to support our organization." The noise increased as confusion, fear, and indecision prowled the room. "My only intent," he bellowed above the din, "is to teach them what is truly important." The tumult was deafening. "MY ONLY INTENT," he finished screaming, "IS TO LEAD THEM!" The words hung in the air, as the crowd was thrown into chaos. Nautas was a mad-man, pacing back and forth, inciting his followers, his fists raised in presumptuous triumph.

Branch stood next to the traitor, holding his ground. People began arguing with each other, heated debates springing up like bubbles in a boiling pot. The quiet man glanced down, trying not to focus on faces. Trying not to take note of who was supporting this evil. It hurt too much. "Who chooses to follow Nautas?" announced Branch abruptly.

The room fell silent as hands were raised. Some quickly, some tentatively. Glances of uncertainty were exchanged, as were looks of disappointment. In that moment, brother was turned against brother. Siblings were torn apart. Best friends were forever separated, and lovers disanointed. A stifling sadness filled the space. Branch scanned the room quickly. It revealed, once again, this group of mutineers was the minority.

Nautas pushed down the resentment he felt, smiling widely and nodding, as if to accept his supporters.

"Then," Branch said definitively, "the separation is complete."

* * *

The office Branch occupied was brightly lit and filled with people. It had been several hours since the final decision was made.

"We are larger, more powerful, and we are in the right!" the austere man standing next to Branch's desk breathed heavily. He was tall and muscled, a serious soldier and fierce friend to Branch. His dark hair, loose and wavy, was wet with sweat. Michael had spent the previous several hours combing the academy, strengthening their supporters. "We should remain here, at the facility."

Branch looked thoughtful, mulling over options. Knowing that making the correct moves from here on out was of paramount importance. "No," he said with finality, "we should leave." Several of the people in the room looked confused, others wore looks of sadness, disappointment, or frustration. Many simply nodded, if not in agreement, then in support of their leader.

"*We* are the majority," pressed the large man. "It is *they* who should leave."

"Force, Michael," Branch interrupted softly, "is not an option at this point."

"*But why?*" Michael questioned, confused.

"Because, my friend," Branch responded sadly, "there are still those who are undecided." His mind flashed to that beautiful face. That face filled with anguish. That face that he believed in. Then others paraded through his mind. The unsure. The struggling.

"The decision was made," countered Michael, shaking his head, "it is done."

"No," corrected Branch, hopefully, "there is still time." He looked up at his closest supporters. Meeting the gaze of several, they each began slowly nodding their consent. "There are still those who will choose good over evil." Dropping his gaze, Branch pressed his fingers to his eyes. He felt a strong hand come to rest on his shoulder. Without looking up, Branch said softly. "I believe in them, Michael."

"All the more reason to stay. To continue recruiting. We can convince more…"

Branch shook his head. "Now that he is operating in the open, Nautas will do anything to retain followers. *Anything*. If we remain…" Branch turned a tortured face toward the large man. "He will destroy those who waver. If we stay, we are a continual threat and he will eliminate anyone who may add to our numbers."

"And if we leave? They will be protected?" It was not a question. Michael was offering a counter argument. If they left, Nautas would still destroy the unsure. That is how Nautas operated. Leaving would not protect anyone.

Branch offered a weary smile. "I understand your thinking, but I know my brother. His numbers are low. If they waiver, he will attempt to regain their loyalty. Not because he values them, but because he needs everyone he can get. To reach his goals requires an army."

The man who had always been an example of obedience and support pursed his lips in thought, then tightened his grip on Branch's neck. "Then we go."

Chapter Two
The Seer

The old, weathered door creaked opened tentatively. Its peeling paint and softened wood evidence of the years it served in the extreme environment of heat, cold and salt spray. Damp morning air intruded unwelcome into the room left exposed by the opening door. Each inch of movement admitted a greater portion of the chilling weather.

The seer stepped resolutely onto the slippery cobblestone path, her bare feet warm against the frigid, unrelenting rock. A building breeze caught hold of her cloak; it billowed in reply, treacherously abandoning its responsibility of offering at least a modicum of protection. Grasping its edges in her smooth strong hands, she halted its retreat and bolstered its confidence.

"There, there," she whispered. "Courage."

Picking her way carefully down the narrow lane, retracing the steps of yesterday, and the day before, and the day before that, she reached the craggy outcropping overlooking the ocean. Angry waves slammed against the shore in their bid to infiltrate the land that always lay just out of reach.

"Evil builds."

The thin covering veiling her head and face slipped in the wind. She allowed it to fall, revealing fine features and long, golden-brown hair. She was an astonishingly compelling woman. Raising her piercing blue eyes slowly and deliberately, she gazed into the murk. Not fear...nor concern. But understanding...calm...sorrow... and perhaps a touch of ferocity flecked her eyes.

The dawn summoned its strength and gathered its forces, glowing first gentle orange then evolving steadily into brilliant red. Building and driving, it burst forth noble and powerful in a sudden explosion of color. The delicate woman stood steadfast between the stunning light and imposing dark, starkly silhouetted by the morning. The bright energy rushed forward, hitting her with force. It bound her clothing to her frame firmly, and a gentle, knowing smile graced her lips. Reinforcements. Inhaling deeply, the seer filled her lungs completely with the warming air. She exhaled, relishing the energy surrounding her, permeating her and every other object it now rested upon.

The darkness screamed its retreat, unwillingly giving way in the face of its enemy. Black fingers clung to the sides of rocks and boulders not yet illuminated by the light.

"Go."

In its last bid for life, the dark relented a bit, melting slowly downward, away from the glorious morning. Taking refuge in the recesses of rocks and crags.

"Depart."

Milky white eyes of evil flashed their hatred at the intruders, narrowing in contempt and resentment. Roaring and grinding his teeth, he spun and fled.

Calm.

The woman closed her eyes. Her mind returned to the gaping jaws of darkness, building, swirling and gaining force in this world. Despair.

Yet there beckoned and twinkled in the gloom: truth and hope. Power and defiance. Goodness and strength. The Children of Light.

Chapter Three
Chicago To Shanghai

October 12, 2009
Chicago, Illinois

"I'll be back in a minute, okay?" Callan looked at her older sister, Alexine, not really sure if she was telling her, or asking permission.

"You can't go by yourself! Anyway, we're getting ready to board." Alexine looked exasperated. Their quick flight from Detroit to Chicago had gone off without a hitch. But the older girl was nervous. Having never traveled internationally, she had no idea what to expect and that unnerved her.

Callan smiled teasingly. Moving her hand up near her face, she curled her fingers slightly, wagging them up and down in a tiny wave, just as their airline escort turned around.

"Uh-uh." The tall, slender brunette shook her head. "We all go together. I'm with you until you board the plane, remember? Never lost a kid yet!"

Callan looked sheepish for a moment, then the three of them joined the throng of people pulsing down the concourse. A few minutes later Callan pushed open the bathroom door. Walking swiftly through the entrance, the little girl pulled up short. There were several people waiting in line. "Good thing they waited outside," thought Callan, noting that two additional people would never have fit in the cramped bathroom. "I hope this moves quickly." Alexine's face flashed in her mind.

A stern looking older woman was eyeing a teenage girl standing at the mirror. Callan could not imagine what was upsetting about the young woman at the mirror. Did the older woman think her skirt was too short? It came to her knees. Perhaps it was the makeup she was applying. "Strange," thought Callan.

A young mother standing in front of Callan held an infant. Bending over to tie a second daughter's shoes, the woman glanced up and smiled. Callan smiled back. Normal people, doing normal things. Why was normal so elusive to Callan? Why didn't she ever feel like she belonged?

Callan walked back through the door more than ten minutes later. The escort and her two charges hurriedly fought their way back toward the gate.

"What took so long?" Alexine shot, once their destination was in sight.

"It was crowded," Callan replied impatiently. When Alexine didn't seem mollified, she added a sarcastic, "sorry!"

The older girl broke into a half smile and shook her head. Her younger, red-headed sister had always pushed limits. This tendency was, in a way, why they were here. She was a special girl, Callan. If she could only learn control, she could be…what? What could she be? Unstoppable? Was that possible? If it was, Callan would get there Alexine thought wryly. Through the sheer exercise of her indomitable, often annoying will.

Born on a beautiful spring afternoon in May, everyone was shocked by Callan's appearance upon her entrance into the world.

"Red?" The midwife had given her mother a quizzical look. "Now, where did that come from?" Both her parents were blond, and her older sister was brunette.

"Mixed up genes," her father finally announced after looking thoughtfully at the little bundle sleeping in his arms. Almost as an afterthought, he murmured, crinkling up his face, "I wonder what's coming up next? Black hair?"

Everyone laughed. But from the very beginning Callan had been...different. It was not just her appearance, she had a personality to match. She was driven, confident, always racing to the next challenge and engaging it with gusto. She had the innate ability to be tough yet gentle, aggressive yet nurturing, confident yet vulnerable. Her family thought of her as fiery; a fiery red-head. In fact, her father nick-named her "Copper-top."

As she grew, her hair softened into blond, but retained those beautiful auburn highlights. "Women pay a lot of money for hair like that!" How many times had people said that about Callan? Family, friends and even complete strangers.

"Now boarding seating group three," announced an airy feminine voice over the loudspeaker.

Their escort hurried the two sisters to the door leading to the jet way. "You two have a great flight, okay?" she gave them one last grin, then stepped back from the entryway.

The younger girl heaved a great sigh. "Well, I'm just amazed we made the flight. Alexine is always making everyone late!"

Alexine let out an exasperated hiss, but softened when she noticed Callan smiling.

They always played this game, and both of them knew it was just that. A game. Alexine enjoyed being "mom" and Callan fit neatly into the "trying pre-teen role."

"I'm a pro-teen," Callan had once remarked, inadvertently mispronouncing the title. Her family roared with laugher but she was oblivious as to why this comment would garner such attention. An explanation regarding the difference between "protein" and "pre-teen" ensued. "Oh," the little red-head shrugged, unfazed by her mistake.

"Have a great flight," said a airline worker in a polite voice as they handed over boarding passes. Alexine smiled in response and the woman at the door returned their ticket stubs.

"53B," read Alexine.

"53C," replied Callan.

Neither of them was looking forward to the fourteen hour flight from Chicago to Shanghai, but it was a necessary annoyance. The people they needed to meet were currently half way around the world. And so, half way around the world they were traveling. So far away from everything they knew. So foreign. But if Callan could find answers, all the frustration would be worthwhile. Alexine was determined to do her part, and getting them both there safely was the first order of business.

"Wouldn't this be nice?" Callan commented as they shuffled through first class, their carry on luggage banging unceremoniously behind them. These passengers had been seated for quite some time and were enjoying pre-flight drinks. They looked like they belonged in first class. A woman with a long, white fur coat, a distinguished man with black hair in an expensive grey suit, an older couple, both of whom were very well tanned. Yes, they all fit in here.

Callan glanced back at Alexine. Her older sister had recently written a phone number in dark blue pen on the front leg of her faded jeans. The little girl giggled.

They would definitely look out of place in first class, and that was fine. Although the front of the aircraft was designed to provide as much comfort as possible, Callan decided she would feel self conscious here.

The first class flight attendant hurried about the cabin smiling and serving. As Callan passed the fur-coat woman, she paused to shift her unruly luggage. The woman wore a clingy black shirt and pants. She was tall, thin, and had very blond hair; it was almost white, and extended past her waist. Her overall appearance was striking.

The woman, who had been reading a fashion magazine, tipped her head back, taking in a full view of Callan. The stranger had, at the same instant, a look of boredom and distaste. Striking, perhaps, but what Callan saw was not beautiful. It was dark.

Callan met her gaze, undaunted and challenging. As their eyes found each other, the little girl instantly wanted to move, wanted to escape that stare. The feeling was powerful; upsetting and infuriating. Confused, she willed herself to take a wobbly step. Stumbling forward, disoriented, the little red-head forced herself to retain control. "Not here! Just keep walking!" Teeth clenched, she fought to stay in her space.

Satisfied, a sinister smile crossed the woman's lips. She returned to her magazine.

Callan continued through the curtain separating first class from economy and shuffled past rows of people caught up in reading, dozing and talking. As quickly as the disquieting feeling had hit her, it left. She dismissed the incident, attributing the odd sensation to stress. Fourteen hours in a plane. Ugh. That was enough to make anyone anxious.

The plane was huge, larger than any she had ever seen, much less boarded. Three sections of seating spanned the width of the aircraft. Three seats sat adjacent to each window, and a center aisle held eight additional spots. The little girl glanced back, noticing a set of stairs leading to an upper level. An upper level?! This aircraft was enormous!

53C... 53C... Upon approaching, she noticed an Asian man sitting in 53A, the window seat. "Hello," Callan smiled. The man glanced up, smiled back, and then nodded his head enthusiastically.

Walking past the row, Callan allowed Alexine to slip into the middle seat, then plopped down herself. Depositing a bulging backpack under the seat in front of her, Callan was thankful to be sitting on the aisle. She had always disliked feeling trapped in any way. Being unable to move unnerved her. This way she could get up whenever she liked.

Alexine put on her earphones, glanced over at Callan, and then shut her eyes.

The little red-head was tired. As other passengers bustled about, stowing carry-ons and finding seat assignments, she fought to keep her own eyes from closing. Within several minutes she had lost the battle.

* * *

It was dark, and something was wrong. She wasn't sure why, but she knew she had to run. No, not run, fly. Get out fast. Callan stumbled to her feet, and pushed off the bed hard.

Whoosh. She was moving quickly, through her bedroom door, then the front door of the house. Long jagged shadows, mammoth trunked and long fingered, leered from front yard trees. Dark and forbidding, they whistled a warning, disapproving of her intrusion. She had to keep going, had to get away. Get away from what lurked in the darkness. It was dangerous, so dangerous. And it was after her. Why?

Whoosh. Callan veered left, traveling toward the driveway. Someplace safe, she had to find someplace safe. The small coop at the edge of the yard stood, silently beckoning. Yes. That's safe. It's dry and warm. The building embodied blissful, sun soaked memories. It was a happy place. Inside the coop in seconds, Callan willed herself to slow and stop. The roosting ducks hissed their disfavor, startled by her sudden arrival.

"It's okay girls, just me," Callan whispered.

She was so tired. The walls of the coop began spinning; the ducks, the walls, the ducks, the walls. She sank to the floor as her eyes rolled involuntarily upward. Safe.

* * *

Callan jumped awake. Jerking sideways, she saw concern etched on Alexine's face.

"You okay?" Alexine whispered, studying her little sister intently.

A flight attendant hurried past the girls, pushing a large beverage cart up the aisle. Reaching her destination, she stepped hard on a breaking lever and the cart steadied.

"Sure, why?" Callan responded innocently, wiping the spit that had spilled out of her open mouth with the back of her hand. Alexine pulled a look of disgust, which Callan completely ignored.

Why did she keep dreaming about that night? It had been the last straw, the reason their mother and father had decided it was time for Callan to find some answers. But why couldn't she let it go? There were plenty of times when Callan...well...flew. Why was *that* time stuck so stubbornly in her subconscious? Creeping through the intervening months to stalk her dreams?

Chapter Four
They can be anywhere

September 25, 2009
Marcellus, Michigan

Her mother, Heidi, had awakened early that morning.

"Something's wrong," she thought, slipping on her robe and slippers then trotting off to search each room of their home.

Alexine was dead to the world in her loft bed, as was typical until noon on the weekend. Walking through the living area, she entered a second bedroom.

Mia and Geoff were both still in their bunk beds, Geoff on top and Mia on bottom, breathing deeply. She stepped back out into the hall and slipped into the last sleeping area.

Hope lay halfway out of the lower bunk bed which sat directly on the floor, her pajama legs pushed up to reveal tiny feet and calves. Although chilly to the touch, she was still sleeping contently. Moving her back onto the bed, then tucking covers around their smallest child, Heidi stood to inspect the upper berth–Callan's bed.

Gone.

Heidi had sensed it the minute she straightened, and panic filled her heart.

The problem with finding a child who can "shift" is that they can be anywhere, especially when they are young.

Making one last thorough search of the house, Heidi stepped outside into the crisp, fall air. The sounds of morning surrounded her. Birds twittered from their penthouse suites, restless for the long flight south. Marsh grasses ebbed and swished in the gentle morning breeze. An occasional car drifted past the house, the noise muffled by the woods separating their home from the road leading to the lake.

"Be still," she closed her eyes and willed herself to quietly ask. "Where is Callan, please." And suddenly she knew.

About a hundred feet off the driveway, behind the garden area, the coop stood stoically. Three ducks milled about the outside run.

"Odd."

Content to sit in their little enclosure, roosting like chickens most of the day, typically the ducks had to be driven out of the small white building. Callan's feathered pets froze as she approached and regarded her closely, their black eyes unblinking.

Walking around the fence, she strode up to the right side of the little shed and opened the door. Heidi could see Callan's white and pink pajamas poking out from beneath a thin layer of straw. She bent down and uncovered her second daughter.

"Callan!"

No movement.

"Callan Marie!"

The girl's eyes fluttered open, she looked around quickly and seemed confused. "What on earth," her mother began in an accusing tone. "Are you trying to give me a heart attack?"

Callan looked sheepish, then remembered. The dark, the danger, the flight, and hiding. "Um, mom, yea, just checking on the ducks." A guilty, unconvincing smile emerged as she stumbled to her feet and began re-arranging hay, giggling nervously.

Her mother raised her eyebrows in disbelief, challenging the little girl to try again.

"I mean," Callan said softly, as if confessing some horrible crime. "I was scared last night, and I…" she trailed off, knowing her mother could complete the sentence and understood perfectly well what happened.

Heidi examined her daughter, trying to decide what to do, how to handle this. She was twelve; so young, but rapidly approaching her teenage years. And this gift she possessed, it wasn't typical. It was *so* powerful. That is what *they* had told her.

Over the years, Heidi learned Callan's gift had the potential to cause a lot of grief. To present myriad dangerous situations. Perhaps finding answers would have to come sooner than later for this little girl. She and her husband, Geoff, had discussed the situation completely on many occasions. This decision had been coming for months.

Heidi stood up, hands on hips, and sighed, "well, it's almost time for breakfast anyway." Smiling down and extending her hand, she pulled Callan to her feet. "Come on, let's get you cleaned up."

Chapter Five
Good News and Bad News

October 12, 2009

"What time is it?" Callan asked, attempting to stifle a yawn.

Her older sister snickered, "that depends on *where* you're talking about. Let's see, it's noon at home, but it's midnight in Shanghai, and I have no idea what time it is where we are right now."

The corner of Callan's mouth twitched upward.

"Because of the fact that I have no idea *where* we are...exactly."

Entertained by Alexine's humorous tirade, Callan dropped her head back and giggled.

"But I do know that I need to get up so..." Alexine motioned for Callan to move.

The younger girl unbuckled her seat belt, swung her legs into the aisle, and stood. "I'll join you on a lap around the cabin." Callan bent over to stretch her legs.

"Let's go to the bathroom first," replied Alexine as she slid across her seat, onto Callan's. Throwing her legs into the walk way, she was finally able to stand.

Callan watched Alexine disentangle herself from their row. "They should call this sardine class, not economy," the little girl muttered under her breath, casting an eye around to ensure no airline personnel were within hearing distance. Aggravating the people feeding her for the duration of the flight seemed an unwise move.

Alexine gave a mirthless laugh, nodding in agreement. Her legs ached from being cramped into the tiny space. When the woman in front of her reclined, Alexine felt as though someone was lying in her lap.

The man occupying the window seat looked relieved as the girls stood. He smiled broadly and began nodding to them, over and over, as he too slid across the seats toward the aisle. Alexine stumbled down the narrow walk way, with Callan following closely behind.

"I wonder if he speaks English," Callan whispered, pulling up close behind her sister. Alexine looked back over her shoulder and shrugged as she slid open the door to a tiny bathroom.

Their lap around the cabin ended too quickly for Callan. "I'm going to stand in back for a few minutes."

Alexine nodded in reply, then took her seat.

There were several groups of people congregated at the rear of the plane. They seemed to be together, taking turns photographing the ground through small, double-paned, semi-frosted windows. What was so interesting? Callan glanced over their shoulders and noted, with a bit of surprise, that all she could see, in every direction, was white. What was it?

"Well, I've got some good news and some bad news."

"What?" Alexine removed her earphones when Callan flopped down beside her.

"Good news and bad news."

"I'm waiting."

"We're flying over Antarctica, did you know that? Ice and snow as far as the eye can see. Anyway, if we crash, the pilots have sub-zero suits so they can walk and get help. Good idea, hey?" Callan nodded hopefully, grinning slyly.

"We're flying over the North Pole?" Surprised, Alexine leaned toward the Asian gentleman to her left in an attempt to look out the window.

"Yea, way to keep up, okay, so the bad news." Callan paused until her older sister turned back toward her. "We'll all freeze to death in a couple of minutes." Callan pulled her lip up in a crooked smile. "Good news, and bad news."

"We're flying over the North Pole?"

Callan wrinkled her brow and shook her head in playful disgust. "I'm going back to watch the students, they're doing some kind of scientific study."

It turned out she was unable to garner any additional information from the people taking pictures and entering data into laptops at the rear of the plane. They were too busy to talk.

The next few hours found Callan becoming increasingly uncomfortable. It didn't seem to matter which way she shifted in her seat, she just could not find a good position in which to sleep. The flight attendant began passing out dinner and she felt herself relax. Food would be a welcome reprieve from the monotony of the flight.

"Chicken with noodles, or beef with rice?" the flight attendant asked.

Their Asian companion nodded at the question, and smiled widely.

"Chicken-or-beef?" the flight attendant repeated.

Slathered in blood red lipstick, her mouth reminded Callan of an out-of-proportion cartoon character's features. She enunciated the words loudly causing several people to turn and stare.

Alexine bowed her head and sighed. "He's not deaf, he doesn't understand you," she thought. "Talking louder isn't going to help."

The man began nodding and smiling again, this time responding in a heavy accent, "beef, beef, shay shay."

Both the girls requested chicken dinners. Although the meal was average, it seemed to taste better than anything Alexine could remember eating recently, simply because it broke the boredom.

As if reading her mind, Callan said, "not bad!" and began to devour her dinner roll. After the flight attendant served drinks and cleared the dinner dishes, the girls fell into a sleepy silence, each lost in their own thoughts. Eventually the in-flight movie line up began playing again and Callan found herself being drawn into story line after story line.

The girls developed a routine; taking several laps around the cabin each time a movie ended. Upon returning to their seats after one stretching session, Callan stared up at the ceiling of the airplane intently.

"You know," she began, "there is no way Uncle James could ever fly to China."

Alexine turned slowly to Callan, studying her as if she were an experiment which had taken an unexpected, surprising and irritating turn. Hour after hour of listening to Callan's thoughts regarding each of the people who walked past their seats, the cockpit crew, school, the weather, the state of the world, and any other subject that popped into her little head, had left Alexine feeling a bit overwhelmed. "What on earth are you talking about now?"

"Claustrophobia," Callan said simply. "There is just no way anyone who is claustrophobic at all could ever ride on a plane for this long. Even I'm starting to get jumpy, it's just not right to be cooped up like this."

Remaining still had always made Callan uncomfortable and Alexine sensed the long flight was pushing the little girl's ability to remain calm. "Well, we'll be landing in a little while," the older girl checked her cell phone for the time. "Like, twenty minutes." Callan seemed buoyed by that thought.

As if on signal, a voice over the loudspeaker announced, "We would like to ask all passengers to return to their seats at this time as we prepare for arrival."

The girls looked at each other with a mixture of exhaustion, relief and excitement.

"I never want to sit in a plane for that long again." Callan adjusted her seat to its upright position and zipped the backpack at her feet.

"Except to get home," her older sister nodded in agreement.

"Yea, to get home." They had not even arrived at their destination, and Callan was already missing the familiar faces of her family and the quiet, small town in which the girls lived.

As they exited the plane, the flight attendant smiled at each passenger and said, "have a wonderful stay in Shanghai," or, "thank you for flying United."

Alexine wondered how she was able to repeat the same greeting, hundreds of times, and still sound sincere. "They must have a class for that," she determined as they exited the plane. It would be a great thing to master; sound and look genuine, even if you are not. She could think of half-a-dozen times that talent would have saved her a lot of trouble.

An airline escort was waiting for them at the gate.

"Hello!" she smiled amicably. "I'm Hermione."

Alexine and Callan glanced at each other in surprise. Hermione was not a traditional Chinese name. In fact, the only person they knew named Hermione was a character in their favorite book series.

"Hello," the girls replied in unison.

Their escort seemed pleased. "Well, let's get going then."

They cleared customs in a matter of minutes, which surprised Alexine. Having never been through the procedure previously, she expected it to take a bit more time. The agents simply took her "customs slip" and passport, studied each intently for several minutes as they glanced back and forth from the papers to Alexine, then snappishly stamped them twice with a loud THUNK. Pushing them through a small hole cut in the glass separating them from their applicants, they looked left to the next person in line. Alexine stood smiling, anticipating something more. But the agents impatiently waved her on and beckoned for the next customer. Callan's experience was similar.

Entering the airport terminal, Alexine immediately spotted an Asian gentleman holding a placard. "KOVAR" was sketched in bright red letters across its surface. He was older, probably in his fifties, and slightly shorter than she. The man looked wrinkly, leathery and worn, like a favorite glove that had seen years of use. She also thought he looked kind. Alexine could imagine him laughing at his grandchildren, and holding hands with his wife. His clothes were plain and clean; brown dress pants and an un-tucked, white button-up dress shirt.

"That's strange." She was expecting a woman to pick them up. What was her name again? Anna? No, that wasn't it. Alexine walked up to the man to investigate as their escort helped Callan manage her luggage. As she approached, she smiled at him. "Kovar?"

The man pointed to the sign and raised his eyebrows. He seemed to be asking if this sign he was holding, with these strange markings on it, meant anything to her.

She nodded and placed her hand in the middle of her chest. "Kovar," she replied. The man looked around as if searching for something. When Callan and Hermione pulled up beside them several seconds later, the man seemed satisfied and smiled broadly.

"I think he wanted to make sure we were both here," Alexine replied to Callan's inquisitive look. "But I thought we were supposed to be meeting a woman."

"Mr. Chow!" Hermione bowed smoothly several times to the man holding the placard. She spoke to the man in Mandarin as he jerked his head forward quickly in acknowledgement.

"This is Mr. Chow," Hermione explained as the girls eyed her expectantly. "He will take you to your contact here in Shanghai. Do not worry," she added, gesturing to the pleasant looking man. "Mr. Chow is a very nice man. Very good driver. Have a pleasant stay in China."

Alexine and Callan thanked Hermione, then followed Mr. Chow out of the terminal into the cool fall afternoon.

"I'm glad customs didn't take forever," Alexine commented as they drove away from the airport. "But I expected…I don't know…more…I guess." She turned to look out the window.

Callan laughed as the cab accelerated and abruptly switched lanes. It was so like her older sister. Always analyzing everything. Always over-thinking the situation.

"Well," the little girl opened her eyes wide, as if in shock, "after Aunt Ruthann's stories about customs in Mexico, I'm glad it went quickly. Can you imagine, three hours of standing in line?" She placed her hands around her own throat and began to mimic throttling herself. As she rolled her eyes upward and stuck out her tongue, Alexine's shoulders shook involuntarily in a tired chuckle.

"Nice," the older girl commented sarcastically, still laughing.

Traffic was thick on the two lane highway. Cars continually stopped and began moving again for no apparent reason. The girls gazed out the windows, soaking in the scenes rolling past.

To Alexine's right, three adults were riding what looked to be some type of moped on the curb of the road, beside the cab. A man was driving, and two women were crammed behind him. Alexine cringed as she realized there were actually four people on the bike. The woman in the middle had her left arm wrapped around a baby's waist. The child appeared to be sleeping and was dangling over the side of the moped, doubled over, it's face hidden from view. He or she could not have been more than two years old.

"That is so dangerous," Alexine thought as they passed. But no one else gave the group a second look.

Alexine glanced to her left and noticed a wide median divided them from the two lanes of traffic traveling in the opposite direction. People were busy picking up garbage, weeding and planting flowers or shrubbery. There were so many workers! Alexine wondered if they were paid for their service or if these tasks were compulsory. How did that work in China?

The gardeners all wore similar yellow outfits and wide, round straw hats which came to a point at the top. Most of them seemed intent on their duties and the result was impressive. Mile after mile of well kept garden areas graced the median into the city.

This contrasted sharply with what lie to her right. As if mirroring the polar opposite of the garden's beauty, there was mile after mile of stark, white, impersonal, apartment-type buildings looming over hundreds of people going about their daily lives. Each window in each building had a metal rod which extended out approximately six feet. Laundry hung on the rods, swaying haphazardly in the afternoon breeze.

The effect of the scene was powerful. In America, this would most definitely be considered a dilapidated slum area. But the people milling around were dressed nicely and moving quickly. They were busy. No one was loitering, no one was standing about, this was not a dead end existence. This was normal.

"Amazing," was all Alexine could manage to come up with.

Callan folded her arms, laid her head against the back of the seat, and fell asleep. Each time Alexine spotted something she found intensely interesting, she nudged the little girl. But by the time Callan awoke the scene had passed, replaced by a fresh one ready to be experienced. Her little sister didn't seem interested, so Alexine sat back and enjoyed the exotic surroundings.

Small trucks piled high with goods, their heavy burdens teetering. Buses crammed with passengers, some sitting, many standing, swaying as the bus surged or lurched. Almost every Asian person that caught sight of Alexine stared unflinching and unrepentant into the window of the cab. Feeling extraordinarily out of place, she diverted her eyes, avoiding their unrelenting curiosity. An overwhelming pity for fish trapped in bowls welled up inside her.

Eventually massive metal cranes loomed in the distance. There were so many littering the landscape the scene seemed surreal. Like a spoiled child's sandbox, filled with construction toys that could easily occupy a hundred children for hours. Alexine remembered reading somewhere there were more cranes in Shanghai than in any other place in the world. That statistic now towered incarnate in front of her.

Passing over a bridge, she could tell they were entering the city. Shanghai, "whore of the orient", lay spread out before them. The city's sordid history earned it that nick-name. So much turmoil, so much evil had flourished here. After reading about this place, it seemed strange to actually be here, thousands of miles from home.

"Okay, time to get up," Alexine shook Callan by the shoulders.

"Yea, yea, I'm not sleeping."

"We must be getting close." She tried to remember the name of the river that separated the old section of Shanghai from the new.

Callan looked around, yawned and stretched as the cab driver exited the freeway, entering the narrow streets of downtown. They were surrounded by small cars, small trucks piled high with various objects, and hundreds of people on bicycles and mopeds.

Although Alexine was sure there were traffic laws, they did not seem to be obeyed or enforced. Somehow, hundreds of vehicles were able to move, flow and function with no noticeable rules or guidelines. The city existed, without realizing that, existence in it's current state, was a blaring impossibility.

As the cab worked it's way toward their destination, Alexine found herself attempting to memorize the route. Suddenly feeling leery, it was a bid to gain control over the situation. The older girl loathed depending on other people, especially when she was unsure if she could trust them. Trust was sometimes a sticky thing.

Realizing quickly she could never remember street names that failed to resemble any familiar words, she searched for objects to mark their path. A book store, a shop with roast duck hanging in the window, a Pizza Hut restaurant, left at the big clothing store complete with neon sign. She repeated the objects over in her head: book, duck, pizza, neon. Just as the landmarks were becoming jumbled in her memory, the direct result of exhaustion, their cab came to an abrupt stop and the cab driver clicked a button on the meter. He pointed to the fare which read 185.

"Whoa, that's expensive," Callan let out a high whistle.

"Yuan," responded Alexine, "not dollars."

"Oh yea," Callan laughed, recalculating. "Whoa, that's cheap!"

Alexine paid the cabbie who was excitedly pointing to a small business, obviously their destination. That uneasy feeling returned, and she suddenly felt strangely vulnerable. They had gotten into a car with a complete stranger. He was dropping them off on a busy street in a huge city half way around the world. Neither of them spoke Chinese, and they knew no one here.

Momentary panic overtook Alexine and she pushed down an urge to refuse to get out of the car. "You're just being silly," she told herself, "come on now, function." Looking back at the cabbie, she stumbled over her words. "Yes...uh... sure. And thanks...um...I mean...shay shay."

Callan gave her sister a puzzled look and Alexine managed a half smile, beginning to relax a bit.

"Sure means yes, and shay shay means thank you. I studied up a bit. You know, it wouldn't hurt you to..." she stopped short. Callan had tossed her a look of boredom, opened the door, and exited the cab.

Letting out a loud sigh, she too opened her door and was engulfed by the busiest, noisiest, dirtiest sidewalk she could have ever imagined in her wildest dreams. She paused mid-breath, forcing herself to inhale only the air which was absolutely necessary, a putrid smell filling her lungs and stinging her throat. They had arrived. Shanghai.

Chapter Six
A Disquieting Introduction

A dragon chime banged against the door emitting a clunking jingle as Alexine and Callan entered the small shop. Shelves of various herbs, plants, bottles, books and even a few cheap trinkets lined the dirty walls of the dimly lit store. She could not imagine anyone shopping here.

A middle aged Asian woman was seated in a bar-stool type chair at the back of the room. She balanced what appeared to be a small computer on her lap, and was typing something into a matching attached keyboard. Alexine had never seen such a small device.

The woman was about Alexine's height, five foot four, slim, and wore dark dress pants and a grey shirt. Alexine estimated she was probably in her early thirties. Shiny, black, mid-length hair hung loose in a curtain, hiding her face from view. The woman looked up quickly, flicking a glance at each girl in turn.

"Just a minute please."

Callan was a bit surprised the woman did not have an Asian accent. Her English was flawless. Aside from this observation however, there was nothing noteworthy regarding the quick exchange. The little girl smiled in response.

In marked contrast, the moment their hostess made eye contact with Alexine, the very second they appraised each other, the older girl experienced a sense of disquiet which threatened to overwhelm her. She felt intruded upon, threatened. Panicking, she fell back several steps in retreat, colliding with Callan.

"Hey!" the little girl protested, "what…" But Callan fell silent when she saw the look on Alexine's face. Puzzled, her eye quickly moved from Alexine to the seated woman. She could have sworn a glimpse of concern flashed across the woman's face, but the next instant it vanished, leaving her wondering if it had been imagined.

Dazed, Alexine attempted to regain control by fingering several items on the shelves. Callan quickly followed suit.

"What's wrong?" she whispered when the woman walked into a back room.

"I…don't…know…." The older girl was still struggling to regain her sense of balance. In addition to feeling she had been violated in some way, Alexine was also struck by the realization that she *knew* this woman. But how could that be possible?

The woman re-entered the front room and confidently strode toward the girls, smiling and extending her right hand in greeting. Callan could not help but admire her sense of surety, and shook their hostess's hand quickly. "We're here to meet Mr. Rippinger." Callan met the woman's gaze boldly, wary as a result of Alexine's strange reaction.

"Ah, yes, I have been waiting for your arrival." The woman bent over slightly in a half-bow. "I am Annalynn and apologize for not meeting you at the airport. I had to take care of something quickly." Annalynn focused her attention on Callan. The little red-head. How long had it been since she saw her last?

Glancing around at the empty shop, Alexine assumed the duty which prevented this woman from picking them up had nothing to do with this store. It was deserted. "The driver found us right away. There were no problems."

Annalynn smiled for the first time; this was a remarkably beautiful woman.

Bright green eyes contrasted sharply with her golden skin and fine features. She reminded Alexine of a modern version of Asian aristocracy she had once seen in a book. Petite and graceful, regal in a way.

Regaining her composure, Alexine decided perhaps she had imagined the previous exchange. She shook it off, returned the smile and grasped the woman's hand firmly. "I guess we're a little tired, that flight is a killer." That had to be the answer: exhaustion.

The woman looked puzzled for a moment, then laughed. "A killer...it is not enjoyable...I agree...much too long."

They had been clasping hands throughout the entire exchange and suddenly this felt very awkward. Alexine released her grip and turned toward the shelves. "Is this Mr. Rippinger's shop?" she asked, searching for something to discuss.

The woman nodded absently. "One of them." Reaching for a waist coat, she slipped it smoothly on. "I was just heading out to lunch." Annalynn flicked off the lights. "If you would like to join me, I can drop you off at the academy afterward."

Alexine and Callan looked down at the baggage laying at their feet.

"Just leave your luggage here, I'll have someone drop it off for you."

A short cab ride later found them sitting on a nearby rooftop dining area, the Bund rolling out below. This area of Shanghai, bordered by the Huangpu river, pulsed rich with history.

Alexine excused herself from the table to peer over the edge of the railing. Across the river lay Puxi, the newly developed area of Shanghai. A haven for business and industry, the Pearl Tower jutted out of the landscape like a bawdy carnival attraction. A huge model of the world flanked the left side of the tower, and skyscrapers provided the perfect backdrop for this gaudy picture. It was amazing to imagine all of this was farmland just a few years ago. Alexine flinched. "Progress," she thought, "is sometimes very ugly."

Looking to her left, she took a deep breath. Here was the architecture she had longed to see: The Peace Hotel, Pudong Development Bank, and the McBain Building. A nostalgic view of what China used to be. It was rising again from the dust of imposed imperialism, violent warlords, corrupt nationalists, and paralyzing communism, determined to regain its former sense of grandeur.

Callan eyed her sister intently from the table. Annalynn had left to use the bathroom, allowing the red-head a moment to relax for the first time since their cab ride. Observing Alexine, her mind flashed back to the scenario in the shop. What had happened?

Experience told Callan it would take a lot to make Alexine uneasy. Although not arrogant in any fashion, her older sister was strong. Quietly confident. She did not scare easily, and what Callan saw in that shop had been a truly frightened Alexine.

"We're just exhausted," she finally decided, tired of mulling it over. Callan stretched out her legs, and tipped her head back to look up at the sky. It was overcast, lifeless and dull. The weather mirrored her mood.

As soon as Alexine and Annalynn had rejoined her at the table, their waiter hurried over to take orders.

"I'll have the fish and chips," Callan smiled up at the waiter as he scribbled notes on his pad of paper.

Alexine was still scanning the selections, "um, yea, me too please," she decided, folding her menu.

"Salad, no dressing, and water," Annalynn ordered, not even raising her gaze from the newspaper which held her rapt attention.

"Of course, ma'am." The server bowed low.

A perfectly pressed man in a tidy suit stood just behind their waiter. Completely bald with an immaculate reddish goatee, he seemed to be training the younger, Asian man somehow. He reminded Alexine of the kind of guy who would carry a man-bag and know all about designer clothes and accessories. She had no idea what nationality he might be, but heard him speaking English. As the waiter excused himself and walked away, the bald man followed whispering what Alexine assumed were suggestions for dealing with foreigners.

Her thoughts were interrupted by two young boys who came belting through the door leading from the indoor portion of the restaurant to the outdoor area. A well dressed woman wearing very high heels was attempting to keep up with the two little daredevils.

"Now, that was a poor wardrobe decision," Alexine giggled as the woman increased her speed and teetered on her stilettos. High heels didn't seem practical in this situation.

The boys reached a small fountain, and the older one dropped a toy car into the water. Several fish darted out of the way of the falling object then resumed circling. The smaller of the two boys began to cry.

"So, where is the academy located?" Callan asked Annalynn, pulling Alexine's attention back to the table. When the older woman failed to answer, Callan glanced at her older sister, obviously annoyed.

Clearing her throat, Alexine reached for Annalynn's arm, touching it lightly. "Are we far from the academy?"

"No, not far at all, maybe four kilometers." The older woman immediately returned to her newspaper.

Alexine shrugged at Callan, an apology crossing her face.

The little girl rolled her eyes and stifled a yawn. "I'm about to drop," she said, as the waiter returned with their lunches. "Do we *have* to go to the academy today?"

"Well, I for one would at least like to see it."

The girls ate hardily, basking in the opportunity to consume food that was not pre-cooked, wrapped, and put on an airplane to sit for hours prior to serving. Half way through their meal, Annalynn finished her article, and let out a disgusted sigh.

"Something interesting?" Alexine asked as the newspaper was pushed aside.

"I do not believe people can be so…" She seemed to search for the correct word, and finally finished, "naïve."

Alexine's simple question seemed to open the floodgates on a tirade which had been brewing in Annalynn for quite some time. "Freedom, everyone wants more freedom, but there must be a balance." She continued hotly, "many cannot be trusted with freedom, they need…"

Alexine finished the sentence smugly, "repression?"

Annalynn pressed her lips together and, wagging a finger at Alexine, gave her a reproving look. "No…guidance. You Americans," she laughed, "so many freedoms, and where has it led?" She threw Alexine a questioning look, immediately responding to her own query. "Problems and chaos. There is no denying it. The state of things! Your country is an infant. China has existed for thousands of years. You think you know more than we know?"

Alexine returned the laugh, graciously bowing out of the pending argument. For some reason, she felt Annalynn was trying to talk herself into believing the words spilling from her lips, as much as her two companions.

Finishing lunch, they returned to street level and Annalynn hailed a cab. The sisters climbed into the back seat as Annalynn entered the front, speaking quickly in Mandarin with the cab driver. Callan assumed she was giving him directions to this "academy". As the cab jostled through narrow streets, the little girl fought to stay awake. It had been twenty five hours since either of the girls had slept well, and Callan was one person who could not function without sleep. A lot of sleep.

* * *

Where was she? It was dark, stormy and cold. Callan stumbled through the damp weeds in a thin nightgown. She was exhausted, and kept trying to push off, to go home, but it was no use. The first trip had used up every ounce of energy she possessed.

An owl hooted and coyotes sang in the distance as the moon, round, bright, and light orange, covered the forest in an eerie glow. The woods behind their home, usually the place they played, were now quiet and scary. Cracking branches and rustling leaves beat against her ears. Trees turned into monsters, and shrubs into ghosts. Confused, she jumped at every disturbance and scrambled down the path she thought led home. Callan's feet met a fallen log and she let out a cry of pain, pushing forward in an attempt to catch herself.

"Mommy!"

The scream sent small forest creatures running for cover. Hands then arms met the hard earth. She was falling too quickly and was unable to prevent her head from smacking the ground with a sickening thunk.

Inside the house Heidi jerked awake, sitting up in bed quickly, full of panic. "Geoff," she whispered urgently, "get up." Her husband's long rhythmic breathing told her he was still asleep. She shook him hard and jumped out of bed.

"What?" he asked groggily.

"Callan."

It was all she had to say. Geoff was out of bed, dressed and sprinting into the darkness thirty seconds later. Heidi had finished dressing, slipped on shoes, and opened the front door, when she spotted them. Carrying their precious little girl in his arms, he was walking toward her through the soggy front yard, pant legs damp from dew. Callan was crying, shivering and covered with mud. Something in Heidi gave and she began sobbing uncontrollably. What was going on? What were they supposed to do?

Although the baby was too young to entirely understand what her parents were saying, the panic and concern in their voices and on their faces left an indelible impression on the little girl. Something was wrong, they were worried, and it was her fault. The warm water, new clothes, and safety that enveloped her as she slept, tucked between her parents, were memories burned into Callan's mind. Warm. Safe. Protected. Home.

Chapter Seven
The Academy

The cab stopped abruptly rousting Callan from deep sleep.

"Mom!" she cried out.

Annalynn turned to look at the red-head inquisitively. They were parked in front of a large, silver, stadium-type building, oval in shape, with a domed top.

"The academy?" The little girl shook her head, trying to will herself into the present. Nodding in response, Annalynn paid the cabbie then got out of the car. Callan nudged Alexine who was slumped against the opposite cab door, sleeping soundly.

"Wha…?" Alexine sat up and rubbed her eyes. "Oh." She opened the door and stepped onto the pavement, swaying a bit. Callan joined her sister, and the two followed Annalynn around the building to a set of stairs which wrapped to the right as they wound up to a second floor balcony.

"We've been using this building for almost four years now," Annalynn began, as if conducting a tour. "We occupy the top two floors. Ground level is a super market. There is a basement which houses a large shopping center."

"Wow, it's huge!" Callan exclaimed, walking quickly to the railing to observe pedestrians milling about below.

"Yes, a big building," Annalynn smiled and continued to walk.

Alexine watched her closely. The woman was proud of this place. This academy was very important to Annalynn, an integral part of her life.

Having remained at the railing to people watch, Callan ran to catch up. Approaching the second level entryway, she slowed her step, surprised to see two police men standing sentry on either side of the door. Police men did not stand at doors in America.

"Nee how," they barked in sober unison. Annalynn produced a card from her pocket, handing it to the guard on the left. Studying her identification for several seconds, he returned it and the three of them were admitted.

The foyer was stark and white with several wooden chairs lining a far wall. Four more security men stood just inside the door, denying entry to anyone without authorization. A desk sat behind them, empty except for an impressive looking computer perched exactly in the middle. The screen glowed brilliant red. Four small yellow stars formed a crescent curved toward a larger yellow star in the top left-hand corner: the Chinese flag. Looking around, Alexine was irresistibly reminded of the apartment buildings lining the highway leading to Shanghai. Stark, impersonal, practical.

Annalynn approached this second set of guards, extended her right arm, and turned her hand palm down. Producing a small device, the guard on the right pressed a button on the machine, activating it, then waved it over the back of Annalynn's hand. Instantly the computer screen sprang to life. It was filled with information, a color photograph of Annalynn displayed prominently in the center.

"Whoa," Alexine eyed the screen. The guards all turned to stare at her in unison, suspicious of her interest in the data. One of them quickly walked to the desk and turned the monitor as the other men waved the group past. The guards. The methods. The suspicion. It unnerved the older girl. They certainly were not at home anymore. Alexine reminded herself they were now in a communist country. Many things were bound to be very different.

As the trio entered the building, Annalynn turned to Alexine. "The best of everything," the older woman tossed her head back to indicate the computer system. Apparently Annalynn was under the misguided notion she was impressed. Quite the opposite, Alexine was mortified.

"RFID chips?" the older girl blustered when she and Callan found themselves alone for a moment. Annalynn had left them in what appeared to be a classroom to find Mr. Rippinger. "Do you have any idea what those things can do?"

Callan shot her a bored, why-do-you-always-have-to-assume-the-worst look. "I thought it was pretty cool myself," the little girl countered, walking around the room.

"Are you at all interested in," Alexine began incredulously, attempting to control her emotions, "what those things are capable of?"

"They just store information Alexine," Callan said, distracted. "Mom uses them on the puppies. It's a great way to identify people too, if you ask me." Callan was investigating the room as she spoke. Opening desks, browsing through what appeared to be textbooks, and rifling drawers.

"And," she continued unfazed, rounding the corner of a neat row of desks and approaching Alexine with a swagger. "No one can steal your identity if it's in-your-hand." Callan emphasized the last three words by pausing between each of them. Hands on hips, eyebrows raised in defiance, she was staring at Alexine, challenging her to refute the argument.

"The inherent implications regarding those *things*," Alexine emphasized the word "things" with as much distain as she could muster, "are astronomical."

Callan gave a hoot of derision, turned and began walking away. "And all I hear you saying is: blah, blah, blah."

Both girls jumped as the door flung open and a tall man walked quickly into the room. He was at least six foot two and very handsome. Lean and powerful, the man was the type of person who demanded attention, simply as a result of his appearance. He smiled at the girls, who stood frozen to their spots.

"Well, hello," he boomed, approaching Alexine first, only because she was closest to the door. These two held promise. He had met enough sillemlem to sense power, and could tell who possessed strong gifts as soon as he met them. "I'm Mr. Rippinger." He paused for effect, as if that fact alone would impress. "You can call me Devin, and I'm assuming you are Alexine and Callan Kovar."

The younger girl strode over and nodded confidently, demanding his attention. "Yes sir," she replied, stopping directly in front of him and taking a wide stance. "And this is an amazing facility."

The man liked this girl. Cocky, confident, attention-seeking. The kind of child who was easily converted. She would make a fine addition.

"Thank you for having us," Alexine smiled, also approaching but more slowly.

"The pleasure is ours," he beamed. "Let's take a look around." Devin led the girls out of the classroom and into the hall. "We began using this facility about four years ago."

Devin wore a condescending expression while speaking of the academy; it's grounds, personnel, and standing in the community. Alexine resented it. It seemed wrong, egotistical, obscene. She felt uneasy about both Annalynn and Devin. Confused and disappointed, the older girl wondered why her parents would send them to these people.

"It is equipped for our specific needs."

"What needs are those?" Alexine broke in, leaving her own thoughts behind and rejoining the conversation.

Mr. Rippinger stopped, turned, and stared at Alexine. She met his gaze; *he* did not intimidate her. She could feel his insecurities, his fears, and his lack of control. It made him vulnerable and weak in her opinion.

"To teach, of course."

Callan was aching for information and found she could no longer resist. "So, you can teach me how to control myself?" Blurted, it sounded like a plea instead of a question.

Mr. Rippinger smiled down at the stammering girl. He painted a knowing, understanding look on his face. It annoyed Alexine. She wondered if he practiced it in front of a mirror each evening. "He's playing her," she thought angrily. "He can tell she's desperate, and he's messing with her."

Leaning motionless against the wall, Annalynn studied the older girl intently.

"We can teach you more than you can imagine," Devin answered. The little girl looking up at him turned radiant, her question fading to glowing expectancy. It was the exact reaction he was hoping to induce. His insides jumped as he attempted to contain his excitement.

Alexine could not help but wonder why Devin was so enthralled with her little sister. Surely there were hundreds of people at this center. Was he this enthusiastic about each of them? Devin threw his shoulders back, pressing himself to his full height, and gave Callan a wink. Alexine thought he looked like a spokesman in a low budget sports commercial.

The group entered a large stadium-type room on the second level. Callan walked swiftly through the doors, eager to glean more information, eager to start learning right now. Her fatigue banished, she breathed quickly in anticipation. Was it true? Could she control this ability that had wreaked havoc with her life since before she could remember? Could it even be something she could use deliberately?

They looked at the floor situated one level down from where they stood. The group had walked out onto a balcony that surrounded the entire gymnasium. Row upon row of stadium stands surrounded them; seating for anyone wishing to view the area below. Annalynn's cell phone rang. Excusing herself, she stepped back into the hallway. The group again focused its attention downward. At least one hundred people were on the floor.

"Shifter training, level four." Devin gave Callan a smug look of pride. "Your class, I think."

At first, Alexine did not notice anything out of the ordinary. The people seemed to be teamed up, working on some sort of exercise. Although there were many individuals below them, the gymnasium was cloaked in an eerie silence. Studying the students below, she suddenly started and gasped. These people were disappearing and reappearing.

Each time one partner vanished, the other would follow suit. Watching more closely now, she realized they were trying to follow each other. Alexine was in shock. This could not be possible. It was as if she was watching a television program, something not based in reality.

Although she knew her younger sister could "fly", Alexine had never actually witnessed it. Callan tended to do it in the dead of night when frightened out of her wits by a recurring dream. She had never been able to do it at will. Because Alexine had never seen it personally, and could not make sense of it logically, she had somehow decided it did not occur exactly how everyone else assumed. Perhaps Callan was just fast enough to span distances quickly. Perhaps she had figured out a way to unlock doors Alexine herself had difficulty getting through. She didn't know, but didn't understand, so she used deductive reasoning to explain it away.

But now the proof lay directly in front of her, daring her to defy it. Her mind reeled. "So many," she kept repeating in awe, as if this mantra would somehow help it make sense. "So many."

Devin watched Alexine intently. "What?" He feigned surprise and smiled. "What did you think you would see here?"

"Uh, I wasn't..." the older girl stammered. What could she say? Maybe some people who could run really fast? That answer, which would have been entirely acceptable thirty seconds ago in the hallway, seemed laughable now. Idiotic.

A shrill whistle blew below and all movement ceased. The people on the floor sat down and directed their attention to a short, stocky woman who appeared to be a teacher. As Devin beckoned both the girls to join him back in the hall, Alexine walked toward the door, astounded, unable to think. It was as if all reason had left the world, and she was now operating in an alien environment. One in which typical rules failed to apply.

Callan's reaction was markedly different. She gripped the railing, paralyzed, only able to think of one word. Normal. Here, in this place, *she* was normal.

In the hallway Devin stopped and turned toward Alexine, inviting her to ask questions. She could not think of one. Nothing came to mind. Callan, on the other hand, was brimming with excitement.

"You can teach me that? Really? REALLY? I can do that? Shift?"

Devin nodded slowly. "That, and much more Callan," the older man grinned. "You, and even I for that matter, have no idea of your potential until we start working."

The little red-head smiled. This was a feeling she could never recall experiencing. It was acceptance, it was belonging, it was knowing you were not a problem. You were something more than average. You possessed power. Her chest heaved in exhilaration.

Devin laughed, clapping the little girl on the back as if to welcome her to the team. She looked up at him, admiration and gratitude beaming from her face. "Perfect," he mused to himself, "like fish in a barrel."

At the very moment Alexine thought she might be sick, Annalynn approached announcing she had arranged for a cab to take the girls to their residence.

"Wonderful!" Devin replied. "We'll see you here tomorrow morning then." After nodding in Alexine's direction, he turned to Callan. Winking, Devin grabbed her by the shoulders. "We'll start tomorrow, superstar," he said, shaking her playfully.

All she could do was nod, sporting a dazed, contented smile. The large man turned and walked quickly down the hall.

Annalynn escorted the girls back to the entrance where they separated and exited the building. The sisters walked down the steps to the ground floor in silence, each lost in their own, opposite thoughts. A cab was waiting for them in the drive. Callan strode around the car and collapsed into the back seat as Alexine leaned into the front passenger window to question the cab driver.

Speaking slowly, she meticulously enunciated each word. "Do you know where we are going?" The cabbie nodded his head excitedly, smiling broadly. He had no idea what she was saying. Trusting the driver had been appraised of their destination, she opened the rear door and slid into the seat next to her sister. The car pulled away slowly.

Gazing out an upstairs window, Annalynn watched the cab pull out of the drive and enter traffic. How long had it been since she had seen the little shifter? Nine years? Ten? And the sister. How could she have missed it? Turning, she walked quickly to a nearby office.

"Enter," came the retort after she knocked firmly. Devin was sitting at a large, expensive, wooden desk which sat facing the door. Fingers laced together, he watched the reader as she purposefully crossed the room. Anxiously awaiting the information she had gleaned, a smile of satisfaction crossed his face.

Annalynn returned the look, but for very different reasons, and took a seat across from him in a hard, wooden chair.

"She's impressive," Devin accentuated his words as if daring anyone to deny them. "I haven't met a shifter with that much energy in a long time. And she's twelve!? Unheard of," he said quietly, almost to himself. "Unheard of."

He jumped to his feet, pacing the room, alternately running his hands through his dark hair, then shoving them deep into his pockets, as if unable to decide where they should be at the moment. Excited, the adrenaline jolted through his veins. "The things I can accomplish with her!"

Annalynn sat rigidly in her chair. Silent, simply staring straight ahead. Something in her mind screamed at her to keep quiet, but she pushed it away. An arrogant, smug monster reared; that part of her which was always egged on by Devin's egotism. She knew it was wrong, but began the game of toying with him none the less.

Devin stopped moving, realizing his excitement was, at best, not being acknowledged. And at worst, being intentionally ignored. "Any thoughts Lynn?" he questioned slowly, wanting some sort of response. Something to indicate she was participating in the conversation. He stopped behind her, grasping the back of her chair, and she stood to turn toward him.

"That's all we have are shifters," she said impatiently. "That's all you can keep." And then, suddenly, her expression changed to one of sly mischievousness. It was wrong. She knew it was wrong to play games with Devin. But he was so infuriating!

"What?" he questioned, stung by the comment, but taken aback by her abrupt change in emotion.

"I don't think she's a shifter," she said simply, toying with the large man. She hated herself for doing it, but couldn't stop now.

"Of course she is!" Devin replied, a bit irritated. "Didn't you hear her?" He paused and cocked his head to the side. "Are you crazy Lynn?"

"No, I think you have that department covered nicely," she snapped coolly. "And by the way, please *control* yourself when they are around, she was reading you like a book."

As Annalynn emphasized the word "control" Devin flinched, glaring at her. "Listen Lynn, *I'm* a shifter, and I know a potential shifter when I see one. And she adores me in case you didn't notice," he added ominously. "Reading me like a book, please!" He shot her a hard look, challenging her to disagree.

This man had the ability to jump from happiness to irritation quickly. As long as the emotion was strong, he was willing to indulge it, and anger was one of his favorites.

"Yes, and I'm a reader…" she trailed off, leaving the implication hanging in the air.

After contemplating these words for several moments, Devin let out a snort. "There is no way that twelve year old is a reader." He shook his head derisively. "No way."

Annalynn smiled more broadly. "Of course she's not," she whispered with distain, relishing her secret up until the last possible moment. Again, the warning flashed through her mind: be quiet! But she couldn't. She had come too far.

"But her sister is."

Chapter Eight
Zeke

Sliding a rigid key card into the reader, Callan turned the handle to the room the girls would call home for the next month. "Hey, it's nicer than I thought it would be!"

Alexine dropped her bags defeatedly as she closed the door behind them and took in their surroundings. It looked like a typical hotel room to her, which, she had to admit, was more than she had expected also.

The room was decorated in placid blues with a bathroom located directly off the entryway to their right. Two single beds, also situated on the right, were separated by a small nightstand. A modest television set sat on a chest of drawers to the left. Large striped curtains, pulled shut over windows just past the beds, cloaked the room in muted darkness. Callan instinctively crossed the room at a clip, flinging them open. She gasped as a torrent of light spilled over their living quarters.

"What?" Alexine shot, still fuming over the way Callan had been taken in by that Devin jerk. "That's his new name," Alexine decided angrily, "that Devin jerk." She glanced up. "Wow!"

The girl's room was fourteen floors up, and from this vantage point, they could see quite a bit of Shanghai. Directly in front of them lay a hutong. Squat and squalid, older neighborhoods such as these were rapidly disappearing from Shanghai's landscape. The short, dilapidated buildings were being demolished to make room for taller, more modern dwellings and businesses. Alexine had read about them in a travel book and longed to see them in person. To say she was disappointed would be an understatement. The books spoke nostalgically about "seeing these wonderful old buildings before they were gone."

"Right," thought Alexine disgruntled. "I completely understand why they're tearing them down, they're horrible!"

Four units comprised each small building, every unit contained a downstairs and upstairs. The top floor of each apartment was divided into two sections; one room, and one open-air area, almost a balcony. It appeared the only running water available in these dwellings was supplied via metal pipes which ran to this outdoor area. Cooking and washing up, therefore, occurred in view of whomever happened to be looking down from the taller buildings surrounding the hutong, and whomever happened to be on their own balcony next door or across the very narrow alley.

A woman walked out onto a balcony below the sisters followed by a teenage girl who sauntered out slowly several minutes later. As the two women initiated a conversation, Alexine wondered what they were discussing. The young girl groomed her hair, slowly and methodically, dragging the brush through it's long, dark-black, shiny strands. She watched the girl intently, her motions calming and reassuring. The older woman busied herself washing dishes and straightening the area. Alexine was surprised to see the women were well dressed. They appeared very normal and seemed out of place standing atop the crumbling dwelling. Like new buttons on a worn jacket. Did everyone in Shanghai live this way?

Across the small, garbage strewn alley separating the two buildings, a man walked onto his balcony. He was wearing loose pajama type pants and a sleeveless undershirt that hugged his slender frame. The man turned on a faucet, filling a bowl with what had to be ice cold water. Picking up a washcloth, he dropped it into the bowl, then wrung it out. As the man scrubbed his face, he glanced up. Alexine and Callan jumped back from the window, jammed the curtains shut, then turned to each other, giggling.

"I feel like a voyeur!" said Alexine.

"A what?" Callan walked quickly back to the door, flicking off the lights to the room.

"Good idea." Alexine whispered, eyes wide with excitement.

The girls again approached the window, now camouflaged by the darkness. They slowly poked their faces through the drawn curtains like hermit crabs emerging tentatively from shells. The man was gone, the mother and daughter were still engaged in relaxed conversation.

"Wow," was the only word they could utter about this strange state of existence.

Alexine had an overwhelming sense of gratitude for indoor plumbing, structurally sound homes, and for the little sister standing beside her. She put an arm around Callan and felt the frustration of the day melt away.

A loud rapping at the door made both girls scream and jump. Callan laughed loudly and dove into bed, pulling the blankets over herself, her antics and giddiness the result of sheer exhaustion.

Entertained, Alexine paused to watch the little girl thrashing around under the covers. The person knocked again and the older girl stifled her own laughter. Walking to the door, she opened it a crack.

"Hello?"

"Hey," replied an attractive young man. She guessed he was nineteen or twenty years old, with blond hair that was a bit too long and straggly for Alexine's taste. She was reminded of the beach bums one might find in California, wiling away the years surfing and bronzing themselves in the sand. Gorgeous, carefree and totally irresponsible.

"I'm Zeke." The young man flashed a perfect smile. "From the academy. Just checking to make sure you're both comfortable."

This boy was quite good looking, well built and athletic. He had an air of confidence and ease that made him even more attractive and Alexine blushed unwittingly.

"Oh, good. I mean, we're good, yea," Alexine stammered in spite of herself. Opening the door a bit wider, she chastised herself for the lame retort. Callan laughed in the background, and Zeke's smile widened.

"Having fun in there?" The young man raised an eyebrow and peered over Alexine's shoulder into the room.

"Invite him in, I can tell he's cute!" This comment was followed, once again, by peels of uncontrolled giggles as the little red-head rolled around in her bed.

"Um, yea." Alexine blushed more furiously. "She's tired and she gets kind of slap happy when…" her voice trailed off as Zeke snickered, and it seemed as if this day was no longer a complete loss.

"Perhaps we could talk down in the lobby? You guys get unpacked, and I'll meet you down there in ten minutes or so, okay?"

"Yea…alright." All thoughts of the hot shower and sleep Alexine had been dreaming of since lunch vanished, replaced by a curiosity about this Zeke. "Ten minutes," she repeated, and shut the door with a soft click.

"Ahhhh!" screamed Callan from her blanket cocoon. She sang in a sing-song voice, "Alexine has a boyfriend, Alexine has a boyfriend."

"Please!" the older girl laughed. "Control yourself! First of all, I'm way too young for a boyfriend. I mean, what would be the point?"

"Ughh, you sound just like mom!"

"Well, she's right."

Callan stopped thrashing around and became very serious, sitting bolt upright in bed. "Yea, I know, but don't you hate that she's always right?"

"Well, I think it's just because she's been here longer than us." Alexine smirked. "I'm sure we'll have all the answers when we're sixty."

"Mom is *not* sixty," Callan looked scandalized, "and you *know* it."

"I know, I know. I just think it's funny to say that. She hates it when we…"

"She's *seventy!*"

Both girls laughed indulgently and began bouncing on their beds.

"I can't believe we're in China," yelled Callan. "Ahhhh!"

Reaching the pinnacle of a jump, Alexine kicked her feet out, landing on her back in the center of her bed with a thunk. "Ouch! Wow, this mattress is like a brick."

"Yea, I thought mine was kind of hard," agreed Callan, punching at her own mattress.

"Well, at least we're here."

"I know...it's weird." Callan was again incongruently serious. Both girls lay still for several minutes, the gaiety so prevalent a few moments before seeped from the room, replaced not by something negative, but by the unknown.

"Well," Alexine finally said, "want to go meet Zeke?" She wagged her eyebrows up and down playfully.

"Sure. I'm starving anyway. Maybe he'll take us out to dinner!"

Alexine eyed her sister incredulously. "We just ate!"

"Don't know what to tell ya," Callan replied casually, "but I'm hungry again."

The girls walked down the hallway of the fourteenth floor, turned left at the end, and found themselves at the elevators. Several Asian women stood waiting, engrossed in rapid dialogue; cleaning ladies employed by the hotel. The women paused, allowing the girls to enter the lift first. Stepping inside, the sisters were closely followed by the loquacious gaggle of women. Callan pushed the "G" button. As they descended in uncomfortable silence, the girls glanced around and smiled. It seemed the two young Americans were much more interesting than whatever it was the women had been discussing previously.

"Bye-bye," said their companions in high-pitched voices as Alexine and Callan exited. They appeared to be excited about conversing in English, and bowed their heads quickly several times.

"Bye-bye," the girls found themselves saying in a similar sing-song voice. As soon as the doors shut, Alexine and Callan appraised each other incredulously. "Bye bye?" they said simultaneously, ruefully shaking their heads.

"We sound like babies," noted Alexine wryly.

Turning, they followed a short hallway to the front desk. Zeke was seated on a couch in the entryway.

"Hungry?"

"Starving!" Callan replied quickly.

"Escaped from those covers, hey? You must be the crazy one in your family."

Callan met his gaze unabashedly. "Yo," she cocked her head to the side, and put her hands on her waist.

Hunch shouldered and humiliated, Alexine rolled her eyes in embarrassment but Zeke just laughed as Callan swaggered out the door, mimicking a cowboy walking with spurs.

"Comin?" Callan drawled over her shoulder.

Zeke looked at Alexine and grinned, gesturing for her to lead the way. Giving him what she hoped was an apologetic look, Alexine followed her little sister out the glass doors.

After leaving the courtyard of the building, the group turned right. They crossed several small side streets, and entered an area of tiny shops. A shoe store, a fabric store, a clothing store, a convenience store. Doors open to the evening, light spilled from the businesses onto the heavily traveled sidewalk, beckoning would-be customers.

Glancing at signs, Alexine attempted to convert prices from Yuan into dollars. "Wow," she whispered to Zeke when she was able to make a calculation in her head. "This stuff is cheap."

"Yea," he replied, not shortly, but uninterested.

Their escort's face slid in and out of view as the group moved past well-lit shops into dark areas between stores, and back again. At once, clearly visible. And then, partly hidden by intimidating shadow. Alexine occasionally stole glimpses at the young man. His angular features, so compelling in the light, inspired the opposite feeling in darkness. She shuttered. Confused, Alexine cast her eyes around for something to divert her attention.

On the corner of the next side street a woman stood behind a silver serving cart. Seven or eight people waited in line to purchase whatever she was selling. Moving closer, Alexine noticed several individuals working in the dirty alley behind the cart, stirring and clanging large, well-worn, metal pots. The pots fit perfectly atop smoky burners, their contents jumping merrily. Beautifully round pieces of dough, the size of softballs, steamed in brown wicker-type baskets.

"Dumplings," said Zeke when he noticed Alexine peering at them. "They're good."

Alexine had read much about Chinese dumplings. She even found a recipe at home and made them for dinner one evening several weeks ago. Her family agreed they were wonderful, but her dumplings looked nothing like these soft, gooey handfuls of white dough. They were pinched closed at the top, the dough twisted to seal in juicy fillings. All of the dumplings were exactly the same size and perfectly formed. They looked like little round packages wrapped for a special occasion.

"Want one?" Zeke pulled two Yuan from his front pocket.

Callan stepped off the curb ahead of them and began crossing the next intersection, failing to notice she was alone. "Cal!" Alexine called after her. The little girl glanced around and, realizing she had left the others behind, made her way back through several groups of pedestrians.

"Man, those smell good!" Callan inhaled deeply.

Alexine wasn't hungry at all, but was anxious to try the little steamed buns.

"Is it safe?" she glanced into the alleyway again.

Zeke shrugged, unconcerned. He looked at the shop keeper, held up two fingers, then handed her two Yuan. Digging around in her apron pocket, the woman produced several small silver coins, handing them over to Zeke. A young man standing next to the shop keeper grabbed a thin plastic bag and plopped in two dumplings.

"Watch out," said Zeke quickly, "they're really hot."

Taking the bag, Alexine grinned. "Shay shay." The woman looked slightly amused, but smiled graciously back.

Several blocks later, the dumplings had cooled enough to handle. "Mmm," Callan moaned. "These are good." She chewed her food loudly, emitting sickening smacking sounds.

"Callan, please!"

"What?" Juice dribbled down the little girl's chin. "These are the best!"

Zeke laughed, pulled several napkins from his pocket, handed them to Callan, then shook his head at Alexine as if to say he understood.

"You're certainly prepared," remarked the older girl, glancing at the jacket from which the napkins had appeared.

"Everyone learns," Zeke commented wryly, "to carry some kind of tissue with them at all times in China. Trust me. Toilet paper and napkins are in short supply."

Alexine flashed him a frightened look as Zeke nodded knowingly.

They passed a huge department store on their right. The blinding neon sign, and blaring English rock song, seemed wrong. Blasphemous at some basic level. "I came to see China, not America!" lamented Alexine.

The ballad belted out and made any chance of conversation impossible. *"You spin me right round baby, right round, like a record baby, right round, round, round. You spin me right round baby, right round, like a record baby, right round, round, round."* A group of young Asians gathered in front of the store. *"I want your loooooove!"* They seemed transfixed by the music and the attractive girls dressed in white and black sequined gowns parading around the entryway. *"I need your loooove!"* The girls strutted on high heels, waving at the crowd.

"Yikes," said Callan when she noticed the sequin-laden models. She shot Alexine an overly horrified look.

"Behave!" Alexine warned through clenched teeth though Zeke seemed entertained by the exchange. "Um, let's keep walking," suggested Alexine. Callan was swaying to the music, waving her dumpling to the sequin girls slowly. Alexine grabbed the hand that wasn't clutching a ball of dough, and dragged the trouble-maker away from the scene. She hoped no one had noticed Callan's condescending display of sarcasm. Or perhaps, just misinterpreted it as sincere interest.

Several blocks later the group found themselves facing a Pizza Hut restaurant. "Ugh," Alexine sighed when she spotted it. "Can't we get away from this kind of stuff?" They turned right and kept walking. More shops. More food stalls.

As dusk fell, it surprised Alexine how many people were still milling about. The diversity of the crowd was similarly astonishing. Well dressed women in high heels, men in suits, boisterous teenagers, workmen in baggy cotton shirts and pants, sedate older couples, bums; a mélange of humanity. "Is it always this busy?"

"It's China." Zeke shrugged. "Lots of people, you know."

"Yea." His response made her feel foolish for asking the question. Not really sure where they were heading, Alexine paused, absorbing the sights and sounds. Looking back at her sister, she noticed Callan standing behind Zeke, swaying slightly.

"Um, you know," the little red-head said dreamily, "I'm going to pass out soon."

"Actually," yawned Alexine, "I am too."

"Well then, tour's over for now. Let's get you two back to your room." Zeke spun around and the group headed back down the street, re-tracing their steps.

Stopping to buy another dumpling for Callan at the silver stand, the shop keeper chortled when they ordered and said something in Chinese to the man who was working along side her. Glancing up at the three of them, he giggled uncomfortably, but looked too embarrassed to laugh for long. Not having any idea what comment the woman made, Alexine imagined it was something like, "crazy Americans just ate...they're back for more!" When Alexine smiled back at the woman and chuckled easily, the shopkeeper seemed delighted and poked her companion as if assuring him it was alright to laugh.

"Thanks for dinner," Alexine told Zeke as they entered the hotel lobby.

"Hey, no problem, I'm here to serve!"

"Well, will we see you tomorrow?"

"You bet, I'm supposed to make sure you get to the academy in the morning."

"Cool, yea, kay, night," said Callan quickly, in complete monotone and abruptly walked away, like a zombie.

No respecter of persons, Callan's propensity to say what she felt like saying and do what she felt like doing was an endearing, maddening and many times, disconcerting facet of her personality. "Sorry about her," apologized Alexine. "She's really tired, and she's a bit...eccentric."

"You both need some sleep." Zeke watched the little red-head intently as she disappeared around the corner. Forcing his attention back to Alexine, he winked, waved, then turned, walking out the door.

Alexine caught up with Callan at the elevator. "Okay, I'm seriously tired," complained the red-head. She was swaying ominously again. The doors opened and the girls were glad to see it was empty. They were too exhausted to smile, laugh, try to remember the few Chinese words they had memorized, or even say "bye-bye." Dragging their feet, they stepped into the elevator.

Down on the street, Zeke pulled out a small cell phone. He dialed and waited. The phone rang only once.

"Hello," answered a deep voice.

"Yea, Devin, it's Zeke."

"And?"

"Walked them around for about an hour, then dropped them back off."

"What do you think of her? The little shifter?"

"She's....interesting." Zeke turned his back on several people who passed, eyeing him inquisitively.

"Yes, and her power is almost palpable, isn't it?"

"Yea, I would have to agree. She's independent, will make decisions completely on her own, doesn't care what other people think. Yea. I'll keep an eye on her. A close eye."

"Good."

There was a pause on the other end of the line. Zeke could tell Devin was satisfied.

"See you in the morning Zeke…nice job."

The phone went dead.

Once in the room, both girls collapsed into their beds fully clothed and fell asleep immediately. Alexine had never been so tired in her life. Everything was fuzzy, and weights had been tied to her arms and legs, encumbering every move. Even the hard mattresses were forgotten as both sisters plummeted into unconsciousness.

* * *

Something was watching. It hid in corners of the darkened room, waiting for movement. Covers pulled up tightly to her chin, she remained perfectly still. Only her eyes betrayed her location; they darted about, attempting to locate the evil, so she could run. Callan wanted to scream, but could only mouth the words, the noise held prisoner by terror. There! Next to the bookshelf!

Whooosh! She was outside, mind fogged with panic. Where is safe? She glanced back at the house.

Whoosh! Her parent's room. Just feet below, her mother and father slept contently. She watched them for a moment and her mother's eyes flickered open. She looked directly at Callan but her face remained impassive.

"Mom!" Callan screamed. But what came out was a whisper, the cry cowered by terror. Her mother didn't answer, but stared at the ceiling fan as if in deep thought. Suddenly her mother jumped, and Callan flung herself between her parents. Warm. Safe. Her eyes rolled back and she was lost again.

Chapter Nine
The Abandoned Box

September 21, 2000
*Marcellus, Michigan * Ann Arbor, Michigan * Sylvania, Ohio*

What was going on? What was happening to her second daughter? So young, so tiny. How did she keep getting outside? They had installed locks near the tops of exterior doors. Locks that adults had difficultly unlatching. How was she doing it? Questioning her didn't help. Heidi re-played Callan's answer in her mind.

"I fly Mom, I fly."

Callan never faltered in this explanation, never changed her story. She flew. This had been happening for so long, it had become a part of their routine. Go to bed, check on Callan. Sleep a few more hours, check on Callan. Wake up early, check on Callan. Heidi was just about to swing her legs out of bed to check on their second daughter, when she gasped, and stifled a scream. In the second it took to blink, she felt Callan fall in between she and Geoff. What just happened?

The little red-head sleeping soundly beside her, Heidi shook her head in an effort to clear it, then rubbed her face hard. Callan must have jumped into bed with them. From the floor at the end of the bed? That was quite a distance for a four year old to clear. Perhaps she had crawled onto the end of the bed, and then jumped. Yes, yes, that made sense. Heidi had glanced at her as she was jumping in between them. Yes.

But wait, she had been staring up at the ceiling when Callan... just...appeared.

Appeared?

Yes, appeared.

One minute she was staring at the ceiling fan, and the next she was staring at her daughter. Above her.

No, that was impossible. She must have jumped.

Lying in the darkness, groping for answers, Heidi entertained any plausible explanation for what she had witnessed. A trick of the light, the remnants of a dream, stress. Nothing was off limits. When the alarm clock rang, she had concocted a neat list of possibilities. None of which eased her anxiety.

Geoff woke early that morning and got ready for work. As he kissed his wife goodbye, he looked over at their second daughter questioningly. Heidi rarely allowed children to sleep in their bed. The kids could bring pillows and blankets in to sleep on the floor if they were frightened, but the bed was typically off limits.

Occasionally Geoff would try to sneak in a child, covering them up and stating innocently as his wife entered the room, "no mom, there's no kids in here! Nothing but us covers!" Both Geoff and the child wriggling under the bedding would giggle, and Heidi would play along.

"Okay daddy, well, time for bed!" Often she would lay on top of the small bump then feign surprise when a little one screamed and popped out.

Heidi stirred and opened her eyes. She acknowledged his confusion but was not ready to discuss it, so she shrugged.

Geoff shook his head, smiled, and kissed her soundly. "I love you."

His intense stare spoke more words than he could ever say. They had been through some interesting things together, and Heidi knew without a doubt that more hills and valleys lay before them. The roller-coaster road of life, terrifying one moment and exhilarating the next. Sharing it with someone you adored, and knew you could count on, was priceless and something she had wondered if she would ever find. And then she met Geoff; they were perfect together.

She smiled softly back at him, her precious husband. The person who had taught her so much about herself. Who had been interested in the parts of her she had put in boxes to be protected and, perhaps, salvaged, if anyone was willing. The love and devotion they shared just kept getting stronger. In a way, it was frightening.

What if she lost him? What if something happened to the children? The fears of every mother filled her mind as the child lying in her arms turned over. She snuggled closer to Callan under the warm, airy comforter. How long could they keep her safe?

"Hi, Mom," said Heidi haltingly on the phone later that morning. She was so tired.

"Hi hon." Marie paused and, sensing the tension in her daughter's voice, quickly added, "what's wrong?"

Overwhelmed by the events of the previous night, Heidi began crying and couldn't speak. The words were trapped in her throat.

"Hello?"

"I'm here."

"Honey, what's wrong?"

"Mom…I don't know…it's Callan."

"What happened?"

"Oh, no, nothing bad, I guess. She's just…well…doing weird things… and…I don't know." What could she tell her mother? That Callan was floating around the house? That, perhaps, she had been floating *out* of the house? For a few years? That was insane.

"Hon, what kind of weird things?"

Her mother's question came calm, as if the odd description and concern were not strange at all. Were, in a way, expected? Heidi frowned, pulling herself together.

"I don't know mom, Callan's…well…" She paused, searching for words that resembled reason but none presented themselves. "She's getting outside somehow. And there's no way she should be able to get outside mom. We have locks on every door. Up high. We can't figure out how she's doing it." Heidi felt guilty about not relating last night's incident, but she was not sure how to put that scenario into words.

"You have no idea how she is getting out?" Marie sensed information was being withheld. That fact alone spoke volumes; Heidi was always forthright and honest, especially with her. A sinking feeling settled over the older woman as her great-uncle's face flashed in her mind.

"None." They had no idea how, or even what, Callan was doing. They were at a complete loss. Heidi ached to give her mother more, without sounding crazy. "When we ask how she's getting outside she always says the same thing." Heidi paused, bracing herself to say the words. "I fly, mom. I fly."

Marie sat down hard in a dining room chair, stunned, as her daughter repeated those words: I fly.

Could it be possible? It had been four generations. So long Marie thought, or perhaps hoped, she had imagined the entire thing. Old memories and ancient manuscripts elbowed their way into her conscience, given power by her daughter's anguish and explanations. Heidi's words brought her back to the present.

"Mom, I'm scared."

An unnerving silence ensued. "Tell me everything that has been happening."

An hour later, Marie slowly dialed her phone. "Hello, Catherine?" she began. "Are you busy tomorrow?" She had thought about it during her talk with Heidi. How to best present the facts she harbored. How to find out as much as she could from Geoff's mother, before driving across the state to see her daughter. To explain things.

"I was wondering if I could come down and talk for a few hours tomorrow?" Marie was sure this sounded strange; she had never invited herself to Catherine's home. Although she had grown up in the same town as Heidi's mother-in-law, they had not been close friends. Catherine was several years older than Marie.

Catherine seemed surprised. "Well...sure. That sounds wonderful. I have a hair appointment first thing in the morning, but after that...." She was still puzzled as she hung up the phone.

That evening Marie walked out to her pole barn. The night was cool and clear and she paused to look up at the sky, pulling her jacket closed. The stars, millions of them, twinkled brilliantly, mocking her building anxiety. She drew a deep breath and steeled herself. The gray building seemed foreboding; her hiding place for the long-held family secret. A piece of information Marie wasn't sure she wanted to expose.

Retrieving the ladder that hung on the wall, she braced it against the roof joist, fifth from the end, and climbed. She peered over the top of the two by sixes, spotting it jammed between the horizontal and roof support.

The small wooden box placed there twenty five years previous was wrapped in a thick, tattered blanket now covered with dust. Abandoned. She had hoped she would never open the box again; hoped she *could* orphan the things the box contained. That somehow, by ignoring them, they would be forgotten. A dream. A fantasy.

Marie paused, hesitant to retrieve the items entombed in wood, sitting within reach. Would it be better for them not to know? To just gloss over what was happening, and hope for the best? Pursing her lips she pushed ahead and un-wedged the package, pinned it under her left arm, and climbed down. As feet met floor, she paused and rested her head on a rung of the ladder. Was there a right decision?

Driving from Ann Arbor, Michigan to Sylvania, Ohio the next afternoon, Marie rehearsed how to best present this to Catherine. After an hour, she gave up. She was just going to have to wing it.

"Hello Catherine." Marie sat the package down at her feet and the two women hugged. As they parted, her host looked puzzled.

"Okay, what's going on?" Last evening Catherine had decided Marie was planning a surprise for the kids, Geoff and Heidi. It was their eighth wedding anniversary this year. Perhaps it was a party.

"Well, why don't we sit down?" Marie offered hopefully.

Catherine walked into the adjacent living room and took a seat on the couch. Marie joined her, finding it difficult to know where to begin, difficult to know exactly what to say. She decided it was best to just dive in. "I have to ask you something about your family."

Catherine's brow furrowed in question as Marie unwrapped a small, old, worn wooden box. She sat it on the coffee table in front of them. Constructed of dark wood, with intricate carvings along the top and sides, the tiny copper colored hinges and clasps looked hand-made. If it had not been so beat up, Catherine was sure this would be a beautiful piece of woodwork. "Wow, where did you find this?"

"Actually, it probably belongs to you."

"Me?" Catherine drew back in surprise. "Why?"

"Well, first I have to tell you a few things, and then ask a few questions. I hope you'll just be patient because this may take awhile, and I doubt it will make any sense." Marie smiled nervously. "After all these years, it still doesn't make sense to me."

Catherine's curiosity was piqued.

"Years ago, when I was about sixteen years old, my family moved to Illinois."

"I remember," replied Catherine distractedly, a bit bewildered by this trip down memory lane. "Didn't you stay behind?" The box on the table drew her eye, beckoned her to study it. To touch it. To open it. Marie's voice startled her...

"Yes, I did."

...intruding on her thoughts, pulling her attention from the object on the table.

"I lived with my grandmother for awhile. I wanted to finish my senior year, so my parents agreed I could remain here." Marie's reminiscent smile slowly faded. "Living with Geraldine was not easy, She wasn't a kind woman and there were many rules I had to follow. I really couldn't do anything."

Catherine nodded, remembering the stern woman. "Weren't you dating Ben then?"

"Yes. He was in the Air Force by that time. When he came home for a week's leave, he stopped by the house to see me." Marie gazed sadly upward as if re-living that day.

"Well, Ben walked in the house and grandma gave him the most disgusted look. 'Boy, you have big feet.' That is what she said to him! Boy, you have big feet? What kind of a thing is that to say? I was mortified. When he left a week later, I borrowed my aunt's car to drive him to the airport. I had to sneak out of the house because grandma hated Ben so much, she would have never let me go."

Bewildered, Catherine asked, "why didn't she like him?" She had known Geraldine Smith was very strict and not at all friendly, but spiteful?

"Ben and his family were German, and grandma hated all Germans." Marie paused, then laughed ruefully. "Her maiden name was Mueller...did you know that? Grandma's maiden name? Well, we tried to convince her that was definitely a German name, but she insisted it was Pennsylvania Dutch! Ridiculous." Marie shook her head. "You see, her son, my Uncle Bill, served in World War II. Ben's dad, Benjamin, also served in World War II, but he was from Germany, so…"

"So they fought against each other." Understanding dawned as Marie shook her head affirmatively.

"Well, not directly, but yes. And Uncle Bill was injured during the war. 'They shot him full of shrapnel!' That was what grandma used to say. 'Those Germans shot your uncle full of shrapnel!' So grandma hated Ben. I'm sure it bothered her when we were married."

Catherine nodded her head in understanding, still perplexed by what Marie was doing here, and what this whole thing had to do with the wooden box resting on her table.

"So…" Catherine lead out slowly, "what is this box?"

Marie shook her head as if suddenly remembering her reason for the visit. "Sorry, sometimes I get off the subject a bit. You know how I am. Anyway, Grandpa Ernie had already died by the time I was a senior, so it was just grandma, Uncle Bill and I living in the old house. One day Grandma must have visited grandpa's brother, Harold. I'm not sure why…and I must have went along." The memory was jumbled and confused, but made such an impression on Marie, she knew it would forever be a part of her. "Harold's wife, Rachel, was at the house." Marie paused bestowing a knowing look on her host. As silence filled the room, Marie waited, allowing it to draw out for several long seconds.

"Oh yes!" Catherine exclaimed. "My mother's sister, Rachel, married your grandfather's brother, Harold." As the recollection dawned on her, she explained, "whenever someone says 'Rachel', I always think of my sister-in-law, her name is Rachel also."

"Of course," Marie nodded. "I forgot. But do you remember anything at all about *Aunt* Rachel and Harold?"

"Well…Rachel was a bit wild."

"Yes, my father has some," Marie paused, trying to think of a delicate way to describe the crazy stories her father had shared, "interesting stories about her. But Harold was an alcoholic, were you aware of that?"

"Not really.

Marie began, her voice sad and forlorn, "he lived in the bathroom stall of a gas station for awhile, Harold did." She spoke slowly, as if working to remember the entire story. "His son used to pick him up each year at Christmas, buy him a clean shirt, and take him home for dinner. But one year Harold behaved so badly, his son decided that the children should not witness their grandfather's…" She broke off. Not sure how to finish the thought, she just left it there, truncated. "Well, Rachel eventually ended up leaving him because of it. In fact, she married his twin brother, Henry."

Catherine nodded. This story was familiar; she must have heard it before.

"Henry was a wonderful husband, and a good father to those children," finished Marie. She shook her head. "Such a sad story."

The women looked at each other, each lost in their own recollections.

Finally Catherine broke the silence, "would you like some herbal tea?" She realized she hadn't offered Marie anything to drink upon arrival.

"I would love some," Marie sighed and followed Catherine around the corner into the dining area.

Walking to the adjacent kitchen, Catherine opened her cupboards and took out two mugs. She dropped a tea bag in one cup and filled it with water. After placing it in the microwave, and pouring herself a cup of coffee, she joined Marie at the dining room table. "It will just take a minute."

"Well, back to that day at Harold and Rachel's home," Marie continued. "Grandma must have been busy doing something. I was standing with Aunt Rachel. Uncle Harold came home, very drunk. I could tell that they were going to argue, you could feel it in the air. But it was the strangest argument I have ever witnessed."

Catherine looked puzzled. "Why was the argument so strange?"

"Well, Harold was the only one actually…speaking."

"What?"

The microwave timer rang and Catherine pulled herself from the story to fetch the tea. She placed the cup in front of her guest then sat down again.

"Thank you," Marie said.

"I don't understand." Catherine narrowed her eyes, confused.

Marie stared into her cup, then slowly shifted her focus upward. Deciding the best course of action was to simply plunge ahead, she took a deep breath and presented her information very matter-of-factly. "Harold was the only one speaking. He came in, took one look at Rachel and started arguing as if Rachel were talking back to him…but she wasn't." Marie looked into Catherine's eyes, trying to gauge the other woman's reaction. It was important she word this correctly.

"I don't understand."

"I remember the conversation so well because it was so odd. Harold looked at Rachel, said, 'no I have not.' He paused for a moment, then said, 'and how would you know that?'"

Marie focused on Catherine, trying to decide if she understood what was being implied. It just needed to be said. There was so much more to discuss. So before she lost her nerve, Marie blurted, "Catherine, Harold was reading Rachel's mind."

Catherine chuckled, but the look on Marie's face remained serious. The laughter died as she realized her guest was not joking. What did she mean? Harold read Rachel's mind? What was that supposed to mean?

"I still don't understand," was the only retort she could muster.

Marie sighed, and slowly reached for the box. She paused for a moment before touching it, as if bracing herself for what was going to happen when she opened the creaky hinges and the contents were revealed.

"Rachel gave this box to me that night, and asked me to keep it safe, but not to discuss it with anyone. It was kind of a family secret, and I was under the impression the box was to be protected, certainly not given away. But, the poor woman was upset. Who wouldn't be? I think she just wanted the entire ordeal to be over; her marriage to Harold, the abilities he had. I think she had had enough."

Catherine watched as Marie opened the box, half expecting something to jump out of the worn container. Both women looked at the contents simultaneously. There was a small book tucked neatly inside, along with several other objects. It was impossible to tell what these items were, as they were all wrapped in a variety of cloths. Marie slowly removed the book on top. It was extremely old and appeared to be some sort of diary.

Leafing carefully through the pages, she caressed them absently. A piece of the past…just sitting in her hand. If it had not been for the disturbing facts contained on the aged pages, she would have considered this a true treasure. As it stood, she had always thought of these writings as a curse. But if they could help Heidi and Geoff, if they could help Callan, then maybe she had been wrong all these years.

There were many entries in the book, and they were not all made by the same person. The writing varied, along with the type of ink. "What is it?" Catherine finally asked, her curiosity brimming.

"It's a journal. A very old journal."

Catherine raised her eyebrows in surprise.

Finding the page for which she was searching, Marie turned to Catherine. "I need to read some of it, and I think it will help you understand."

October 10, 1891   *Kilmacthomas, Ireland*

As this year is on the point of closing, we find ourselves unable to dwell in the place of our birth. Peace alas has away from us. Although it breaks the heart to consider leaving this, the land of our forefathers, little choice we have. The leaders of the churches have rallied forces, initiated efforts to disenfranchise us of everything we hold dear. "Heretics," cry they. "Abominations." Though we plead, they be deaf to our entreaties. It is our hope that we find peace, safety and security in America. To be sure, it's better for us to be there nor over here. That our children can live in a land of liberty and overcome fear. This book, with the others, will make the journey with us. May God deliver us safely to freedom. May the just endeavor to which we have dedicated our lives, and for which we suffer, prosper.

Brenna Mccree

Catherine jerked her head back in surprise as Marie revealed the author. Brenna Mccree.

"Mccree? Did you say Mccree?"

"Yes. The Mccrees were your great grand parents, correct?"

"On… my… father's… side…." Catherine's surprise caused her to speak slowly, thoughts and possibilities reeling through her mind. "Um… may I?"

"Of course." Marie carefully placed the book in her hand.

The entry by Brenna was written in beautiful, long, perfectly angled cursive at a time in history when writing was an art form that required time, skill and patience. She appeared to have written it with a quill.

"Wow," breathed Catherine, running her hand softly over the page. "It's strange to be reading something written so long ago. By someone to whom I am actually related."

"Like holding a bit of history."

"Yes!" she smiled brightly. But as quickly as the smile had been born, it faded. Replaced by concern and confusion. "They had to leave? Why? What else does the book say?"

Marie raised her eyebrows and glanced upward at the ceiling, as if skimming over the contents of the worn diary quickly in her mind. She pursed her lips in concentration. Most of the things she remembered were painful, tainted with sorrow. But there always existed a glimmer of hope. "A lot," she finally answered seriously. "A lot. And," she gestured into the still open box, "there are more books."

"Wait…" Catherine diverted her gaze, deep in thought. "Rachel was not related to the Mccrees. Rachel was my aunt on my *mother's* side. The Mccrees were on my *father's* side. Why would *Rachel* have this book?"

Marie smiled appreciatively, pleased Catherine was picking up on the incongruency surrounding the box and its contents. "I'm not sure. Other books in the chest concern both sides of your family. Some contain historical information. There are instructions in some of them which I don't understand at all. The box is a collection of writings about people with abilities. And many of those people are, in one way or another, related to you."

Catherine was stunned. "What? Why? Who collected them?"

Marie shrugged. "No idea. But I know your family is a large part of this puzzle, and I also know mine has at least a little to do with it. I think we can safely add the fact that these books did not come together by coincidence. Someone searched for them. Someone made it a point to bring them together for a reason. It's the only thing that makes sense."

Catherine nodded, still completely perplexed.

"And I must admit, I felt guilty for keeping them, kept thinking I should give them back to Rachel, but she had been so adamant about my taking them out of her sight. I doubt she would have welcomed seeing the chest again. She could have asked for it at any time! I would have returned it!" Marie pled her defense, even though no one was accusing her of anything.

"And then, she was gone." Marie still remembered the day she discovered Rachel had passed away. At a loss regarding what to do with the box, she hid it and forced the experience from her immediate attention. The memory would sneak out, sometimes, when it was least expected. The circumstances surrounding how she acquired it, all of the things she had discovered, smacking her in the face out of the blue. Like yesterday. When Heidi called.

"But these things belong in your family. And I think what is written in them can help Geoff and Heidi. I think they need to read the books," Marie finished.

Catherine stared down at the item in her hands. Her family. Her history. People she had never met, but to whom she was indelibly drawn. The feeling was overwhelming. But how could these things help Geoff and Heidi? What did *they* have to do with antique chests, diaries and history books?

"As if this wasn't enough," Marie laughed sardonically, "I need to fill you in on a few other things." The smile melted into concern. "And then tell you about Heidi and Geoff's problem."

"Problem? What kind of problem?"

"It's Callan… and it has a lot to do with this information." She gestured to the chest and it's contents.

Catherine drew back in her chair several inches in surprise, as if what Marie had just said jolted her backward. "These books?"

"It has to do with the reason the Mccrees were persecuted in Ireland. The reason they had to leave their country. The reason Harold could read his wife's mind. And the reason Callan's causing…well…" Marie searched for the appropriate words. She finally smiled and gave a little nod, "a stir."

Catherine's head was spinning. A man who could read his wife's mind. A hundred year old diary. Her grand daughter in trouble. What on earth could all these things have in common?

"Start from the beginning Marie," replied Catherine, "and make it slow, I am so confused."

Chapter Ten
Talents & Gifts

"The Mccrees had certain…talents…that made them…different from other people," began Marie tentatively.

"They were in show business. A trained dog act I believe, and they also danced." Catherine vaguely remembered hearing stories. Her brother, Don, knew more about the family. She made a mental note to call him and arrange a visit.

The women had moved downstairs. It was more comfortable here, with a couch and two soft chairs. Whenever the grand children came to visit, this was the space they occupied most of the time. The home to television and toys, it was every child's perfect place.

Marie searched for the right words. She did not wish to sound insane, but was not sure she could avoid it. "The Mccrees and our Uncle Harold had something in common."

Catherine was nodding her head, not in agreement, but to acknowledge she had heard what was said.

"As I told you, our Uncle Harold could read minds. No… that's not exactly right." She wanted to be as precise as possible. "He could experience things they experienced, sometimes only a fraction of a second after they experienced it. So, it was almost like he was reading their mind. And he was very good at it, his ability was quite strong." Marie looked at Catherine, and raised her eyebrows as if to ask, "do you believe me?"

Catherine was not sure what to think. This was impossible. She did not believe in ESP or any other such nonsense. "Okay, for the sake of argument, let's say Harold could tell what someone was thinking. And, let's assume that these diaries contain proof that the Mccrees had," she broke off, searching for the word, "oh yes, 'talents,' also. What does any of that have to do with Heidi and Geoff?"

Marie took a deep breath, thankful they had made it this far. "These 'talents' that both the Mccrees and Harold possessed are sometimes passed down through generations." She continued only when Catherine nodded slightly. "I think our grand daughter, Callan, has a similar gift."

"A similar gift?"

"Yes. In a nut shell, what I believe has happened is that Heidi and Geoff have inadvertently brought together two families that have strong…abilities. Harold, of course, is Heidi's great-great uncle and the Mccrees are Geoff's relatives. So, Geoff and Heidi's children, perhaps, have a greater chance of having similar…abilities."

Marie shook her head. Abilities. Talents. She kept using these words. What else could she call them? And what would she think if the tables were turned? How would she react if this conversation were reversed, and Catherine was the person attempting to explain the unexplainable?

"I know this sounds impossible, but I think I'm right, and I think the kids could use our help."

Catherine was unsure. Her motherly instinct told her that if her son were in trouble, she would be there for him. But common sense told her nothing could be wrong simply because what had been proposed was unfeasible.

"I'm going to Marcellus today. I've got to explain this to Heidi and Geoff. Would you be willing to come along?"

"I guess I could," Catherine answered slowly. "And maybe you could re-explain it to me at the same time."

Catherine called her husband, Geoff Sr., and told him she was going to Marcellus to visit Heidi and Geoff. He was, predictably, surprised.

"What?" Geoff Sr. scratched his head. His wife was rarely spontaneous, and a three hour trip, to the other side of the Michigan, just for a quick visit, was strange to say the least. "By yourself?"

"No, actually, Marie is here and we're driving together."

"Umm, okay." Totally confused, he shook his head and hung up the cell phone. A nearby co-worker shot him a questioning look and the older gentleman shrugged his shoulders. "The wife."

The man smiled knowingly. "Yea, can't figure mine out either."

Both men laughed.

Catherine climbed into Marie's dark blue Toyota Forerunner. The corner of her mouth turned up wryly as she recalled the flak Marie took from her family regarding this car.

"Get that off my lawn!" Marie's brother, Charles, would yell, teasingly, whenever she visited. A union steward for the UAW, he was an adamant proponent of buying 'American' cars. Marie's husband, Ben, had the unfortunate circumstance of working for Toyota and was able to help his children purchase leased vehicles from the company. Most of the kids took advantage of the discount, including Geoff and Heidi.

One year at a family reunion, Charles's yard was full of Toyota automobiles.

"I'm going to loose my job if anyone drives past here!" he yelled in greeting, striding across the lawn toward the hulking figure of his brother-in-law, Ben. Charles looked around as if expecting union spies to pop out of nearby bushes.

Ben swaggered up the lawn confidently. He was six foot two, very ample, and jovial. Embracing his brother-in-law fondly, and amid reciprocated blows to the back, the large man laughed. "True... true..." Ben smiled slyly then looking around as if taking mental inventory of the cars now parked three or four deep on the lawn. "They do make those pieces of junk you build look bad." Both men chuckled, again pounding each other between the shoulder blades as they walked through the doors leading to the swimming area.

Catherine's smile faded. "How are you doing Marie?"

"Great!" The uncomfortable silence that enveloped the two women startled Marie, and she glanced toward the passenger seat. Catherine's concerned look spoke volumes. "I'm good," she said more seriously. "Really."

It had been two years since Ben's death, but everyone still asked her how she was doing, still gave her that same look. Was it ever going to end? She knew they were worried about her but she was fine.

"Well," Marie began, wanting to change the subject. "Let me try to explain more about the situation while we drive."

"That would be great. I would really rather not seem baffled when you try to tell Heidi and Geoff about this."

"It *is* overwhelming," Marie agreed.

"And confusing," Catherine nodded.

"And unbelievable."

Over the next two hours, Marie summarized what she knew, and what she suspected, about both sides of the family.

"So, my family has a long history of these people with special… abilities," Catherine said, a question in her tone.

"Yes, it appears to run in certain genealogical lines." Catherine seemed more comfortable with the particulars, and Marie couldn't help but think that had to be a good thing.

"And your family has some people with these…talents… too," Catherine again posed the statement as a question.

"Exactly."

"And, there are different 'gifts' people can have?"

"From what I understand. I definitely don't know everything," said Marie as they pulled into the driveway in Marcellus, Michigan. "Only what I've read in a few of those books. And some things from another conversation I had with Rachel a little while later."

Catherine tilted her head in question.

"After reading some of the books, I had so many questions. I went to visit Rachel to try to find answers."

"And?"

"She wasn't pleased, and wouldn't divulge much, but she mentioned a few things Harold had told her." Again Marie focused to remember, her recollection of that day hazy and muted. She had felt like a detective that day. Sitting at the dining room table with Rachel, aching for answers to the questions the books generated, scrambling for clues, trying to piece together an intricate puzzle full of danger and intrigue. It all seemed so far removed; a story to which she was inextricably drawn but from which she was completely insulated. Safe. Until now.

"Harold attended a school for a few years, but ended up leaving for some reason. He learned to control and channel his ability there. The place changed the way he looked at his talent. Before, it had been a curse. It frightened people. Made him an outcast. He had to hide it. But there he became convinced that it was a gift. I'm sure he told Rachel more, but she shared very little. Two things stood out. Maybe she thought they were important. First, that *everyone* in the world has certain abilities."

Catherine pulled a puzzled look and Marie shrugged her shoulders, not entirely sure about the ramifications of that statement herself.

"Second, that when people with strong abilities have children, those children are watched carefully and great things are expected of them."

Catherine considered this a moment, then looked down at the tattered book in her lap. She ran her hand over the cover absentmindedly. "Then what about Rachel and Harold's children? Shouldn't they have been really… different?" Different seemed like a strange word to use, but it was the only one that surfaced.

Marie was nodding and wore a forlorn smile. "Yes, but, they were completely normal, and that may have been part of the problem."

Chapter Eleven
The Intruder

October 13, 2009
Shanghai, China

Several hours after the girls left the academy to return to their hotel, Annalynn and Devin entered the lift together. When the elevator closed, Devin opened a small door at the bottom of the control panel. He waved the back of his right hand in front of a red laser, Annalynn followed suit. A clicking noise emanated from the reader as a panel below the laser slid to the right to reveal another set of floor buttons. They were small and dark green in color. Devin pressed the number thirteen. The panel closed and the lift began moving downward quickly.

Annalynn shifted her weight to move closer to Devin. "Don't say anything about them," she whispered in a menacing voice. "We need to get more information first."

"Afraid I'm going to steal your thunder?"

Annalynn let out an incredulous but controlled sigh. She forced her face to remain passive, glancing at the security camera in the upper left hand corner of the elevator. "You're such an…" The sentence trailed off as the lift slowed and the doors parted. Berating herself for sharing the information regarding the older sister, she took a breath and tried again. "Devin," she said with as much self control as she could muster. "If he asks a question we can't answer yet, we'll look very stupid."

The hallway which appeared was dimly lit, but the walls were painted bright white which reflected light well. Devin stepped out quickly and turned right. Annalynn's legs were shorter than his. She lengthened her stride, but the efforts were futile. Surging forward, she struggled to keep up. "Trust me," she almost seemed to be begging, "we shouldn't say anything yet."

The large man stopped abruptly in front of a heavy metal door on the left. He turned, looking down into her pleading face. He gave her a swarthy grin, placed his right hand on the doorknob, opened it quickly, and walked in ahead of her.

The room chosen for full board meetings was stark white, mid-size, and more rectangular than square, with a long table spanning almost the depth of the space. Harsh, fluorescent lighting ran parallel with the table. There were no plants, no shelves, nothing except the heavy, wooden table, at least thirty metal chairs surrounding it, and a clock hanging on the wall. All but two of the seats were occupied. Devin and Annalynn quickly found their places near the closest end of the table as nine o'clock struck. Clearing her mind, Annalynn forced herself to remain calm.

The dark figure seated at the opposite end of the room faced away from the group. As the clock chimed, he slowly turned his swivel chair. Annalynn jumped as his features emerged from the shadows which kept their unsavory secret until this moment. A suffocating silence entombed the shocked occupants. Annalynn marveled at the transformation; she had seen him just days ago. Whole. Darkly handsome. But now…

Now he had an eerie gauntness about him as though a horrific disease had ravished his body and left him consumed. The man at the end of the table was tall and wiry, with harsh features. The skin on his face stretched taunt across his skull, his black eyes were sunken and overshadowed by his now protruding brow.

His eyes.

Those eyes that had been an arresting shade of stormy blue. Those eyes that had captured Annalynn on the day of decision were now coal; the long table and its occupants reflected in their perfect darkness, like a mirror that could penetrate their very souls. Haunted, she shuttered. His dark hair was slicked back, elongating his forehead. The man still wore his signature black suit and cloak, but what was inside had changed. Degenerated.

Slowly raising his arms, he placed them on the table. His hands were large and powerful, as if they had spent a lifetime engaged in hard labor. But not coarse, as one would have supposed. They were soft, complimented by well manicured nails. A compelling blend of harsh and soft, masculine and feminine. Moving to rest his elbows on the table, he placed the palms of his hands together as if praying. Purposefully leaning forward until his lips touched his index fingers, their leader closed his eyes as if in thought.

The dark man remained in this posture, still and silent, then took a deep breath, his mind racing to the space occupied by Annalynn. She sensed his approach and braced herself, her thoughts clear. Calm. The anger and frustration of just moments ago in the hallway had been compartmentalized and filed away. Hidden from him. The horror at seeing him now, pushed aside. She resisted his intrusion. Resented it.

A small smile stole across his lips. He opened his eyes and they appraised each other for a moment.

She opened her mind, just a bit, keeping her foot wedged against the door, preventing the barrier from totally admitting him. The intruder.

"*Why?*" he thought.

"*Out loud,*" she answered in her mind, giving him an intent gaze.

"Alright, we'll play it her way," he mused to himself, entertained and satisfied at the same time. He liked this woman. He had won her, despite her strong ties to Branch. Annalynn's defection had been the icing on the cake. She was the only person in the world who could completely devestate his brother, the only person who could hurt Branch so deeply. Nautas relished this victory above all others.

The dark man nodded his head slowly and turned his attention to the other reader in the room; the woman sitting half way down the table from him. She was tall, and had very long, blond hair. It was almost white. A striking woman. She also knew he was coming, and turned her head toward him, welcoming him. He did not know which he preferred; someone who challenged him a bit, or someone who went willingly. He closed his eyes.

"*What do I need to see? Show me what you saw. Take me.*"

The room slowly began spinning around the two of them, increasing in velocity until in an explosion of light, the scene abruptly changed. The dark, solemn boardroom was gone. He was in an airplane, and it was morning.

A pretty petite girl with strawberry blond hair walked toward him, carrying a backpack. When she stopped to shift her luggage, he tipped his head back to appraise her, a look of boredom and distaste masking the interest that bubbled inside him.

What powers did she possess? What were her weaknesses?

The girl met his gaze, challenging him. She did not fear.

Ahhh, arrogance, I love that character trait. It makes them weak.

She would dread him soon enough. He gazed into her eyes and entered her mind. She was not ready for him, and seemed stunned for a moment. Then she wanted to shift.

A shifter? Interesting. How old was this girl? She could not be more than twelve, perhaps even younger. Very interesting.

He journeyed further. Evenings filled with fearful dreams of dark threats. Moving away from them; to the woods or the shed, safe places. His head pounded as he relived night after night filled with terror and flight. He relished the feelings coursing through his being.

This was a child! This was a baby who could shift!

Filing that discovery into his memory, he directed his attention to what was happening. As each scenario played in his mind, horror washed over him like waves in an angry ocean. But then there was safety and warmth.

No!

He concentrated to jump ahead. Frustration, anger, impatience, resentment.

Yes, that is what I am looking for.

But it was time to leave, he needed to return. As he pulled back he felt the strong connection to family, and especially to an older sister.

That could be useful.

Haltingly he allowed it to engulf him in an attempt to discover how he could manipulate it to his advantage.

Love. Attachment. Enough.

He needed to leave now! Sharp pain shot through him and he wrenched himself away. The girl walked past, and he returned to reading a fashion magazine.

Back in the boardroom, the meeting continued. Only a fraction of a second had been spent gleaning the information the white-haired woman possessed. Nautas nodded his approval to her.

"So practical," he thought condescendingly. "If only we never had to speak; it would save so much time." His gaze flicked back to Annalynn for an instant.

"New arrivals?"

"Yes, Mr. Balak," Devin replied quickly.

Nautas had changed his surname several days ago, hoping to rid himself of any human connection. Nautas Balak. He enjoyed the sound of it. Enjoyed hearing others refer to him as Nautas Balak. Yes, a good name.

"Five this week, two today," Devin answered.

"And the sisters?" Nautas directed the question to Annalynn.

Staring down at some papers on the table, Devin was unaware Nautas addressed the woman beside him.

"Staying at housing unit five," Devin answered before Annalynn could speak. "Zeke is their..." feeling the energy in the room change, he looked up, too late, "...tail for now." The last words were spoken softly, broken by fear.

As Devin's voice trailed off, Mr. Balak slowly shifted his eyes from Annalynn...to Devin.

Devin moved uncomfortably in his seat as the room filled with a feeling of disquiet. It pressed down, and he found it difficult to breath, difficult to think.

Nautas's anger bubbled. The darkness in the room lingered for several moments until it had served its purpose, then the man at the end of the table swept it away and continued with his questioning.

"Annalynn, I would like to hear *your* thoughts."

Nodding, she glanced at Devin, daring him to contradict her, then returned her focus to the end of the table. "They are promising, but we'll need time to evaluate the situation."

"She's a powerful shifter," Mr. Balak replied succinctly, "and very young."

"Yes." Relieved Nautas seemed interested in only the younger girl, Annalynn none-the-less winced at their leader's surety regarding Callan's abilities. But the younger girl was a shifter and would be safeguarded by that fact. It was Alexine who would need protecting.

There were several moments of silence, as if the dark man were allowing her time to expound on her thoughts. But she met his gaze firmly, revealing nothing more.

"Keep me informed," he finally answered, satisfied. He trusted this reader. *She* had chosen *him*.

"I will."

"And the other three that arrived?" This question was directed to Devin who was still attempting to gather his wits.

He swallowed and answered haltingly, "yes, a changer who is nineteen."

"Good, good."

"A traveler who is twenty-three."

"Hmmm." Nautas pushed his lips together and narrowed his eyes slightly. He considered the possibilities. When the dark man nodded, Devin continued.

"And," Devin paused, glancing around nervously. Speaking quickly, the last statement was quiet and subdued, "a healer. She's twenty-one."

Mr. Balak looked over slowly, meeting Devin's gaze. The large man's eyes shifted nervously away.

"Don't waste anyone's time with her," Nautas snarled, as if offended to be speaking the words. "She's useless."

Not wanting to become even more of a disappointment, Devin responded quickly and with finality, "of course sir, she'll be gone in a month."

"No! Sooner!" Nautas barked, leaning forward as everyone in the room jumped. The dark man settled back into his chair. "And when she leaves," Mr. Balak continued slowly and silkily, unwilling to close this subject quickly, "it *will* be *without* her gift." The words he spoke smacked of sadistic evil, the menacing smile that stole across his lips confirmed his command.

This healer was to be harmed. Annalynn's conscience seared, as she fingered the seam of her pants nervously. What was happening?

"*You* will take care of that personally," Nautas hissed threateningly. "Do you understand me Devin? There are to be no healers admitted to the academy. None."

Although he was not looking at the dark man hurling hate at him, Devin could tell that the leader of the group was staring. Boring a hole into his being from the end of the table. Devin dropped his gaze further and nodded somberly, "of course, sir."

"Good…good…very good Devin." He spoke the words as if stroking an animal, a pet.

Their leader changed the subject quickly. "And the others…anything noteworthy?"

"Classes are going well," Annalynn responded, suppressing her urge to flee the room. "But we may want to consider another instructor."

Nautas raised his eyebrows in question.

"There are now about 95 shifters upstairs, and over 400 underground." Her argument with Devin, her surprise regarding Nautas's appearance and icy presence, his instructions to Devin; all emotional blows that pushed her off balance. She fought to retain control of her options and emotions.

Although Annalynn typically hid it well, today had been too much. She had always felt a certain level of distain for shifters, now those feelings poked through as she spoke. Shifters were impulsive, emotional, and generally found it difficult to reign themselves in. The irony regarding her own inability to maintain a neutral façade buzzed just behind her train of thought, annoying her.

The dark man's lips turned up slightly in a tiny, triumphant smile. He sensed her animosity and relished it for a moment. "They are the workers," he responded soothingly, as if giving Annalynn remedial lessons in leadership. "They get things done, Anna." He paused thoughtfully. "You feel they are beneath you, you feel they are not as developed, not as useful, perhaps, as readers?"

Her heart skipped a beat. Control. She had to control herself and get through this meeting. Concentrating and suppressing her impulse to breath more quickly, she plucked her words carefully. "They are the soldiers, sir," she stated, as if relenting a point. "As long as they have a strong leader," she inclined her head toward him, "they will be a mighty army."

His smile broadened. Flattery. How un-like Anna. "Spoken like a true diplomat," he said, clapping his hands together softly and chuckling. It was not a joyful outburst, but an evil thing that lurked in the room, setting the other occupants on edge.

"Mr. Wu, how are things in the libation business?" Mr. Balak asked, emphasizing the word "libation" as if it were quite entertaining.

Annalynn relaxed, out of the hot seat for a moment.

A small Asian man in a light tan suit seated midway down the table responded, "ahh, yes, good." He spoke in heavily accented English. Pressing a button on the computer sitting in front of him, the man donned a satisfied grin. "Beddy good. We have acquired nine new places business. We are own sixty-eight percent market by end month."

"And our friends in the government, they are comfortable with this… situation?"

Mr. Wu smiled broadly, "they appreciate beddy much many contributions we extend. Yes, sir, they comfortable with arrangement."

"It is amazing what one is able to procure in only several days." Their accomplishments since the split were staggering, the dark man himself was surprised by their success. He looked knowingly around at the group. "As if it were meant to be."

The rest of the meeting centered around various other methods to raise funds, which means could best support their endeavors. Each person reported on their sphere of responsibility in turn.

"I love China," Nautas remarked at the end of the meeting. "Such a charming place to stage a coup."

The members sitting around the table looked satisfied, and perhaps a bit relieved.

"Well," the dark man rose from his seat quickly, "I won't be back for a month. I have…things which much be attended to." Chairs slid back from the table in a cacophony of sound as small groups of individuals formed impromptu meetings to iron out details and make minor decisions.

Their leader passed Annalynn and whispered, "I'd like to see you in the hallway."

Mr. Balak strode through the door, as Annalynn woodenly rose from her seat and followed. Turning right, they moved toward the elevator. The noise their foot falls made seemed deafening in the silence, the cadence pounded in Annalynn's head, reverberated in her chest.

"Things are going well. In fact, better than I anticipated." The speed with which he had been able to take over the academy, the way all his ideas had come to fruition, it meant he had been right all along. He knew it! The fools who opposed him, where were they now? Perhaps… he was capable of *more* than originally planned. Perhaps… *much* more.

And his crowning achievement: *they* had found *him*. They, the repositors of ways and means to attain all he had ever dreamed of. All he longed for. He was ready, worthy. The past several days with them had been illuminating. So much to learn! So much to find! Having taken the first of the four oaths, he intended to plunge ahead and finish the course. Why had he waited so long? It was as if, for the first time in his life, he had a mission. A definite path laid before him.

The split at the academy had initiated the process, had been his offering; proof he was willing to sacrifice. And his offering had been accepted. If only he had known it was so easy to prove himself, he would have instigated the division long ago. Maybe years. But, what did it matter? The process initiated, now it was *he* who needed to embark upon the seldom-traversed path. His eminent rise was not hampered by anything or anyone; it was totally under his control. The road that would lead to domination, to unprecedented power! He pulled himself back to the present.

"After only several days, the security systems are up and running, the technology we have introduced is…staggering." The dark figure stopped abruptly, heady excitement filling him; the things he had learned. "The power." He spoke the word reverently, caressing it. "It's just sitting there, waiting to be harnessed, to be commanded. It is eternal in nature Anna! Always there, surrounding and engulfing all."

He knew she could not completely comprehend these facts. But perhaps… soon…she too would realize her potential. Would rise and take the next logical step. Yes, she would follow him.

"Waiting for those who will take it. For those worthy to claim it." Turning slowly to face her, Nautas grasped Annalynn's chin with his right hand. She was *his* now. "Us Anna. We will do it…together!" Tipping her head back, he moved in slowly.

Annalynn's heart raced as the distance between the two of them disappeared. He was so close, too close. She turned her head slightly to avoid contact, feeling as if he would engulf her if she relented.

What was happening? As they drew closer to each other, darkness shadowed Annalynn's mind. She felt vulnerable, isolated, confused. Knowing he was not trying to read her, Annalynn realized that his mere physical presence had become overpowering. What had happened over the course of the previous few days? How had he changed so quickly? What had he become? In desperation she clung to the first memory that rushed forward to defend her. *"I believe in you. I believe in you."*

Nautas smiled, he could feel the woman's heart pounding. When she turned her head, he brushed his lips against her ear. "Us," he repeated softly. She wanted to play coy? That was fine with him; he enjoyed a well planned challenge. It was how he had won her.

Annalynn pulled back to look at him. Several days ago she had been fairly sure of her decision. But now... Nautas continued, too blinded by his obsessions to notice her hesitation. He turned and began striding down the hall again, beckoning Annalynn to walk by his side.

"The technology necessary for full control is only several steps away." He was drawn to this fact with immeasurable passion. "I can feel it." Glancing at the beautiful woman next to him, Nautas smiled. Being back in this place, his place, he could sense it's potential. It was intoxicating.

The dark man paused at the elevator, turning toward his second-in-command. The things they would accomplish together. Nautas relished these thoughts for a moment, then returned to business. There would be time enough to contemplate that later.

"The sisters," he began slowly as if mulling things over, "they are not to leave us." He looked down at Annalynn, his face now expressionless.

She met his gaze, trying to decide how to respond. "Nautas," she said, imploring him slightly, "perhaps..."

But he cut her off. Looking at her sternly, as one would a naughty child, he repeated, "not to leave us Anna." He had made his decision. It was absolute and not open for discussion, even by her. There would be few additions at the academy now that the separation was complete. Painfully aware Branch had halted the influx of students, Nautas realized they needed to retain every possible candidate. Especially these two. Fortunately his brother had been unable to stop the arrivals this week. He would make the most of that situation.

The dark man's mind flashed back to the little girl in the airplane. There was something about the child. What was it? The answer was elusive, as if it were hiding behind the next corner. Yet, as he approached, the memory fled and took refuge in another spot. What was it? A child that shifted. *A child that shifted.* It was possible, of course. It happened sometimes. It was just...rare. And this girl. Nautas could not shake the feeling of deja' vu. This girl.

Annalynn watched as her dark leader disappeared several seconds later, melting into the surroundings like a chameleon. He was gone, she sensed his departure. Dropping her head, her eyes affixed to the floor, she inhaled deeply. It felt good. She wondered how long it had been since she was able to breath, to relax enough to completely fill her lungs with air. How long?

Nine years ago they had agreed to keep the little girl a secret; Annalynn was immeasurably grateful for that stroke of inspiration. He had been right, after all. He had been right about everything. Everything.

Confused regarding what her next step should be, angry with herself for divulging so much to Devin, she stood in the hallway, alone, her mind reeling.

"Not to leave," she repeated to herself. "Not to leave."

Chapter Twelve
Shifter Training

"It's time to get up, it's time to get up, it's time to get up in the morning! It's time to get up, it's time to get up, it's time to get up today!"

Callan was belting out their mother's "morning song" as she jumped up and down on Alexine's bed. Both girls loathed the revelry, with it's sing-song melody line. Their mother only used it on special occasions like weekends or holidays. It seemed appropriate for Callan to sing it now.

"Wake up!" yelled Callan. When her older sister failed to rise to the screaming, she let out a sigh of frustration. "Come on! It's already eight o'clock!"

Alexine mumbled something incoherent and rolled over in bed.

"Ughh!" Callan stomped back into the bathroom as someone knocked sharply at the door. The little red-head turned toward the sound, but before she could make a move, her older sister had swooped into the hallway, wrapped in a blanket.

"Yes?" Alexine inquired through the small crack when she had opened the door, just an inch. The door strained against the security chain put in place the prior evening.

"Good morning," came the decidedly confident voice of their escort, Zeke.

"Good morning Zeke. We'll be down in a second, Callan's still getting ready."

The red-head let out a burst of disgust. "Yea right!" She rounded the corner from the bathroom into the entryway, scandalized, but Alexine had already shut the door.

The girls stared at each other for a moment. Callan wore an ugly, disgusted look but Alexine's playful demeanor melted the little girl's resentment. They both laughed.

"We're in China!" they screamed together, grasping hands firmly then jumping up and down in glee.

Several minutes later, Callan announced she was going downstairs since *she* was ready and that Alexine should "hurry it up." The little girl prepared to leave their room to the anguished cries of her older sister imploring her to wait. It was to no avail.

"Perhaps tomorrow we'll wake up when we're called," replied Callan condescendingly, cocking her head to one side. She grabbed her sweat shirt, then turned back to glance around the room for something she might have forgotten.

Hurling a nasty look in her direction, Alexine hurriedly pulled on clothes, falling over in an attempt to shove a foot into the leg of her jeans. "Ouch!" She hit the floor hard.

Callan looked wickedly down at her sister struggling on the carpet. "Well, hello Zeke," the little red-head said in a high-pitched voice, mimicking the conversation she anticipated having with the attractive young man. "Oh no, Alexine's still getting ready, she has a very hard time getting up in the morning. Kind of lazy if you ask me, but what a beautiful spirit." The little girl placed her right hand over heart, smiling with sickening sweetness.

"Callan!" Alexine yelled. "You wouldn't dare!"

Taking a deep bow, the little girl slammed the door as she left.

"Good morning," she sang out approaching Zeke in the waiting area downstairs.

"Hey, Callan."

"Wow, he really is cute," she observed silently. "Thanks for taking us out to dinner." Callan gave Zeke a perfunctory curtsy. "I was seriously starving to death." Zeke laughed, prompting the little red-head to give him a half-grin. She was typically able to win people over with her dry, playful, sometimes unexpected humor.

"Where's Alexine?"

Callan considered her options. Should she rat out her sister? It would be such fun and she completely deserved it! When Alexine stumbled onto the scene, she and Zeke could giggle at her. Sighing heavily, she decided today would begin mercifully. A part of her resented the show of good will. "Oh, she had trouble getting her contacts in, she'll be down in a second." Alexine owed her one. A big one.

"Good morning," the older girl beamed several minutes later as she approached the two of them sitting on the couch, "sorry I'm late."

Zeke rose, but Callan remained seated, her expression a mix of disgust and impatience.

"Good morning."

Looking past Zeke, Alexine gave her little sister a questioning glance. What had she told him?

Enjoying the tension displayed in her sister's eyes, Callan decided to have a little fun at Alexine's expense. "So you got them in okay?" Callan asked, knowing Alexine would have no idea what she was talking about.

"Huh?" Alexine smiled sheepishly at Zeke.

"Your contacts," said Callan, feigning disinterest while brushing at imaginary lint on her shirt. "You got them in okay?"

"Oh...yea...they can be such a pain when my eyes are dry."

One of Alexine's attributes Callan enjoyed; she caught on quickly and knew how to play along.

"Well, the taxi is waiting ma' ladies." Zeke bowed low and motioned for them to exit the building ahead of him.

Donning an aristocratic air, Callan stood, lifted her chin and looked down her nose. Their escort smiled. "And could you see to it Jeeves," she began, "that the room is tidied and at precisely 72 degrees upon our return?" The animated girl pranced out the door like a princess as Zeke shook with silent laughter.

This girl was refreshing. He liked her.

Stepping down the stairs, Alexine resisted the urge to scold Callan for overindulging her ego.

"So, what can we expect on our first day?" asked Alexine as the taxi pulled away.

"You'll get a tour of the facility, and then they like to get you right into classes."

Callan's face spread into a smile. "You mean I get to start today?"

"Yep." Zeke grinned back at her. "Why waste time?"

Callan clenched her fist and shook it as if she had just won a competition. "Yes!"

"What will I do all day?" Alexine had been slightly worried. In the back of her mind, she always wondered what would occupy *her* time while Callan went through this…training.

"Oh, don't worry," replied Zeke reassuringly, "you'll be busy."

"But with what? It's not like I have a gift or anything."

Zeke laughed.

"What? What's funny?"

The young man turned in the front seat to look directly at her, "Alexine."

He said her name softly, almost in a whisper. Alexine enjoyed hearing it. She decided Zeke could say her name anytime.

"Everyone has a gift. *Everyone.*"

Then he smiled. Not a joking smile, but a kind smile. An accepting smile. A flirtatious smile? She blushed and was glad he turned away in time to miss it.

* * *

"Well, hello there," Devin boomed as Zeke lead the girls into his office. "And thank you Zeke."

"No problem, sir," the young man replied officially. "I'll see you at lunch." He left the room quickly, closing the door behind him with a snap.

Devin finished making several marks on the papers sitting in front of him, picked them up, opened a drawer, and dropped them in roughly. "The tour," he said, as if making an announcement. Rising from his chair, the large man walked around his desk. "Are you ready?"

"Yes!" replied both girls.

Devin turned right into the hallway after leaving his office then slowed approaching the door just down the hall. "This is Annalynn's office."

They continued. As they passed a door, Devin explained who used the room, and what subject they taught, but did not break stride.

"Mr. Boyson's classroom. Changer training level two."

The girls looked at each other for several moments, then shrugged when Devin offered no additional information regarding what "changer training level two" meant.

"Ms. Clarvink's classroom. Tutoring in any subject."

That was easy to understand.

"Ms. Kerry's room. Traveler theory level three."

Traveler theory? Alexine felt she should be taking notes to ask questions later.

"Mr. Malark's room. Shifter prep level one."

Callan paused at the door and touched it. Shifter prep level one. She had no idea what that meant, but it was connected to her ability. She was a shifter. The word sounded good; powerful and slightly mysterious. She repeated it again and again in her mind. Shifter. I'm a shifter.

"Ms. Jang. Reader training level two."

"Devin, are we going to learn about all of these things?" Although the large man seemed intent on a quick tour with few explanations, Alexine could not help but pose the question. Her mind raced. How many abilities existed? What did all of these new words mean? Traveler? Changer? Reader?

The man leading them stopped and turned. "Yes, of course," he answered dismissively, turned and began walking again. "You'll be brought up to speed on everything."

More rooms, more words neither girl understood.

Devin stopped as they again approached his office. "As you can see, the building is oval and the hallways circle around, so we're back where we began."

Callan smiled up at him.

"Here we go again." Alexine did not like Devin. She had hoped the exhaustion of the day before had clouded her judgment. That upon seeing the man today, she would realize she had been too harsh. Nope. Definitely didn't like him. Arrogant. Condescending. And kind of, she hated to admit it, well...not too bright.

The large man smiled as he turned toward her and Alexine smiled back. "Nice," she thought guiltily, trying to force herself to look at him in a new, more forgiving light. "That will be my project," she decided, "to like Devin." They walked toward a set of stairs leading down to the first level. "I wonder if someone can teach me that," she mused. "Liking Devin, prep level one. Was that offered?"

Escorting the girls past more classrooms on the bottom floor, Devin again threw out the name of the teacher and what subject was taught. And again, the words fell foreign on Alexine's ears.

They stopped in the cafeteria where workers were busy cleaning up after breakfast.

"Have you girls eaten yet?" Devin asked after a quick look around the room.

Callan spoke up. "Nope, but we're not hungry anyway."

"Couldn't have anything to do with all those dumplings last night, could it?" Alexine whispered sarcastically as the group left the cafeteria and moved to the large auditorium they had looked down upon the previous day. It seemed bigger now that they were standing on the ground floor of the spacious area.

"Wow," Callan ignored her sister's comment and spun in a circle, taking in the entire room. "It's huge!"

Devin glanced around, "yep."

"Do you use this room for anything other than," Alexine searched for her words, "um, what we watched yesterday? Uh...shifting practice." She looked up at the seating surrounding the auditorium on the floor above, picking out the spot where they stood the day before.

Devin fell silent. This took Alexine by surprise since he tended to answer questions quickly, often before the person asking the question stopped speaking. Turning back toward him, she was shocked to see a look of...what? Fear?

"Well, yes," he stammered, then gathered himself. "We do use it for *shifter training*." Devin emphasized his last words as if handing her the proper term, then paused for several seconds. "And, we also have meetings in here occasionally." Just a hint of tension filled the air.

Turning, Devin walked quickly toward the door they had accessed to enter the room. When Callan shot Alexine a questioning stare, the older sister shrugged her shoulders. What had she said?

Once they entered the hallway, Devin seemed to relax. "The only training that requires a lot of space is shifting. So most of the classes occur in the smaller rooms on both floors."

"Oh." Callan nodded her head, encouraging Devin to elaborate. He seemed entertained by her enthusiasm, but said nothing more.

As they passed the security personnel, Alexine winced. She chanced a look at Callan, who gave her an annoyed stare. "What?" Alexine mouthed silently. "I don't like it!"

"Shhh," Callan mouthed back not making a sound either, then shook her head "no" emphatically.

"Well, let's head back to my office. We can fetch your temporary badges, and get started."

Before the group had a chance to mount the steps, a short, dark haired woman approached at a clip.

"Hello Mr. Rippinger." She winked at Alexine.

Although the gesture seemed strange, Alexine was instantly comfortable around this stranger. She had a motherly feeling about her. A kind, caring aura that seemed to permeate the surrounding space. Noting unexpectedly that she was grinning back at the woman, Alexine nodded a greeting, feeling self-conscious.

"Elizabeth," Devin replied, acknowledging her with a slight, somber nod.

The woman turned her attention to the girls looking expectant.

"Yes," answered Devin, anticipating the question. Flourishing his hand to introduce them, he announced, "this is Alexine and this is Callan. Callan will be joining you today. She's a shifter."

Directing his comments to the girls, he inclined his head toward the newcomer. "Elizabeth instructs Shifter Training Level Four which, I believe, you are prepared for Callan."

Elizabeth raised her eyebrows in interest. "Really? Level Four first day? Well, let's get started then," she said jovially. "I was headed that way." She grabbed Callan by the arm, pulling her along.

"Wait!" Alexine's outburst was louder than intended and a bit demanding. On alert, the guards spun to face the group as Elizabeth stopped and turned back around.

Bristling under the irritated gazes of the guards, Alexine continued more humbly, "are…are we going to meet up for lunch?" It was the first thing that came to mind.

"Oh, yes dear, we'll see you at lunch!" the shifting teacher announced happily. The pair trotted off down the hall, Elizabeth at her quick step, still holding onto the little red-head.

As Alexine watched them leave, the panic that gripped her as Callan was unexpectedly dragged off evaporated. It was replaced by a sense of security. In fact, Alexine guiltily admitted, she was even slightly entertained watching her little sister attempt to keep up with her new instructor, Callan's short little legs moving quickly to maintain the frantic pace.

"And as for you," Devin began, "Annalynn wanted to…" he paused as if attempting to find the correct words, "…get to know you better."

Alexine felt slightly uncomfortable about this. Since their first meeting, and the overwhelming fear that possessed her in the small store, she had been planning to avoid Annalynn. Added to this recollection were the impressions Alexine felt in her presence. Annalynn seemed to have a lot of tension brimming just below the surface; turmoil and struggle. It made the older girl nervous. But instead of attempting to bow out of this arrangement, Alexine heard herself say, "oh, yea, that would be good."

"Well then…until lunch." Devin jerked his head in the direction of Annalynn's office. "Just knock."

Nodding nervously, Alexine walked down the hall then turned and rapped on the door.

"Come in."

The older girl took a steadying breath and turned the knob.

The office was decidedly more feminine than Devin's. Several plants sat on shelves attached to the walls, while small photos of lavish landscapes and angular city scenes adorned the top of a light colored wooden desk. Annalynn sat in a computer chair facing away from the door gazing out the window.

"Good morning," said Alexine tentatively, bracing herself for the uncomfortable feeling she feared would barrel toward her without warning. Annalynn stood and turned. The beautiful Asian woman looked tired, sad. Disappointed? Alexine did not feel as intimidated.

"Good morning," she answered back, and motioned to a large, couch sitting against the wall. The older girl took a seat placing herself at the far left and Annalynn sat beside her, quite close.

"Well," began Annalynn. "I think it would be a good idea for us to get to know each other before you begin _your_ training."

Alexine could not disguise her surprise. This was a different person sitting beside her. The woman had become someone else. Someone that did not make her feel like squirming in her seat and inventing an excuse to leave. Someone whom she wanted to know better. How could this be? Clearing her mind of the thoughts regarding Annalynn's sudden personality change, the confused girl suddenly realized what had just been said.

"I'm sorry…did you say _my_ training?"

The reading instructor had expected this reaction; the young lady had no idea she too possessed abilities. Annalynn enjoyed breaking the news and smiled. "Yes, of course. Unless you are not interested in developing your skills."

Alexine looked around the room, searching for another person, assuming there must be someone else to whom Annalynn was speaking. The instructor laughed and Alexine could not help but join her. It was as if the older woman had not enjoyed herself in a long time and truly needed to be happy for a few moments.

Annalynn composed herself and began. "From the moment I met you, I sensed you had a special gift."

Alexine had no idea what this woman was talking about.

"It's not exactly your talent that makes you special," Annalynn gazed upward as if searching for a way to explain something difficult to the young woman sitting beside her. "It's the person you are."

"I'm sorry, but I'm completely confused. The only reason I'm here is because I needed to bring Callan. She's the one with the…abilities."

Annalynn smiled at her again. This girl was so refreshing, innocent and sincere. Talking with Alexine was like a breath of fresh air, and Annalynn realized she missed being around people with these qualities. Her mind was suddenly filled with the image of a tall, well built man with light brown hair streaked with gray. He had compassionate eyes. She pushed the picture away. "You have a gift that is very strong."

Alexine shook her head "no."

Annalynn nodded her head "yes" insistently. "Alexine, you're a reader. But it's not this gift alone that caught my attention. You have an innate ability to relate to people, to understand them, even without reading them. If you're successful at fusing these tendencies with your reading ability, I have no idea how far you'll be able to progress. Because I've never met someone exactly like you."

Alexine again shook her head "no."

Annalynn again nodded her head "yes." But this time she laughed. "And if you don't stop shaking your head, we're both going to get very dizzy!"

Chapter Thirteen
Hippy-Girl

"What have *you* been doing?" asked Callan as she joined Alexine at the lunch table.

"Hanging out with Anna."

"Anna?" the younger girl repeated, scowling. "Who the heck is Anna?"

"Annalynn."

"Oooh." She gave Alexine an overly-impressed look dripping with sarcasm. "Since when do you refer to an instructor by a pet name?" The older girl stuck out her tongue, and Callan laughed. "Seriously, who have you been with?"

"She's really nice, actually. I like her."

"What about yesterday in the shop? She scared you." The little girl flashed back to those moments in the little store and Alexine's disquieted demeanor. It had unnerved even Callan, who was not shaken easily.

"I don't know. But now that I've gotten to know her a little..."

The girls sat in silence for several moments. Bewildered, Callan took a breath and broke the trance, "well, I'm starving, so let's go get in line."

"Yea," agreed Alexine, pulling her mind from what happened yesterday in the shop. They both stood.

The cafeteria at the academy was a large room located adjacent to the auditorium. Home to ten long tables, the room was obviously a popular gathering place; young adults filled almost every available space. A buffet lined the far wall, and many older, stern-faced Asian women stood behind the food bar serving students.

Several people looked at Alexine and Callan questioningly as they moved through the crowd. Glancing around suspiciously, the younger girl whispered, "why are they staring at us?"

"Well, it appears that we are pretty young to be here. Haven't you noticed?"

"Nooo..." Callan drew the word out slowly while attempting to inconspicuously look around. "I hadn't noticed." Raising her eyebrows in surprise she added, "but now that you mention it," it was as if she was seeing the people surrounding them for the first time, "you're right!" she whispered, wide-eyed.

"Can't pull anything over on you, can we?" Alexine chided, snorting. Callan flashed her a mock-angry look and they both giggled.

The girls approached the buffet. "Um, what is that?"

"Not sure," Alexine gave the little red-head an intimidated look, but wiped it quickly from her face upon noticing the kitchen staff eyeing her microscopically. She continued in a low, monotone voice, "once we get back to the table, do you want me to try it first?"

"Please."

They both smiled at the Asian woman holding two plates in her hand. She stared at them as if awaiting orders so the girls nodded their heads when the woman pointed at the first serving dish on the table. It was piled high with brownish, spongy, oblong objects.

"Eggs?" whispered Callan appallingly.

"I hope so," Alexine spoke out of the corner of her mouth. "But why are they brown?"

The woman took a step to her left and proceeded to look questioningly at the girls as they passed each serving tray. Not wanting to offend, they allowed her to dish a bit of everything.

"That was painful." Studying her plate, Callan laughed nervously as they walked back to their seats.

"Okay…here goes…" Attempting to force down the food she placed in her mouth, Alexine warned, with a miserable shake of the head, "don't try the squishy white stuff."

"Thanks," responded Callan gratefully, picking at the items on her plate.

"The white gobs of dough, are…"

"My favorite!"

"Yea, dumplings."

"Mmmm," Callan moaned in pleasure. "Think we can smuggle some home?"

"Don't think they would travel well," the older girl smirked.

Other than Callan's noisy chewing, the two sat quietly enjoying their lunch and taking in the commotion surrounding them. Alexine estimated there were at least a hundred people in the room, including teachers and staff.

"This place is impressive." Alexine pushed her plate back, wiping her mouth with a napkin.

The little girl sitting next to her took another big bite of dumpling, then looked around to survey the scene. "Ughm," she mumbled, her mouth full of dough.

"Ugh."

"Wha…?" garbled Callan defensively, still chewing.

"Stop! You're going to make me sick!"

Callan smiled teasingly, her mouth still full of food.

Sitting back, Alexine looked around the room, trying to discourage Callan's antics by ignoring them. An older teenage girl with long, straight, brown hair was sitting at a table by the exit. Wearing a canvas, floor-length skirt, the girl irresistibly reminded Alexine of a hippy from the 1970s. The girl gazed down at a textbook and seemed on the verge of tears.

"Maybe we should talk to her," Alexine noted, momentarily returning her attention to Callan who was still heartily eating her "favorite."

Callan swallowed hard. "Who?"

"Thank you for not talking with your mouth full," Alexine threw in. Nodding in the direction of the hippy-girl she answered, "that girl over there."

As both sisters turned to look, a familiar, large, well built man entered the cafeteria. Devin made a bee-line for the table nearest the door and sat down heavily next to the miserable girl, speaking quietly to her.

"Maybe Mr. Rippinger will help her," shrugged Callan hopefully. "He's nice."

Alexine furrowed her brow and frowned, not optimistic. They resumed eating. The older girl could not stop thinking about the young lady now sitting next to Devin. Who was she? Why was she upset? Both girls spun in surprise as the teenager noisily slid her chair back from the table, it's metal legs screeching in opposition, then ran sobbing from the room.

Callan looked confused. "What the heck?"

Glancing around the cafeteria, Devin pushed his own chair back. The young lady's outburst had caught everyone's attention, but the moment Devin stood, students diverted their eyes.

"Are they afraid of Devin?" Alexine wondered. Looking around, she noticed a short, dark woman standing in a far corner. It seemed she had been watching the exchange with interest. The woman turned her head slightly, locked eyes with Alexine, and winked without changing her expression at all. It was a secret wink. A wink that no one else was intended to see. Caught off guard by the unexpected exchange, Alexine looked down and focused on her food.

"Callan," she whispered without raising her head, and making a concerted effort to keep her lips motionless.

"Yea?"

"Is that lady in the corner your teacher from this morning?" She continued to speak quietly and as inconspicuously as possible.

"What?"

"Shhh!" warned Alexine, eyes wide. "That lady...in the corner..." Alexine jerked her head slightly in the direction of the short woman. "Isn't that your..." she fumbled for words. "The lady that teaches you to...you know...to do your thing?"

Callan gave Alexine an are-you-crazy look, then said sanctimoniously, "shift...she teaches me how to shift. You can say it."

"Whatever!" hissed Alexine. "That's not the point...it's her...isn't it?"

Callan whirled in her seat, to face the corner.

"Don't be so obvious!" Alexine whispered harshly.

"Yea, that's her. Mrs. Gary," intoned the little girl, bored. She turned back toward Alexine and let out a hearty laugh. Her older sister was hunched over, face inches from her plate. She resembled a turtle who longed for nothing more than to see the inside of it's shell. Sometimes Alexine was so odd.

"Listen secret-agent-lady," she giggled, "loosen up!"

Alexine's anger bubbled. Why was her little sister so oblivious? Why couldn't she see that something was wrong with Devin? Was something going on in this place? Something sinister? The older girl sat upright. Fine. She was alone on this, that was just dandy. She was here to watch over Callan, to protect her, and she was going to do it. No more secret-agent-lady. What was she afraid of?

Turning back toward the well-built man, Alexine thought he looked smug and satisfied. Who was the girl he upset? She was determined to find out. Devin noticed Alexine staring at him, and as their eyes met Alexine willed herself to watch. To hold her gaze steady. "Yea, I caught you," she thought. "So much for working on liking you more." Devin's expression instantly changed to one of over-exaggerated concern. "Too late. You might fool Callan, but..." The muscular man strode toward the girls. Alexine followed his every movement and he seemed intimidated by the attention. Weak.

"How is your first day going?" he asked jovially, standing over the pair.

"Better than hers," Alexine shot quickly before Callan had a chance to answer. Devin ignored the comment as Callan scowled reprovingly.

"Have you learned *everything* yet?" The question was directed at the red-headed shifter.

The little girl laughed. A little too loudly, and a little too long by Alexine's account. "You have got to be kidding me," she thought miserably. "He's up to something...strange. And why is he so interested in Callan?"

"Well," Devin continued to tower over the girls, "I would like to invite you both to attend a class next…together." He finished the sentence looking directly at Alexine as if expecting to catch her off guard.

And he did. It surprised her. She had made this trip to watch over Callan. They were a team and should stay together as much as possible. But it seemed that was not going to happen if Callan was in shifter training most of the day. "Good," she heard herself reply, her anger returning. Concentrating, she scrutinized Devin thinking, "I know something's going on." Perhaps if she focused enough, he would feel it. "I'm watching you."

Callan's reaction to this turn of events was the polar opposite of her sister's. Disappointment clung to her features as she slouched on the bench. "I thought I could go back to Mrs. Gary's class." She put on her most pathetic pouty face.

"Hold your horses, there's plenty of time for that!" Devin laughed.

The little girl frowned at him, but he just smiled back. "You *do* need to develop that *amazing* talent of yours."

As Callan nodded vigorously, Alexine felt like making a loud, gagging noise.

"But you both need to learn some basics also. So, if you're finished, I'll take you two to your next class."

As Alexine gathered the trays, Devin and Callan headed toward the doors, the little girl looking dejected but following obediently. Walking behind them, Alexine passed the table where the altercation had taken place just minutes before and noticed a textbook abandoned on hippy-girl's chair. Only hesitating a moment, she sat the trays down, grabbed the book and slid it into her backpack. Hopefully she could return the item and find out more about this girl. Specifically, why she was so miserable here, and what the heck the large man had said to upset her so. Alexine jogged to catch up with Devin and Callan.

"You can leave your dishes here," instructed Devin. He and Callan paused when they realized Alexine was not behind them. Rushing up, she left the trays on the stainless steel table and the three of them entered the hallway.

Devin led the girls up a set of stairs to the second floor. Turning left at the top, they walked almost half way around the circular building, stopping at a door on which was affixed the number "12."

"Mr. Rush instructs this class," Devin informed the girls, opening the door and motioning the sisters to enter. "Academy overview."

The room was stark and sparse, a recurring theme which made Alexine feel she had been transported to a time and place where art and beauty had been banished, driven away, deemed not useful and unnecessary. Small school desks and chairs lined up in perfect rows faced a wall which supported a large blackboard. The board was abnormally clean, devoid of any markings or even that stubborn veil of chalk dust. Antiseptic. Alexine's hopes sagged. This seemed like an austere room in which obscenely boring subjects were expounded upon relentlessly.

Almost entirely obscured by a gray, metal desk near the far wall, a very tall man slowly stood. The girls jumped as he began to move, surprised by his presence. The man peered at them over a set of small, black rectangular spectacles. Mr. Rush was thin with light, almost translucent skin, and slicked, black, short hair. Dressed in dark dress pants and a striped grey dress shirt which was buttoned all the way to the top of his slender neck. When he straightened to his full height, Alexine was irresistibly reminded of a spindly daddy long leg spider.

He walked toward the group fluidly, lifting his feet high as if stepping through deep snow. As he approached, the man smiled and extended a hand. His gait and appearance cemented the image of the eight legged predator firmly in Alexine's mind. Looking over at Callan, she noted a horrified look marring her little sister's features. Luckily, the man standing in front of them seemed not to notice. Or, perhaps, not to care.

"New students," Devin said matter-of-factly, looking first at Alexine then at Callan. The words were clipped. He had always been uncomfortable with this man.

"Good," the lanky man rasped, appraising the girls as if they were his next juicy meal. Callan laughed nervously.

"I'll leave them in your very capable hands then," Devin finished and strode off just as Zeke walked through the door. Mr. Rush returned quietly to his desk.

"Alexine!" Zeke said playfully.

She blushed immediately. Glad not only to see him, but relieved someone else had entered the room prior to Devin's departure. She didn't relish the thought of she and Callan being alone with Mr. Rush.

"And of course, Lady Callan," the handsome boy droned aristocratically, bowing low.

The tension from a few seconds prior vanished as Callan threw all of her weight onto her right leg, cocked her head to the side, placed her left hand on her hip, and mimicked shooting Zeke with her right index finger. He roared with laughter as she clenched her teeth together and make several clicking noises at him.

"Always a pleasure," he shook as he took his seat.

Callan turned to face Alexine who rolled her eyes at the red-head in disgust. Spinning on the spot, the little shifter strode over to the chair directly behind Zeke. But instead of sitting down, she quietly walked behind the older boy and began moving her eyebrows up and down.

Alexine froze and shook her head slightly, a panicked look crossing her face. "Pleeaassee," she thought, "don't embarrass me!"

Callan laughed silently, then began making kissing motions at the back of Zeke's head prompting Alexine to turn a violent shade of puce just as Zeke looked up at her.

"Are you alright?" he asked seriously.

"Um, yea, fine."

Nodding his head deliberately then smiling as if aware of some secret hidden from everyone else, he opened a notebook on his desk and began writing. "Oh, and Callan," he added nonchalantly, not glancing up from his work. "There's a mirror at the front of the room. Handy for seeing everything going on behind you."

The little girl raised her gaze slowly, only now noticing a long mirror which spanned the front wall, just above the chalkboard. It had to be thirty feet in length. When she looked down again, Zeke had turned around in his chair and was staring at her condescendingly. He had seen the whole thing. Called out in her own game, Callan sunk mortified into her seat, eyes wide in embarrassment.

"Serves you right!" Alexine whispered angrily, taking the desk to the left of Callan.

Zeke snickered.

Chapter Fourteen
I Fly, Mom

September 22, 2000
Marcellus, Michigan

"There must be an answer." Heidi had repeated the mantra out loud at least ten times this morning, trying desperately to conclusively explain last night.

Callan sat at the island on a bar stool eyeing her. "I want Daddy," she answered back, seriously.

Heidi laughed and walked to her youngest daughter. Taking the little girl's face in her hands, she tipped her head up so the two were staring at each other. "Do you know the answer?"

The little girl smiled up at her. "Daddy work."

"Yes sweetie, Daddy's at work. Where's Mommy?"

"Mommy home."

Heidi turned as she heard the front door open, immediately recognizing her mother's voice. "Mom?!" she called from around the corner. Scooping Callan into her arms, she walked into the dining room. "What in the heck?" she asked incredulously. Her mother and mother-in-law stood in the doorway, smiling slyly.

"Good afternoon dear!" Marie removed her shoes, walked up quickly to kiss both she and Callan on the cheek, then quipped, "thought we'd stop by for a little visit!"

"What are you two doing here?" Heidi asked, baffled.

Her mother-in-law laughed. "Hey, it's your mother that does things like this! You know me, I plan things in advance!" Catherine removed her shoes and inched up to Heidi and Callan. "Come see Grandma?" She extended her arms toward the child. Callan beamed and threw herself forward. "Yea…" Catherine purred, holding the baby close, "come see grandma." The child clung to her grandmother's neck, burying her head in the woman's warm shoulder as they both rocked soothingly back and forth.

A warm feeling filled Heidi as they surrounded her small child. Callan was safe for a moment. Protected. Suspended in a bubble created by three strong, able, determined women who were each ferociously dedicated to protecting her. Heidi could sense it, feel it. As tears threatened to betray her, she blinked them back and spoke quickly. "So…what brings you two to Marcellus?"

"Oh," replied her mother, "just thought we would come over for lunch!"

They walked into the piano room and each took a seat on the old couch the couple had inherited from Geoff's grandmother. It was threadbare and extremely out of date, but treasured. A constant reminder of Geoff's roots; where he had come from. Heidi gave her mother a forced smile.

"Oh, alright," Marie relented, "we thought we could help."

Catherine stood and walked back to the front door. Retrieving a satchel, she pulled out the old, worn box, offering it to Heidi. The younger woman reached for the strange object. It was beautiful. Intricate detailing lined the sides and top.

"Wow," Heidi breathed, recognizing it as a very old example of a hand-made storage box. "I've seen these before," she offered, "in pictures. Typically they were made to hold things of extreme importance."

Marie nodded her head absent-mindedly, her thoughts drifting off to another time. "Extreme importance," she repeated distractedly.

"Mom?"

Returning to the present, Marie nodded. "Go ahead and open it."

Heidi unclasped the latches and carefully tipped the top.

An hour later Callan clomped back into the room for the ump-teenth time, an armful of blankets trailing behind her. Wrapping around her feet as she moved, they threatened to topple her at any moment. She arrived in the middle of the room and dumped her load on the ever-growing pile of items painstakingly carted from toy room to this spot. Turning to her brother, she covered Geoff Junior up as he lay prone on the floor. The baby boy smiled and closed his eyes feigning sleep. "Nite nites," whispered Callan, as she giggled and patted him on top of the head.

"She's such a little care taker," commented Marie as she watched her grand children play. Callan's natural mothering ability never ceased to amaze her. "I'm serious…you can't teach that, you're born with it!" The other two women smiled indulgently. They each seemed relieved to take a break from the subject that had held their attention for the last sixty minutes.

Heidi gazed down at the kids. Her mother was right, Callan was definitely a little mom. From stuffed animals, to Baby Geoff, to little rodents she found outside. Heidi longed to talk about normal subjects like this, longed to provide details about Geoff's new words and Callan's latest painting, but her mind kept being pulled back to the problem they were attempting to solve.

"So…" Heidi said slowly, placing her hand on the old diary, and reluctantly beckoning them back. "What you're saying is that Callan is…altering…somehow…so that we can't see her. And she's able to change locations in that state?"

Marie turned away from the children and toward her daughter, biting her lip absently. "I know it sounds impossible. But yes," she finished resolutely.

"I fly mom, I fly." Heidi repeated Callan's answer to herself. "No it does not sound impossible actually. It is the only logical answer."

Catherine stared at her daughter-in-law in disbelief, mouth hanging open. "Just like that?" Catherine asked, surprised. "You believe her, just like that?"

Heidi inhaled deeply and let out a long sigh. A tired, defeated smile touched her lips as she exhaled quickly, producing a noise somewhere between a laugh and a grunt. "I have been thinking about this all night and all morning mom." She reached over and touched Catherine's arm. "It's the only logical answer. Believe me, I've tried to come up with something less…extreme. But you weren't here last night. You didn't see her…just…appear, and then fall into our bed."

Heidi felt very far away as she re-lived the events of the previous evening. It was useless trying to explain it. She looked deeply into Marie's eyes. Before the two women arrived, she already knew this was something amazing. Something not easily explained. Something which would affect not only Callan but the entire family, and not only for a few years but…forever. Her mother's nod was almost imperceptible.

Chapter Fifteen
Answers

"The lake is beautiful today." Marie turned her face toward the water as the breeze blew back her hair. "So serene."

As the sun reached its afternoon climax, the gray water of early morning gave way to deep blue. So blue, in fact, that small waves skating the surface crested black. Blinding light glittered from ripples, flashing like Fourth of July sparklers, as the three women followed a bend in the road that ran along the shore of the lake.

Callan and Baby Geoff enjoyed taking stroller rides around the lake in the afternoon while Alexine was at school. If they planned it just right, they could meet the school bus on the way home. Heidi typically used the time to get in an hour of exercise and collect her thoughts. She always felt better after walking along the lake; the weeping willows that lined the road opposite the lake proper, the occasional beaver they spotted swimming in the pools of connecting water, the people they knew simply as a result of traversing the same path over, and over, and over. Heidi loved it all. Today her mother pushed the double stroller that held the two children.

"Perfect for skiing, it's like glass." Catherine still regretted she and her husband, Geoff Thomas, had not purchased a particular house on this lake several years ago when it was offered for a song.

As if reading her mother-in-law's mind, Heidi piped in sarcastically, "yea, wouldn't it be great if you could get a house on the lake for super cheap?"

Catherine gave Heidi a mischievous, side-ways glare, then laughed, "never going to live that down, am I?"

Considering this question for a moment, Heidi tipped her head up to watch a flock of geese flying in V formation. Their dark forms moved effortlessly against the light blue sky. She truly loved living in Marcellus. "Nope," she said suddenly, in answer to her mother-in-law's question. "I doubt it."

"If you could go back in time," Heidi said, as the five of them came to the end of the road and made a loop around the cul-de-sac, "let's say, one hundred and fifty years, and tell someone that one day, we would be able to talk into a little box and someone on the other side of the world would be able to hear us, and talk back," Heidi smiled, "they would think you had lost your scruples!"

The older women laughed and nodded in agreement. "Things have changed a lot in the last one hundred and fifty years," Catherine concurred. "That's for sure!"

"And," continued Heidi, "we know that human beings utilize only a fraction of their potential. I mean, that is a documented scientific fact." Heidi seemed deep in thought, and hesitated.

"What?" questioned Catherine. She and Marie looked confused.

"I don't get the connection," said Marie, bewildered.

Brow furrowed, Heidi stared ahead, focusing on several small birds sitting atop a telephone wire. The same type of birds had dive bombed her for a week last spring during morning walks. Barn swallows were so protective during nesting season.

"Well," she said haltingly and then paused as if deciding whether or not to continue. What was she afraid of? Questioning…thinking…those were good things. She pushed through her hesitation and heard herself say, "well, we read in the bible that we're supposed to be 'perfect'."

Catherine stopped walking, and everyone else followed suit, pausing in the middle of the empty road. Catherine looked at Heidi, questioningly. "Okay, I'm officially lost. What do cell phones and human potential have to do with a bible verse?"

"It says, 'be ye therefore perfect, even as your Father in Heaven is perfect.'"

"Yeesss?" said Catherine.

Heidi turned to look directly at her mother-in-law. "I don't think He was kidding...when He said that." As she spoke, it was as if the way were being illuminated one word at a time. The truth of her string of thought lighting the way. Each word followed the last easily... naturally. "I don't think He was telling us to do something we could not do." Yes. That felt right.

"Okkaaay," replied Catherine, still unsure about where this conversation was headed.

Marie observed the exchange with a mixture of interest and unease.

"Well, that verse really says it all, doesn't it? We're supposed to be perfect, like He is perfect." Heidi paused, "that is what it says, right?" She waited for a reaction that failed to materialize. "Well, that *is* what it says, right?" Heidi pressed. Silence.

After several seconds, Catherine answered cautiously, "I think we're supposed to be the best people we can be."

Mulling that over a moment, Heidi pursed her lips as if tasting something slightly sour. "I think it may be more than that," she replied. "We're supposed to be perfect, that is what it says... *perfect*."

"What does this have to do with Callan?" asked Catherine, a bit exasperated. She took hold of the stroller handles and began walking, pushing the children forward. Glad to be moving again, the kids giggled as Heidi and Marie fell into step beside her. Catherine was not sure why, but this conversation was making her uneasy.

"Well, we know He can do *anything*, right? We know He *is* perfect." Heidi posed the question to her mother this time.

"Yes," answered Marie deliberately, her interest in where this conversation was headed piqued. "Definitely."

"So, if God is perfect, and He can do anything, and we're supposed to be perfect – we're supposed to be like Him – I guess that means that maybe we can..." Heidi allowed the suggestion to linger for several seconds.

"Then it follows that we, too, are capable of doing amazing things," Marie finished the sentence for her daughter, contemplating the implications of this statement. After a minute, she nodded, as if coming to a decision. "Yes...I believe that...we're supposed to follow Him."

"Callan can do things that we don't entirely understand," Heidi stated firmly. "And that is not a bad thing, not something to be feared. It is a miraculous thing, a good thing. She's supposed to develop her talents, not bury them. Right?"

A somber silence followed as the three women considered the answer to this very important question. It seemed right...somehow. But then...fear. It swooped down on them. Lurking behind nearby trees. Sinewy tendrils of doubt and panic growing toward the group, slowly, deliberately. Be afraid. Run.

"Fear is the opposite of faith." Marie's statement pulled the others out of their thoughts, and the bright afternoon engulfed them once again.

Heidi drew a deep breath. "Fear is the opposite of faith," she parroted. "*Fear* is the opposite of *faith*," she repeated thoughtfully, as if the words contained an element of power. Fear. Faith.

The sun felt warm on her face, she was with the two women she adored most in the world, and she felt close to finding answers.

Chapter Sixteen
A Poisoning

"Are you coming to sleep soon?" Geoff flopped over in bed to face his wife later that evening.

The kids were tucked in, the dish washer running, the clothes spinning in the washing machine, and Heidi was on the computer. An evening like any other in the Kovar house.

Earlier that afternoon, the three women returned from their walk and immediately began pouring over the information contained in the mysterious, ancient box. Two books contained historical data. They skimmed over these volumes quickly, returning them to the chest. There was a book outlining an organization. It's hierarchy, guidelines and operating procedures. Having nothing to do with their situation, the women glossed over this also. But there were several diaries dating back hundreds of years. One of them contained names very familiar to one or all of the women. Heidi was enthralled.

Genealogy had always been a favorite subject and these books were a treasure trove of information; pieces of history you could hold in your hand. The pages pulsed with power, answers, and a connection to people who, in their own ways, had made possible the very lives these women were living. It was awe-inspiring. Heidi devoured the information, looking for answers to questions. But the books simply generated more unknowns.

"Sillemlem. Have you ever heard of that word before hon?" She had been typing key words fervently into search engines for at least an hour. "Or Sil, for short?"

Geoff gave her a look of disbelief, then laughed. "You're the English person, remember? I have a tech writer at work!" Turning back over in bed, he focused on the movie he started several minutes before.

As the familiar theme song filled their bedroom, Heidi giggled. "<u>Back to the Future</u>...again?" The trilogy was Geoff's favorite, and they had watched each one many times.

"What?" he shot indignantly. "It's a classic!"

"Yea." Turning ruefully back toward the computer, she typed "www.google.com." Maybe...just maybe. "Sillemlem." Taking a deep breath, she hit the enter button and the computer whirred into action. "We found the word in a diary."

"Mmm."

"Geoff?"

"Mmm?"

"There was something about today... I can't figure it out."

"Mmm?"

"Geoff!"

Forcing his attention from the television, Geoff tried in vain to focus glazed eyes on his wife. "I'm listening," he said, unable to completely concentrate. It had been a long day at work, and he was so tired.

"My mom told me a story today. Said she visited with her grandfather's brother, Harold, while she was living with her grandmother."

"So?"

"Well, it's just that…" Heidi fumbled, trying in vain to organize the time line in a way which removed all doubt from her mother's recollections. "My mom lived with her grandmother in 1966. Harold got divorced and left Sylvania in the early 1950s. It just doesn't make sense."

"So your mom's a liar?" Geoff smiled, not able to imagine his mother-in-law fabricating anything.

"Of course not," Heidi answered, picking up on the sarcasm. "She described the events so vividly, in such detail, but I just don't see how…it could not have happened the way she…"

"Finish a sentence."

"It just doesn't make sense," Heidi clipped.

At one o'clock in the morning, she crawled into bed, exhausted and disappointed. Her search fruitless.

* * *

"Here's something that might interest you," said Nautas, sitting in a classroom in London, England. Thousands of miles away from the Kovar home.

Rolling his eyes, the man's younger brother slid closer, scanning the computer screen.

"Marcellus, Michigan. A woman named Heidi Kovar."

"What?" asked Branch, confused.

Nautas rubbed his chin as if pondering some deep question. "She was on the internet for hours searching for…well…searching for us." The man froze, lowered his voice, and appraised his brother evenly. "Sillemlem. Now there's a word you don't see everyday." Eyes narrowed intensely, the two men stared at each other for several protracted seconds then Nautas laughed. "Don't you just love the information highway?"

"How do you know she…?"

Turning toward his younger brother, Nautas opened his eyes wide, flashed a guilty look, then held up his hands in mock surrender.

"You didn't," said Branch, an accusing tone accompanying his angry glare.

Nautas smiled condescendingly, and shrugged. "It was easy, easy, easy. I am Google, did you know that? A cache poisoning. And the beautiful thing about it is," the man continued, his haughty grin hitching onto a knowing nod. "No one knows about the glitch. Amazing, isn't…"

"What!?"

Sighing and suddenly loosing his sense of humor, the older brother snapped, "it will be helpful."

It was a transparent attempt to pacify him, and Branch saw right through it. "No!" he hissed. "It's wrong!"

"Come on," drolled Nautas, turning back toward the screen. "It's not a big deal."

"Nautas," said Branch after calming himself for several seconds, "people should be able to ask questions without being investigated. It's wrong."

"What are you afraid of?" The older man closed his eyes, bored by this repetitive argument.

"It has nothing to do with fear. It's about privacy, it's about not having someone looking over your shoulder all of the time, it's about freed…" He never finished the sentence.

Nautas stood and whirled toward Branch. Lunging down, he spat, "shut up, you fool," and didn't look back as he stormed from the room, his dark cloak billowing behind.

Branch sighed heavily. Why did this always happen? He didn't intend to upset his brother. He tried to be patient, tried to explain his point of view. Was he really being too bossy? Was he really allowing fear to dictate his actions and beliefs? Were any of the accusations Nautas hurled at him when they argued true? Dropping his head into his hands, he rubbed his temples with his thumbs.

As if in answer to questions posed only in his own mind, a melodic voice said soothingly, "he's wrong."

Branch's head jerked up. She was standing in the doorway, outlined by the light from the hallway. Branch thought she looked like an angel and his face softened as Annalynn walked slowly toward him.

"Sorry," she began guiltily. "I overheard the end, and for what it's worth..."

"We're always arguing. I just don't understand how it happens." Shaking his head, Branch interlocked his fingers and buried his face in his hands. As if, somehow, they could become a barrier that would afford him protection from the storm developing between he and his brother.

Annalynn pulled up a chair beside him, glancing at the computer. "Heidi Kovar, who is that?" She sensed he needed a change of subject.

The relationship between the two brothers had been deteriorating for some time, Annalynn did not completely understand the reason. There was something lurking below the surface of the confrontation, a source of contention initiated perhaps long ago. Thus far, Branch had never shared it with her. And she had never asked.

He did not move.

Annalynn studied him. The man had sandy brown hair that always seemed slightly windswept. Although no one would give him a second look on the street, he was handsome in a carefree, accidental way. In a way that entailed you getting to know him first.

Branch sat up and frowned, confused. "What?" Completely forgetting the initial cause of the fight between him and Nautas, the young man followed Annalynn's gaze to the screen.

They both studied it for a moment. Heidi Kovar. Marcellus, Michigan. It appeared as though she had been searching for answers about the academy, and questions about children possessing the ability to disappear or fly. Her final query comprised one word, "Sillemlem." It sat there on the screen, awaiting an explanation.

"Sillemlem? What is that supposed to mean?" Annalynn asked, confused.

Branch's gaze slid sideways as he answered distractedly. "It's an old term, used hundreds of years ago. A code name. But few know its meaning now, and where it originated."

Although she found this piece of information fascinating, Branch seemed unwilling to divulge anything more. "Children?" she finally continued, her attention returning to the computer. "Is that possible?" She turned toward Branch and searched his face for answers.

"Yes...although it doesn't happen often." He was so tired. So disappointed.

"How did he get this information?" Annalynn ran her finger along the computer screen as she read.

Branch's answer seeped irritation. "He set up some sort of program that tracks and redirects queries posted to major search engines."

"You're kidding me!"

"No," he said angrily, "unfortunately I'm not. He's set up hundreds of fake websites that mimic legitimate sites. The people accessing them have no idea he's watching them. He's poisoned the name servers so that..." Branch broke off. It wasn't important.

"Creepy. But isn't that..."

"Illegal," he finished, nodding his head wearily. "Yes."

Annalynn sighed and relaxed her shoulders, as if trying to accept a questionable truth. "Well," she began, attempting to sound positive, "it looks like this poor woman is desperate for some answers. Maybe we could help her."

The defeated look on Branch's face caused Annalynn's stomach to twist. "I know you think Nautas's methods are wrong but..." She never finished the sentence.

Branch's gaze shifted slowly until he was staring directly at her, as though seeing her for the first time. As though suddenly he didn't know her. Shaking his head incredulously, he croaked, "*I* think he's wrong? Am *I* the only person who thinks he's wrong Anna?"

The hopeful look slid from her face. She shook her head, as if she wanted to agree with him, but words escaped her.

Disappointment struck Branch like a blow to the chest, the fight abandoning him. Deflated he wondered if he were alone in what he believed. No...in what he *knew*.

"Not you too Anna," he said, seeing a hint of uncertainty in her face. He could always read her like a book, and what he saw now made him lose heart. Dropping his head to avoid having to look at her, he whispered, "not you too."

When she didn't answer, Branch turned slowly back toward the computer, closed out the window and deleted the file created by Nautas. He rose and left her there, alone in the dark. But he couldn't wipe the information from her mind that readily. Heidi Kovar. Marcellus, Michigan. A child that could disappear.

Watching Branch pull himself from his seat and drag out of the room, Annalynn sat in deserted darkness. What was right? What was wrong? She wasn't sure she knew anymore.

Her mind flitted to the many things she needed to accomplish today. The relocation had begun two weeks prior. Moving an entire academy was a chore everyone loathed, yet it happened every four years, like clockwork. This had been the schedule of her life, spelled out in four year increments. It was tiring, and she never felt like any *place* was home. The people who surrounded her, who had raised her from infancy, her friends, they were home.

Turning back toward the computer screen, she stared transfixed at the blank display. She grabbed a piece of paper before she lost her nerve, jotted down the information still fresh in her mind, then pocketed the scrap. Was it the right thing to do? Something told her this woman needed help. This woman *wanted* to be found. It wasn't like Heidi Kovar was trying to hide from them, she was searching *for* them. That made it alright, didn't it?

Even though she eventually convinced herself it was acceptable, it still took several days for Annalynn to build up the courage to make the call.

"Hello?"

The voice at the other end of the line was friendly and bright. Optimistic. Instantly, Annalynn felt she had made the correct decision, though explaining this feeling to Branch was going to be another matter. She pushed that fear from her mind to concentrate on the task at hand.

"Um, hello Mrs. Kovar." She had rehearsed this conversation many times. "My name is Annalynn and I'm calling from the academy." After several seconds of silence, and wondering if the connection had been lost, Annalynn said, "hello?"

"I'm here," replied the woman. "I'm sorry, you just kind of…caught me off guard."

Annalynn laughed nervously, stammering a bit. "Yes…I'm sorry also…you are interested in our organization." It was not a question, it was a statement. She had bet Heidi Kovar from Marcellus, Michigan would seize the opportunity to discuss her situation; this child that disappeared, that flew. Annalynn had been counting on this because, unfortunately, no matter how many times she role-played this discussion, she could think of nothing else to say beyond this point. Fortunately, her assumption had been correct.

Over the course of the next forty-five minutes, the two women, separated by thousands of miles, discussed the details of their lives. The conversation ebbed and flowed naturally. There was no hesitation, no fear, just honest inquiry and sincere concern. When Annalynn hung up the phone, she felt as though she and this Heidi woman knew each other well. Even though Mrs. Kovar was a bit older than she, Annalynn felt as though they were, in many ways, similar. And most importantly, she knew she had helped.

Approaching Branch later that evening, Annalynn was aware she had one chance to convince the man that Callan was worth checking into. How she had been located was irrelevant.

"So, I made a phone call today," she began, when they had settled into seats in the cafeteria at dinnertime.

"You did?" he replied lightly, fingering lesson plans, and Annalynn braced herself.

"To Heidi Kovar."

Branch paused, his gaze glued to the papers in front of him. When his eyes met hers, they were challenging. "Nautas does not have good intentions Anna. You do know that, don't you?"

She did not respond, and was sure he took note of her failure to answer the very direct question. "I think we have a three year old shifter on our hands Branch. That has to be worth looking into."

He narrowed his eyes in question. "You're sure?"

"Sure enough to talk to you about a very touchy subject," she said matter-of-factly, eyes wide.

Branch took in a deep breath. A three year old shifter. This was more than just "worth looking into." This was "must look into." He grudgingly nodded his approval to Annalynn and the young woman smiled warmly at him.

"I know we're supposed to help Branch. I can just feel it."

* * *

Early the next morning Branch put in a call to the United States.

"Charlie?" He had waited until the office was clear, increasing the likelihood that this conversation would remain private.

"Yea?" answered a friendly voice on the other end.

"I think we may have another one."

Charlie sighed. "Does all of this mean what I think it means?"

"I don't know," Branch croaked, "but it feels like things are on fast-forward, doesn't it?"

"I thought it was just me," the voice replied unsteadily.

Branch paused several seconds, then said reassuringly, "this isn't a bad thing Charlie. It's what we've been waiting for."

"Keep telling me that, alright?"

Chuckling, Branch replied, "Well, I need a favor."

"Of course you do."

Chapter Seventeen
Protecting the Innocent

"I don't know how you managed this," said Branch for the hundredth time as he and Annalynn landed at the Kalamazoo airport several days later. She laughed easily, taking Branch's arm and he smiled at her.

"Hey, let's look at the bright side."

"And that is…"

"We won't get lost in the terminal." Motioning toward the small airport to which they had taxied, Annalynn squeezed his arm as Branch laid a strong hand on hers.

Branch laughed loudly, enjoying the opportunity to escape the tension at the academy. Satisfied, Annalynn pressed her head back into the seat as the airplane came to a stop.

"Shall we?" Branch invited as the fasten seatbelt sign was extinguished.

The forty-five minute commute from Kalamazoo to Marcellus was pleasant. Country settings always calmed Annalynn; the lush, green trees. Rows of crops stretching in fields. The smell of fresh air, unencumbered by smog and engine exhaust. She felt more at home during their drive than she had the previous four years living in London.

The car traveling in front of them created a soft slip-stream, causing the long grasses gracing the edge of the asphalt to sway back, then bow in deference to the passing autos. Annalynn found herself mesmerized by the movement; swirling shades of green, spattered with vivid yellow wildflowers. This was a beautiful place.

* * *

"Thank you so much for coming," said the slender woman who answered the door.

Blond, with shoulder length hair, she balanced a baby boy on one hip. In blue jeans and a light sweater, the woman struck Annalynn as being vibrant and welcoming. Annalynn and Branch smiled their greeting.

"Please come in." Heidi stepped backward into the ranch style home.

"Mom!" The little red-head's screech reached them before the child herself appeared around a corner. Pulling up short at the presence of two strange visitors, Callan appraised them carefully, sizing them up, her innocent eyes wide with intrigue.

"This is Callan." Heidi smiled down proudly at the precocious child.

Squatting to get down to her level, Branch looked into those eyes and they gazed at each other for several seconds. Deciding the newcomers were no threat, but loosing interest quickly, Callan raced off to find her older sister.

"She's a little fireball," Heidi laughed, as they moved into the living room and sat on the couch. "But I'm concerned about her. Something could happen. She could get hurt. We could lose her."

Her normally calm demeanor shifted whenever Heidi thought about her little girl. Losing a child, every parent's nightmare, became all too possible when Callan disappeared. "Is there anyway to protect her?"

"I think we can help," answered Branch.

Annalynn nodded in agreement, but Heidi had the sense they both harbored concern as well.

"We have some family diaries that explain a bit about these things." Things. That word seemed ridiculous, and yet she had used it over and over again during the course of the previous few weeks. Heidi felt out of her element. What words did these people use to describe what they were able to accomplish? Not wanting to sound foolish, but at the same time wanting to be perfectly clear, she sighed in frustration.

Callan needed help. She had no time for pride or for beating around the bush. "Okay, I don't know the terminology for a lot of these things." There was that word again: things. This time she laughed. "But I understand a bit about them, and I'll do anything to help. Not only to keep Callan safe, but to encourage her to use this ability, to develop it."

Branch relaxed. This woman was refreshing. He detected no fear or recalcitrance regarding Callan's ability. She was ready for answers, and seemed willing to accept direction. Looking over at Annalynn, he smiled grudgingly, admitting he was glad she had initiated contact with the Kovars.

"Well, if it is alright with you, we would just like to spend some time here observing. Having met so many people with abilities, we can typically pick them out fairly quickly." What he left unspoken was that children, especially three year olds, who could exercise even a portion of their gift, were extremely rare. Unsure the same rules applied in this situation, it was the best he could do: watch.

"I knew someone…" Heidi faltered, unsure how to phrase her statement and question. Deciding the simplest way would be the best, she continued, "…that could read other people's minds." Her guests were unfazed by this, as if reading minds were an everyday occurrence. Heidi found this wildly humorous, but contained herself. "Could you try to do that with Callan? Read her mind?"

Branch and Annalynn shook their heads simultaneously, smiling assuredly.

"Actually," began Annalynn, "children under the age of eight can not be read."

"They can't?"

"No."

Again, the answer came in unison and Heidi was unsure where to direction her attention. A part of her wanted to delve into exactly why children couldn't be read, but pragmatism pushed that option out of the picture. If it couldn't be done, then it couldn't be done. They needed to focus on Callan and finding answers. "Okay then, let's go watch her."

* * *

"It is good we came," Branch said thoughtfully several hours later, sensing Annalynn's gaze and sardonic smile even though she was not looking in his direction.

His companion crossed her arms, as if taking credit for the decision. Annalynn had felt they needed to make this trip. That for some reason, this trip was vital. And Branch had, in his own way, just admitted to that fact also.

Having moved outside, the adults sat on the front lawn watching the children cavort happily. Callan and Alexine raced from the large rock in the front yard toward the onlookers. As they crested the hill, Alexine fell back several paces and growled to the delight of her little sister. She was a tiger, with a voracious appetite, ripping after her prey. The younger girl screamed in panic and ran even faster, eager to escape an untimely fate.

Throwing herself into his arms, as if she were being pursued by a truly wild beast and he was the safe place, Callan gripped Branch tightly. She giggled wildly and clung to his chest in a bid to, somehow, hide in the folds of his shirt. When she relaxed her death grip, Branch smiled down at the child in his lap who began massaging his cheeks.

"Nice...nice...nice."

Branch smoothed Callan's straight, red hair, pushing it back out of her eyes. He answered, in a soft voice, "yes...nice...nice." The little girl smiled and squirmed to get free, eager to repeat the game.

"I am under the impression," Branch began confidentially, as the two girls bounded away, "that your daughter has amazing potential. I have never seen, or even heard of a child her age being able to shift." Heidi would have learned Callan's ability was rare eventually, so he decided she might as well know, now that he was certain. There was no sense in keeping it from her. That the child could shift, and had not injured herself as of yet, conveyed a lot regarding her level of mastery. Shaking his head in wonder, Branch laughed and laid his hand lightly on Annalynn's shoulder, as if to congratulate her on a job well done.

"Do you think she does it intentionally?" asked Annalynn, who instantly accepted Branch's unspoken apology.

"Definitely," he answered quickly. "I think her mother is correct. She does it when she is afraid."

"This ability is putting her in jeopardy." Sobered by these observations Heidi continued, "so what can I do to protect her?"

Branch thought about the question a moment. This was certainly a unique situation, but he had been entertaining ideas and possibilities. Since the realization and ramifications regarding what kind of child he had been cradling in his arms hit him, wonder and foreboding sent his instincts into overdrive.

"Alright," he began, "we need to figure out a way to, A) give her a protected place to go when she shifts. And, B) keep her safe until she's old enough to harness her abilities." Branch sat back, laughing at the incredulous looks he had garnered from the two women on either side of him.

"Oh..." said Heidi sarcastically, "is that all?"

Annalynn laughed and nodded, "she's right Branch, how on earth are they supposed to accomplish this?"

"That ladies," Branch said smacking his knee, "is what we are going to figure out right now."

Two hours later, they had formulated a plan. Amid breaks to play with Alexine, Callan and baby Geoff, the three came up with some guidelines.

"She needs somewhere safe to go," suggested Branch. "I would suggest somewhere outside the house. That is where she typically shifts, correct?"

Heidi nodded her head thoughtfully. Somewhere safe. Outside. The idea developed in her mind as she spoke, "what if we got her an outdoor pet. An animal that would live in a shed?" Her mind raced...an animal that would live in a shed? What animal would live in an outdoor shed? Or...perhaps...*animals* that would live in a shed. "How about...chickens...or ducks?"

"Do you think she would like them? She would want to visit them often?" Annalynn asked, studying Heidi intently.

"Definitely," replied the older woman. "I doubt I could keep her away."

"Then, yes," Annalynn agreed, "a shed would be a safe place." She directed her comment to Branch as if attempting to convince him of the idea.

"That's a start," he answered, "but I think you'll need more than one spot she'll feel comfortable. We need to stop her from popping up in the middle of the woods where she is difficult to find and can easily be injured. Because she is small she is unable to travel great distances, she shifts slowly, but that will change."

Heidi was caught off guard. Change? Callan will travel farther as she grows? Before she was given a moment to pose this question, Annalynn interjected, "how about the garage?"

"That's two," Branch nodded, "she'll need something to pull her there though. Something that holds her interest. Something she loves." He looked at Heidi steadily.

Her question banished, Heidi contemplated this latest problem. Something Callan would want, in the garage. "The cat."

"Okay, good, now maybe a third place, not inside a building," suggested Branch.

Heidi turned her attention toward him, confused. "Not in a building?" she repeated, questioningly. "But wouldn't a building help protect her?"

Shooting a glance at Annalynn, Branch entered her mind quickly. "*Should we warn her?*" Branch's concern for this gifted little girl had grown in the few hours they had spent in the Kovar home. She could be incredible, and that would make her dangerous; a potential threat. But at this point, it was anyone's guess what that could mean.

"*No,*" Annalynn answered slowly, "*I don't think it will help. If they came after Callan, no one here could protect her anyway. Why worry them?*"

Branch paused, weighing his next words carefully. "*Charlie checked her out last week for me,*" he finally revealed, hesitantly. "*She isn't being tracked. If no one finds out about Callan, she's safe.*"

"*You put a seeker on Callan?*" Annalynn replied, surprised and hurt. "*And you didn't tell me? Why?*"

"*The fewer people who are aware of these things, the safer Callan will be. You know that.*"

"*So that includes me now, Branch?*" Annalynn's irritation shifted into sorrow. "*There was a time when you trusted me with everything.*"

Pulling back, Branch turned toward Heidi, taking her hands in his.

"You two just read each other, didn't you?" she asked, narrowing her eyes and studying him intently.

Branch flashed a tired smile. Additionally, it bespoke guilt and surprise. "Yes, we did," he admitted. "You're familiar with readers?"

She ignored his question. "Two people are able to hold private conversations if they are both readers?" This prospect was both fascinating and exciting to the older woman.

Branch nodded. "Yes."

"The more I know, the more I can help my daughter."

Although phrased as a statement, Annalynn knew that she was, in a way, posing a query. Annalynn responded thoughtfully, "yes. But Callan's definitely not a reader. And I would be cautious about giving her too much information as she gets older."

Puzzled, Heidi turned toward Annalynn, "why?"

Annalynn looked at Branch, silently turning the responsibility of answering over to him. Taking a deep breath, he began, "children and teenagers are not notorious for making great decisions," Branch smiled wryly.

Heidi let out a tired laugh. That was certainly true.

"Knowing too much about these abilities can harm some children and teenagers," Branch added knowingly.

"They can try too much, too quickly," put in Annalynn. "And, they tend to take chances because they feel they're invincible."

Branch nodded his consent. "They need to be taught about their abilities, and how to use them, in a safe environment. That is what we do at the academy."

"Yes, I know a little bit about the academy," Heidi glanced toward the house where the diaries lay safely in the wooden box. "My great-uncle was trained there...but..." she shifted her weight uneasily. "Well, I think he left early." Heidi's thoughts flashed back to that evening, so long ago. The little house. Harold's heart-broken wife. The one-sided argument. So much pain. It seemed odd to share personal feelings and facts with these people who were complete strangers. But she found herself divulging more information. "He was an alcoholic, and ended up putting that before anything and anyone else."

"Realizing your potential is sometimes difficult to live with," suggested Branch delicately. "I don't know exactly what happened with your great-uncle, but we have lost many to self-destructive tendencies."

"Alcohol, drugs," said Annalynn softly, as if reliving painful memories. "Sometimes they use substances to run from themselves, or to cope with how they are viewed by others. Feared by others."

"These abilities," Branch added, "are a huge responsibility. Some people are just not able to live with that. Or worse," he continued, almost as an after-thought, heaving a heavy sigh, "they don't use them to help." He flashed Annalynn a look full of meaning. "They use them to hurt, to control. For pride, selfishness."

Heidi flinched. To hurt?

"Everyone is born with abilities," added Annalynn, deep in thought, "but few use them to serve...to do good. Some allow them to fade, some are robbed of their talents." A sadness descended on the three people sitting on the ground.

Heidi was confused. Everyone was born with abilities?

Annalynn shook her head as if clearing away negative images and coming back to the conversation. "Young children are also easily misguided."

It took Heidi a moment to register Annalynn's latest concern. The past few days had been filled with so much new information. She felt overloaded, as if there was not time to glean what was necessary. Use them to hurt? How did they use them to hurt? Talents taken from them? How? Misguided? Misguided by whom? Annalynn threw out yet another problem before Heidi could form these most recent questions tugging at her.

"And...giving some people details regarding their abilities, is like trying to teach calculus to a five year old."

"They just aren't ready for it yet," agreed Branch. "When we receive new students at the academy, we work with them to see if they are prepared to progress."

"You wouldn't give sharp scissors to a child and tell them to run," threw in Annalynn.

"Or a gun to a criminal and tell him to be good," added Branch darkly.

Sensing the turmoil and concern that filled Heidi, he paused and collected his thoughts. They were giving her too much. People had to learn these things slowly, to digest them, to build their knowledge one layer at a time or it could be overwhelming.

The man whom Heidi had invited into her home this morning, whom she had just met six hours ago, posed a pointed question.

"I guess what it comes down to is this: you have to decide if you trust us."

Looking into Branch's eyes, Heidi realized she had made that decision hours before.

Chapter Eighteen
Denique

"So you feel better now?" Geoff asked, grinning at his wife later that evening after returning from his second job at the gym. He took her into a bear hug, picking her up off the ground momentarily.

"Yes! It was wonderful."

"Good!" he nodded, pulling her into the kitchen. "I'm going to get dinner, and you're going to tell me all about it!"

An hour later, Heidi had explained everything she learned that day. Referring to notes jotted down quickly after her visitors left, she covered Callan's abilities, the implications they held, Branch and Annalynn's suggestions, and even the uneasy feeling she had about some of the things that weren't explained entirely.

"I don't know, I learned so much. I doubt we could have gone over more."

"But?" Geoff lead, sensing his wife's hesitation.

"But...I got the feeling there was more I should know." She shook her head, and pursed her lips. "I don't know, maybe not. Or...maybe not yet." Rolling her head to stretch her neck, she focused on relaxing and letting the feeling go. "One thing is for sure, we're a lot better off now."

"Yes," said Geoff, walking up to his wife. He ran his hands through her hair and leaned in close. "I love you," he whispered, his eyes brimming with affection.

Heidi smiled playfully, "I love you more."

After he had finished eating, Geoff stopped by the children's rooms to wish them goodnight, then collapsed onto the bed in he and Heidi's room. Picking up the novel he was reading, Geoff opened it absently and found the spot where he had left off the day before.

"Well, tomorrow is Saturday so we should start getting things together," Heidi suggested as she walked from the bathroom into their bedroom. "I would like to get her safe places set up as soon as possible." Climbing into bed, Heidi ran through the list in her mind: shed, garage, big rock in the yard.

"We'll need to go over to Peterson's to get the chicks and ducks. She has to have something that pulls her to the shed." Heidi was speaking more to herself than to Geoff. They had been planning on using the old out-building currently sitting orphaned on the edge of their property as a chicken coop anyway. Branch and Annalynn's visit just hastened the process. "How are we going to move that thing?" Heidi rolled onto her side to face her husband.

Looking at her and smiling, Geoff set his book down. She gave him a sheepish look, so caught up in this process she had not realized she was interrupting his reading. He shrugged good-naturedly. "Let's call Todd Thomas. I'm sure he'll know how to do it."

She laughed. Mr. and Mrs. Thomas were good friends. Todd was a huge bear of a man who, in his day, Heidi was sure had been quite intimidating. Now he was just a big marshmallow who helped everyone with anything. If it had ever been done before, Todd had done it, or helped do it, or invented the machine that had done it for the first time. "Actually, that's a great idea," she kissed Geoff on the forehead.

"Thanks!" he beamed, smiling as if very proud of himself. Picking his book back up, he promptly began reading again.

"Blasphemy?" Heidi made a face. "That's an odd title for a book."

Geoff turned the book over to look at the title on the front cover. Blasphemy. "Yep," he said dismissively, focusing on the novel.

When she was sure he wasn't looking, she rolled her eyes.

* * *

"We'll just pull it with the truck!" said Todd, as he and Heidi studied the old shed the next afternoon.

His jean overalls were wore white in places, the result of endless hours of work, most of which had been accomplished in the service of others. What was once a brilliant red and white checkered flannel work shirt also bore scars of being over utilized, its collar frayed with age. But this was Todd; use something up completely, never waste. Resting his hands under suspenders which curved abruptly around his ample midsection, he rocked back and forth on his feet, silently making decisions about the project.

Geoff had run into town for a few other items: a litter box and heating pad for the cat. Winters in Michigan were sometimes frigid. They were counting on the heating pad, nestled snuggly in a blanket laden box, to entice the cat when temperatures plummeted. In addition, he was purchasing feeders, mash, a baby pool, and a watering container for the chicks. And of course, the chicks and ducklings themselves. This left Heidi to work with Todd.

"How?" she asked, almost afraid to hear the answer. The lines etched deeply in Todd's face became more pronounced as he frowned, pondering that very question. The skin on the older man's face was growing thin, translucent; undeniable proof he was getting up there in years. She didn't want to imagine not having him around.

"Sink an eye into the base, hook up a tow chain, drag it." Todd was so confident concerning his methods, he gave them a forceful nod. "Yep. Corban!" he shouted, beckoning the young man who accompanied him. "Grab one of those big eyes in the toolbox!"

Todd had a serious habit of keeping teenage boys, whom he thought were lackadaisical or destructive when left to their own devices, busy completing odd jobs as his helper. It was an endearing trait and one appreciated by many a parent.

In one easy leap, a teenager with long, brown, curly hair jumped into the bed of the truck. He was a large, powerful boy who irresistibly reminded Heidi of a gorilla. She grinned. The boy scrounged around, a cacophony of clinks and clatters filling the air as parts of Corban popped in and out of view over the sides of the vehicle. Metal hitting metal, large items being shoved and shifted, and then, "ah ha!" He emerged with the biggest metal eye Heidi had ever seen.

"Whoa!"

"That should work!" Todd accepted the piece of metal from Corban who had lumbered over, one hand holding the eye, and one hiking up his pants which threatened to drop every few steps. Todd turned over the piece of steel in his hand examining it closely. Throwing it up in the air, he caught it and smiled. "Yes it will!"

"Okay, here we go!" the large man yelled to the younger boy whose duty it was to watch the tow chain which tethered the shed to the truck. Thick links of chain strained as the slack lengthened out and the weight it bore was realized.

The dirt of many years partially entombed the lower portions of the small building, drawing it down into the soft lawn. The shed creaked and groaned as it was coaxed from the only home it had ever known. Reluctant to relinquish it's captive, the sod surrounding the base of the shed held firm.

"Come on," Todd breathed, pressing on the gas peddle, then letting off, in an attempt to slowly break the earthy ties and rock the prisoner free. The spot seemed hesitant to release it's quarry. Todd repeated the process, twice, three times, four times.

"The trick is, not to ruin the shed!" he yelled to Heidi over the roar of the engine. "You've got to be easy on them," he said more softly, to himself.

"There you go!" Heidi cheered as the dirt foundation surrendered, clumps of grass, roots, and mud trailing behind as the small shed obediently followed the powerful vehicle. Wanting to put the little building on the far side of the garden, Heidi hoped they could maneuver it into the space she had designated. It turned out they could only get it in the general area. After pulling then pushing it with the truck, the shed sat just feet from the perfect place.

"That's as good as we can do." Removing his hat, scratching his head, then smoothing thinning white hair, Todd pulled the cap back on and turned to Heidi.

She beamed. "Thank you so much! We really appreciate it!"

Todd nodded, as if satisfied with the effort. A hard working man of few words, he barked, "whelp, let's go," as he climbed back into the truck with his young helper.

Heidi waved as they abruptly left.

* * *

"It's close." Geoff surveyed the new chicken coop when he returned home. "Won't it work?"

Heidi shook her head. "It's completely out of square with the garden!"

"So what?" Geoff shook his head at her.

"It bothers me."

He eyed the shed for a long time. His wife could be truly exasperating. "Let's talk to Billy," he sighed. A neighbor down the street who had done some work for them in the past, Billy owned several very big toys. The front end loader came to mind on this occasion. "I'll run down and ask." Geoff hopped into his car.

As her husband pulled out of the drive, Heidi called, "Alexine!" The little brown haired girl looked up at her from the back yard. "Bring Callan!" she shouted, intentionally sounding overly excited. She hoped her enthusiasm would spur the two girls into quick action.

Alexine looked around, searching for her little sister. "Come on!" She plastered a big grin on her face and nodded. "Let's go see mommy!" Callan seemed to understand some sentences, but body language and facial expression still played a large roll regarding whether the little girl would cooperate...or not. Taking her hand, Alexine lead Callan down the driveway.

"I have a great idea!" Heidi squatted down to address the girls and the two children looked at her in anticipation. "Let's get the chicks and ducklings set up in the den!" She had been planning on keeping the little birds in the house for several days until they were old enough to withstand the evening temperatures. A decision which would cause more work than she imagined, but Heidi wanted to make sure the little bundles of feathers didn't freeze to death. Even with a warming lamp, she was unsure the little guys would be safe outside.

Alexine began bounding up and down screaming. "Yea! Yea! Yea!"

Not sure what was so exciting, but assuming it was something really good, Callan joined the revelry. "Yea, yea, yea!" They ran to the front door where Geoff had deposited the baby chicks and ducklings along with their supplies.

"Okay," whispered Heidi, holding a finger in front of her lips to shush the girls. "We have to be quiet because Baby Geoff is sleeping!"

The girls both gave her serious looks; they understood. Getting the items into the den, the chicks and ducklings into the baby pool, the food and water situated, and the warming lamp adjusted was not the problem. The problem was keeping the birds *in* the wading pool. The girls wanted to carry them around. They enjoyed playing with the fluffy little balls of feathers. This situation went from bad to worse when baby Geoff woke up.

Walking into the den and depositing a little chick into the pool for the twenty-seventh time that afternoon, Heidi decided this was undoubtedly going to work. These little creatures had captured the interest of all the children. Callan in particular was drawn to them.

Geoff returned with Billy less than a half hour later. They made quick work of moving the shed into place. The only hitch occurred when Billy drove over a small, neatly placed pile of rocks on the edge of the woods near where the shed now stood.

"Mickey!" Callan screamed, running to her mother. Clinging to Heidi's leg, she tipped her face up imploringly, tears pooling in her eyes. "Mickey!"

Heidi leaned down to comfort the child. Did she really remember? It had been over a year since Mickey died. Callan was so young when it happened. Could she really remember where they buried him?

Pointing at the front end loader desecrating their old dog's grave, Callan continued wailing. "No! Mickey!"

Heidi was shocked. She scooped up the little girl, smoothed her hair, cooed, and rocked in an attempt to calm her. The pair turned their backs on the commotion. When the men were finished, Heidi and Callan returned to the area and carefully replaced the stones that marked the little dog's resting place.

"Okay," Heidi crooned, reassuringly. "It's okaaaay...see?" Callan seemed instantly content and bounded away into the front yard. Geoff, who had been inspecting the shed's position, shot her a quizzical look.

"She remembers that we buried Mickey here," Heidi frowned, a incredulous look creeping unbidden across her features. She still couldn't believe it.

"No," he replied shaking his head doubtfully.

"Yea," she countered emphatically.

Geoff furrowed his brow, his gaze moving from his wife to the little red-head running across the lawn. "Wow." He shook his head again in disbelief. "Weird. Well, what's next?" Geoff rubbed his hands together quickly in hurried anticipation. He seemed to be enjoying this.

Saturdays tended to drive Geoff a bit stir-crazy. His life was extremely busy and not having something to do, even on a day off, unnerved him. There had been times Heidi assembled a quick list of things she "desperately" needed from the store, just to get him out of the house. She smiled at the man who became more endearing each year they spent together.

"The cat. She loves that stray, so we need to set up a spot that will attract the cat."

Geoff nodded, eagerly accepting his new assignment. "In the garage, right?"

"I think Killer will pull Callan there, don't you?" She threw a quick look at the big, grey building.

The feral cat which had adopted the Kovar family several years previous had been dubbed Christine immediately. Heidi wasn't quite sure why the cat reminded the children of her sister, but the name stuck. It wasn't until they took the animal to the vet that they discovered Christine was a boy.

"Perhaps Christopher?" the vet remarked laughing.

Recently, the animal had been re-christened Killer. His penance for feasting on rodents and then lounging luxuriously on the front steps, fat belly abnormally distended, earned him the title. Alexine preferred to call him Chris, but the rest of the family stuck with the more suitable name.

"Definitely. She loves that indolent cat." Geoff made off for the garage.

"I'm going to get lunch ready," Heidi called after him. Not breaking stride, nor turning around, her husband waved his hand above his head in acknowledgment.

"Can they live in here forever?" pleaded Alexine as she and Callan sat down next to the little pool in the den. Heidi had popped her head into the room on her way to the kitchen, quickly counting to ensure there were no peepers being carted around the house.

"No," replied Heidi with finality. "Only for a little while, then they'll go out to the coop."

"They'll be lonely!" the little brunette complained, looking sadly down at the small puffs of feathers scratching around.

"You can visit them everyday," suggested Heidi, smiling. "I'm going to make lunch, what would you like?"

"Ramen noodles!" yelled Alexine.

"Noobles!" mimicked Callan.

That night after putting the kids to bed, Geoff and Heidi worked on ideas to pull Callan to the rock.

"Why the rock?" asked Geoff, puzzled.

"Branch wanted her to have a spot where she wouldn't be in an enclosed space. He acted like she needed a place to go where she couldn't be trapped. An open place."

"Trapped?" repeated Geoff, surprised. "Trapped by what?"

Heidi shook her head, "yea. That is what I wondered too. We never really discussed it. I had so many questions and there was so much information. We ran out of time."

Geoff shrugged. "There's nothing here to hurt her," he replied, unconcerned.

"Yea." Heidi was unconvinced, but temporarily shook off her misgivings. "Actually!" she said slyly, "the other day, I heard some soccer moms talking about a mountain lion!"

Geoff smiled. "Actually, I've heard the same thing. You never know!"

In the end, they decided the rock was their family meeting place in case of emergencies. It worked. The children always ran to the rock whenever a fire or other disaster was simulated. In addition, Heidi took the kid's yearly pictures somewhere in the vicinity of the rock. The rock became a Kovar thing. "Safe" when they played tag, the fortress for king-of-the-mountain games. Even the cat hung out near the rock, which Heidi found wildly ironic since he had a lovely home in the garage.

* * *

Several months later, the phone rang in the afternoon.

"Hello?" answered Heidi, instantly realizing they had a bad connection as the line crackled ominously.

"Mrs. Kovar?" asked the staticy voice on the other end.

"YES?" Heidi spoke loudly, hoping her voice carried through the din.

"It's me…Branch."

"HELLO!"

"I wanted to check in with you. How are things going?"

"Great! Thank you for all the help!"

"You're welcome!" he yelled over the poor connection. "I can't talk long, but I wanted to let you know how you could reach me."

Heidi was relieved. After her guests left, she realized she had no idea how to find them again. In fact, the more she thought about it, the more strange it seemed. A woman, contacting her about her little girl, just when she was desperate for help? Branch and Annalynn show up and she just invites them into her life, not knowing who the heck they were? They leave and she has no information regarding how to contact them. It was all very odd, but for some reason, she did not feel uncomfortable. Logical, pragmatic Heidi felt fine about it. Now *that* was weird! Heidi quickly jotted down the number. "I'll keep it in a safe place!" she answered, her mind immediately turning to that ancient, wooden box. The repository for so much vital information.

"Oh, and one more thing," Branch said.

"Yes?"

"This may seem strange but, I would ask that you not tell the girls about our visit. Please don't tell them our names either. The fewer people who know about this, the better."

"Why?" Heidi asked, perplexed.

Branch paused, unsure how to respond. "Well, we talked about children knowing too much."

"Yes?"

"It will help keep Callan safe. The less she knows, the less *anyone* knows, the better."

"Alright," Heidi agreed, still confused.

Branch hung up the phone and turned toward Annalynn. "She knows how to find us," he said, a hint of relief in his voice. "How could we forget that?"

Following the move from London to Venice, the academy was thrown into chaos. Having just realized the Kovars had no way to contact them again, they were relieved to get through quickly.

"And she knows to keep things quiet," he added in a low tone, glancing around. No one was within earshot.

It was a precaution many leaders of the academy were now taking to protect potential recruits. Too many situations were up in the air. There was too much dissension to risk innocent children's futures.

And these children they were finding! Branch could not help but believe the time had come; they were arriving. Denique. The last. Finally. He had not shared these feelings with Annalynn, but felt deeply impressed that these were the little ones they had been waiting for.

"Good," she replied. "And things are going well?"

Nodding, Branch looked at his phone as if he could view the events across the world in it. "They seem to be."

"Well then, you're still sure we should keep this a secret? Tell no one?"

"Yes," answered Branch quickly and seriously. "You have to promise me Anna. We need to protect her. If they find her…" Branch's mind flew to his brother and the frightening turn Nautas was taking. Grasping Annalynn by the shoulders, he drew her in. "Just trust me on this, please," he implored.

Annalynn's gaze drifted to the left…and remained here. She softly whispered, "I do."

Chapter Nineteen
An Escape

October 14, 2009
Shanghai, China

"Well then," began Mr. Rush several minutes later, taking his place at the front of the room.

As other students in the class produced notebooks and pens, Alexine felt dreadfully out of place. She looked over at Callan.

"Um, excuse me," Callan said suddenly, raising her hand as she spoke. Everyone in the room turned to look, but if Callan noticed the attention, she completely ignored it. "I don't have any paper or…"

The comment trailed off as Mr. Rush quickly took several long spidery strides to his desk. Alexine stifled a giggle. Now that the room was full of people, this man seemed less threatening and more absurd. The spindly man opened a drawer retrieving two pads of paper and two pens. He returned to the front of the room, walked around Zeke's desk, and stood directly in between the two girls. Smiling unpleasantly down at Callan, he handed her a notebook and pen.

"Thank you," Callan said politely, giving him a curt nod as if she expected nothing less. She turned to the first page.

The instructor raised his eyebrows looking both surprised and perhaps a bit entertained. Inclining his head as if to say "you're welcome" he placed paper and pen in front of Alexine then walked back to the front of the room.

"Um… thanks?" the older girl said timidly to his back.

"Now that we're all prepared," his eyes found Callan and Alexine then flitted away, "let's begin."

Alexine looked down at the pad of paper on her desk. Picking up the pen, she began writing her name on the cover. A-L-E-X-I-N-E   D-A-N-Y-E-L. She had always liked her middle name, variously pronouncing it Danielle and Daniel at different times during her life.

"For the benefit of our new students…"

Alexine felt the class's gaze and glanced up quickly. Mr. Rush was again staring directly at she and Callan. Her little sister ignored this latest bid to focus attention on her, and continued flipping through the pages of her notebook absently. Alexine looked at Zeke, surprised to be the center of attention again, and they smiled at each other. She blushed furiously, and immediately regretted allowing herself to gaze at him a bit too long. It was one thing to blush in front of several people, quite another to do it in front of a classroom of strangers.

Callan chose this moment to look up and saw the exchange but remained silent. Failing to take advantage of any opportunity to poke fun at Alexine killed her, but her ego still stung from being humiliated several minutes before. The large mirror at the front of the class. Better not push it.

"I would like to quickly cover the basics." As Mr. Rush finished, he turned toward the board and began scratching words onto it's surface:

Shifters. Readers. Changers. Travelers.

Alexine watched him write the words with unfeigned interest. Finally!

Answers to questions that had been irritating her since their perfunctory tour by Devin the day before.

The small awkward man turned back toward his students and locked eyes with a small girl. She had jet black, perfectly smooth hair, fine features, and almond eyes that turned slightly upward. Her complexion was flawless, the color of milk chocolate. She was sitting in the middle of the room.

"We'll get rid of her today," he thought to himself. "New students in the room, how could she resist?"

The girl was pretty and petite, Alexine noted, and seemed to be of middle-eastern descent.

"Ms. Huda?" the instructor intoned.

She raised her eyebrows in surprise.

"Can you please tell us about shifters?"

The girl contemplated her position for a moment. If she answered honestly, it would give them a perfect excuse to expel her from the program, or worse. She wasn't sure she believed the rumors circulating about holding cells in a basement no one knew about, but *was* sure she did not care to find out.

Mr. Rush's motives were transparent; he had asked her to answer in hopes she would dig her own grave. "Because," she thought angrily, "being honest? Well, one could get themselves in a lot of trouble for that." Rohbiha had seen it time and again over the course of the past several days.

What was it Jiana said before *she* disappeared? Oh yes, "they don't want to know what you think, they want to know what *they* think." No room for opinions. No interest in input. The roommates had agreed, in the dark protection of their quarters, that thinking was now banned at the academy.

She laughed to herself, why had she made the decision to stay? She was tired of their games. Tired of this place. She ached to escape. Mr. Rush wanted an answer? She would give him an answer. She had changed her mind.

"We might as well have a bit of fun with it," she thought haughtily. The young lady stood solemnly, and stared ahead stone-faced, answering his query in robot-like fashion. "Shifters posses the ability to control themselves at a molecular level." She glanced around, waiting for someone to challenge her. No? Not yet? Well then, I'll continue.

"They are all able to become the air that surrounds them. In that respect, they seem to disappear, although they remain in their space." Nothing earth shattering there.

"Most shifters have the ability to alter their molecular structure in other ways, thereby simulating inanimate objects. By 'becoming' the objects they are moving through, they have the ability to travel through walls, windows, anything that is not living." Basic question, basic answers. The girl braced herself for what was surely coming should she continue.

"A few shifters reorganize themselves into, and can thus pass through, living things; plants and animals. " The stillness that followed unnerved the girl. That shouldn't be surprising. Everyone was aware of that. Perhaps they knew what would follow. Was she that obvious? Hearing no opposing view, she continued stoically.

"The only people who can see shifters when they alter are other shifters who are similarly altered," she paused, "and seers," she added, steeling herself for the rebuttals she knew would manifest themselves quickly. Several people in the room sighed loudly, some let out snorts of derision, still others covered their eyes.

Mr. Rush flushed with pleasure. "Seer-ship is, of course, disputed." His tone was ominous; a perfect match to his piercing glare. "You are, I assume, aware of that."

The teacher turned away, and as he did so, the small girl flashed an irritated look that was gone in an instant. If Alexine had not been staring at her, she probably would not have seen it. Did the girl disagree with Mr. Rush? And what the heck was a seer? *And* why did Alexine feel like there were suddenly a lot of angry people in this room? She had not noticed that before. Had she been distracted? *And* why did they all seem to be mad at this girl?

This place was strange. Alexine felt as though she were on a roller-coaster. One moment, she felt safe at the academy, like it was the right place to be. The next moment, she had an overwhelming urge to run from the building. As if she had been thrown into the middle of something she did not understand; an unwilling pawn in a mysterious game.

The petite girl continued, uninvited, as the energy in the room changed perceptibly. "The most advantageous form shifters can use is air, because nothing can affect them while they are thus altered."

Mr. Rush turned slowly back to appraise Rohbiha, his face unreadable. It seemed to Alexine that he was irritated, but at the same time exhilarated. He had just caught something in his web.

Rohbiha again continued, unabashed. "In this way, shifters can protect themselves from attack."

The instructor smiled wickedly. "That's enough," he said, but his tone conveyed the opposite. He wanted her to continue, wanted her to go on Alexine thought, but why? Several students in the room mirrored the instructor's excitement, as if anticipating an entertaining event to take place momentarily.

Alexine was so confused. She looked around, as if someone must have the answer, and she needed only to meet the gaze of that particular person. Zeke faced away from her, toward the girl, though his profile was visible. His eyes flitted from the girl, to the instructor, and back. He seemed both concerned and very serious, almost as if *he* were in charge of the class and should put a halt to this exchange. The girl did not seem to care whether or not anyone wanted her to continue, she had more to say.

"Shifters are the individuals whom typically get the job done."

"Ms. Huda," the instructor interjected, suddenly uncomfortable with the power he had relinquished to this rebel. Perhaps his desire to rid himself of this nuisance had overcome his sense of reason. She had the floor and could do some serious damage. There were new students in the room, and it was anyone's guess which side they would choose. He chanced a glance at Zeke too late. Zeke was not pleased.

"They are the workers. They are the soldiers," Rohbiha said quickly, as if ticking off a list.

"Rohbiha may I see you in the hall?" Mr. Rush bumbled. He needed to remove her from the equation. His second nervous glance toward Zeke went unnoticed by anyone else.

She ignored him, placing her right hand slowly on her desk. Studying her hand for a moment, she finally uttered, in a low, deep, challenging voice. "They also tend to be the most *expendable*." She emphasized the word, bringing her head up deliberately as she spoke it, to meet the instructor's agitated gaze.

"Ms. Huda that is enough!" The little man boomed.

She continued, narrowing her eyes defiantly. "… as they are more prolific than other…"

The instructor took three long strides and grabbed Rohbiha by the arm. She stopped speaking momentarily, then looked up at him, daring him to stop her. An unrepentant smile curled her lips upward.

"They are the sillemlem," Mr. Rush's eyes flashed at the mention of this strange word, "that are most often taken advantage of." The pretty girl looked accusingly around the room. "Used." She locked eyes with several other students. "Victimized." The girl was impassioned, forcefully hurling her charges, condemning both the people and the place. The pretty girl tipped her head up to look Mr. Rush full in the face. He was still grasping her arm firmly. She finished menacingly, "because of their blind loyalty" Rohbiha and Mr. Rush stood toe to toe, each held in the others challenging gaze, as others in the classroom glared at the girl. Her offensive description regarding shifters had obviously hit a nerve.

Mr. Rush displayed a wicked grimace. "Yes," he said softly, leaning down to whisper in her ear. "Finally we discover where your loyalties lie."

Rohbiha smiled up at him slyly…and disappeared.

The room was thrown into chaos as Mr. Rush's arm jerked suddenly, and then he was blindly grasping the air, flailing as if he could somehow find something that was no longer there.

She pulled her arm sharply away from his grasp as she altered. "You've done it now," she thought, "get going!" Rohbiha moved toward the window and was through it in an instant.

"I've got her!" a young woman from the back of the room shouted, vanishing.

"No!" yelled the instructor, sounding panicky. "Just let her go!" He whirled, searching for students who were no longer visible, grasping for control of the class which was now in turmoil. Turning toward Zeke, he pleaded for instruction, direction of some kind. Zeke simply shook his head slightly in disgust.

Alexine jumped to her feet and spun around wildly, fear filling her as she realized this was an escape of some kind. Were people forced to stay here? She turned quickly toward Callan. Her little sister seemed transfixed, studying the events unfolding before them intently, completely calm.

"What's going on?" whispered Alexine, leaning toward Callan.

The little red-head looked at her sister, winked, and then…she was gone.

Chapter Twenty
Trust

"Never do that again!" Alexine said threateningly when the girls were alone in the hallway thirty minutes later. "What were you thinking?"

Class ended abruptly after Rohbiha disappeared. Alexine had hoped Zeke would volunteer to escort them somewhere, anywhere, or at least offer an explanation regarding what had just occurred. Instead he bolted through the doorway as soon as Mr. Rush announced class was over for the day. The other students then filed out quickly leaving the two girls sitting in their chairs, alone, wondering where they should go, what they should do, and what had just happened.

"What do you think that was about?" asked Alexine accusingly, sensing Callan knew more than she was letting on. "And where did you go?!"

Callan shrugged non-commitally, "I don't know what it was about, and I was just checking things out." This uninformative response earned her an exasperated look from her older sister.

"What in the heck is up with you?" Alexine could not take it anymore. Callan seemed much too relaxed about these events, much too willing to accept things that weren't right.

"Alexine, listen to me," Callan said seriously. "You just need to take it easy. We don't know the whole story."

Alexine was incredulous. "Take it easy?" she said loudly. "Take it easy?! Are people are being forced to stay here? That girl in the cafeteria was sobbing after Devin talked to her, why?" Alexine looked imploringly at her little sister, begging for whatever information Callan may have garnered. Her questions were met with an empty silence. "Every time I walk into this building, I can feel something... bad. And you expect me to 'take it easy'?!"

Callan turned and walked away down the hall.

"Don't you care that something is really wrong here?" hissed Alexine to Callan's retreating figure, then followed after her in a huff.

The little girl stopped, dropped her head slowly and turned back around. Eyes downcast and fixated on the floor, she spoke in a whisper, but her words were serious and intense. "Do you trust me?"

Taken aback by Callan's change of tone, Alexine thought about the question for a moment. Her little sister had always been impulsive, had always had trouble controlling her emotions. She ran head-first into challenges, often times not contemplating the repercussions. But she had a heart of gold, and Alexine loved her dearly. "Yes," Alexine answered firmly, ripping the answer from her heart because her mind was reeling. "Yes, I do."

Callan's shoulders relaxed and she sighed as if a heavy and ill-fitting yoke had been taken off her back. A wry, tired smile graced her face as she looked up slowly at her older sister. It surprised Alexine. Perhaps Callan shared her concerns, shared her fears about this place. For some reason, it made the little girl look older, more mature.

"Thanks," Callan said.

Alexine could tell her trust meant a great deal. That somehow, her trust, and the bond that existed between she and her sister, were of paramount importance.

That many things hinged on it. *Why?*

"Remember that, okay?"

Alexine was puzzled, but before she was able to ask any more questions, the little red-head stated with finality, "we need to find Devin."

Even though Devin was the last person Alexine wanted to see right now, Callan said it with such confidence that she didn't argue.

"We need to get back to our room, and we need Devin to do that," the little girl said, as if thinking out loud.

And Alexine was relieved to agree.

* * *

The hot shower felt wonderful and Alexine was not looking forward to getting out. The water seemed to melt away some of the tension that had been building all day long, not to mention soothing the exhaustion she still felt. She had never imagined jet lag could affect her so profoundly. It felt as if she was walking around in a daze, and she wondered if her sleepiness was affecting her judgment.

It had to be.

Perhaps she was more sensitive than usual because she was so tired. Perhaps she was reading the situation wrong. Now that the girls were back in their room, things felt safer. Settled.

They had found Devin soon after the "incident." That was what they had started calling it, the "incident." He arranged for a ride back to the hotel, and even had dinner delivered to their room.

Callan smiled when Alexine relented, "that *was* pretty thoughtful of him."

"He's not so bad after all then?" the little red-head laughed at her older sister's defeated look.

Alexine was confused. When she went with her gut instinct, she felt they needed to get away from this place. But Callan didn't seem convinced, and Alexine was so tired. It was perplexing, and for the first time in her life, the older girl was not sure what was right and what was wrong. She felt lost, and it was an uncomfortable experience.

"My turn!" Callan smiled when Alexine emerged from the bathroom soaking wet.

"Mmm, that felt so good."

"Wait up for me. We can talk."

"Yea." Alexine pulled on clothes, turned down her blankets, and fell into bed. She was asleep before she pulled the covers up to her neck.

* * *

The sun fell hot on her face as Alexine looked around the yard. Mom was in the garden, humming a familiar tune, although for the life of her, Alexine could not remember the name of the song. Callan ran along the driveway chasing baby Hope, as the latter giggled wildly. Geoff wandered around the edge of the lawn, picking long stems of grass and using them as swords to attack the weeds still standing: soldiers of an opposing army. Mia followed behind him, the cat hot on her heels. Everything was calm. Perfect.

Alexine waved to her mother, who looked up and smiled then a horrible noise interrupted the peaceful scene. It sounded like an annoying, grinding car engine. Alexine looked around for the source of the tumult but could not locate it. Walking into the yard, she continued her search. Where was the noise coming from? It vibrated into her head. Please be quiet. It's so nice here. Please be quiet. Alexine felt someone shake her shoulders.

* * *

"Mom?" she said quietly. "Mom, what's that noise?"

Laughter.

Opening her eyes, Alexine looked around, puzzled. Where were the kids? Where was the garden? Where was mom?

"We have to get up," Callan said sleepily, still giggling. "Come on."

A dream. It was only a dream. "Ugh," Alexine sighed. "I can't get up, I just went to sleep."

Callan let out a tired, bark of a laugh. "Yea, me too." She stumbled into the bathroom.

The swish of water running in the sink was mesmerizing. Unable to keep her eyes open, Alexine unwittingly slipped back into darkness.

"Alexine!" said Callan loudly. "Seriously, we have to go!"

As her eyes fluttered opened, she was greeted by a vision of Callan, fully dressed, hair brushed, arms folded tightly, looking very irritated.

"Okay, okay," said Alexine dreamily.

Callan pulled the covers off Alexine's bed. The chill air hit her exposed skin and she instinctively curled up into a ball, whimpering. Admitting defeat, the older girl rolled to her right and fell onto the floor, hitting her head against the small cabinet on the way down.

"Ouch!" she whined, rubbing her forehead.

"Serves you right! You have five minutes."

Dragging into the bathroom, Alexine washed her face and brushed her teeth. Going to bed with wet hair had caused Alexine's normally misbehaved locks to look even more crazy. She frowned into the mirror, smoothing the stubborn mass with her hands but it stood back up defiantly. Wetting it down was the only way to regain control. She turned and kneeled in front of the tub.

"Ouch!" she cried again, banging her head on the faucet. This was not going to be an good morning, she could tell.

Chapter Twenty-one
Jealousy

Stepping into the taxi several minutes later, Alexine had misgivings. Was she really going to walk through the doors of the academy again? Was she really going to expose she and Callan to whatever lurked there? She shut the car door quickly, realizing that if she thought about it for too long, she would turn around, take the elevator up to the fourteenth floor, and lock herself in their room.

The taxi ride was monotonous. They happened upon an extremely careful driver and Alexine missed the younger, crazy guy. If they were headed back for more weirdness, they might as well get there quickly and get it over with. Drawing it out was like torture; providing more time to create fantastic scenarios of intrigue and mayhem.

Meeting them at the front door security check, Devin escorted the girls to the cafeteria for breakfast in silence. He seemed tired. "Didn't get enough sleep?" Alexine finally questioned as he turned to leave them. The large man stopped and gave Alexine an irritated look that immediately cowed her into silence.

"Whoa," she whispered as he walked away. "He's grumpy."

Callan shrugged, disinterested.

Of course, her little sister understood being grumpy in the morning. All it took was the red head missing several hours of precious sleep and she turned into the main character from some intense horror movie. Thrashing around, screaming in irritation and defiance, it could be quite comical. As she thought about it, Alexine realized this had not held true since they left home. Callan was first up this morning, ready to go. She had tolerated the long walk the evening they arrived, which seriously cut into her sleep time. Was the little girl that excited about being in this place? Being able to find out more about her ability?

Alexine tried to put herself into Callan's shoes; possessing an uncontrollable propensity that wreaked havoc with your life, that made you different, that no one else understood. And having an older sister who resented your gift to an extent. Why?

"Because you're jealous." The words came to mind automatically.

"No I'm not!"

"Yes, you are."

"Am I?"

Alexine and Callan developed a routine over the course of the next few weeks. Aside from hitting her head every morning on the bed stand, which seemed to be a habit, even Alexine had to admit they *were* learning a lot.

"The incident" which had shaken Alexine considerably seemed to be an isolated event. No one else challenged an instructor, no one else voiced dissenting opinions regarding the academy's teachings, no one else "escaped."

Not that Alexine would know if people were disappearing; she didn't associate with any other students. But additional "escapes" hadn't happened as far as she knew, and Alexine hesitated even using the word "escape" anymore; it didn't seem as if anyone were being held prisoner. She was under the impression that she and Callan could pack up and fly home whenever they liked.

When first introduced to Mr. Rush, Alexine had been uneasy. Following the disturbing events during that first day of class, she decided to stop attending, and no one noticed her absence. Or, if they did, they didn't care that she was playing hooky, so skipping his class didn't seem like a big deal.

Perhaps as a result of her ditching "Academy Overview," she was not invited to attend any additional lessons either. But that was fine with her; sessions with Annalynn had become quite enjoyable. They spent two entire days discussing the process of reading someone when the older woman asked permission to read Alexine. Hesitant at first, she agreed.

"Okay, typically, in the beginning, you must have some type of connection," began the instructor, repeating what she had already taught the younger girl. Pulling her chair up so the two sat directly across from each other, the older woman took her seat and grasped Alexine's hands.

Alexine giggled uncomfortably. It had taken several days for her to adjust to the fact that most Asian people had no sense of personal space. They all tended to stand very close, and to speak very close. Alexine had also become accustom to being stared at; it seemed staring was not considered rude in the slightest bit.

"So," Annalynn continued, "the easiest way to start is to grasp hands."

Alexine nodded, remembering the steps. Sitting this close to Annalynn, she hated to talk. "What if I have bad breath?" she thought nervously.

"Okay," the instructor began, "when you are first learning, the best thing to do is feel compassion for the person you're trying to read. Compassion is a very powerful emotion, it brings you close to the person for whom you feel pity."

Alexine again nodded. She knew they had gone over this, but her anxiety made it difficult to remember these pieces of information. What was this going to feel like? Compassion. Yes. She was so nervous.

"As you become proficient, you won't have to use your emotions as much," Annalynn instructed, thinking of Nautas. When was the last time he felt compassion for anyone? "Okay, here we go…one… two…three…"

The room stopped spinning, and Alexine swayed in her seat. Collecting herself, she felt that familiar sense of disquiet; as if something had happened, but she couldn't quite remember what. As if someone had taken advantage of her, but the memory of the event had been erased. She stared at Annalynn and her temper flared. Face contorted with anger, she said accusingly, "you read me the first time we met!"

Annalynn leaned back in her chair and nodded slowly, contemplating her next move. This was an unforeseen situation. Her student was extremely agitated. Thus far, Annalynn had not experienced Alexine's anger and in a way, it surprised her. Afraid Alexine would walk out if she attempted to justify her actions, Annalynn decided silence was her best option.

"I hated it!" shouted Alexine.

"We read everyone who enters the academy," replied Annalynn mechanically, still trying to get a handle on the situation. The excuse sounded lame, ridiculous, even to her.

Alexine pulled back in surprise. "You shouldn't!" she insisted, her voice high pitched and cracked.

"It's the fastest way to appraise the situation," Annalynn heard herself say. The words felt wrong, even as she spoke them. They were Nautas's words, his excuse for violating the students coming into the academy. His excuse for entering anyone's mind, in fact.

"Well, it's wrong," shot Alexine loudly, shaking her head and wagging her finger at Annalynn, as though she were a naughty puppy.

Realizing that relenting was her best move, Annalynn replied, "you're right…you're right." She hoped her response would diffuse the situation, and was not surprised when she admitted to herself she agreed with the girl. It *was* wrong.

It took Alexine several days to forgive Annalynn for reading her in the shop the day they arrived. But she finally decided it wasn't worth arguing about. It was over. The woman tended to be the bright spot in Alexine's day and she hated to alienate her. If she were to be completely honest, sitting around the building for hours was monotonous in the extreme. And that, admitted Alexine ruefully, was the primary reason for excusing the older woman.

After spending more than a week with Annalynn, Alexine sensed her instructor was somehow different than most of the people at the academy, although she couldn't put her finger on just why.

So, the reading continued. And although the sessions were still quite disconcerting, Alexine felt she was learning more about this ability by actually experiencing it. Almost as if it were becoming a part of her, as if she were being physically altered by it in some small way.

Focusing on history quickly moved to the forefront of her academy instruction. Although Alexine had always found the subject boring, Annalynn had a way of bringing it to life. Actually, the history that Annalynn taught was unlike anything Alexine had ever encountered. It centered on individuals who impacted the past and their abilities, as opposed to broad overviews of events.

Alexine was coming to the realization that every person who ever stood out historically was *special*, or at least, that was Annalynn's opinion. Carl Jung, George Washington, Houdini. Reader, shifter, changer. Annalynn also seemed more open minded regarding the types of abilities in existence. Some of the instructors had their favorites; the ones they dwelled on most of the time. And some were only willing to acknowledge several; ignoring, or sometimes denying other abilities existed. This puzzled her, and she often wondered why. She found herself asking a lot of basic questions and Annalynn, at least, was content to answer some of them.

The terms filled her mind, there was so much to learn. She flashed back to the first few minutes of Mr.Rush's class on their second day. The teacher had listed what Alexine later learned were his four acceptable abilities; the ones he was willing to discuss.

Shifter was the first one, the one that had caused the "incident," the people that were taken advantage of. Used. Her baby sister, Callan. Chills ran down Alexine's spine at the thought that someone might someday use Callan. Certainly not if she had anything to do with it! "Easy girl," she thought as the blood rushed to her face. She pushed those somber thoughts from her mind.

Reader. That was the second one. Annalynn was a reader. Annalynn thought Alexine was a reader, which was hysterically amusing. She was currently learning more about this ability than any of the others.

What was the third one? Alexine racked her brain trying to remember. Oh yes. Changer. She and Annalynn had discussed it briefly. Changers were able to alter the structure of an object, changing it into something else temporarily. Whenever the subject of changers came up, Alexine was indelibly drawn to the proposition of changing everything into big, pudding-filled crème puffs; her favorite dessert. Now that would be cool.

And the final ability? Traveler. That was the last one Mr. Rush had listed. She hadn't learned about travelers yet. Visions of people, suitcases in hand, walking around the world flashed through her thoughts. She smiled. Surely not.

There had been four on the chalkboard, plus the one that had irritated Mr. Rush when it was mentioned in class that day: seer. He hadn't seemed too impressed with the suggestion that seers truly existed. Other than what the renegade girl mentioned about them, that they can see shifters when they are altered, Alexine knew nothing about these seers.

Although she had not learned specifically about healers, she heard the term mentioned in passing, and imagined they could heal people. It made sense, seemed logical. For some reason, Devin got bent-out-of-shape about healers. Alexine could not, for the life of her, understand why. What would be bad about making people feel better?

One day in class, Annalynn hinted there were several more abilities, and that combinations of talents created additional hybrids. It had made Alexine giggle, thinking of people in these terms, like they were crops, or livestock, which could be altered and developed into stronger, more disease-resistant strains.

All-in-all, she found the information fascinating, and maintained detailed notes in an attempt to keep everything straight in her head. Shifter, reader, changer, traveler, seer, healer. Periodically running through them aided her endeavors. On occasion, she would request additional information or insight from Annalynn, but more often than not, her instructor dodged the questions, intimating there would be time to delve into each ability later.

Even though the sessions with *Annalynn* were positive, Alexine still felt as though something were amiss at the *academy*. But she could never figure out exactly what.

Meanwhile, Callan loved shifter training and appeared to get along very well with her instructor. Relieved that things had settled down, and glad to see her sister enjoying their stay, Alexine hesitated questioning Callan about the academy, but questions still plagued her.

Did she feel uneasy as Alexine did at times? Were there instances when things just didn't seem quite right? The few times Alexine tried to start a conversation with Callan about the place, the fiery little red-head abruptly changed the subject. She assumed the little girl wasn't interested in discussing anything negative about the school. Callan seemed to *love* it here.

* * *

"How many of those do you think you can eat today?" Alexine asked as Callan bit into another dumpling one day at lunch.

"Actually, they're different this time." Callan did not bother swallowing prior to answering.

The older girl had become accustom to what would have been completely inappropriate table manners at home. Almost everyone in China slurped, gulped, or devoured food loudly. Alexine smiled; Callan was certainly in her element in that regard.

"You should try them." Callan pushed her plate of food across the table.

"Thanks." She was hungry, and there were few acceptable options at the buffet today. The girls ate breakfast in tired silence for several minutes. How Alexine longed for a piece of fresh fruit. Although readily available from several shops near their hotel, fresh fruit and vegetables were never served at the academy. She had assumed it was a safety precaution.

"Hey, there's your friend," said Callan lazily. Still holding her dumpling with a fork, she extended a little finger toward the entrance.

Alexine frowned in question, then turned in the indicated direction. Hippy-girl had just walked through the door of the cafeteria. Alexine had not seen her since that day she stormed out of the cafeteria, sobbing. For some strange reason, it seemed everyone was intentionally ignoring and avoiding her.

"I still have her book!" Alexine watched the girl take a seat, far away from any of the other students. "I feel sorry for her," she mumbled, mostly to herself. "It doesn't seem like anyone wants to talk to her, sit by her, or have anything to do with her."

"Mmm," replied Callan, still chewing and totally uninterested.

"I'm going to keep her company," announced Alexine, smiling. "Want to join me?"

"Umm…no," replied the little girl quickly, as if Alexine should have known better than to ask.

"Why not?!" demanded Alexine, the smile fleeting from her face. Perhaps she could guilt Callan into it. "How would *you* like to be alone?" This wasn't like Callan. For a moment, Alexine thought she had her.

"Um…" Callan looked up at the ceiling, drawing the word out as if considering the proposition, "…no," she finished again quickly, giving Alexine a look which fell somewhere between disgust and irritation.

Surprised, the older girl shot back, "whatever," and stood.

Chapter Twenty-two
I Believe in Her

"Hi," Alexine intoned tentatively.

Hippy-girl slowly looked up, appraising her for several moments as if performing a thorough check; noting Alexine's strengths and weaknesses, sizing her up. Although strange, this examination did not bother Alexine. A lot of students seemed to do this. She stood still, allowing the girl to collect important details. Hippy-girl smiled and Alexine felt instantly at ease.

"May I sit here?" asked Alexine, motioning to one of the many empty chairs surrounding the girl.

"Sure."

Although Alexine expected the girl to show some degree of relief for the company, she seemed non-pulsed about having a guest. Perhaps she was wrong, perhaps the girl didn't want someone to sit with, perhaps she wished to be left alone. Alexine unzipped her backpack and produced the book she had taken from the girl's chair several weeks ago. At least she could return the item.

"I think this is yours," Alexine slid the text across the table.

"Yes…it's been missing for awhile," she replied, giving Alexine a quizzical look. "Where did you get it?"

"Back when you had that…discussion…with Devin…" she stammered, unsure how to term the emotional exchange. "You left it on your chair. I grabbed it for you, but then didn't see you again."

Hippy-girl thought for a moment, then snorted in derision. "I've avoided the cafeteria since then," she offered. "It's too easy for him to catch me when I'm alone here." Hippy girl looked around, ducking slightly, as if searching for someone she really didn't care to see.

"You stormed off so fast that morning…" Alexine left this sentence open, hoping the comment would encourage the girl to discuss the events of that day. Anger flashed across the girl's face, but she seemed unwilling to speak of the altercation with Devin.

"So," said Alexine after several moments of silence, "when did you get here?"

The girl seemed to relax a bit. "Actually, I arrived a few days before you."

"What?" Alexine was shocked. She was not sure why, but was under the impression the girl had been here longer.

"How is your head?" Hippy-girl posed the question without looking up, offering no segue between subjects.

"It hurts," she replied automatically, confused at the sudden change of subject. "I'm such a klutz when I'm tired."

The girl smiled weakly as if thankful for the chance to find something funny.

"Do I have a big bruise today?" Alexine touched the area on her forehead which was now black and blue, compliments of her nightstand. She immediately regretted pushing on the sore spots. "Ouch," she winced.

"Actually, no, your hair hides it completely."

Alexine had painstakingly arranged her hair that morning to cover the little blue knots collecting on her head. "Good. I was hoping it...." her voice trailed off. If her hair covered the bruises, how did this girl know about the angry lumps? She heard herself say, "how did you..." but was cut off.

"I still feel a bit lost in this place too," hippy-girl stated, as if to agree with a statement which had not been voiced.

When Alexine eyed her questioningly, the girl smiled. She seemed so relaxed. So at ease with herself. Her smile wasn't forced. It wasn't something fake she pulled out of her pocket and slapped on at appropriate moments. It wasn't one of those smiles people wear sometimes that make you feel uncomfortable, because you can tell *they* are uncomfortable. Hippy-girl had an innate ability to make her feel calm, as if they were old friends. She was genuine. Although this penchant for jumping from subject to subject was unnerving.

"This place," repeated the girl, absent emotion. She looked around the room as if examining it. "Yes, this place."

Alexine's stomach lurched into her chest. "You don't like it here either?" she whispered, working to restrain herself but excited by the prospect that someone, anyone, agreed with her.

"You want to know what happened that day...here in the cafeteria...with Devin," said the girl, returning to their original subject so quickly Alexine was puzzled for a moment.

"I just thought I could...help...or something." A lame excuse for wanting to hear the story, but it was the only thing she could think to say. It was ludicrous really, how could Alexine help?

The girl looked knowingly at her. "It's okay, I'll tell you." She glanced sideways. "They want me out of here." Anger and resentment seethed from her words. Hippy-girl looked toward the ceiling. "No, that's not entirely it," she said, re-thinking her position. "They're trying to convince me I shouldn't be here at all. That my abilities are..." she searched for words, "weak and useless." Hippy-girl nodded as if satisfied with her appraisal of the situation. Bringing her hand up to her face, she cradled her chin, partly covering her mouth. "Weak and useless," she repeated, her eyes wandering from side to side. She looked conspiratorial, as if formulating a plan of attack.

"Why would they do that?"

Hippy-girl's eyes stopped wandering. They narrowed and stared straight ahead as she thought hard for a moment, then suddenly her expression changed. "Not sure," she said in her happy voice, dropping her hand and sitting back in her chair, a smile spreading across her face.

It was as if Alexine had just asked her any old question like, "what is your favorite color?" The change in emotion caught her off guard, and she laughed at the ill-fitting retort. Holding a conversation with this girl was certainly a unique experience. "Aren't you upset about it?" Of course, the answer was obvious. But Alexine was not sure what else to say.

Hippy-girl raised her eyebrows and cocked her head, as if to say "what do you think?" "I guess I just try to make the best out of situations," hippy-girl shook her head knowingly. "I figure that if I buckle, then they win, so I'm putting up with it for now."

"Well, I have to admit something," said Alexine softly. "I think something is seriously wrong here." Instantly she had hippy-girl's attention.

"Yeeesss…." The word was drawn out, giving her more time to process Alexine's opinion and formulate a response. "Yes, things are now…strange…" She wrinkled her forehead in thought for several moments, and then shrugged as if giving up. "You know," she said feigning disinterest, "aside from the fact that they're trying to drive me out!" She sighed. "I don't know, I've seen some things and heard some things that lead me to believe…" Hippy-girl went silent as she and Alexine watched several students pass the table. When they were out of earshot, she picked up where she had left off, "that something BIG happened a few days before we arrived, and we're seeing the results of that."

Alexine jerked her head back in surprise. Something big?

"Yes," began hippy-girl again, nodding impressively, in answer to a question Alexine had not voiced. "And I honestly don't think we belong here."

"I agree," whispered Alexine, leaning in close. The bubble of anxiety that had been gradually building in her mind seemed to deflate a bit. Someone understood what she had been feeling all along, someone else felt things weren't quite right, and someone seemed to know a lot more about it than she did. Alexine liked hippy-girl. She liked her a lot.

Hippy-girl reached toward Alexine, placing a hand gently on her forehead. A complete stranger touching her head in public would have normally been very uncomfortable, but for some reason she felt warm, and safe. What was it about this girl?

"Want me to help with those bruises?" hippy-girl asked non-chalantly.

"Um… sure." Maybe this girl had some sort of cream in the huge, colorful purse she carried. Alexine could picture the girl producing a little tube of arnica, the homeopathic remedy her mother sometimes used on bruises. She had always been dubious of it's ability to heal.

Hippy-girl smiled. The hand resting on Alexine's forehead felt warm and comforting. It relaxed her so completely her eyes slowly shut. When she opened them, hippy-girl withdrew.

"Let's talk more later," she said, scooting her chair back and standing.

Alexine had the strange sensation that a lot of time had passed while her eyes were closed. She looked around, a bit confused. Objects came into focus, then blurred again, but everything seemed in order. Had she lost a contact lens? Callan was still sitting where Alexine had left her although she had been joined by the shifting instructor, Elizabeth, and they were engrossed in deep discussion.

"I have to go endure a class with an instructor who is going to spend the entire time belittling me." Hippy-girl threw Alexine an exasperated look.

Her words sounded as if they were spoken from the bottom of a metal barrel. Shaking her head to clear it, Alexine turned toward the voice and concentrated on the form in front of her. Instantly it zoomed into view and everything was clear again. She was relieved when it remained that way. Swaying, she tipped her head back to look into her new friend's eyes. Hippy-girl cocked her head to one side, studied Alexine intently for a moment, then jerked her head once, as if satisfied. Flashing a self-conscious smile, Alexine suddenly feeling a bit like a class project.

"I would hate to be late for my daily dose of criticism!" Hippy-girl started toward the exit just as Alexine remembered something.

"Hey!" Standing, she took a few steps toward her new acquaintance.

Hippy-girl turned back, eyebrows raised in inquiry.

"What's your name?"

"Bethia." The eccentric girl smiled. "It's Bethia... Alexine."

She watched her new friend open the door and disappear. Bethia. Alexine turned to rejoin Callan at the table across the room noting that the shifting instructor retreated when she saw Alexine approaching.

"New best friend?" her little sister asked sarcastically.

"What is your problem?" Alexine watched Elizabeth walk away. Why had the teacher left so abruptly?

"None of the instructors think she should be here." Callan threw her head in the direction of the table Bethia had recently abandoned. "They all say she doesn't have any ability at all."

Alexine's eyebrows knit together as she appraised her sister in surprise. Callan was acting just a bit too snotty for her taste. "Oh! No one is as good as Devin's little star shifter?"

The red-head's face remained impassive, as if she were deciding how to answer her older sister's question for a moment. "Nope," she finally answered matter-of-factly, "guess not."

"What? Who are you?!"

"There's nothing wrong with realizing you're good at something Alexine," Callan lectured. "All I'm saying is that you shouldn't hang out with just anyone here, it's a bad idea."

Alexine folded her arms in defiance, wanting desperately to deflate her little sister's ego.

"People could get the wrong impression," Callan finished.

Alexine could not believe what she was hearing. Had someone kidnapped her sister and replaced her with this egotistical little brat sitting across the table? As Alexine fumbled for a reply, Callan stood to leave.

"Think about it." The little girl picked up her things and rushed off.

Alexine plunked down into her seat, dumb-founded, and completely alone. What had just happened? She struggled with feelings of betrayal, disappointment, shock and anger for several minutes. Lugging the backpack over her shoulder, she collected her tray and headed for the exit in complete confusion. She wasn't hungry anymore.

As Alexine walked to Annalynn's office, she tried to make sense of Callan's condescending opinions. Alexine was glad she had not told her little sister what Annalynn suspected. She had not divulged the fact that Annalynn believed Alexine to be a reader, even though it had been several weeks since Annalynn voiced this opinion.

What would Callan say about *that*? Would she laugh at *her*? Would Alexine suddenly be placed in the file with Bethia? The file of people who shouldn't be here, and with whom no one should associate? The file of people who thought they had abilities, but actually had the unsavory disease of being normal? Alexine's blood boiled as she climbed the stairs. Who in the heck did Callan think she was?

"You have to take Callan to China."

Several months ago, in their living room at home, her mother and father sat Alexine down to break this news. She thought they were crazy. China? They had to be kidding. Nope, they weren't.

"You have to take her to *the academy* so she can learn more about her *abilities.*"

Academy? Abilities? What were they talking about? Always getting into trouble, always running around outside in the middle of the night, always ending up in weird places, was that now called an *ability*? Alexine had always thought of it as juvenile delinquency.

So here she was, as far away from home as possible, feeling uneasy about the place, abandoned by her little sister, who it appeared had suffered a complete personality reversal. By the time Alexine knocked on Annalynn's office door, she was fuming.

"How did you sleep?" asked Annalynn as Alexine threw herself into the extra chair.

She gave Annalynn a hard stare. Annalynn was part of the problem. Annalynn was part of this place. This place that had turned her sister into a moron.

"That good?" Annalynn laughed. When the girl scowled back, the laughter in the room met an uncomfortable demise.

"You know," said Alexine, irritated. "I'd really appreciate it if you would stop doing that when you don't ask permission. When you don't even warn me! It's uncomfortable, and it feels like you're intruding."

Alexine was on a roll. When the lesson just wouldn't take off, Annalynn became impatient. Asking questions of her student had not gotten them anywhere. Alexine was so angry! She thought a quick read might shed a little light on the subject. Witnessing the girl's indignant reaction, Annalynn now regretted her decision. Teenagers.

Alexine rose from her chair and paced in front of the reader's desk. "Like you just fling open the front door to my house and walk in." Alexine mimicked throwing open a door, and stepping forcefully over a threshold. The frustration she had brought into the office that morning had taken hold and claimed a life of it's own. "And...I don't know," she continued angrily, spitting out the words slowly, one at a time, her voice rising as she spoke. "I could be standing there...naked...and you just barge in!" Her chest heaved as she allowed her fury and resentment to swell. "What makes you think I *want* you to know how I feel?" Alexine threw her hands in the air, addressing the ceiling. "And don't I have the right to say, 'No!? Sorry!? You can't come in today!?'"

Annalynn leaned back in her chair. Alexine was right, of course. It was wrong to read someone without their consent. But they had come so far since their first meeting. Annalynn had read the girl almost everyday for the last two weeks, why was today different?

The older girl's foul mood was beginning to wear on her. What happened to the girl she had enjoyed so much during their lessons? Who was this person standing in front of her? And which was the real Alexine? The instructor thought she knew, but this person was trying her darndest to convince her otherwise.

"The easiest way to teach you..." Annalynn began, stopping short as she was cut off.

"Is to get into my head!" yelled Alexine. "Leaving nothing unexposed, browsing around like I am some kind of library that is opened for you to explore at will!" Alexine pointed an angry, accusing finger. "You're a peeping-tom!" Breathing heavily, her expanding wrath becoming overwhelming, she knew she needed to leave before anything *really* horrible occurred.

"What is going on today Alexine?" Annalynn asked, shaking her head in confusion, her voice full of genuine concern. "What happened?" she implored. "Maybe I can help."

Somewhere in her mind Alexine knew what she was doing was wrong but she didn't care. "When was the last time *you* were read Anna?" She shortened the name to be intentionally disrespectful. If this woman could poke around inside Alexine's mind, she could call her Anna. "Did *you* like it?"

Annalynn flashed back to the last board meeting; Nautas coming to her, and her refusing him entry. Guilt washed over her; she was Nautas, and Alexine occupied her position. No, that wasn't entirely accurate. Nautas didn't force entry, Nautas respected her decision to deny him entrance. Did that make her worse than Nautas? She shuttered at the thought. What *had* she become?

"You feel vulnerable…exposed…not to mention nauseous!" The girl began another tirade. "It's not like you can stop someone from doing it!!!" Alexine made her decision hastily; she was leaving. Grabbing belongings, she stormed from the room, slamming the door behind her.

Annalynn sat riveted to her chair, convicted as she listened to her charge's feet falling heavily on the hallway floor, growing more and more quiet as the girl stomped away. Annalynn dropped her chin to her chest in defeat.

"Yes…you can stop someone from doing it," she said softly to her student, even though the young woman was not present. Annalynn spoke to the Alexine she had been working with before today. She spoke to the girl full of humility, patience, and kindness. "You will learn," she continued. "And you too will have to choose your path."

The events of the past few weeks had exhausted Annalynn. Unsure and floundering, her conscience burned. She questioned every decision, every move she had made. Second thoughts did not sit well with her, she always thought of herself as resolute, sure of her path. Introspection had always been her Achilles heel. A single tear dropped on the desktop. It's this place…it's evil. "What have I done?" Covering her face with her hands, Annalynn quietly sobbed. "And what have I become?"

On the other side of town, Branch felt Annalynn's anguish and dropped to his knees. "I believe in her," he pleaded, "…I believe in her."

Chapter Twenty-three
The Market

"Hey Alexine!" bellowed Zeke.

She looked down at him from the top of the steps as he murmured something into the cell phone held to his ear, then hung up. Flicking the phone back together, he stuffed it in a back pocket. The attractive girls surrounding Zeke soured Alexine's mood even further. The center of attention, the guy everyone wanted to talk to.

"Or, date is more like it," Alexine told herself, angrily. Good. She could be mad at Zeke next. Her anger had become another person; walking along side her, chiding her into action, poking and prodding in an attempt to incense her further. She didn't care, and allowed her anger to accompany her, embracing its company. Lumbering down the stairs, she purposefully avoided Zeke's gaze, choosing instead to throw the nastiest look she could muster at the girls surrounding the handsome boy. The comments which followed didn't surprise her. In fact, she quite enjoyed them.

"What the…?"

"What's her problem?"

"Who is *that?*"

Zeke ignored the angry outbursts. "I'll talk to you guys later, kay?" he said, running after Alexine.

"What's going on?" He panted to keep up with the frantic pace she set. "Where we going?"

Alexine stopped so abruptly that Zeke ended up half way down the hall before he realized he had left her behind. Laughing, he strolled back slowly, a bit self-conscious.

Alexine didn't find it funny, failed to return the gesture, and instead offered an irritated look she hoped would anger even a saint.

"Whoa girl!" Zeke breathed, putting his hands up in surrender. "Now, settle down. What on earth did *I* do?" Folding his arms, he shot her a challenging look, indicating she was not leaving without an explanation.

Trapped, she faked left, then lunged right trying to walk past the human wall standing impenetrable before her. He caught her by the arm and she stopped immediately.

"Let…go…of…me…" she said menacingly, heatedly snapping out each word.

Anger. Yes. Her invisible companion roared in appreciation, goading her gleefully.

She glanced from Zeke's face to her arm, held tightly by his large hand.

"Not…until…we…talk…" he replied, using the same slow tone, but replacing the anger with firmness. He eased his grip on her. They stood in the hallway, challenging each other. Finally Zeke broke the impasse. "I want to take you somewhere. Let's leave your stuff here though, we'll walk."

Alexine heard herself say, "I don't want to go anywhere with you," even though she did. And although she spoke these words of refusal, her tone over powered them. She desperately wanted to get out of this building, this horrible place.

She felt violated, afraid, trapped here. And she wanted Zeke to make things better.

He could sense that, knew it, and nodded in understanding, his expression softening.

The invisible person at Alexine's side sneered; he was loosing control of her. No.

Stowing her backpack in an empty room, the two left the building and walked to the street.

"Yea, he's got her." Devin spoke into his phone as he watched the pair leave from a second story window. "He knows what to do, take it easy," he said dismissively. "She'll be fine, you know women. They get all riled up once in awhile." The large man laughed condescendingly. "Hello? Hello?"

Punching the "end" button, he jammed the phone into his pocket and yelled, "women!" to the empty office. "Annalynn's never been able to take a joke."

Devin became thoughtful. Pulling his cell phone back out, he pressed the three button, speed dialing. "Front door," he said, speaking slowly. "Bar...Fangbang...shay-shay."

Devin descended the steps leading from the second to the first floor. Throwing the security personnel a disinterested glance, he pushed open the front doors. The driver was waiting.

Several blocks away, Alexine slowed her step and Zeke followed suit beside her, not speaking. She needed time to settle down and the long walk would allow her to blow off steam. Almost an hour later, the tension had eased and Zeke felt comfortable trying again.

"Now," he began quietly.

Alexine stopped. Staring straight ahead, her arms folded tightly across her chest, she burst into tears. Zeke moved toward her. Running his hands gently down her shoulders, he pulled her into his arms. "It's okay," he said soothingly, encircling her completely. "It's okay."

Sobbing silently, Alexine pushed her face into his chest. Had they only been here a few weeks? It felt like months. She couldn't take it. She wanted Zeke to worry for her, to take care of her. His powerful embrace was reassuring. She unfolded her arms and held him, her arms under his, her hands reaching around his back and grasping his shoulders. He was hard, and strong, could protect her. "I need to go home," she said defeatedly. "Home."

Zeke chuckled quietly. "Please," he pushed her back to look her full in the face. "You just got here."

Alexine managed a tired, apologetic look. "I'm sorry. I..."

He shook his head. "Don't. You're tired. I'm telling you, jet lag!"

They both laughed, Alexine, reluctantly.

Releasing her, Zeke shoved one hand into his pants pocket. "No, seriously though, it takes awhile to adjust."

She smiled half-heartedly, looking down at the ground as the things she had said to Annalynn came racing forward. She was mortified. How could she ever face her instructor again? She had been another person, had lost complete control.

"Come on," said Zeke, sensing she needed a diversion. "You've never even seen the market. How can you visit Shanghai and not hit the market?"

Zeke began walking backward tortuously, weaving back and forth, motioning for Alexine to follow, a devious look painted on his face. "Come on," he coaxed, wagging his eyebrows up and down. "You know you want to."

She laughed.

Huaihai street was crowded as they made their way east toward the river. As time passed, Alexine settled and began browsing through shops. She finally felt a bit more…free. "Luggage!" she squealed, spotting a storefront across the street. Zeke laughed when she looked at him longingly.

"Alright, alright," he relented, leading the way toward the baggage.

"I'm not much of a purse girl." Alexine fingered several small bags. "But I'll tell you what. I want luggage with wheels." She mimicked carrying a heavy suitcase, recalling the excursion through the airport.

"It's cheap here," offered Zeke, shrugging, "but plan on it falling apart within a year."

Alexine scowled, "really?"

Raising eyebrows, he looked at her knowingly. "Had a friend who bought one of those," he pointed to an over-sized gym bag with wheels, "and it actually broke after he pulled it a few blocks from the shop!"

Alexine shot him a scandalized look. Engrossed in their conversation, she did not notice the tiny Asian woman approaching from behind.

"You like?" The question caused Alexine to jump. "I give you good price!" she said in clipped English.

"Oh…" Instantly uncomfortable with the intrusion, Alexine stumbled, "um…I don't know." She pointed at suitcases near the front of the shop. "Maybe some luggage?"

When the small woman turned away to grab the closest piece of baggage, Alexine mouthed the words "help me" to Zeke. He offered nothing but a smirk in return.

"You could give me a hand here!" Alexine scolded several minutes later.

Zeke seemed unfazed by the pushy tactics of the shopkeeper. He just ignored her and strolled out the door. Alexine followed, bolting from the shop and the tiny woman followed them into the bustling crowd.

"Good price!" she called shrilly, grabbing for Alexine's arm.

Zeke reached behind and took hold of Alexine's hand. She clung to him, picturing the ludicrous scene in her mind. A comical tug-of-war between the tiny shopkeeper and the well-built young man, with Alexine stuck in the middle.

"Okay, seventy-five… good price… friend price!"

Alexine flushed a more brilliant red as Zeke pushed his way through the crowd in front of them. Eventually the woman gave up, returning to her store disappointed.

"I'm not looking at anything else!" She glanced behind quickly to make sure they had escaped.

"Yea, right!" Zeke tossed back over his shoulder. "You just have to learn how to do it," he insisted as Alexine shook her head. "You'll enjoy it soon enough. All girls do."

"Doubt it!"

"Uh-huh, told ya so," teased Zeke dryly fifteen minutes later as Alexine paused in front of a store filled with trinkets.

She threw a playful, nasty look in his direction. "Not going in," she countered, melodically. "Just looking." The shop owner spotted her and began making his way toward the front of the store.

"Better get going then." Zeke motioned in the direction of the Asian man moving toward them.

"Yikes!" She fell into step behind Zeke as they moved back into the flow of pedestrian traffic.

"Here it is." The pair slowed their step, approaching a large intersection. The corner of Huaihai and Xizang bustled with activity, but did not resemble a marketplace.

"The market?"

"No," laughed Zeke, "our next turn!"

Alexine let out a sigh.

"Oh, come on!" he said jokingly. "You needed a walk anyway...to cool down. You scared me this morning crazy girl!" Zeke winked at her and turned right onto Xizang as Alexine's face fell. She had behaved like a lunatic.

Several minutes later they passed a Burger King. "Food," said Alexine wistfully. "Normal food." Pulling out her cell-phone, she noted it was only 10:30am.

"Are you hungry?!" Zeke seemed incredulous.

Pausing, she took inventory of her body. It was odd but, ever since their arrival in China, Alexine never truly felt hungry. She simply knew she should eat by watching the time. "Nope. But... it's like... whenever I pass something having to do with food...that's familiar..."

Zeke laughed. "I remember. When I first got here I missed regular food so much. Pizza, hamburgers, salad."

"You got used to things in less than a month?" The academy training program lasted only 30 days. Although she hated to think of Zeke leaving, his time had to be drawing to a close.

"Yea...well...I adapt quickly," Zeke answered, then glanced around as if disconcerted by the discussion.

Alexine grew serious. "I don't want you to leave, but your training has to be ending soon."

Zeke began walking again. "We're not far from the market now," he said, obviously wishing to change the subject.

She felt sorry for him. He must be upset about leaving. It was apparent he loved the academy, and he also seemed to know everyone. He seemed to know everyone quite well.

"Hey, Zeke?"

"Yea?"

"How long *have* you been here?" She tried to appear as uninterested as possible, but really wanted to know how much more time they had together.

"Hasn't been too long, but seems like forever!" he answered, neatly skirting the question. "Hey, I'll tell you what," he again changed the subject abruptly. "I'll take you to a restaurant after we're done shopping. You'll love it."

"Kay." Something was wrong. He was hiding something. Why? Was he afraid she would be upset about loosing him?

When they crossed Xizang, Alexine stopped and looked around. What sat before her felt familiar. "Where are we?"

"Actually, we're close to your hotel." Zeke motioned further down the street.

"Yea," Alexine laughed. "For a minute, I thought I was going crazy."

The dumpling shop they had visited their first night in Shanghai. The clothing shops that sold items for 10 Yuan, or about 1 dollar. The shoe shop stuffed with brand name knock-offs. The tiny convenience store Alexine visited to purchase water bottles.

They walked past the hotel's courtyard, coming up on some more small stalls. Alexine had not ventured south of the hotel yet and was pleasantly surprised to see even more varied goods. A store dedicated to plants and flowers, varieties Alexine had never laid eyes on previously. A miniscule restaurant that sat, at most, fifteen patrons. Several people were gathered round a table slurping noodles, but they all appeared to be employees.

"Are those?...." Alexine trailed off, approaching an old man leaning back precariously in a rickety wooden chair. Thirty or more tiny plastic cubes sat next to him on a decrepit table. She leaned close in curiosity. "Crickets?"

Huge crickets, actually. The imprisoned bug's droning kept cadence over the constant murmur of the people milling around as the old man flashed a yellow smile displaying a mouth absent many teeth. Alexine smiled back warmly, feeling slightly guilty that her teeth were white, straight and still intact, the result of expensive orthodontic work. "Man. My brother would absolutely LOVE one of those."

"Unfortunately, you aren't supposed to take them home."

"I know, I know…but he would die." A loud clicking noise emanated from the cubes as the bugs attempted to jump in their fruitless bid for freedom. Alexine suddenly felt sorry for them. They did not understand what was happening. They only knew that they were trapped.

Moving down the street, she noticed that everyone was carefully stepping over any water they encountered on the sidewalk. "They don't step in the water?"

"Water?" Zeke said, teasingly. "You never know *what* it is. But it's probably not *just* water. That's the problem."

Although Alexine's mind screamed, "NASTY!" she contented herself with, "ohhhh." She stepped over a trickle of… something…originating from one of the shops. The liquid meandered around bumps in the concrete, finding the path of least resistance, until it spilled over the edge of the sidewalk and onto the road. "That's important to know," she stammered, not able to stop the sickening look which overtook her features as the two of them picked their way south.

A fancy bakery bloomed on the corner of the next side street. Alexine stopped to look through the large picture window at gorgeous, intricately decorated cakes. White cakes. All sizes, but all round. The same. No variations. No creativity.

Three women stood behind the counter dressed in neatly pressed, white knee-length dresses and matching caps. Absent their frilly aprons, they would resemble nurses. The shop was devoid of customers and seemed completely out of place in this neighborhood. White. Uniform. And sterile.

Alexine shook her head. This was Shanghai. Polar opposites existing side-by-side. The old, the decrepit, the people floundering in heart-wrenching poverty right next to the new, the shiny, the younger, upwardly-mobile, emerging generation, jabbering into cell phones. The antiseptically clean coexisting with the profoundly filthy. It was mind-boggling.

"Here it is." Zeke too had paused at the corner.

"The market?" Alexine playfully questioned again, pulling herself away from the shop window.

"No," Zeke played along. "Our *next* turn."

Alexine trudged behind him as he headed east. "Fang bang?" Alexine looked up at the street sign.

"No," Zeke seemed entertained by her accent. "Fahng Bahng."

She studied the sign more closely. It definitely said "Fangbang." Alexine attempted to pronounce the name with an Asian slant. "Fong bong?"

"Um...closer..." said Zeke dubiously, shaking his head as if relenting a point, "come on."

As they moved down the street Alexine immediately noted this was not an area typically traversed by tourists. Surrounded by Asian people, the two of them stood out like a sore thumb, yet no one paid much attention. Alexine was grateful for that.

Clothing lined the right side of the street. Laid out neatly on blankets, men's suit coats covered a half block of sidewalk. Women's dresses came next. Shoes. Coats. Handbags. Everywhere people were bartering; money and goods trading hands in rhythm. The street had a pulse of it's own, ebbing and flowing, the most basic form of capitalism imaginable. Alexine looked around. Now this was China. This was what she had come to experience. Relishing the commotion, she unconsciously slowed her step.

Noticing his charge lagging behind, Zeke followed suit.

Neither Zeke nor Alexine was aware of the large, dark man scrutinizing their progress from behind a window glazed with the filth of who-knew-how-many day's worth of accumulated pollution. Devin sipped his drink. Zeke had managed to calm the girl down, he was a capable soldier. The influence he exercised over certain people impressed Devin.

Devin himself had never mastered the art of deception, had never been smooth enough to win loyalties absent fear. Well, unless you counted Callan. Devin smiled as he thought of his littlest soldier. But she was a mere child, wrapped up in the excitement of harnessing her ability. Devin pondered his shortcomings as Annalynn's waspish words flung themselves at him. Her criticisms burned into his memory. People didn't like him, didn't trust him, saw right through his charade. Who cares! *He* was the master of the academy. *He* had garnered a portion of Nautas's trust and approval. *Him!*

As they crossed an intersection, Zeke and Alexine moved into a decidedly different area. Homes? Looking around, Alexine again became tense. In America, any place this run-down would be considered a slum. In addition, it would be very dangerous to stroll into such an area, yet Zeke seemed nonplused.

They passed more entrepreneurs set up on the side of the road, trinkets laid out on coverings spread over the walkway. Alexine wanted to stop, to look, to experience, but was afraid of being accosted again by a highly motivated seller. A picture of the luggage woman grasping her arm less than an hour ago returned. "I give you good price! Friend price!" She kept moving.

Attempting to be inconspicuous, Alexine glanced out of the corner of her eye to the left. A very old and thin, wrinkly man sat perched on the front stoop of a doorway. His bony knees jutted out abruptly in front of his emaciated body. Thin, tenuous arms stuck out of a dirty-white, sleeveless undershirt. The shirt flowed coarsely into crumpled, dark pants and his head, covered in sparse white hair, lay on his chest.

Slow and steady, his rhythmic breathing revealed he was sleeping. At the moment, oblivious to the dichotomy surrounding him. Unconsciousness his protection against the reality imposed upon him and his family. An impotent ancient guardian standing sentinel in front of a home with a blanket for a front door, and glass-less windows. Alexine shuttered. It was heart-breaking.

In the alley to their right, a young woman held a little boy by the arm as he toddled beside her. He was probably less than two years old, dressed in a grungy t-shirt, no pants, and simple black cloth shoes. The child peered up at his mother and Alexine felt as if she were somehow invading their privacy. But the woman looked non-chalantly over her shoulder at Alexine, then turned her attention back to the baby.

She had been told about the split pants babies wore in China. They were just what they sounded like; pants split at the middle allowing parents to prop the baby's legs apart so they could relieve themselves without making a mess or requiring diapers.

The tiny bare bottom clumping away from her indicated some people didn't even bother with them. Alexine found herself thinking that it was, actually, quite practical and definitely lead to less garbage. But water trickling across sidewalks sprang to mind, and she found herself reconsidering that opinion.

Winding their way through the hutong, the road became more and more narrow and took several hair pin curves morphing into more of a wide sidewalk, impossible for a car to fit through, she determined. As if to refute her last thought, she looked up to see a small automobile winding it's way through groups of people, furniture, and goods jammed against the buildings lining the street. Pushing themselves against a wall, she and Zeke stopped to allow the car passage. It came within inches of them and appeared to be precariously close to scraping an old brick building on the other side of the "road." Alexine flinched, expecting to hear a grinding screech as car scraped building. She was relieved when the automobile passed.

A dirt road lay to their left. It ended abruptly at a decrepit stone wall several hundred yards away; a partition protecting this microcosm of feudal China from the lull of unrestrained change and progress. Shanghai's skyline of soaring buildings towered just beyond the ancient barrier. It seemed odd that a dirt road wandered through the middle of a city inhabited by millions. Was this situation repeated anywhere else in the world?

De-feathered, un-cooked, headless and footless ducks dangled dead-weight from ropes thrown over support beams in the roof of the building on the corner. Alexine wondered how long they had been hanging there, and if the people who consumed them would become sick. How long could a duck hang without being refrigerated? Alexine wished she could find a nice, safe restaurant that offered Peking duck, she had wanted to taste it since first reading about it. Now, that would be an experience. Eating Peking duck where it originated; in China. They kept walking.

A small produce stand lay to their right. Two men; one older and one young bustled about inside arranging goods. Father and son?

A well dressed man ahead of them held a small dog in his arms. He moved toward them cooing at the animal, a small lap dog, who returned the affection by licking at his owner. Alexine suddenly realized something. This was the first pet she had seen in China.

A pristine high rise apartment building abruptly marked the end of the lolling hutong district. Towering dull-black iron fence posts sharply guarded the dwelling, screaming that this place was for a select few. The man with the dog walked through a gate in the forbidding fence.

"The elite?"

Raking his gaze up floor after floor of steel, concrete and glass, Zeke nodded slowly. Intently. He seemed irritated by the thing.

They stood on the curb of Ring road, the pair of them, waiting for the light to change. Alexine was glad to leave the older area. Although intriguing, it made her nervous. Several people stepped out, against the light, and dodged cars as they crossed four lanes of traffic.

The signal changed so she and Zeke walked into the busy intersection. Although the stop light gave them the right-of-way, they still had to work their way around several automobiles, and allowed a few bikes to claim ownership of the most direct path to their destination. A brightly colored arch marked the west entrance to the market.

"Is *THIS* the market?"

"Yes, Alexine, *THIS* is the market."

Here shops operated out of actual buildings. Small, short, compact, it seemed they squeezed as many areas as possible into the existing space. More trinkets, dishes, chop sticks, hats, clothing, silk robes and pajamas, jewelry, food stalls of every type, jade carvings, pearls. Alexine was under the impression that anything and everything could be purchased in this complex.

She stopped at a stall to her left. Huge bugs and other figures frozen in molten plastic shapes stood on a display case at the front of the shop, silent and still. Bees, small crabs, scorpions, beetles, creatures that Alexine had never before laid eyes on, having met their demise for the sole purpose of becoming paperweights.

To her right, across the street, a silk shop caught her eye. Brilliantly colored kimonos and other articles beckoned her.

"I don't know where to start!"

"Don't worry, we'll come back again."

The pair wound their way east, penetrating even further into the market complex. Ahead, Alexine noticed a middle-aged man hocking whole coconuts from a wooden trolley. Driving a knife into the soft spot in the husk, then twisting to create a hole, the man inserted a straw and handed over the drinks to customers.

She stopped to watch the transactions. Five Yuan, that was what people were paying, about sixty cents. During the few weeks she had been here, Alexine noticed that often times, foreigners were charged much more than Asians for goods and services. She typically didn't mind paying a bit more, assuming she was helping the economy with her donation. But today she felt like standing up for herself, like refusing to be taken advantage of anymore.

Approaching the man, she held out a 5 Yuan bill, and gave him a take-it-or-leave-it look. He appraised her, sighed, and the exchange was made. Slurping on the refreshing coconut milk, Alexine smiled. It was delicious.

Turning north, she gasped. People thronged the shops lining both sides of the street. It was even more crowded here.

"So many people!"

"Actually, it's not that bad today. It's slow."

Alexine frowned dubiously.

"Yep," he asserted, in response to her doubt. "I'm serious."

Still holding the coconut, Alexine looked around for a garbage can. She noticed several other people with coconuts simply discard theirs on the ground. Where had she read that China was really pushing to train their citizens to keep things clean? In one of the many books poured over prior to traveling, she was sure. Wanting to be a good example, and unable to just toss garbage on the ground, she held onto the heavy object. Fortunately she spotted a large, plastic wheel-barrow type receptacle on the side of the road several minutes later. She relinquished the coconut, grateful to be rid of her burden.

A half an hour later, Alexine and Zeke turned right into a narrow alley. A young girl selling neckties operated a booth on the left. There were hundreds in every hue and design.

"Okay, I've got to stop for this!" Alexine imagined her father beaming at the ties she gave him upon her return. He loved ties, especially unique ones.

"Umm…how much?" asked Alexine, approaching the shopkeeper. She couldn't have been more than fifteen years old. Alexine noted vendors all seemed to know what "how much" meant, probably in several languages.

The girl produced a calculator and plunked out several numbers; the preferred method for bartering in China. She turned the contraption toward her potential customer, eyeing Alexine inquisitively.

"Ten?" Alexine peered at the figure displayed on the gadget.

The girl nodded, pointing at the amount.

"Ten?" She turned to Zeke. "Is that right? Ten Yuan?"

"Yea."

"That's cheap," whispered Alexine.

"It's okay," he whispered back playfully out of the corner of his mouth. "You can speak normally. I don't think she understands English."

Alexine shot him an impatient look for making fun of her. "I want to get twenty."

His eyes flew open in disbelief. "Twenty? For who?"

"Everybody! Are you kidding me? That's like…a dollar a piece!"

Zeke shook his head in exasperation as Alexine began selecting ties. The young shop keeper, keen on the sale, helped her leaf through the bundles of silk. Moving to the right, she noticed there were more around the corner. Smaller ties for children.

"Geoff!" she thought excitedly. "They would be perfect! Wouldn't it be great if…" Alexine froze.

A man sat on the steps in the doorframe of the adjacent building. He was not shabbily dressed, as Alexine would have expected of a cadger. There was something different about him. Something…

Several Asian people walked by. He watched them intently, almost longingly, then lowered his head as they passed, their animated conversation filling the narrow alleyway. The man glanced toward her, then again diverted his face, readjusting his position. There was nowhere to hide.

Half the man's face was red. Violently red. What could have caused such an injury? Alexine was racked with pity as the realization dawned on her; part of his face was burnt away. The man's right eye rotated around in the socket, mimicking the movements of his left eye, but Alexine was sure that he could not see out of it. Both the upper and lower lids were absent, leaving his eyeball protruding awkwardly from his skull. Uncovered, dry and streaked with angry red veins, the eyeball rolled toward her again. Again the man turned away. She wanted to cry. She wanted to run up and hug him, tell him he was her brother and she accepted him no matter what, tell him to stop looking away.

"Find anything good?" asked Zeke, rounding the display. His joviality seemed irreverent. Disrespectful.

"Um…yea!" Alexine blurted, attempting to recover. Not wanting Zeke to see her upset, she began sorting through ties, blinking back her welling tears.

"How about this one?" Zeke held up a little silk dragon tie.

Glancing sideways only slightly, and trying to sound grateful, she said, "perfect." The lump in her throat ached, screamed at her to cry and get it over with. Instead she swallowed hard.

"I'm ready." Laying the ties in front of the shopkeeper, Alexine counted out 200 Yuan quickly. The woman accepted the payment, folded the lengths of silk gently and placed them in a plastic shopping bag, then handed them over with a smile.

Two-hundred Yuan, for gifts. Two-hundred Yuan for unnecessary items. How much would that money mean to some of the poor people she had encountered? To the toothless cricket seller? To the old man sleeping on the porch? To the man sitting yards away from her in black despondency? This place; it made her feel guilty almost all of the time. Her fight with Callan, the abuse she had heaped on Annalynn, these people who were consigned to live in pain and poverty, no way out, they each paraded before her. Guilt, guilt, guilt.

Folding a ten Yuan bill up into a small rectangle, she turned from the stall as she and Zeke began moving through the alley.

The injured man raised his head slightly to take them in as they passed. His ritual, repeated day after endless day; watching the whole people pass him, not disfigured, not burnt, not held prisoner by experiences that would not fade and a body that could not heal. Their conversations and laugher haunted him, mocked him.

One more step. One more step. Zeke moved past the man, completely ignoring him. Alexine walked on Zeke's left, sandwiched between Zeke and the man now eyeing them sadly. One more step, and she would be past him. She bent in his direction. They were face to face and he stared into her eyes. Pressing the ten Yuan bill into his hand, all she could see was that face. That tormented, red, burnt, ashamed face, as their surroundings began spinning wildly around them. What was happening?

Chapter Twenty-four
Evil Revealed

The Asian man walked toward the front entryway.

"Wait!" A beautiful little girl raced up behind him, grasping him around the legs. "Papa!" she cried frantically. He patted her backside twice, smiling sadly.

The child's mother, his wife, approached them rapidly and grabbed the young girl snatching her up. "Learn something while you're there!" Her words were spit, sharp and judgmental.

How had this happened? All he could do was nod, regretfully. Not sure what was worse, the contempt in his wife's eyes or his baby girl's whimpers, he turned quickly and left them there.

Once in the street, he looked back toward the house. Burning it into his mind, he wanted to remember the place his life had truly began. Would he ever see it again? Would he ever see them again? His mind turned to their child; innocent, few cares. If he failed to return, what would the future hold for her? If these accusations were not cleared, she too would be doomed.

The man mopped his head with the back of his sleeve as he walked, it was going to be another sweltering day. He would rather run one hundred miles in the burning heat than report to the cadres. No choice. There were very few choices he made on his own anymore. It was the way things were, the way they had to be. It was for the good of the country. As the man left his home, Alexine was drawn along with him, as if tethered by an invisible, binding cord.

Push. Crawl. Push. Crawl. Push. Crawl. Pitch black, two miles down into the belly of the mine. Chipping at the coal, the fuel that ran the country; his work, penance for incorrect thought. What was wrong and what was right? Pull. Slide. Pull. Slide. Breaking into glorious sun only to dump the basket of black rocks onto a slowly growing pile on the surface, and then blackness again. Push. Crawl. Push. Crawl. Chipping. Loading. Pull. Slide. Pull. Slide. Blinding light. Dump. Hour after hour. Day after day. His appearance betrayed his young thirty-one years; he was an old man.

Enduring the humiliating "struggle meetings." Brutal sessions designed to reform his way of thinking. Self criticisms so immense and detailed, he was unsure of reality. Had he truly done all the things to which he admitted? Everyone interrogating him seemed so sure of his culpability, they had to be right, didn't they?

The endless written dissertations of guilt which seemed to become more horrific and incriminating each time he put pen to paper. He had not truly done these things, had he? Yet they were never good enough for his captors, never acceptable, never enough.

Bound and gagged, deprived of food, shelter, sleep. Was he improving? What horrid crimes had he perpetrated? Having an opinion? Thinking? No! This was incorrect thought! That was why he was here. He was guilty. Guilty.

Push. Crawl. Push. Crawl. Chip. There was a flash of light and pain, excruciating pain. Hands instinctively flying to his face, he tried to scream as heat seared his lungs, but no sound escaped. His ears filled with the pounding explosion as he was engulfed in flame and flying debris. Clambering backward away from the devastation, he scrambled toward the surface. He had to get out, had to locate the opening, had to claw and fight and do whatever was necessary to find freedom. His little girl's face flashed through his mind. Get to the surface, you must live! Rocks cut deep gouges into his knees, hands and arms in the frenzied search for escape, then all was benevolently dark.

Months of healing, his existence now just day after painful day. Longing for the times he walked to work. Wanting to wipe the sweat from his brow. Aching to recall a life free of agony. No escape from the anguish, his constant, unrelenting companion. The entity that never left him and prodded him into becoming someone else. Impatient. Brooding. Self-focused. Angry.

Slowly becoming accustom to the torment, only to realize that physical pain was not the end. Robbing him of himself, of his personality, of who he wanted to be, was not enough either. No.

The expressions on stranger's faces. The horror in children's eyes when he passed. The wife that could not cope with his uselessness. The little girl screaming as she was torn from him *again*.

"Papa!"

Pain. He wanted to die. Gone. Everything was gone. His body, his wife, his daughter, himself. Gone.

Days flowed into each other. Living on the change people tossed at him, too disgusted to approach. Accepting the coins, their offerings, defeated. They threw the money in his direction, grateful for their own fortune. Grateful they were not consigned to sit on this stoop broken and disfigured. Grateful they were not him. He wasn't sure why he was still alive, he could end it anytime he chose, but something told him to live. Live.

Alexine fell backwards as they separated. Her head still spinning, the man slowly came into focus. He was frightened and had that surprised look of…disquiet. As if he weren't sure what had just happened, but knew it was something strange. Something that violated him in some way.

"I'm sorry!" she whispered, clumsily getting to her feet. "I'm so sorry!"

"What happened?" barked Zeke angrily, spinning back toward them and shooting an accusing look in the beggar's direction.

"No!" Alexine burst into tears rounding on Zeke. "He didn't do anything!"

Zeke didn't look convinced. Wheeling around, Alexine met the man's gaze and her heart sank. He turned from side to side, like a cornered animal searching for escape. He wanted to disappear, to melt into the building, but there was nowhere to go. No reprieve.

"I'm sorry!" she heard herself say again, through tears. "I'm sorry!"

Zeke grabbed her arm, dragging her down the alley to the street ahead. Alexine threw one last desperate look behind them, wanting to ensure the man was alright. She watched as he rose, unsteadily, to his feet and tottered off hastily in the opposite direction.

Once around the corner, the powerful young man turned and pulled Alexine close. "What happened?" he demanded, his voice menacing through clenched teeth as he shook her by the arms. No longer welcoming and full of comfort, Zeke's embrace was now forced and harsh.

Alexine didn't like his tone, and her biceps ached where he gripped them. Instantly corralling her emotions, she pushed pity and guilt down into the deep recesses of her mind. She had a situation to deal with… now.

"I…" Alexine stammered. Why did she suddenly feel trapped? Why did she suddenly feel like not telling Zeke anything? "I fell over." It was a lame excuse, and she knew it the second it escaped her lips.

Zeke squinted at her, unconvinced. "Fell over?" he repeated, eyeing her dubiously.

"Yea." Alexine pulled herself back a bit, retreating in both anger and fear. She wanted to get some space between she and Zeke. "He didn't do anything, I just fell."

"And you were saying, 'I'm sorry,' because…" Easing his grip, Zeke slid his hands down her arms and grasped her wrists, waiting for her to finish the sentence. Alexine felt like a prisoner, being held by living hand-cuffs no key could open.

"I…uh…startled him…I think." Yes, that sounded good: she startled him.

"Yea." Disgusted and doubtful, Zeke glared at Alexine accusingly.

"Maybe we should just head back?" Looking down at the strong hands wrapped around her wrists, she no longer wanted to be alone with Zeke. Suddenly she didn't trust him. She was walking around, alone, with a stranger, half a world away from everything familiar. Did anyone even know where they were? They needed to get back.

Zeke loosened his grip on her and nodded tetchily. "Let's get a taxi."

He was so angry. Why? "Okay." Alexine fell contritely into step behind the young man.

Zeke did not look back to ensure she was following. In another situation, she would have left him, simply walked away, perhaps given him a lengthy piece of her mind to boot. How dare he take that tone with her! How dare he put his hands on her! But right now she needed him. Stupid. That is what she was: stupid. *She* had put herself in this situation; this very vulnerable, dangerous situation.

Several taxis passed before one stopped. Leaning into the window, Zeke handed the driver a business card and he looked it over then nodded, agreeing to take the fare. The driver returned the small piece of paper to Zeke as Alexine climbed in the back seat. Zeke took the front and the car raced west toward the academy. Alexine had never been so thankful for a fast driver. Get back to the academy. Get the backpack. Find Callan. Go back to the hotel. Then what? Run? Escape? Would they let them go?

An overpowering sense of guilt filled the panicky girl as they pulled into the parking lot. So worried about what her next step should be, so taken aback by what happened in the alley, so tired of the emotional roller-coaster she had been on all day long, she had forgotten the angry fit she subjected Annalynn to earlier that day.

The car was still rolling to a stop when she opened her door and exited, leaving Zeke to pay for the taxi. She took the front steps two at a time, pausing outside the door at the security checkpoint. Would they admit her? Would they know she had caused quite a ruckus earlier? Conformity seemed to be the order of the day here at the academy, she was sure a rebel would not be welcome.

One of the guards had seen her approaching and dialed Annalynn. He nodded and hung up the phone. "Let her in," he told another man standing at the doorway. Following this instruction, the front guard beckoned her inside.

She thanked them, hurrying past. Finding the room where her backpack lay abandoned, she retrieved it quickly. Next step, get Callan; shifter training in the auditorium. Her mind raced. Get out of this building, get out of this place. Turning the corner upstairs, she stopped dead. Annalynn stood just outside the door to the auditorium, arms folded resolutely across her chest.

"Welcome back," she said evenly, cocking her head to the side.

Caught off guard, Alexine searched for a reply. "Thank you." It sounded hollow and insincere and Alexine sighed loudly. "Listen, I'm sorry for earlier. There was no excuse for it, I just let my frustration get the better of me." She couldn't afford to make Annalynn angry, couldn't afford to fail in her plans to leave this place. She needed to make peace with her teacher, find Callan, and run.

Alexine paused, hoping the older woman would fill the silence, but those hopes were in vain. Annalynn stared at Alexine as if weighing her words, contemplating her next move. Fumbling, Alexine stammered, "it's just like…this place. It makes me feel…" She stopped, dropping her gaze to the floor. She wished she could climb into a hole and hide. How could she explain how she felt here? Wrong? Angry? Afraid? And why was she confiding any of this to Annalynn? One of the people responsible for this place? She was supposed to be trying to fool Annalynn, to pacify her, to remove her from the equation so she could plunge to the next step: find Callan.

The reader shifted her weight slightly then walked toward Alexine. Bracing herself, the young girl wondered what was coming. Leaning close, Annalynn whispered one word.

"Evil."

Alexine's head jerked up. "Excuse me?" She did not understand.

Giving her a knowing, intense look, the woman leaned in again and repeated the word, adding a hushed explanation.

"Evil. This place…it's evil."

Chapter Twenty-five
Confessions & Confusions

Annalynn pursed her lips emitting a quiet shushing noise. Turning her head slightly, she glanced at a security camera mounted to the wall, close to the ceiling. Alexine took note of the move and understood; they were being watched.

"You should be sorry!" said Annalynn sharply. "Come!"

Alexine played along, dropping her head then following the instructor dejectedly down the hallway.

Safe in the privacy of her office, Annalynn relaxed. "No cameras in here." She stopped and appeared to be concentrating for a moment. "No one listening either."

"What's going on?" asked Alexine, momentarily forgetting her previous outburst and the attendant guilt. "What do you mean… evil?"

Annalynn sighed heavily. "It's actually a very long story that began years ago." She wore a look of concern, but finished abruptly, "I can't tell you anything else."

"Why?" Alexine resented this feeling of confusion, of being excluded. There seemed to be very few answers and a mountain of questions sitting in her path, resolute and insurmountable. Residual anger from this morning's argument with Callan and the ensuing altercation with Annalynn lingered. The frustration she felt over her experience with Zeke, her guilt regarding the injured man, it all suddenly boiled over and exploded. She was finished with the secrecy, the lies. "What's happening?!" she shouted, impassioned. "Tell me!"

The older woman hesitated, held momentarily by her pupil's ferocity. This passion would serve the girl well once she was presented with the decision; once this talented child understood everything and choose good over evil. She stared at Alexine, making quick decisions and sizing up the situation.

"You can be read easily, Alexine." Annalynn's retort was measured, tentative, and thoughtful. She was unsure if even this piece of information should be divulged. "It would be dangerous for you to know too much. Dangerous for you," she paused to emphasize the point, "and dangerous for me. Can you accept that?"

Alexine had not considered the possibility of information placing her in jeopardy. "I guess so," she answered through narrowed eyes. "But who would read me? And if they did, why would I, or you, be in danger?"

Annalynn looked sadly at the young lady standing in front of her. "I can't tell you that." She had revealed enough. "But I can do something. Sit down."

Disappointed, but walking obediently to her chair, Alexine took a seat. Annalynn pulled her own chair up to face the younger woman and grasped her pupil's hands, as she had done many times before. "Today you learn how to stop someone from reading you."

"You can stop someone?!" Alexine was shocked. It had never occurred to her that she could protect herself from intrusion. "Really?" Light seemed to fill the room, sweeping away a portion of the fear Alexine felt. She could stop it from happening! *She* could be in control!

"Yes," the older woman replied seriously, "most of the time." She took Alexine's hands in hers.

"Most of the time? Why not all of the time?" The younger girl dropped Annalynn's hands and shot her a questioning glower. "And why didn't you teach me this before?"

Annalynn sighed, contemplating her student. "Some people, who are very talented, very powerful, can *force* their way in, so…no…not all of the time. And in order to repel a reader, you must be equally powerful, have equal ability."

Alexine could not place Annalynn's expression. Anger? Resentment?

"As to why I didn't teach you this previously; before you can hope to prevent a read, you must understand reading yourself. This is what we have been working up to. You must also be fixed in your determination to stop someone," she lingered, then smiled wryly. "You may not have your mind completely wrapped around reading yet, but after witnessing first hand your emotional range today, I believe passion may push you through. I think you can do this."

Alexine blushed, but nodded thoughtfully, considering these pieces of information.

"So, are you ready to get started?"

Slumped in her chair ten minutes later, Alexine pushed cool finger tips into warm eye sockets, as if she could somehow force the pounding in her head to relent and abandon its attempt to cause a horrid headache. "This is tiring!" she complained, exhausted. It had been a long, draining day, she had not eaten lunch, and this "repelling" business was hard work. She understood why they had waited so long to attempt it. It felt impossible.

"You're actually catching on quite quickly." Annalynn hoped her encouragement would stave off the defeat evident in her student's expression. "I can feel you pushing back, trying to deny me access."

"Really?" asked Alexine hopefully, grabbing for the life line of words, under the impression she was dreadful at keeping people out of her mind. "I've always been bad at keeping secrets," she admitted quietly. "I thought this might be the same type of thing."

"Actually…no. It has more to do with will power, sense of self, confidence." She looked admirably at her young charge. "And despite your age, you possess an abundance of all those attributes." Annalynn smiled and nodded slowly. "I'm impressed." Alexine's weary grin warmed her heart. This was the girl she enjoyed. "And I need to thank you," she noted somberly. "Earlier today…"

Alexine cut over her. "I'm really sorry about earlier today," she bit her lip. "It was a weird morning. I met that hippy-girl, Callan was horrible, and this place…" She stopped, looking around. "This place makes me crazy," she whispered, as if the walls could take note of her perfidy.

"No. I needed to hear what you had to say. You were right about everything." Alexine shook her head, but Annalynn continued. "I shouldn't read people without asking first, it's their right to refuse."

The older woman seemed to be focusing on something just above her head, but when Alexine turned to see what that something was, she noted nothing out of the ordinary.

"A person's freedom is more important than anything."

Several moments passed and Alexine felt she should remain quiet; as if talking would somehow intrude on Annalynn's thoughts. The silence was not uncomfortable. Somehow, it was filled with meaning. The older woman finally met

Alexine's gaze.

"Alright, now let me give you some ideas about how to keep someone from…."

"A person's freedom," Alexine repeated deep in thought. "Annalynn!?" she rushed, the events of the market coming to mind. "Zeke took me to the market today. We saw a man there." Alexine's mind momentarily flashed back to the man's mangled face. He was trapped by his outward appearance, held prisoner by the hand life had dealt him. She closed her eyes to picture him more clearly, part of her never wanting to see him again, but another part needing to memorize every line, every shape. She knew, somehow, that calling him back from the past would imprint him indelibly in her memory. And that he needed to be there, in her mind. He was now a part of who she was. "His eyes…" her stomach twisted with pity. "He was injured."

Annalynn's own eyes narrowed inquisitively.

"I…" Alexine stammered, "I…think I read him."

Annalynn's expression changed immediately. Tipping her head back, and furrowing her brow, she cocked her head to the side and sized Alexine up for a moment. "You're sure?" The question came out as a whisper.

How could Alexine not be sure? She nodded somberly. "Everything started spinning," the words escaped slowly, as if feeling their way forward to best describe what had occurred. "At first I thought I was going to be sick, and then we stopped." Stomach aching and head beating more furiously, she groped to describe the scene.

"It was…it was…him and I…the market had disappeared." Alexine's eyes darted back and forth, working to remember exactly what had occurred. "It was like we were tied together; I had to follow. In a way, it seemed like I understood what he felt and was aware of his thoughts. Horrible things were happening to him. I wanted to help, wanted to stop it." She shook her head, confusion growing more and more prominent on her face. "Does this make any sense?"

When Alexine again caught sight of Annalynn, the older woman was smiling. Warm and secure, it was the type of smile her mother wore a lot while observing her children; that proud, gentle, knowing smile. Alexine jerked back, blinking tears. "What?"

"You felt compassion for this man," Annalynn stated simply. "What is the first step to take when you wish to read someone." It wasn't a question, she knew Alexine had the answer, and so continued. "Did you touch him?"

The girl nodded slowly, forcing her mind to rift through every reading lesson they had undertaken. Compassion. Physical contact. Alexine slumped in her chair. "It upset him," she said morosely. "I felt horrible."

Concern crept into Annalynn's features.

"And then Zeke thought the guy had done something to me." Alexine found her instructor midway through the sentence. At the mention of Zeke's name, Annalynn's expression hardened. "I fell over and when we came out of it, I was sprawled on the sidewalk." She shrugged. "I guess Zeke thought he had tried to hurt me or something."

The pained expression on the injured man's face returned to the front of Alexine's mind. She cringed as the overwhelming sympathy she had felt, when Zeke turned on the man, again reared its head. The urge to cover him, to protect him from Zeke's fury surged inside her once again. "It was so sad," she said close to tears. "The man didn't know what had happened, and when Zeke got mad, he wanted to hide, but there was nowhere to go. Trapped. Oh Anna," Alexine sobbed, unable to control her emotions.

Unlike earlier in the day when Alexine had used just part of this woman's name out of disrespect, this time she called upon it as a result of the affection she felt. This time she used it because she realized she loved this woman, and, as of a few moments ago, trusted her. The other words Alexine longed to speak, the apologies which needed to be voiced were held prisoner as her throat involuntary closed and tears streamed down her face.

Annalynn leaned forward and hugged her. "It's alright," the older woman crooned soothingly. "It's alright...shhhh." They rocked sideways in rhythmic motion, reminding Alexine of home.

Alexine smiled, remembering the time she and her mother ran to the supermarket late one evening. Her mother began rocking while standing in line at the checkout. She looked ridiculous; swaying in the aisle, back and forth, back and forth.

"It's a habit!" Mom had given her a playful swat. "Wait until you have kids!"

Alexine sighed. She missed her family, missed everything familiar. Relishing the feeling that someone else was in charge, someone else was taking care of things, even if it was just for a moment, she pressed into the reader; her only available support.

They separated just enough to allow the instructor a view of her student. She raised her eyebrows in question. "Okay, then?"

Alexine nodded, sniffling. When Annalynn flashed her a knowing grin, the younger girl squinted, wondering what the her instructor was hinting at. "What?" she posed suspiciously.

"You're a reader," Annalynn stated as if saying "I-told-you-so."

"I guess." She had suspected it for awhile, but the fact was now undeniable. Looking sheepishly at the floor, she was still not sure if this was a good thing, or a bad thing.

Suddenly all business, Annalynn grasped her student's hands. "We need to get busy. Keeping someone from entering your mind is an important ability for everyone to work on, but it is *especially* important for all readers to master."

Alexine nodded knowingly, although she could not come up with a reason why readers would need to protect their memories more than anyone else.

"Unfortunately several people are aware of your ability." Thoughtful and guilt ridden, she filled in, "no one knows the extent of your power though." She had merely told Devin, in her fit of pride, the girl was a reader, but had kept him completely in the dark regarding Alexine's progress. "But," she said, a bit annoyed, "they'll figure it out soon enough."

Who were "they?" Alexine wondered. The people behind the security cameras? Devin and Zeke?

"The first step is realizing someone is approaching," Annalynn began. "Do you know what that feels like?"

Alexine concentrated. They had worked on repelling for almost a quarter hour, and yet she had not paid attention to feeling Annalynn's approach, having focused so intently on clearing her mind or diverting her attention. "I just know that all of a sudden I feel kind of sick and then I feel disturbed afterward." Alexine dropped her head to the side and stared up at the ceiling, thinking. "Do you know that feeling when you're going to the bathroom and someone just walks in?"

Annalynn snickered.

"What?" Alexine asked, slightly hurt.

The older woman nodded knowingly. "Yes! Yes! That is exactly how you feel when someone reads you!" She straightened and took a deep breath. "I've never thought about it in those terms before though," she laughed. "But before you're read, you can actually feel someone coming. Let me show you…okay?"

The women held hands as instructor approached student. Just prior to entering her mind, Annalynn stopped.

"There. Did you feel that?"

Alexine's eyes widened in surprise. "You were coming!"

"How did it feel?"

"It felt like…" Searching for words to describe what had just occurred was difficult. "You know someone is staring at you, you can just tell, and you start to become self-conscious." She thought hard. "Like…why are they looking at me?"

Annalynn nodded her head. "Cement that image in your mind, that is your warning image."

"My warning image?"

"Every reader has a different warning image, something unique to you. Something that tells you when another reader is approaching."

"Everyone's warning image is different?" Alexine said the words "warning image" as if trying them on for size; slowly, not sure she was using the term correctly.

"Yes. Because being approached feels different to each person. It's a unique experience." Annalynn slid back in her chair. "Let's try it again. When you feel me approach, just think about how it feels, where you are, what is happening, and keep that image in your mind." Annalynn looked at Alexine intently. "Ready?"

"Wait. So all readers have a warning image?"

"Yes."

"What about normal people?"

Annalynn's eyebrows traveled up her forehead as the word "normal" was mentioned. "Normal people?"

Alexine realized how insulting her phrase sounded even as she spoke it and smiled apologetically.

"So, we're not normal now?" The older woman smiled, waiting for a response.

"I didn't mean…well of course we're…"

Annalynn shook her head, waving any thoughts of an apology away. "Normal people don't have a warning image," she stated matter-of-factly, emphasizing "normal people" as if quite entertained by the newly coined term for non-readers. "They will simply experience the feelings associated with being read. Now, let's get started."

Alexine felt her coming. She was sitting in class at school and someone was looking at her. Where were they? Self-conscious and embarrassed, she wanted to smooth her hair, wipe at her nose, cover up a blemish, anything to clear away whatever it was which caused this person to focus on her. Annalynn pulled back.

"Do you have it?"

"Yes. I think so."

"Okay, now, let's try it again." Annalynn paused to gather her thoughts. "This time, when you feel me coming, you need to do something that makes you feel safe in regard to your warning image."

Alexine frowned. "You lost me after 'this time,'" she said, trying to decipher what she viewed as a convoluted set of instructions.

"Alright." The instructor took a deep breath. "Describe your warning image to me. We'll figure it out together."

Alexine blushed. "It is…" she was hesitant to finish her thought.

Ticking off a list etched into memory, Annalynn completed her pupil's truncated explanation, "embarrassing, makes you feel self-conscious, like someone is intruding, a bit frightening. I know Alexine. The feelings are the same for everyone, the image is just different."

The older girl nodded, "ohhh," relieved in a way she was feeling the right emotions, pleased she was getting it. This was more difficult than anything she had ever attempted, and if this warming image was different for everyone, it had to be nearly impossible to teach.

"Alright. Now tell me about where you are, what you see."

Alexine closed her eyes. "I'm at school, in a class, and someone is outside the room, standing at the door. They are looking at me." Now that she was cognizant of her warning image, the feeling when Annalynn approached was easy to recall, to describe. Strong and upsetting, she hated to even talk about it.

"There's something wrong. My hair is sticking up…or I have a zit…or…" she paused, not wanting to continue, "there's a booger on my face," she whispered horrified. Alexine's eyes flew open when her teacher giggled. She glared at Annalynn, angry and hurt.

"I'm sorry!" The reading instructor was trying desperately to control herself.

Alexine forced an annoyed look.

"It's just that…" Annalynn began snickering. "I can picture that, and I feel so bad for you!" She covered her face with her hands, as if this would somehow protect her student from further embarrassment, yet she continued to laugh.

Although Alexine tried to maintain it, the hurt slowly melted away. The mirth filling the room was contagious.

Taking a breath, the older woman looked at the younger, momentarily plastering a serious look on her face. "I'm sorry…" Annalynn began, stifling a giggle. "It's just that…" she couldn't help it, and began laughing again, promptly pulling a deep breath in a bid for self-control. "It's just that…" again she was unable to continue. Leaning forward she hugged Alexine, giddy. "I'm sorry," she kept repeating. "Oh Alexine, I'm so sorry!"

Alexine threw arms around her instructor and broke down herself. Laughing had never felt so good.

"Boogers!" Annalynn wailed, tears falling down her face, shoulders shaking involuntarily. "Boogers!"

Several minutes later, the older woman grasped Alexine's hands once again. "Okay, seriously now," she tried to force her expression to match her words. "Let's work on this."

Bouts of raucous laughter had given birth to an elevated level of relaxation. Annalynn had no idea why boogers had been so funny but was grateful they were now able to start again, refreshed and ready. She sensed this was the perfect time to teach Alexine how to protect herself.

"This time," she began, withdrawing her hand momentarily to wipe away the remnants of a happy tear stubbornly clinging to life, "when you feel me approach, you need to act."

When Alexine scowled, Annalynn tried to elaborate. "You need to do something, anything, that allows *you* to take control of your feelings in that classroom. Does that make sense?"

The young lady sitting across from her searched for understanding, but slowly shook her head "no."

"Let me explain my warning image. Perhaps that will help."

Alexine nodded her head in relief.

"I'm in my home and there is a knock at the door."

Alexine shut her eyes to concentrate and felt her instructor involuntarily shutter. Surprised, she opened them to find the older woman had also closed *her* eyes and was deep in thought.

"I'm very afraid," Annalynn continued, knitting her eyebrows together and shaking her head. "But I know that someone is coming in. I have a choice," she said firmly, abruptly changing her tone. "It's up to me to deny them entrance." Annalynn was impassioned, defiant. "All I have to do is prop my foot against the door. YOU… CAN'T…COME…IN!"

It was a command, and Alexine jumped at the ferocity of her words. The instructor opened her eyes slowly, and Alexine was caught off guard by the intensity of her teacher's visage. It conveyed a commitment the young girl had not witnessed on too many occasions. Alexine refused to divert her eyes, wanting to experience as much of this power as possible. The feeling was incredible.

"You *have* to believe in yourself," said Annalynn. "When you do, there will be very little denied you. You will be able to do amazing things." Annalynn's voice trailed off. "Do you understand now? Did that help?"

Alexine nodded her head deliberately, still fixed on her instructor. Yes. She needed to be resolute, confident, impassioned.

"Let's try again."

Annalynn approached the younger woman. Opening the door, she strode across the classroom. The reader was shocked she had gained entrance so easily. A few minutes previous, Alexine did not even know what a warning image was, and she had done a better job repelling then!

She spotted her pupil sitting near the front of the room and wondered if the girl typically sat in a seat nearest the teacher. The agitation Alexine felt was apparent; her hands fluttered from her hair, to her face, to her nose. She straightened her shirt, glancing down at her chest. When their eyes met, Annalynn shook her head quickly, shooting Alexine an annoyed look. *"No,"* the instructor thought fiercely. *"There is nothing wrong with you. Stop me!"* Annalynn approached the younger woman slowly. Why wasn't she reacting?

Frozen, unsure what to do, much less how to do it, Alexine ran through her lists. Clear my mind? Distract myself? This experience was so different than what they had practiced just a short time ago. This was real. This was physical. This was a place…not just feelings and thoughts.

The young girl stood to face Annalynn, but her instructor kept coming, kept walking toward her, not breaking stride. Another step, another step, the two were now mere feet from each other. What should she do?

Alexine abruptly flashed back to that feeling which filled the room when

Annalynn explained her warning image. Passion. Defiance. Ferocity. Annalynn had protected herself by bracing her foot against the door. The reader was already in the room, she had already gained entrance, and she looked angry about it. Disappointed that Alexine was standing there, inept and undecided.

"Do something now!" Annalynn thought.

Stronger than any words that had ever been spoken to her, the command pierced Alexine, reverberating through her mind like an angry wave through undisturbed waters. In desperation, she drew back her arms.

What was wrong? Why was Alexine allowing her to approach? How had she gained entrance into the classroom so easily? Why was she just standing there!?

Annalynn hurtled backward. "Anna!" the younger woman yelled as her instructor was catapulted out of her chair. It happened in slow motion, as if Alexine could catch her, stop it somehow, if she only moved quickly enough. Flailing, the girl grabbed only air. What had just happened?

WACK! Smacking her head on the office floor, Annalynn screamed in surprise and pain, then rolled onto her side cradling her head in her hands.

One moment they were in the classroom, the next they had returned to the office. "Anna!" Alexine screamed again, bolting from her chair and shoving Annalynn's seat out of the way to reach her. Kneeling next to her teacher, unsure what to do, where to touch, she cried, "I'm sorry! I'm sorry!"

Annalynn curled into a ball still holding her head in her hands, and began shaking slightly. Petrified the older woman was seriously injured, Alexine rolled her over cautiously to get a better view. Perhaps she should run and get help. What was the number for 9-1-1 in China? The instructor looked up at Alexine, she was laughing but her face was still a mask of pain.

"Holy crap Alexine," she blustered. "What was that?!"

The young lady shook her head, tears springing to her eyes. "I don't know...I'm so sorry Anna! I'm so sorry!" she sobbed. "Please...let me..." She grasped Annalynn's arm as the woman attempted to stand.

Pulling herself together, Annalynn stumbled to her feet, gingerly rubbing the angry knot rapidly enlarging on the back of her skull. "Uhhh," she sighed, feeling the injury swell under her fingers. "Ice pack," she sputtered, dazed. "I need an ice pack."

Alexine burst back into the room several minutes later carrying a plastic bag full of ice. It had taken what seemed a lifetime to convey the request to a confused kitchen staff. Finally, in exasperation, she had flung open the freezer and began pointing.

The older woman was sitting in her chair, head resting on her desk top. She was still exploring the injury carefully with her fingers but looked up as Alexine entered.

"Are you alright?" Alexine handed over the ice packed baggie.

"Yes. I'm fine." She softly laid the cool compress on the back of her head. "What happened?"

Alexine's mind whizzed back to the classroom; Annalynn approaching, unsure of what to do. Annalynn was disappointed, angry that she just stood there. The first thing that came to mind.

"I pushed you," she answered quietly, an imploring, apologetic look crossing her face. "I'm sorry. I didn't know what to do! I didn't think it would..."

"Pushed me?" Annalynn repeated, surprised. She raised her head from the desk and sized up Alexine. "What do you mean... pushed me?" Her eyes narrowed.

"Well," Alexine winced. "I just..." the girl made a motion of drawing back her arms, and then shoving an imaginary object. Looking back at her instructor, she explained, "a lot of times, in soccer, when the bigger guys are coming at me, and I know we're going to collide, I just...." again, she repeated the motion of pushing something which did not truly exist. "It's the best way to avoid getting bull-dozed by an opponent."

"Impossible," Annalynn whispered to herself. She had never witnessed a complete amateur physically affect another person during a read. Never seen anyone so young, trying to repel someone else, harm them in reality.

Of course, there were always the feelings involved, and one could argue that those feelings generated certain physiological changes; rapid heart beat, elevated blood pressure, sweating, neurological alterations. She had seen individuals being read fall over, simply because it was a bewildering experience. But a child, who had not even mastered reading yet, possessing the ability to slam her backward during a repel?

She shook her head, as if to answer her own unspoken question. It took years and years, patience, dedication, work. Searching her memory banks she opened up old lessons, conversations, even theories. Nothing bounded forward to cast light on the convoluted questions now descending on the pair of women.

"Impossible," she whispered again under her breath then glancing at Alexine. All color had drained from the girl's worried face, so Annalynn smiled at her reassuringly. "I'm alright. I just don't..." Alexine looked petrified, so she stopped. The girl was already upset, perhaps it was better for her not to realize what had just occurred. "You know what?" Annalynn said, trying to infuse the situation with normalcy.

Alexine threw her a fearful look.

"I'm starving, are you?"

The young reader nodded her head and sniffed. She didn't want to repel anymore. She didn't even want to be in this room anymore. She was horrified.

"There is a great little restaurant not too far from here. Let's go out to eat."

Again, Alexine nodded, reaching for the tissue box on the desk.

Annalynn need to talk to someone about what had just occurred. She needed answers, answers that only one person could provide. But she couldn't imagine him ever forgiving her.

Chapter Twenty-six
The Interrogation

"What did I tell you?" Annalynn asked as the waiter set large salads in front of both women.

The instant they entered the restaurant, Alexine experienced palpable relief. It was a normal restaurant; well, normal for Alexine. There were no reptiles in aquariums, destine to be chopped up and served on a platter. There were no pungent smells emanating from the kitchen. And as they walked to their table, she, Alexine, was not the center of attention as often was the case when the confines of the academy were left behind. Offering salads, sandwiches, soups and malts, <u>Fresh</u> was...familiar. It was just what she needed.

Somewhere in her brain the warning regarding not eating any fresh vegetables or fruit replayed. When she learned the Chinese sometimes used human waste as fertilizer, Alexine had decided to play it safe.

Of course, she had no idea that several weeks of eating doughy dumplings, oddly preserved eggs, canned meats, bread, and overly cooked vegetables would eventually wear down even the most determined person. She whimpered each time they passed a fruit stand and looked in longing at the people daring enough to consume the beautiful varieties of produce China offered.

Alexine didn't want this salad...she *needed* it. Diving into the greens with gusto, the first fresh food she had eaten in what seemed like ages was wonderful. She couldn't do anything but chew and smile as Annalynn smirked at her.

"Thank you," Alexine murmured through bits of romaine lettuce, tomatoes, cheese and cucumber. She reddened, immediately thinking of Callan and how piggish her little sister had appeared when she talked while eating.

Focusing on the large, white, concave plate loaded with vegetables, she quickly devoured them, only to regret not enjoying it more when the waiter whisked what was left of the entree away several minutes later. She sighed, pushing back into the bench seat and peering to her left out of the large window which spanned the wall from top to bottom. Breathing deeply, gratitude for things she typically took for granted filled her; lettuce, cucumbers, salad dressing, simple things.

With dinner finished, she took time to scrutinize her surroundings. The restaurant was decorated tastefully, with gleaming tables and crisply dressed waiters. It seemed quite a number of foreigners frequented the eatery. A dark haired woman on a cell phone clogged past their table, trailing bits of conversation as she passed. "Yes...make sure they have everything delivered to my office..." Alexine relished hearing her own language and basked in the moment. It seemed an odd thing to enjoy so deeply and find so reassuring; words, simple phrases.

Wondering if the lavatories were up-to-standard, she excused herself to use the bathroom. Although set up in a very different manner, the bathroom was quite nice. Walking down a hallway and turning to her left, she entered a door-less room with two long, deep sinks mounted on the opposite wall. An Asian man washed his hands in one of the basins as she glanced around and pushed through a door to her left. It wore the outline of a woman wearing a dress.

Several minutes later, she walked back through the bathroom door and re-entered the communal room with sinks. Scrubbing her hands, Alexine glanced into the mirror. She shook her hair back to reveal her bluish bruises, but furrowed her brow instead, then ran a wet hand over her forehead; no pain, no wincing. Gone? Running her hand over her head again, she frowned. They *were* gone.

Upon returning to the table, she continued covering her newly developed list of gratitude: real toilets, not the Turkish-style which were so prevalent in her present surroundings. An exciting novelty upon arrival, Alexine had affectionately dubbed them "squatties," but the holes in the ground had grown tiresome quickly. Clean bathrooms were definitely on her list; ones without waste spilling out of them which forced occupants to hold their breath as long as humanly possible to avoid inhaling rancid air. Sinks had to be included also; they were often conspicuously missing from public restrooms. Soap. Milk shakes. People who knew the area and could cart you around the city. She looked fondly over at Annalynn. The positive thinking helped, she felt better than she had all day. Enjoying the time away from the academy, away from Zeke, Devin, and for the moment, even Callan, she drew in a calming breath. Callan.

* * *

Hours later, in their room, the little girl was still harping on her older sister.

"What happened today?"

Apparently Alexine's tirade in Annalynn's office, her storming out of the building with Zeke, and returning in a huff was breaking news at the academy. Why couldn't she have been more discrete about the entire ordeal?

"What happened?" This time, it sounded like more of a demand than a question.

"I told you…it was nothing!"

"Well, Devin heard you screaming at Annalynn. And several girls saw you storm into the street with Zeke."

Alexine cringed as her sister painted a vivid picture of today's events. She had hoped they would remain private.

"By the way, I don't think you made any friends there." The little red-head shot Alexine a condescending look. "I personally saw you barge back into the academy, followed closely by Zeke who, by the way, looked mad as a hornet!"

The older girl rolled resentful eyes at the mention of Zeke's name.

Pausing, Callan glared at her sister suspiciously, then continued, pulling together pieces of the scenario which played out earlier that day. "Then Zeke rushed to Devin's office…" Callan left the sentence open ended, knowing she had unearthed a bit of information which warranted exploration. "Alexine, what did you do to make Zeke mad? I thought you liked him?"

Alexine stood, tired of being interrogated by this little nit. "Listen Callan," she began angrily, the emotions born earlier that day creeping into the present. "I don't like Zeke, and it would be good if you stayed away from him."

Callan fell back as if taking a blow, then flashed an incredulous look.

"And," continued Alexine, surging to prevent questions, "Devin's not on the up-and-up either…I don't think."

It was Callan's turn to stand. "So, what you're basically saying," began the little girl nastily, "is that I can hang out with that hippy-freak," she held up her index finger.

"Her name is…"

The sentence was sliced off by the little red-head who decided it was her turn to dominate the conversation. "You." Callan added her middle finger. "And your precious Annalynn." She extended her ring finger. "Who, by the way, is as much a part of the academy as Devin or Zeke!" Callan could not believe her sister could be so myopic! What right did she have to dictate whom Callan could befriend? "Three people." She wagged her fingers in Alexine's face. "That's what you're saying, right?" The little girl crossed her arms angrily. "Out of all the people at the academy, you've cleared *three!?*" The words were fired from deep within Callan, born of resentment and anger.

"Yea!" Alexine shouted, unsure how to respond. Put that way, it did sound rather foolish, but she knew she was right. She knew they needed to be careful. It wasn't just her being paranoid, Bethia agreed. Annalynn admitted to it!

"No," answered Callan, suddenly calm. "It's time you learned that even *you* can be wrong." She grabbed tennis shoes and began pulling them on. "It's time you learned that you shouldn't judge people you don't even know." She picked up her jacket. "It's time you learned that you can't make decisions for everyone else."

The words cut into Alexine. They were her own worst fears, the criticisms she often hurled at herself, searching her soul for proof of their existence. Although probably guilty of all those things, she was right this time. And it was so important Callan took her seriously. How could she convince the little girl standing, stony faced, in front of her of that fact? Something told her to stick to her guns, but calm down.

"Listen Cal," she said softly, using her little sister's nickname. "I'm worried." Working to keep her voice even, pushing down how passionately she felt, Alexine continued. "The academy...something's just not right there. I'm afraid...for you...for me...for everyone."

Callan listened intently while she spoke, mulling over words. After a long stretch of silence, the little shifter replied quietly, almost whispering, "you said you trusted me."

Their eyes met. The words seared Alexine more than any others Callan had voiced tonight. She *had* said she trusted the little girl. But did she truly? Did she *now*?

Callan turned away, afraid her older sister would see too much. She had to protect Alexine. "Please..." She wanted to tell her more, but knew doing so would be imprudent. "Please remember. You trust me." Without looking back, Callan walked to the door. It closed quietly behind the little shifter as she left the room.

Across town Annalynn was undergoing a similar interrogation. After Zeke reported how poorly things had gone with Alexine, Devin burst into Annalynn's office, demanding to know what had happened.

"Listen Lynn," he said ominously. "You and I both know how important those two are to Nautas." The large man pulled an annoyed face. "I personally have no idea why the older one matters," he said throwing his hands in the air. "Callan *is* young, and she's pretty good," he searched for an explanation as to why Callan was of such import, but came up with nothing solid. Perhaps it was because of her age. Perhaps she could be better trained since she was beginning so early. Whatever the reason, Devin knew Alexine and Callan were not to leave. That had been made abundantly clear. "You know as well as I," he began, a fleck of fear in his voice, "the consequences for disappointing him."

Annalynn dropped her head back, eyes fixed on the ceiling. Several of Devin's words leaked through to her. "Callan...you know...consequences..." She was relieved to be alone in her thoughts, relieved Devin couldn't intrude on her feelings, couldn't enter her mind. Ever since being thrown out of her chair this afternoon, Annalynn had been racking her brain. If she had not experienced it herself, she would have been dubious.

How had Alexine accomplished it? And with no training! The only person with whom she could explore possibilities was unavailable. She didn't dare contact Branch now. Devin was suspicious, she could feel it. She wasn't even sure Branch would speak with her. She didn't deserve his attention, much less his trust, or his acceptance. Alexine was, at least for now, a puzzle. Could the young lady defend herself if the situation warranted? Should she try to get Alexine and Callan out *now*? Would the younger sister agree to leave? Too many questions, too many unknowns. Devin was still rambling when she tuned back in. She snorted; this man pacing before her was completely obtuse.

"I really don't see what's so funny!" he boomed, slamming his hand on her desk. The photos residing there jumped, clattering as they toppled over.

Annalynn didn't flinch, didn't move, but slowly lowered her gaze, like a wildcat defending its territory. Her eyes met his. "It's under control," came her cutting retort. "And if you insist on behaving like a child," she hissed, "you can leave."

Her reprimand took him aback. "He'll return soon," Devin said evenly, in a bid to justify his behavior. "He'll want to hear about our progress." The panic in his voice was obvious and he resented it. It made him sound weak. He waited for Annalynn to share something, anything about her pet project; Alexine. Appearing uninformed when Nautas had questions was more than unadvisable, it could be deadly. The older sister was bound to come up during the next meeting. There was something going on. Annalynn was concealing something. What was it?

It seemed silly to play these games, silly to pretend she cared. The reader didn't anticipate *being* at the next board meeting, didn't anticipate seeing Nautas again, at least, not as a follower. And if they did meet…well…she did not anticipate surviving. It was a brutal thought, but she wanted to be honest with herself, claim responsibility for her initial decision, and accept the consequences of her subsequent reversal. That was that. Annalynn had a new focus: getting out as many people as possible. Doing it quickly. Doing it soon.

"*You* had better not disappoint him then," Annalynn said, forcing a small smile.

Devin's mind moved back to the last board meeting, recalling Nautas's displeasure over a simple misunderstanding. What would failure on his or Annalynn's part invoke? He didn't want to find out. Anger burned in his gut, his chest, then worked its way up and exploded. "I don't plan on it!" he yelled. "Callan's progressing quickly, she's amazing!"

She watched the large man grope for control, knowing it would, as typical, be elusive. A part of her pitied him. If someone couldn't master themselves, how could they ever hope to progress? She involuntarily shook her head.

"What?" he spat.

"You want to know about Alexine," she said simply. "Can't you just ask?"

Devin frowned at her, not wanting to admit she was correct. "Well?" he blurted, working hard to keep both his irritation and interest concealed.

"I…don't…know," Annalynn replied slowly, as if deep in thought. She needed to diminish Devin's interest in the young lady; he was a weak link and could make things difficult. Hoping to satisfy his curiosity, and divert his attention, she continued. "It feels like she's a reader, but no matter how hard we work…" Annalynn left this thought dangling, hoping Devin would grab the bait and run. She paused, but didn't have to wait long.

"Ha!" Devin sputtered. "I knew it!" A smile split the shifter's face as forced barks of nervous laughter filled the office. "Worthless. I knew it when I met her…she's completely worthless." The man wheeled in front of Annalynn's desk, suddenly energized.

Feigning offense, Annalynn scowled at Devin. "I didn't say that!" she shot back, raising her voice slightly for effect. "It might just take a little more…"

Devin cut over her. "Face it Annalynn," he grinned, basking in the thought that perhaps next time Annalynn would be in Nautas's cross hairs, and he would be commended for his outstanding work with Callan. "You were wrong." He turned, flung open the door and walked out before she could retaliate.

Hopefully this would buy her some time.

Chapter Twenty-seven
Haggard Comrades

Alexine was up half the night waiting for Callan to return. Where on earth could she be? As much as the thought grated her, she hoped the little girl was at the academy. It was better than imagining her baby sister wandering the streets of Shanghai. She pretended to be asleep two hours later when the key-card slid into the reader, the door handle clicked, and Callan entered the room. Things were calm and they needed to stay that way for awhile. No more arguing.

Alexine hugged the little girl the next day when they separated for classes. Stiff as a board at first, Callan wrapped her arms around her older sister after a few moments, then squeezed hard. Pushing her little sister back, both girls laughed.

"Hey!" Alexine yelled as Callan began walking away.

"Yeah?"

"I love ya sis." It was a bit embarrassing, sharing her feelings in the middle of a hallway, but it was important.

Callan's paused, her eyebrows knit together in surprise, then she smiled. "Love ya too, girl." She turned away thoughtfully and disappeared around the corner.

Alexine groaned as she walked into Annalynn's office. The instructor was pulling on what appeared to be a bright red motorcycle helmet. Already donning several bulky winter coats, she resembled a deranged Eskimo.

"I said I was sorry." Alexine covered her eyes with her left hand and shook her head. Thinking this must be a joke, she laughed. "A helmet Annalynn? A helmet?"

The older woman looking at her didn't crack a smile. Surely this must be a joke.

"Are you sure?" Alexine whined as the two women sat face to face, their chairs pulled close to each other. "I don't think we should do it again. It was awful."

"I'm sure. You must learn to control this, so let's get started."

Annalynn knew giving Alexine more information placed the girl in a greater degree of danger, so she formulated training designed for three purposes. First, to clandestinely uncover just what this little reader was capable of. Second, to work on honing those skills in the event using them became necessary. Third, encouraging Alexine to focus so completely on the second task that questions regarding the academy were chivied out of the way.

"Okay, Alexine, tell me what happens again."

Alexine sighed and spoke in bored monotone. "I'm in the classroom, you walk in, you get angry, I panic, I push you." She had gone over it a million times in her head since yesterday. Classroom. Intruder. Panic. Push.

"Okayyy." There was more, something of which the younger girl was not cognizant. Could she tell Alexine? Or, was it something her student needed to figure out on her own? "Let's go then."

"Whap!" The sound reverberated through the room. Pulling herself up from the floor, Annalynn swayed slightly returning to her seat. Again and again, Annalynn was flung around the room. "I should have put a mattress down," she thought, ruefully.

Alexine had stopped getting up to check on her instructor forty five minutes previous; she was exhausted. Slumping in her chair, the younger girl allowed her head to drop forward.

"What do you feel?" The same question posed each time the exercise was completed.

"Like something is wrong with me…I'm vulnerable…no one is there to protect me…and I need to defend myself." The same answer repeated each time the question was posed.

Annalynn nodded her head, encouraging the young lady to explore the feelings fresh in her mind for what seemed like the hundredth time.

"You're angry and disappointed I'm not doing anything," she sighed quietly, fumbling to re-word what had been said over and over again during this session. "I'm upset you're there, judging me. You're intruding…I didn't let you in."

"Yes, yes," prompted the instructor softly as the young girl, out of sheer exhaustion, sliced open her inner-most feelings, laying out extremely personal thoughts, fears and inadequacies.

Locking eyes with the older woman, Alexine was suddenly animated and intense, her exhaustion dissipating. "No," she said slowly…thinking. "No." Adrenaline pulsed through her veins as the realization formed in her conscious. Something had changed. She thought for a moment, allowing the epiphany to develop. Somehow, over the course of the last two hours, anger had disappeared, and it had taken frustration with it. "I'm not mad anymore." Alexine started, surprised by another thought, "and neither are you."

Annalynn nodded slowly, smiling. Finally, they had arrived at the next fork in the road, ready to move to a more advanced level. Annalynn had been analyzing and re-analyzing everything which occurred yesterday. Hatred and impatience; they were both negative emotions she recognized while formulating her plan the evening prior. She had brought them into Alexine's classroom, introduced them as if they were old, haggard comrades.

"The anger, although it focused your energy and allowed you to throw me around originally, was holding you back. It's a negative emotion Alexine." The older woman shook her head in regret. How had she been so foolish to make anger a part of the equation? "You would do well to not indulge it…*ever*. Anger will *always* lead you down paths you do not wish to tread…*always*."

The disquieting feeling that Annalynn was feeding her morsels of something truly important, vitally important, lingered on the edge of Alexine's attention span. Anger, hatred, impatience; they are bad. Something Annalynn herself had learned through painful experience. But Alexine was too tired to think anymore, too tired to connect thoughts, too tired to even move.

"Please," she whimpered, "can we be done?"

"Yes," replied the only person whom Alexine felt she could count on, confide in, trust.

The reading instructor wore the disappointed look of someone trying desperately to convey an idea of utmost importance to another person who just wasn't capable of internalizing the information. Her shoulders sagged. So much more to teach. So much more to learn. Would they be able to do it before… No sense in worrying about that now. It was time to call it a day.

"Tomorrow we will continue to develop your sense of control."

It was ironic, really. How many times had others tried to teach her? How many times did those lessons fall on deaf ears? It was the crowning irony of growing older. Learning to deal with the next generation, recalling that you were once in their position.

Annalynn winced as she ruefully flipped through the memories of her own training. Always thinking she knew it all. Actually believing there was precious little wisdom anyone older could pass on. Where had those feelings of invincibility gone? Why was it that, as time ticked by, she became more and more aware of her fallibility? Alexine's voice pulled her back to the present.

"Kay," was all the younger girl could manage to say. She pushed off the chair slowly, dragging her feet all the way to the couch. Groping for her backpack, then finally grasping the shoulder strap, she swung it over her back, glancing at Annalynn. "Eight o'clock then?"

"Eight o'clock. Sleep well."

Annalynn had just finished putting her protective gear away when there was a knock at the door.

"Come in," she called suspiciously.

The door swung open and Devin stopped in the entrance, his bulky frame filling the rectangular space. Annalynn sighed. She didn't feel like dealing with Devin. Tired and sore, she was looking forward to a long, hot shower and sleep, lots of it.

"Quite a racket today," Devin said, eyebrows raised. Annalynn detected the question even before he spoke. He was fishing for information. Disappointed their last conversation had failed to curb his appetite for any tid-bit he could use against her, Annalynn's mind whirred, racing to find an explanation for the noise.

"Thought we would concentrate on self-defense," she said, musing that it was the truth. "Since we aren't getting anywhere with reading, I thought we could kill some time with a good work out."

A slight crease appeared on Devin's brow. Did he believe her?

"Mmm," he grunted, nodding. "Workout."

He was not falling for it. Feeling she needed to take control of the situation, Annalynn cocked her head to the side. "Is there something I can help you with?" she asked curtly, folding her arms. When he failed to answer, she said, "Devin?"

"Nope," he replied, turning, then walked out of the room, closing the door softly behind him.

Annalynn dropped her gaze, tension creeping back into her thoughts. So many dangers, so many problems.

Chapter Twenty-eight
Worthless

"Yes sir, I'll see you then."

Devin pushed the end button on his phone. Something was going on, Annalynn was not being up front with him. She spent every waking moment with Alexine. And that din today in her office? A work out? The woman had to believe he was a moron. Devin bristled at the thought. She had always believed he was beneath her, had always treated him like an ignorant buffoon.

"Well, I'm smart enough to pick up on the fact that you're up to something." Full of animosity and resentment, he hurled the statement at his bare office wall, as if the reader were present to take the abuse.

The large man leaned back in his chair and clunked his feet up on the desk. Smiling wickedly he recounted his conversation with Nautas. Their leader had seemed too interested in his observations. If Anna had been working on something for Nautas, Devin doubted the phone call between he and the dark man would have lasted almost twenty minutes. If Nautas truly trusted Annalynn, there would have been fewer questions.

Devin indulged himself in a self-congratulatory nod. He had never spoken with Nautas for so long. As far as Devin knew, few people had. Nautas tended to operate alone, leading his followers with little input from outside sources. A strong leader. A leader who needed no one else on which to lean.

Enjoying the feeling of being useful, Devin inhaled deeply. Yes, Nautas was pleased with him, and it felt good for a change. He only had a little time to gather more information, to prove his case. It was Devin who should be in charge at the academy. Splitting that position between two people was a bad idea, he had known it from the beginning. Especially two people as different as he and Anna.

Yes…Anna. Perhaps *she* would enjoy a taste of the dark man's disappointment. Perhaps that would smack down her ego a bit. Devin humored himself for several minutes, running through scenarios in his mind. Each of them included an angry Nautas, a guilty Annalynn, and a triumphant Devin. The *only* one in charge of the day-to-day operation of the academy.

Down the hall, Annalynn fidgeted in her office. So much to do and so little time in which to accomplish what seemed to be insurmountable tasks. Priority number one, though, had just become throwing Devin off the trail. Why did the insufferable man choose now to figure things out?

Annalynn was waiting at her office door when Alexine reported for class the following morning. "We need to diminish Devin's interest in you, and we need to catch him before he leaves."

Alexine flashed her instructor a questioning look.

"Just follow my lead," Annalynn whispered as she stepped past Alexine, being careful to turn her face away from the security camera as she spoke. The two women set off toward Devin's office, Annalynn blazing a trail down the hallway.

Mulling over the plan in her mind she tread toward the man who, she imagined, was sitting in his comfortable chair completely unaware of what was steaming toward him. Annalynn realized popping Devin's turgid ego had inadvertently become a likely possibility, if all came off without a hitch. A tinge of guilty pleasure floated in front of her for a moment, but she dismissed it. This was not personal. This was necessary.

She had hoped to have at least a few minutes with the girl; time to explain, to offer suggestions. But Devin's meeting this morning had been moved up. If they didn't catch him early, they would miss him completely. "Perhaps," she thought, "it's for the best." Alexine would be more convincing if she were truly perplexed. She would catch on, play along, Annalynn was sure of it. The girl was sharp.

Devin scrutinized the exchange between Annalynn and her student. When it became evident they were heading in his direction, he slowly closed the drawer which housed his security monitor and set his briefcase back on the desk. The meeting would have to wait. Puzzled, he boomed, "enter!" at the rap on his door.

Annalynn walked briskly into the room, followed closely by a recalcitrant and confused Alexine who drug behind the older woman like an obedient pup. Devin followed the pair as they entered but remained seated.

"To what do I owe this pleasure?" he drawled in a lazy, bored tone, folding his arms across his chest and leaning back in his chair.

Annalynn flashed him an innocent look, then stated matter-of-factly, "she's yours for the day." With that said, the older woman turned on her heel and strode quickly out of the office leaving Alexine glancing around nervously and Devin fumbling for a retort.

"Hold on a second!" he yelled down the hall, belting after Annalynn like a little boy attempting to catch up with an older sister. How did she always manage to turn the situation around? How did she continually swipe control from his grasp? His large hand closed like a vise around her arm as he spun her around roughly. When Devin realized Alexine was hot on his heels, he loosened his grasp slightly.

Annalynn gave him a serene, questioning look. "Yes?" she said cordially. He was squeezing her arm so tightly there was no doubt in her mind it would leave behind a bruise, evidence of Devin's impatience and frustration. But she ignored his grip, determined not to voice her discomfort and give him the satisfaction.

"Wha.." he stuttered, searching for words. "What's…going on?" he finally finished, anger and confusion hampering his ability to speak. Devin's breath came in gasps, partly a result of his dead run down the hallway, and partly a result of his indignation.

Annalynn entered Devin's mind forcefully. Thrown back several steps in surprise, he dragged her along. The pair teetered on the edge of falling over each other, narrowly avoiding plowing down Alexine in the process.

"You remember what Nautas said!" The volume and intensity of Annalynn's accusation surprised Devin as much as how violently she had entered him. *"I've been trying to convince her to stay!"* The large man's head pounded in unison with the reader's recounting. *"We're supposed to keep them both here! You want them both? Fine!"* She pulled back, leaving him alone to his thoughts, confident her point had not only reached it's mark, but left an impression which would not fade for some time.

Devin made a concerted effort to steady himself. He wore that look now so familiar to Alexine. The disquieted look of someone who had just been involuntarily read.

"You want more information about Alexine?" Annalynn began coolly. "Doubted my explanation regarding her lack of abilities?" she leaned in and whispered so the younger girl would not hear. The reading instructor pulled back, raising her eyebrows and lowering her head, she gazed up at Devin like a school teacher scolding a student. "You don't believe we were working on self defense yesterday?" She shook her head as she spoke, mimicking Devin's doubt regarding Alexine's training. The older woman looked purposefully at Alexine for a moment, then returned her attention to Devin. "Well…" she said with finality, shrugging her shoulders, "your turn." She pulled a quick grin, reminding Alexine irresistibly of the Cheshire cat, reclaimed her arm slowly removing it from his grip, and strode away.

No longer a being of flesh and blood, Devin stood anchored to his spot, as if chiseled out of concrete. Alexine watched as the wheels in his head creaked to life; first digesting what had just happened, and second, trying desperately to come up with a game plan.

"So," he began, smiling awkwardly at the young lady standing next to him. As quickly as the grin appeared, it abandoned its owner, leaving him looking uncomfortable and impotent. He had hoped that, miraculously, an idea would spring to life if he spoke. Nothing. He drew a complete blank.

From the moment they entered Devin's office, Alexine had a vague idea of her roll in this charade. Judging from Annalynn's comments, Alexine deduced Devin had been asking questions about her training. It was a stroke of genius actually; throwing the situation in his face, thereby robbing Devin of the control for which he so desperately yearned. "If nothing else," Alexine thought bemused, "Devin has to admire her moxy."

One look at the man standing next to her told Alexine otherwise. Devin's expression changed from foolishness, to anger, to contemplation, to curiosity. But no admiration, not even for a micro-second. The large shifter eyed Alexine unabashed, as if she were a strange toy which held secrets he needed to explore. No, needed to expose. She felt uncomfortably like a bug under a microscope.

"It's apparent she's uneasy," thought Devin, "and unsure how to react to being unceremoniously dumped on another instructor. So, what are they hiding?" He still could not believe Annalynn would do this. What was she up to? He considered the possibilities for a moment. Perhaps he could turn the tables on Annalynn, perhaps this was a stroke of luck which could be used in his favor. He now had an entire morning to gather information, an entire morning to collect shreds of evidence to aid in his bid for control of the academy.

Alexine cleared her mind and quickly replayed the events of the past several minutes, she didn't have long to make decisions. Throughout the tirade with Devin, Annalynn had been giving her clues regarding how she was supposed to behave, directions concerning what Annalynn wanted Devin to believe after he spent the day with Alexine. What had she said?

Something about Devin wanting to know more about Alexine. No problem, she could give him oodles of information, loads of unimportant facts. Something about lack of abilities. Again, she had this covered. Although Alexine now realized she was truly a reader, faking normalcy would be a piece of cake. Working out yesterday. Her mind flashed back to the Tao Kwon Do class she and Callan took years ago. "Okay," she steeled herself, "I can do this."

Fishing for ideas regarding how to procure the evidence he so desperately desired, and not knowing where to begin, Devin asked, rather officially, "so, where did you two leave off yesterday?"

Alexine was reminded of a substitute teacher whom had once taken over her math class. The woman had few ideas regarding how to handle the group of kids, much less what to teach. She relaxed a bit; this was familiar territory. "Actually," she thought brightly, "this little game may be fun." "How about reading?" Alexine replied, a little too innocently she thought. Darn it! Devin didn't seem to notice. It was the word *reading* that caught his attention.

"You're...a...reader?"

"Well," she took a deep breath, and her words tumbled out. "Annalynn really thought that I felt like a reader, you know, not really felt, I mean, she didn't feel me or anything, but more like, sensed it, you know, anyway, so we worked on me reading for hours and hours, you know, at first she tried to explain it to me, you know, how to go into someone's mind." While speaking these last few words, Alexine closed her eyes serenely, placed her pointer fingers on her temples and sat in silence for several moments.

Glancing up at Devin, it was all Alexine could do to control herself. The mixture of incredulity and disappointment, combined with his dumbfounded expression was hilarious. Alexine knew she was on the right track. She racked her brain trying to duplicate the mannerisms of several ditsy girls from school. The "you know" was one of their pet segues. It drove Alexine mad.

Dropping her arms to her side and allowing them to hang lazily, she took another deep breath and started in again, speaking quickly. "But she actually wouldn't give me any more time, you know, so, maybe we could try the reader thing again? I really think that if I had some more time, you know, I could really get it because I think, you know, that I've always had kind of a knack for that sort of stuff, you know, people watching, and figuring out what people think, and stuff like that, you know." She made a concerted effort to take very few breaths, having learned that the amount of rambling a teenage girl was capable of producing exactly equaled the annoyance level of any adult male within ear-shot. She loved using this tactic on her father.

Devin wasn't quite sure how to respond. The girl had said so many words, yet conveyed very little information. He was still trying to process when Alexine started up again.

"Have you ever just sat somewhere, where there were like, a million people, and just watched them? Wondered what they were thinking? I've always loved doing that, so I guess I've been trying to read people for a long time, yea, I think the reader thing would be a really great place to start, you know, because Annalynn did think I had potential in that area, you know, I don't know, it just seems like a..."

Holding his hands up in surrender, Devin shook them in an attempt to quiet the incessant prattle. "Okay, okay," he kept saying softly, hoping she would be silent. Alexine bull-dozed over him, pretending she didn't hear.

"...good place to start today, start fresh, you know, with someone new, and I have actually been thinking of some ways we could..."

Still shaking his hands, Devin repeated her name in a quest for control. "Alexine? Alexine?"

"...try to prove or disprove my abilities as a reader, you know, because I was thinking that it would be really awesome to be a reader, although those changers sound good too. I was thinking how, if I were a changer, I could like, totally change things into cream puffs which are my absolute favorite..."

Devin was beside himself. A part of Alexine felt guilty. Even at her young age, she realized that men had difficulty understanding, dealing with, even tolerating the awkward stages in which every young girl eventually found herself entrenched. And the incessant talking, Alexine thought ruefully, that drove most of them to the brink of insanity. As if, somehow, the organized, compartmentalized minds of most men experienced overload when exposed to the wandering, meandering, disorganized, often completely irrelevant thought processes of young ladies. Unable to make sense of it all, their brains shut down in a last ditch effort at self-preservation. She decided to cut Devin a break. "Oh," she paused, as if suddenly realizing there was someone else in the room. "Yes?"

"Alright," he said quickly, trying desperately not to allow too much time to pass before speaking again. Somehow knowing that, if he left any quiet time floating around, Alexine would claim it and run. "Let's try your ideas."

Alexine shrugged and smiled, looking happily around the room. Spying two chairs in front of Devin's desk, she turned them to face each other, trying to read Devin's expression the entire time. Was he nervous? Excited? A bit lost? She decided it was probably a combination of them all. "Okay," she instructed, "so you sit here." She patted one of the chairs. "And I'll sit here." Alexine plopped down in the opposite seat.

Devin approached cautiously, lowering himself slowly into the chair Alexine had indicated was his. Although less than a foot from each other, Devin tried, in vain, to maintain as much space as possible between he and the young girl. She grabbed his hands and closed her eyes.

Devin had rarely experienced such discomfort. Having listened to the young girl twitter for the last few minutes, his suspicions regarding her had softened. His first inclination, that this girl was nothing, had suddenly become a possibility once again. It was maddening; he felt like a bull being lead around by the nose.

But, if Alexine had no abilities, then why was Annalynn so interested in her? If the girl was useless, what else could the pair of them be up to? And, most troubling, what if he were wrong? What if this young lady was, in fact, a reader? Scenarios swam through his thoughts; possibilities and their attendant problems.

One fact was indisputable; he possessed information Alexine could not be allowed to procure. There were banks in his memory to which she must be denied access, and he had always found repelling readers difficult. If Alexine could take his thoughts, he was placing himself in grave danger with this little exercise. This was supposed to be a good day; a day to collect information about Annalynn, a day to prepare for Nautas's arrival. Instead, he found himself petrified of a pubescent child.

"Now," Alexine said, "you think of something, and I'll try to read you."

Alexine felt the man's hands tighten, his breathing quicken ever so slightly. This huge man was afraid of readers? Turning that bit of information over and examining it, Alexine decided she was not surprised. Being read was not a pleasant experience most of the time. Her mind flashed back to the afternoon she and Callan had arrived in Shanghai; the shop, and Annalynn.

She also suddenly realized, when you were able to enter someone's mind, their physical stature was obsolete. In a way, it leveled the playing field. Devin struck Alexine as the type of man who was completely comfortable using physical intimidation. Devoid of that tactic, what would he use?

All of these theories seemed solid, but there was something else. Devin knew a lot about what was going on at the academy. That was it! She knew it! There was a part of Alexine that trembled in anticipation of reading Devin, longed for answers which were sitting just inches away, unprotected, available. He wouldn't be able to stop her, would he? Could she actually do it? She certainly did not feel compassion for Devin, nor pity, both important emotions which enabled her to read at this point in her training. She sighed. It didn't matter anyway, it was out of the question. The less accurate information Devin had on Alexine, the better. He could not discover she was a reader.

Something in Alexine's stomach turned over uncomfortably. It disturbed her when she realized that, if she were to be truly honest, she would have liked to read this man. Even if she did not have permission, even if he opposed it. She was tempted to steal his thoughts and insights. The prospect was so alluring.

"It's not right!"

The words she screamed at Annalynn upon discovering the woman had read her without permission. Not right, very true. But it beckoned her, none-the-less. Enticed her. Alexine felt a guilty blush invade her cheeks; she had judged Annalynn so harshly that day. And here she was wishing she could do the exact same thing. She pulled herself back to the present and the task at hand, not wanting to think about that anymore.

Alexine heard Devin's stomach growl. Time to make a fool of herself.

"Yes," she began, still holding his hands firmly in hers. She started to sway, like a charlatan fortune teller swooning in an old movie. "I'm getting something now…you're thinking of food…you're very hungry and you want food." She droned on slowly, deliberately. "You want lots of food…food is important when you're hungry…and you're thinking that food would be a good idea right now…and…your favorite food is…"

Alexine paused, her mind unintentionally scanning the breakfast buffet in the lunch room downstairs. She blurted out the first thing that came to mind, and almost laughed when she spoke the words.

"Chicken feet…your favorite food is chicken feet." She opened her eyes expectantly and smiled at Devin who wore a look which fell somewhere between irritation and bewilderment.

"Um…"

Chapter Twenty-nine
The Enemy

Annalynn roared with laughter. Alexine had reported directly to her office this morning, having been instructed to do so by Devin.

"Tell me more!" the reading teacher choked, trying to catch her breath.

"Well…" Alexine stammered, attempting to keep herself under control as well. "Devin thought it would be a good idea to go down to breakfast after that. Even though I wasn't hungry, I agreed. It gave me some time to consider my next move."

Annalynn had managed to stop laughing, but still giggled occasionally, hand over mouth, as Alexine recounted the previous day's events.

Pressing back into the couch, the younger girl put her hands behind her head, a self-satisfying smile crossing her face. "Then we went back to his office. He wanted to continue the 'work out' that you and I had started." She pictured what had happened next and shook with silent laughter for a moment. "Boy, what a fiasco that was! I haven't sparred since I was about eight years old, but I'm bigger now." Recalling the look on Devin's face when he challenged her to "not hold anything back" sent Alexine into a fresh peel of laughter. She had followed his instructions to the tee. "He…was…limping… when…I…left!" she managed to eek out.

The women enjoyed the moment for several minutes but then, slowly sobering, Alexine flashed her teacher a serious look, the light moment gradually dispelling. "He really pressed to find out exactly what we have been up to. That's what all of this was about. It wasn't about teaching me, it was about gathering information."

"I know. I need to gather some information of my own." Annalynn was now stark serious also, and speaking more to herself than to her pupil. Who remained at the academy whose loyalties lie, not with Nautas, but with Branch? Was a plan being put into play at this very moment? Should she attempt to contact whoever was spearheading the initiative?

Alexine wondered where Annalynn's thoughts had lead, and her own mind raced. How could she help? She didn't know very many people at the academy; this was intentional. Avoiding contact with almost everyone had kept her safe. Sane. It was as if by distancing herself from everyone associated with the place, she was able to hang onto the ledge, cling to life. Being pulled in with them would mean a long fall and a sudden demise. She knew it. Could she assist in any way? "I don't know anyone here," Alexine began, feeling useless, "except…" Her mind turned to Bethia. She *thought* the eccentric girl could be trusted. "Perhaps…."

"No Alexine. You talk to no one. We trust no one. *I* observe, *I* collect information, and *we* prepare. We need to be ready."

"Ready for what?" Alexine scowled. "What is going to happen?"

Annalynn shook her head, anticipating the questions. "No details for you. Your job is to learn; reading and repelling. That is what your focus should be."

Alexine slouched. The recurring theme: Alexine is told nothing, kept in the dark. She understood the reasoning, but couldn't help being just a little resentful. Her retort was unenthusiastic. "Okay."

Annalynn sighed thoughtfully. Sending Alexine out amidst the chaos that reigned at the academy seemed irreparably unfair. Her only protection rested on the fact that she knew very little. If the worst happened, and she was read, what would her memories divulge? The only person who would be implicated was Annalynn, that is where the trail would begin and end. No information. No additional names.

And the girl herself? Alexine was young, had just begun her training, and was gifted. Nautas may feel Annalynn was beyond hope once her treasonous decision was unearthed, but the girl? She was a clean slate and Nautas would do everything in his power to keep her, win her over himself. Annalynn knew it. His arrogance would override sense, and the little girl would be safe. Pardoned at least long enough for the opposition to liberate her, and the academy. At least long enough for Branch to return and lead them, as was his right.

"I'll see you after breakfast," the young lady said as she turned the door handle. Stepping over the threshold, she glanced back at Annalynn. "I'm starving." The statement was posed in full view of the unrelenting security camera which captured both her entrance and exit from Annalynn office.

Annalynn similarly stepped out into the hallway, feigning exasperation. "Yes, Alexine," she droned, trying her best to appear flabbergasted with what was supposed to be yet another trying conversation with someone who was un-trainable. "Report back after you eat."

The young girl smiled brightly as the door closed slowly. Suddenly stark and foreboding, the room contracted around the older woman. It was as though when Alexine departed, she took hope and faith with her. Settling into the seat behind her desk, Annalynn glanced around self consciously. She hated the quiet; like a tomb after mourners departed to re-join the living, leaving her there to deal with her decision. It was in the quiet Annalynn felt full responsibility for her choice.

She took a deep breath, shaking her head at the haunting image. Focus. Annalynn knew Branch, understood him completely. He would not abandon them, he simply could never do that. She was sure Branch had a plan, and it was more-than-likely being put into action even now. Who was facilitating? Who was helping? And who was sympathetic to Branch's cause?

There *had* to be opposition. It would have been impossible to completely eradicate Branch's influence over the occupants of the academy. Impossible. All of her plans, her assumptions hinged on this belief.

It took Annalynn forty-five minutes to begin compiling a list of people who, she felt, could possibly harbor mixed allegiance. All of the individuals on the list were present on decision day; they had elected to remain with Nautas. But, for one reason or another, Annalynn felt positions could have altered, minds could have been changed. Or, even better, she theorized, some perhaps remained at the academy under the guise of loyalty when actually their plans were to thwart the dark man's intentions.

Annalynn mentally ran through each name on the list. The question surfaced again: should she contact them? She smiled sadly. A melancholy, sorrowful sentiment cloaked her like a wet, woolen coat, weighing heavy on her thoughts. She slouched under the burden, the fight abandoning her. She would not have been on the list of hopefuls lying quietly on her desk. She doubted anyone would suspect her of harboring support for Branch, much less affection for him. Not anymore An involuntary tremor ran through her body and she buried her face in her hands.

Annalynn had not seen Devin since the morning she dumped Alexine in his lap. The situation was to her liking; the less she interacted with the man trying to build a case against her, the better. Her stomach somersaulted uncomfortably the next day when they came very close to colliding in the cafeteria.

"Good morning," the large man stammered, trying to regain control of a tray full of food. He mirrored her embarrassment. Steadying his load, Devin looked at her questioningly. "You're coming down for breakfast?"

Annalynn rarely visited the cafeteria, preferring nearby vendors or restaurants. Devin seemed surprised and wary. Annalynn could picture him rushing up to his office and recording this information, pouncing on anything out of the ordinary which concerned her. She fought the impulse to shake her head and roll her eyes. "Actually," she said truthfully, "I'm looking for Alexine."

Devin cocked his head slightly in interest. "Why?" he tried to sound nonchalant.

"Her training didn't go very well yesterday," Annalynn lied, frowning and glancing around the room. "And she's late today."

Devin pulled a disgusted smile. "You're wasting your time Anna," he said condescendingly. "I called it from the beginning. The girl is worthless."

Annalynn's temper flared and she flashed him an irritated look. "We have to keep her here, remember? Perhaps you'd like another shot at training her? Anything on your schedule today?"

She felt a pang of guilt as the color drained from Devin's face. A part of her wanted to burst out laughing. Alexine's recounting of the day Devin had spent with her had been hilarious. Obviously the young girl had not done the day justice. Judging from Devin's reaction to the possibility of facing another session with Alexine, Annalynn had to assume it was more horrible than words could describe. The hulking man stalked away indignantly. "Serves him right," she whispered under her breath. "Now where is that girl?"

Scanning the room several times, she finally spotted Alexine sitting across from an unconventionally dressed girl. She strode toward the pair quickly and, walking up behind Alexine, put her hands on her hips.

The young lady was deep in conversation with the strange looking girl. They were both bent so far over the table, their heads almost touched. Excited whispers filled the air around them, although exact words were unintelligible. So engrossed in whatever they were discussing, the girls were oblivious to Annalynn standing impatiently behind Alexine, now tapping her foot on the tile floor.

"You're late," she finally said accusingly. The young lady jumped and spun around, spilling her milk. It pooled, and began running the length of the table. Out of the corner of her eye Annalynn noticed a cafeteria worker running toward them, towel in hand. "Come," she said threateningly.

The girl dressed in a brightly colored t-shirt and long skirt raised her head confidently, inclining her eyebrows in question. Then her brow furrowed, a deep crease forming between her eyes. She addressed Alexine.

"Aren't you going to introduce me?" she said politely, and with emphasized control, her eyes never leaving Annalynn.

"Uh, yea," Alexine stuttered. "Bethia this is Annalynn. Annalynn, this is Bethia."

A warning pounded in Annalynn's head. Was it her imagination, or was this strange girl *very* aware of who she was? Annalynn's first impulse was to read this "Bethia" on-the-spot, but she reluctantly resisted the urge. Fragments of Nautas's practices were so alluring and, after embracing them, difficult to abandon. Forcibly, she ejected the man and his methods from her thoughts.

"Annalynn is my tutor." Alexine glanced between Annalynn and Bethia. A feeling of mistrust and anxiety filled the air between her instructor and her new friend. It completely confused Alexine.

This outlandishly dressed girl knew something, it was undeniable, and it made Annalynn anxious. There was too much at stake. Perhaps she had not given Alexine enough direction. The desire to leave this girl's presence settled over Annalynn as she voiced her command. "My office...now." Turning on her heel, Annalynn stalked away.

Alexine remained very still, studying her instructor intently as she left. Turning a questioning look to Bethia, she frowned. "What's going on?" She had not intended for it to sound so gruff, but her bewilderment had quickly turned to fear when Annalynn retreated so hastily. It wasn't like her. Alexine was surprised to note Bethia wore an expression similar to the one plastered on her own face.

"How long have you been working with Annalynn?"

Alexine sat back in her chair, taken aback by the question and the tone. "Why?"

"Annalynn is at the forefront of everything wrong here Alexine," the girl whispered urgently. "She...is...the...enemy!"

Nodding her head, Alexine dropped her eyes, re-living that day in the hallway. After her frightening experience with Zeke, she had been shocked at Annalynn's confession that the situation at the academy was dire. It was imperative Annalynn's allegiance to the academy was not called into question by anyone. Devolving any information about her change of heart placed both Annalynn and Alexine in terrible danger. She knew this. But it was time to make a decision. Could she trust Bethia with something so crucial?

They had to figure out who was friend, and who was foe. That necessitated taking some chances. Annalynn had told her not to ask questions, not to divulge information, to lay low, but perhaps she could help. As she weighed her options, Alexine searched her heart; she felt this girl was trustworthy. She wasn't sure why, but a secure feeling settled over her. It was as if something, someone, were confirming her hopes. Alexine leaned in close and whispered almost indiscernibly in Bethia's ear. "She's changed her mind."

As Alexine left the cafeteria, Bethia's mind flew into overdrive. How could she contact him? He needed to be warned; Annalynn was definitely switching sides. This information could change many things.

Chapter Thirty
A Flicker of Fear

After Annalynn's appearance and abrupt exit from the cafeteria, Alexine and Bethia agreed to meet later that day. Alexine then reported to Annalynn's office, as instructed.

There was something about the odd-looking young lady that unnerved Annalynn. She was not an innocent by-stander, that much was certain. She knew more than Alexine realized. The question was: was that good, or was that bad?

"I don't want you involved," Annalynn pleaded after Alexine recounted her feelings about Bethia. How she just trusted her, but wasn't sure why. "You haven't told her anything, have you?"

"Well, we talk about the academy. How something is wrong here, and I kind of told her that you and I agree." It was a half-truth.

"You give information to the wrong person and," Annalynn shook her head slowly, "very bad things happen quickly." The instructor looked thoughtful, then relaxed slightly. "But since we're both still here, and in one piece... Just please leave this to me. Give me your word."

Alexine paused. "I can't do that."

"Alexine, we've been over this. You shouldn't know too much."

"Or what?" the younger girl leapt to her feet, suddenly incensed. "You and I are in more danger? That's a lie, it makes no sense. I know you've switched sides Anna. If someone reads me, you're..." She did not want to finish her thought, so she allowed it to trail off. "So, this isn't about *me* protecting *you*. This is about *you* protecting *me*. In case you haven't noticed, you're not the only one willing to put themselves on the line." As Annalynn rose from her chair and walked around the table, Alexine followed her approach. She thought her instructor looked older, more worn, than the first day they met.

Annalynn's jaw worked as she clenched her teeth then sighed, "we'll finish this discussion later." Her final comment in the argument was clipped and impatient. Alexine was a stubborn girl. She wasn't going to win this debate now and she was too tired to keep trying. "So let's get started." Eyeing Alexine thoughtfully for a moment, Annalynn finally sat down in the chair opposite the young girl.

"Okay." Hesitant, but wanting to abandon the impasse, Alexine too sank back into her seat, wondering what new, and predictably uncomfortable scenario was about to unfold. When the woman sitting across from her looked perplexed, Alexine glanced around the room self-consciously, half wondering if Annalynn was about to re-open the argument. "What?" she finally asked, her eyes still darting about.

"I want you to try something for me," Annalynn said slowly, as if contemplating the implications of her request.

"Okayyy."

"I want you to go into your classroom," she began again, staring at something invisible hanging unseen in the air just above Alexine's head. The younger girl fought an intense desire to turn around and find out what was so compelling. She knew nothing was there.

"And then I want *you* to come and find *me*," she finished. As she spoke, the instructor lowered her gaze, eying Alexine soberly.

"Find you?" Alexine repeated, perplexed.

"Yes, find me and pull me into your space."

Once again, she had spent a sleepless night formulating the next day's training. Although she was comfortable with the younger girl's ability to repel most readers, Annalynn was becoming increasingly interested in the boundaries of this girl's capacity. Having already been surprised by her expertise in exerting physical force during a repel, the instructor now wanted to turn her attention to other skills the girl possibly possessed.

"The problem is," Annalynn said, a bit unsure, "I've never been able to do it myself, so I won't be much help."

An hour later, the women sat across from each other, exasperated. What Annalynn had hoped Alexine would be able to figure out fairly quickly had morphed into what appeared to be a monumental task.

"Let me try again," Alexine whispered, breathing heavily. "Maybe if I....." Her thought was cut short by someone rapping harshly on the office door. Both women jumped in surprise, Annalynn flashing Alexine a quizzical, concerned look.

Devin pushed open the door the moment Annalynn turned the handle.

"So Anna," he began, officially. "How's the training going today?"

The look he threw in Alexine's direction made her skin crawl, but she met his gaze, undaunted. Distain, distaste, and something else. Just a flicker of...what? Alexine wrinkled her forehead in surprise and uncertainty. Fear. Why would Devin fear her? Was he truly convinced she had no power? She had worked so hard to prove she was incompetent.

Alexine dropped her gaze, suddenly realizing she was supposed to be worthless. Not confident, and certainly not impassioned. She was sending mixed signals. She was supposed to be a ditz who babbled on and on about everything and nothing of importance. Devin continued to study her even after she turned away, she felt his probing gaze surround her.

"And I can help you...how?" Annalynn stated evenly, pulling Devin's attention from the younger girl.

"Nautas is returning." He allowed the tension in the room to build, coaxing it on, encouraging it with his silence. His eyes never left the reading instructor. The words were pleasant, but his presence was challenging. This woman with whom he was forced to share power, his equal at this moment, soon, very soon, would be his subordinate.

Annalynn could tell he wanted her to ask "when", so she resisted the impulse. "I understand," she replied instead, never missing a beat, her cool façade completely convincing. "I'll be ready." But under the surface, her blood boiled. Why would this man mention Nautas's name in front of Alexine? What was he playing at? What else was he willing to splutter in front of the girl?

"Really?" he said sarcastically, tipping his head, and raising his eyebrows in question. "Well...we'll see."

The color rushed to Alexine's face and she was grateful to be facing away from the large man bearing down on them. Darkness. The emotions pulsing through the room were suppressive, leaving her uncomfortable. She wanted to run. Nautas? Who was Nautas? She had the uneasy feeling she did not want to know.

The door knob clicked and Devin sauntered away, satisfied.

Alexine turned toward Annalynn, surprised by the fear on her teacher's face.

"I've got to think," the older woman said quickly, speaking more to herself than anyone else. She placed a hand on her forehead as if, somehow, it would increase her ability to formulate a plan. "Think. Think." She ran her hand through her hair, pulling it back off her face. "I'm going to need to do something, but I'm not sure…" Annalynn shook her head, failing to finish the thought. "Perhaps find out where everyone stands. But we can't trust anyone," Annalynn said nervously, "especially not your sister, I'm afraid." She was rambling.

Pausing to compose herself, she registered Alexine's look of concern; it had deepened at the mention of Callan. But there was no time for niceties. "She's a shifter," Annalynn stated the obvious fact, bracing herself for the other words which needed to be spoken. "I'm not saying Callan's made a bad choice yet, but shifters are notorious for following." Annalynn turned away from the young girl and her pained expression, and finished in a whisper, "they're the soldiers."

Alexine flashed back to those horrible events which had unfolded in the classroom upstairs several weeks previous. She replayed the statements voiced that day. Statements she had committed to memory. "They are most often taken advantage of…victimized…because of their blind loyalty and trustworthy nature."

Not Callan. Not her baby sister. She would never knowingly align herself with evil. This rebuttal popped into Alexine's head automatically. But another thought had been lingering just outside her consciousness since the first day they reported to the academy, and now it begged to be recognized. Would Callan support evil *unknowingly*?

"There's something else," Annalynn said hesitantly, coaxing Alexine back to the present. "You must learn how to pull people in Alexine. It's very important." Visions of Alexine being unable to defend herself against what Annalynn felt was now speeding toward them haunted her. "You must learn how to protect yourself…protect others, go on the offensive if necessary. Do you understand?"

Alexine looked fleetingly impatient. "I understand, but can't you just tell me…"

"Things might happen," Annalynn spoke over her, and when Alexine opened her mouth to talk again, the older woman interjected, "don't ask questions."

The young girl clenched her jaw. She thought she understood what Annalynn was saying, of course, but ached to know more. Wanted to be a part of this plan. Wanted to help.

And how was she to learn this pulling-people-in thing? Who could teach her? What was she supposed to do? More confusion and still no answers. Alexine stole a glance at Annalynn who remained visibly unsettled. A pang of guilt tweaked her conscience and, pushing her own impatience away, she finally relented. "Don't worry, I'll learn."

Her instructor seemed to relax a bit.

It seemed odd for Alexine to be reassuring Annalynn. Feeling it had something to do with whoever was coming, Alexine blurted out the question before she had a chance to change her mind. "Who is Nautas?"

Annalynn looked at her intently for several seconds, unblinking, as if paralyzed.

"Annalynn?" Alexine said as the silence stretched uncomfortably long.

The older woman shook her head. "Things are going to get bad…the next few days…we need to figure out…" Once again, she didn't seem to be able to complete a thought. "We need to be gone when he arrives," she finally finished. "You do not want to know who he is."

The words were punctuated. Firm. It was a definitive statement intended to end the conversation. Alexine understood there would be no more questions about this man. They needed to be gone. No discussion.

Alexine spent the next day observing. Annalynn had told her not to get involved, but she had refused to agree, so she wasn't being deceptive in any way. "Just uncooperative," she thought guiltily.

Some students were easy to peg. Zeke and his cronies…obvious. And others, the way they treated fellow students and instructors. Alexine grouped them with Devin. But there were several who struck Alexine as being different. She discovered their names by a combination of eavesdropping and innocent questions and jotted them down on a scrap of paper.

Alexine fingered the list of names in her pocket after entering the girl's bathroom. Although there were not supposed to be cameras in the lavatory, she was taking no chances. Unfolding the list carefully, she removed it only when she was locked securely in a stall. It contained only a handful of possibilities.

"John Seid," she mouthed the first name silently. "John Seid."

Chapter Thirty-one
John

Callan gave her older sister a puzzled look as Alexine settled into an adjacent seat in the cafeteria.

"Since when do you eat lunch here?" she asked. "And where is Annalynn?"

"Up in her office," Alexine responded non-chalantly. "Thought I'd pop down for a few minutes...see my favorite sister." She tried to look sincere but Callan's disbelieving look told her it would be impossible to deceive the little red-head. Luckily, it appeared Callan was going to let it slide.

"Yea. Okay."

"So," began Alexine haltingly, "who have you been hanging out with lately?"

The little shifter paused mid-chew and again threw her older sister the same incredulous look. "What's going on?" she demanded. "Like I can't read you like a book."

Alexine put on the most innocent face she could muster. "Nothing's going on. We just haven't talked in awhile. I want to catch up."

Callan began chewing again, but kept her eyes on Alexine. It made the older girl self-conscious. Unsure of what else to say, she decided to go with the direct approach. "Do you know a guy named John Seid?"

Dropping her chopsticks on her plate in impatience, the little girl whispered menacingly, "what are you up to?"

"Just wondered if you knew him," Alexine replied, realizing she sounded anything but innocent now. "I wanted to talk to him."

"Why?" Callan asked quietly. "And how did you get his name?"

"How do you know him?"

Sitting back in her seat, Callan mulled over whether the answer to that question would compromise anything, or anyone. Deciding it would not, she said slowly, "he's a shifter." Not taking her eyes off Alexine for a moment, Callan noticed her older sister's flicker of excitement. Something was going on. "You going to tell me why you're asking about him?"

Callan knew him! Alexine felt a wave of relief wash over her, but then she paused. A shifter; they were followers, not to be trusted. Should she go ahead with her plan; try to figure out where he stood? She made her decision quickly. Perhaps Anna was being a bit too cautious. Perhaps they should give some shifters a chance. Perhaps even Callan?

"Can you introduce me?"

"No," Callan said quickly, completely uncomfortable with this line of questioning. Alexine was up to something, albeit clumsily. She was so obvious! "And whatever you're up to, stop it," Callan said under her breath as she rose to leave. "What you're doing is dangerous," the fiery red-head mumbled between clenched teeth, trying to get her point across forcefully, but at the same time, not call attention to their conversation.

Alexine panicked, what had she done? Although she had told Callan she trusted her, sometimes she wondered if that was just wishful thinking. Grasping for damage control, Alexine furrowed her eyebrows and remained calm. "What in the heck are you talking about?" she asked, sounding thoroughly confused. "I can't ask about a *boy*? Boys are dangerous now? Why? Is he bad or something?"

Callan sank back down into her seat. "Boy?"

"Well," began Alexine more convincingly. "Zeke is definitely out of the picture after that market fiasco."

Callan nodded her head still wary. Alexine had made it perfectly clear she didn't trust Zeke, and wasn't interested in getting involved with anyone from the academy. This entire conversation was extremely fishy, but she decided to play along for the moment. "Looking for a boyfriend?"

"Of course not!" Alexine said defensively. "Just a friend...you know...and I saw this kid the other day," Alexine lied, and blushed furiously for it, but perhaps Callan would assume the characteristic blotches of purple were the result of discussing the boy.

Had Alexine actually relaxed her earlier demand that the girls remain aloof from almost everyone at the academy? Did being completely alone for a bit help Alexine to realize that complete isolation was not the answer, and was almost impossible?

The little red-head smiled deviously. This preference for hanging out with boys, as opposed to girls, was something she and her older sister had in common. They both got along very well with most boys, and fairly well with a few girls. She had never really pin-pointed the reasons why. Both the girls were confident, athletic, to-the-point. It seemed as though the funny games most girls played didn't sit well with them. They were straight forward, liked to get things out in the open, honest. Callan was pulled back to the present conversation by her sisters halting words.

"He's...cute..." she smiled, "but I don't know anyone else here, so I was hoping maybe you knew...never mind," she finished quickly. "It's a dumb idea."

Callan stared at her incredulously, unsure what to think. John? Cute?

* * *

"John?" Callan said confidently as they approached a crowded cafeteria table.

A stocky young man with short reddish-blond hair glanced up. He resembled the rugby players Alexine's uncles watched on TV. Her mind returned to one of the games she had witnessed. A jumbled mass of power, pushing and contending with each other in a tightly formed circle. Fingers clenched into neighbor's shoulders, muddy shoes dug deep in rain laden fields, powerful, massive thighs and calves straining to alter the course of an oft times brutal game.

He was taller than she, and twice her size. Wearing a rust colored plaid shirt, jeans and tan work boots, John was slowly chewing on a straw, his jaw pulsing. It appeared he hadn't shaven for a few days, and the coarse stubble on his face matched his hair color perfectly. The area just below his bottom lip was a bit darker and thicker than the rest of the growth.

Alexine approached timidly, just behind her little sister. This was not the type of boy Alexine would typically find attractive. Athletic, she liked. But more like soccer athletic, basketball athletic. Not the small mountain of a man sitting before her. No wonder Callan had looked at her as if she were insane when she suggested Callan introduce them.

"This is my sister, Alexine." Callan turned toward her older sister shaking her head in wonder. "She wanted to meet you."

John stopped chewing on his straw, holding it tight in his teeth. His questioning eyes darted back and forth between Callan and Alexine several times. Finally settling on Callan, he threw her a wary look.

Callan shrugged her shoulders and rolled her eyes as if to say, "I have no idea."

"Well…nice to meet you Alexine…um…pull up a chair guys…I mean…girls."

The group spent the remainder of the hour discussing their experiences in Shanghai and the interesting cuisine they had each encountered since arriving. Interspersed here and there were impromptu debates regarding which talent was the most important, which required the most skill, and which would be the best in myriad situations. Alexine found herself having a wonderful time despite the urgency of her task. It felt good to just be a normal kid again. "Well," she thought ruefully, half-grinning, "normal for this place anyway."

Her mind periodically returned to the paper folded in her pocket. Alexine was surprised to find most of the people on her list were sitting here…at this table…with John. That could not be a coincidence. Perhaps her work for the day would be easier than anticipated. If she could just talk to one of them, she was confident they would be privy to the mind-set of the others. These people all seemed very comfortable with each other.

Alexine was surprised, and a little hurt, that Callan had not told her about them. Had it been the argument in their room that spurred Callan's secrecy? Alexine *had* grouped everyone in the academy together, pegging them all as bad characters. Had she been wrong in her assumptions?

"Well," said John, at five minutes to one o-clock. He pushed his chair back, its legs scraping the floor noisily, "time to get back."

Several people murmured their agreement and began stirring.

John found Callan in the crowd. He wrinkled his eyebrows in question quickly. Almost imperceptibly, Callan shook her head in retort. His features relaxing a bit, he looked at her intently, pleading. She shook her head again and shot him a nasty glare, then turned away. John sighed. "Hey Alexine," he said, disappointed. "You want to walk with us to the gym?"

As the group left the cafeteria, John noted that Callan stuck very close to her older sister. Obviously, she wasn't taking any chances. The situation at the academy was spiraling, John could feel it. Although he understood the reasons behind Callan's reluctance to give her older sister information, it frustrated him. If they could just talk to Alexine, explain things, he was confident they could convince her to join their cause. She would not be a threat, he knew it.

Slowly the group dwindled down to a handful of people. Students bid their farewells, turning into various classrooms scattered along the hallway.

Looking to his right, John was surprised to find Alexine staring at him, studying him. He smiled playfully at her, the corner of his mouth twitching, and she quickly dropped her gaze to the floor. His gesture earned him a scathing look from Callan who was walking alongside her sister. She shook her head menacingly, and again mouthed the word "no." Glowering, he slackened his pace, falling behind the group.

"I'll catch up in a second," John announced, turning into the bathroom. The group continued on to the gym, filing in and stashing back-packs and bags around the perimeter.

"Well," Callan turned to her sister, "I'll see you tonight then."

Alexine nodded, smiled, and gave the small girl a squeeze. "Thanks sis," she said sincerely.

"Yea," stumbled Callan, "no problem." She winked and walked to the middle of the floor where the other shifters had gathered.

Exiting the large gymnasium, Alexine turned to her right. The meeting with Bethia was upstairs. Heading down the hall she almost ran smack into John. Surprised, she stifled a scream. "Oh my golly John!" she said, flustered. "You scared the heck out of me!" John had dropped from the crowd prior to their arrival at the gym. What was he doing here? Past the boys lavatory and past the gym entrance?

"We need to talk." The words were whispered and serious. "Your sister would kill me if she knew I was doing this," he continued quickly. "Too many cameras here, we'll need to meet tonight."

He moved closer, glancing up at the monitor mounted near the ceiling directly behind Alexine. Smiling for effect, he advanced, forcing her back against the wall. Her heart skipped as John placed his hand on the wall beside her, the veins on his arm standing out as he leaned in closer. "Pretend I'm asking you out," he said in a low voice. "Smile back at me and nod."

Alexine followed orders, confused at this turn of events.

"Five-thirty, at the dumpling place near your hotel." The space between them disappeared when John bent his arm, his ample bicep flexing under the pressure. "Callan will still be here, at dinner. I'll find you," he whispered, his face inches from hers. The intensity alive in his clear green eyes caused Alexine to flush pink as the temperature in the room climbed. She had not been aware of how large John was until he stood so close. She looked up at him obediently.

John winked then, pushing off the wall to right himself, walked past her toward shifter training. Alexine stood there, glued to the spot for several minutes, and now very weak in the knees.

Chapter Thirty-two
Blind Dates

Alexine was still in shock when she entered the classroom upstairs.

"You found it," Bethia said matter-of-factly, "good."

The odd girl had her face buried in a book, she didn't look up. Alexine was not surprised to see Bethia sitting on the floor cross-legged, shoes off, with her tan gauzy skirt billowed around her. Books scattered haphazardly encircled the girl, completing the effect. She reminded Alexine of a flower that had dropped some of its petals.

Glancing at her watch the older girl noted, "and right on time."

Bethia remained very still, listening intently, as Alexine made a full confession regarding the list, and the events involving John. When she finished, the eccentric girl's expression made Alexine even more wary of her predicament. Concern.

"I don't think you should meet him," Bethia said seriously. "It's just not a good idea."

Alexine frowned in confusion. Perhaps the warning was warranted. These people were, to an extent, merely chosen at random. But she wasn't going to *give* them any information. She was asking a few questions, that was all. Yes, but the questions weren't innocent and wouldn't be taken as such. She was tired of arguing with herself. "Am I supposed to work on this?" Alexine asked no one in particular, pulling the list from her pocket. "Am I supposed to help?"

The older girl shook her head. "No, you're not," she said, gently taking the list.

Alexine was surprised how easily she relinquished it. "But I need to help, somehow. I need to do something! I'm tired of just sitting here, knowing nothing."

"Tell you what," Bethia touched Alexine's hand lightly. "We'll figure it out together. Trust me," she said soothingly.

Alexine blanched at the words: trust me. Who could she truly trust anymore? Annalynn who kept her in the dark? Callan who was embroiled in a group of people who seemed really wonderful, but were bound together somehow; students in an academy gone awry? The young woman sitting before her, of whom she could not be absolutely sure?

Bethia watched Alexine's face carefully, picking up on the turmoil roiling just beneath her tearful surface. Obviously Alexine was not going to let this go. How could she prevent things from getting out of hand? "I'll do it for you. I'll check up on these people for you. I'll find out."

Alexine's heart leapt. "Really?"

"Yes," Bethia replied thoughtfully. "It's safer for me."

"Are you sure?"

She nodded her head, the list disappearing into a fold in her dress.

"Thanks. But don't tell them anything, okay? Just find out if they like what is going on at the academy, that's all I need to know."

"I understand what we need," Bethia smirked at her. "Leave it to me."

"So what about John?" Alexine asked uncertainly, remembering her "date" at the dumpling stand. "Won't he think it's weird if I don't show up? I can't bring any attention to myself."

"I wouldn't worry about it." The healer felt she was pushing her luck. The list, yes, she could give answers about a list. But she had to be cautious. If she took care of John also, Alexine may become suspicious. She was supposed to be a loner, that was her roll. Why would a loner agree to pry into a group of student's opinions *and* meet another student for a clandestine rendezvous? Way too conspicuous. Alexine could not be given information. She was a wild card; sitting out there like a rabbit in the middle of a busy road. Only ignorance and the fact she was not moving in any direction was protecting her. At this point, the cars just kept rolling over and missing, but one step the wrong way… "Guys get jilted all the time. And what could he know? Nothing, that's what. I've been watching him. He's definitely not involved in anything here, no way. Just wanted to get you alone, I suppose. When you see him next, just say you changed your mind."

That just didn't sit right with Alexine. How would *she* feel if *she* were stood up? "I don't know. I don't want to hurt his feelings."

Bethia let out a humorless laugh. "Alexine, do you hear yourself?" Her incredulous look included just a fleck of impatience. "What's more important…you and Annalynn's safety…or hurting a boy's feelings?"

Alexine diverted a guilty gaze, her focus flitting right, then left. "When you put it that way…"

"This is a serious situation," Bethia continued, dropping any evidence of light-heartedness. "Hurt feelings should be the least of your concerns."

Alexine nodded in agreement. Of course, Bethia was right.

* * *

At five-o'clock that evening, Bethia slid back into the shadows of a recessed door directly across the street from the dumpling shop, completely concealed. Shaking her head in disgust, she watched John approach the stand slowly from the north, ducking into an alleyway to await Alexine's arrival.

"What is he thinking?" Bethia asked herself, irritated. They could not afford mistakes at this point. She pulled the dark shawl tightly around her head and abandoned her hiding place. Overshooting the stand, she crossed the street and quickly walked an additional block east. Turning right, then doubling back around, she approached John from the rear.

The alley was cluttered with dirty pots and pans, restaurant refuse and rancid water. Like so many other places in China, there were no animals. No cats, no dogs, no rodents. She shuttered considering the reasons behind the creatures absence.

Moving slowly, Bethia's feet were almost silent as they made contact with the concrete. Honking horns and the murmur of people moving about the street created the perfect distraction.

"The answer was *no* John," she said quietly just inches behind the young man who was intently watching the street. She emphasized the word "no," drawing it out, punctuating it.

John jumped at least six inches off the ground and slipped when his feet once again met the earth. Regaining his balance, he spun on the spot, ready to attack the intruder now flailing at him. Bethia grabbed at his shirt instinctively when he stumbled, releasing him just prior to being thrown sideways by his abrupt turn. Fortunately for her, John pulled up prior to striking.

"What are *you* doing here?" he whispered, realizing she was not the enemy, but surprised and angry none the less.

The older girl gave him a long, hard stare. "I know who you are. I know what you're a part of. And I know what you are about to do. So, I think the more pertinent question is, what are *you* doing here?" When the young man scowled, Bethia ordered, "let's go…this way," and the pair retreated back down the alleyway.

"Too many people have worked too hard on this John, you're throwing a wrench in the works," she began impatiently. "What were you thinking?"

"You're involved? Why were you brought in? To spy on us?"

"Keep your ego in check tiger," Bethia drawled drolly. "I'm not here to take over. I'm the contingency plan, that's all." The young man still appeared disgruntled, but calmed down quickly, anxious to make his case.

"If we explain things to her," he implored, "what we're trying to do," John trailed off then looked sternly over at Bethia. "I know she would agree." When his companion failed to respond, but merely eyed him steadily, her face impassive, John stopped and tipped his head back.

The stance emphasized his thick neck, the tendons of which were pronounced and taunt. Although appearing to study the sky, the shifter's eyes were glazed and unseeing. As if trying to put a questionable concept into words, he mumbled, "Annalynn's playing coy, but that girl is *powerful.* I can feel it." John rounded on Bethia, leaning in to whisper, "I think Devin has his suspicions regarding her abilities too. We could *use* her on our side!"

"Since when do you put any stock into Devin's opinion?" Bethia asked shortly. "Please don't tell me you trust his take on the situation at all."

"No, of course not," John replied quickly, disgusted. "He's a schmuck." The powerful young man began walking again and grabbed Bethia's arm to pull her in tight. "But word is Nautas is eager for she and Callan to remain at the academy," he whispered urgently, a tinge of concern evident in his voice. "That has to mean something."

"Of course it does," Bethia replied curtly. "But what you were about to do tonight? Was that smart?" The older girl stopped walking again, forcing her companion to pull to a halt. She took hold of him and shook his wide shoulders roughly, but he barely moved. "This whole thing tonight is just between you and me. My anonymity is mandatory. Understand? I'm trusting you. No one is to know about me, no one. Okay?"

John nodded seriously. "No problem."

"And from now on, you leave this alone…understand? No one is to know about your little plan either."

"We should win her *before* they force her to stay!"

"So, let me get this straight," Bethia began sarcastically, readying herself to present a list of problems in a logical pattern. Shifters! They were so frustrating! "You want to jump the gun on Nautas," she raised her eyebrows and gave him a half-smile that said "probably not smart." A huge understatement. "You want to force Annalynn to show her hand, when no one is truly sure about her. And you want to give an inexperienced *reader* a ton of information," she emphasized the word "reader." "John!" she finished, exasperated, "readers are *read*. An untrained reader is an open book; they can't protect their thoughts!"

The young man nodded morosely. "But are we sure she's a reader? She might be a…"

"Absolutely sure."

"How do we know?"

"We know." She paused, waiting for the shifter to look at her. "John?" He intentionally diverted his attention. "The only reason you aren't having to disappear right now is because I stopped you from making a huge mistake."

"Yes Bethia…I understand." It was droned in a monotone, as if spoken just to get the healer off his back. He wanted to ensure Bethia registered his dissent. He did not agree.

"Shifters!" she blurted, exasperated, and began walking again, taking his arm then tossing her head in frustration. "You guys just don't think!"

John laughed playfully. "And perhaps that is why we are protected."

"And perhaps that's why you require a leader to constantly pull back on your reins!" The comment was snapped, but lent a little playfulness to lighten the blow. A true statement, but one you had to make carefully.

John stopped and looked at her in mock astonishment, tinged with a hint of hurt. His eyebrows raised, his mouth agape. "Et too Brute?" He shook his head playfully. "Why doesn't anyone give us shifters a bit of credit?"

"After tonight, John," Bethia again looped her arm through his. "You're going to have to earn your credit with me." She sighed, "coming out here after you…as if I don't have enough to do!"

Chapter Thirty-three
Read Me

"I'm not letting this go," Annalynn frowned at the obstinate girl sitting opposite her, "promise me."

"I can't."

The older woman heaved an incensed sigh. "Promise me."

Alexine considered her options. They had been arguing for fifteen minutes and she was growing weary of the tit-for-tat, back-and-forth. She had already tried to help and failed. Developed her list, only to abdicate the responsibility of investigating the names to Bethia. Made a date to talk with John, only to stand him up. Who was she kidding? She wasn't getting anywhere. So, why was she locking horns with Annalynn on this? Just to prove a point, which, she admitted, was childish. They had better things to do with their time.

"Okay, fine, I won't poke around…anymore."

Annalynn's shoulder's relaxed slightly. "Promise me."

"I promise."

The older woman inclined her head toward Alexine, her eyes contracting sharply. "What do you mean…anymore?"

"Well, I have to be honest," Alexine said quickly, before she could change her mind. "You know…Bethia?" she began, fidgeting.

The instructor jerked her head back in surprise. Brow creased, she cocked her head to the side, as if contemplating a situation gone horribly awry. "Tell me you didn't say anything more to her."

"Um, I didn't."

Annalynn inhaled deeply, then exhaled in a relieved shoosh.

"Don't be too pleased," replied Alexine, wincing. "I wasn't exactly honest about what I had already told her the last time we spoke."

Annalynn considered this, then, realizing the implications she said sharply, "keep talking…fast."

The ticking of the clock seemed loud and disruptive as an uncomfortable silence filled the room. "I told her you…changed your mind."

"WHAT?!" Annalynn jumped from her seat. "You didn't. Tell me you did not tell her that."

"I trust her." The assertion came out small and feeble.

"Well, I don't!" the older woman spat back.

Alexine sunk in her chair. She was operating in a cocoon with no input from anyone except Bethia. The decisions she made up to this point had seemed sound…until now. Now, they seemed fool hardy and reckless. She was just trying to help, just trying to do…something, anything. How could she tell Annalynn that she felt useless, all of the time. Worthless. Ignorant.

"I'm sorry."

"Okay," the reading instructor worked to control her frustration. "Something is up with your friend Bethia. She is more than she appears."

Doubtful and confused, Alexine opened her mouth in retort but was silenced.

"She is either sympathetic to the group who opposes what is going on at the academy...."

Alexine interrupted her instructor. "No...I don't think so...she came right around the time we did. I don't think she knows anything about groups. No one even talks to her."

Annalynn controlled her impulse to tell Alexine that *when* someone came into the academy did not matter, and that things were not always as they appeared. That the people they were fighting were tricky, dishonest, conniving liars. And they were smooth, so smooth. "Okay, then perhaps she's simply against anything having to do with Devin."

That seemed plausible. Alexine knew Bethia detested Devin. "That must be it."

Annalynn left the third possible scenario unspoken. Bethia was working for Nautas. Anna saw this as a distinct possibility. It would be just like the dark leader. Perhaps he was not getting his information from Devin, but from his spy, Bethia. Then why hadn't he made his move yet? Perhaps he's waiting. For what? Annalynn could not fathom an answer.

They sat in pondering silence for some time.

Mulling over her relationship with Bethia, Alexine felt she could trust the eccentric girl. She was not sure why, really. It was unlike her to form an opinion with no base in fact, with very little reason. Operating solely in the emotional realm was foreign to her. She was practical, pragmatic, almost to a fault. Did she trust Bethia simply because she felt threatened here? Did she trust her because she *needed* to trust someone? *Anyone?* Shaking her head, the only answer she could come up with was, "I don't think so."

Looking over at the young girl seated opposite, Annalynn heaved a sigh. "Okay," she began, a hint of exasperation in her words. "You're going to promise me again, swear, that you will leave this alone."

"I will."

"You won't talk to anyone about this. You won't do anything more."

"I won't."

Annalynn shook her head, disgruntled.

The clock again intruded upon them, beating it's rhythm relentlessly into Alexine's head. Tick-tock. Tick-tock. Tick-tock. Annalynn stared at her as if waiting for additional reassurance.

"I promise."

The older woman's face relaxed slightly. The damage was done, there was nothing more to say. Annalynn was unsure if this move on Alexine's part would make a difference this late in the game anyway. "I think we should get you out of here." She knew it was the only way to keep Alexine safe. Remove her from Nautas's grasp, then hide her. Just until things settled down. Just until things returned to normal.

"Not without Callan."

"I don't know if that's possible. At this point, I doubt she wants to leave."

"Well, then, I'm staying too."

"Alexine, Callan is safe. She agrees with what is happening here."

"Anna, what *is* happening here?" It was a plea, an entreaty. She ached to understand.

Her instructor flashed her an incredulous look, then shook her head impatiently. "No. We are not having this conversation again. Just think about what I've said."

Alexine looked stung, but Annalynn could not allow personal feelings to govern this situation. If Alexine knew too much, she might make a concrete decision regarding her loyalties. At this point, should she be stripped of her memories and leanings, Nautas may still think he could turn her. The dark man may still think he had a chance to convince her that his way was more…logical, that his way was more…safe. Nautas was certainly adept at twisting the truth.

Annalynn knew Alexine would make a better choice than she herself had made. And when Alexine was fully informed, and made that decision with all facts presented…Well, if the girl was still at the academy, and if the academy was still under the dark man's control, Nautas would destroy her. No question. Her only options to keep Alexine safe were to hide her from Nautas, or to prevent her from learning too much.

Annalynn sighed, then softened noticeably. "I want to show you something. I want to share something with you."

"Share?" Alexine was confused at the abrupt change in subject.

The older woman stood and walked around her desk, taking a seat in the chair opposite her young charge. Their chairs.

"Yes. Share."

The younger woman shook her head in confusion. "Share what?" she asked. Annalynn's hands were empty, there was nothing in the vicinity.

"Share who I am…where I have come from…why I am here." Annalynn needed someone to understand, to sympathize with her decision. If she did not make it out of the academy, she wanted a piece of her to survive, to live on and explain her change of heart to Branch. She needed him to know. Annalynn had already thought it through. This information was personal, it in no way implicated Alexine. Nautas would discount it as the sentimental ramblings of an emotional woman, should he procure it, nothing more.

Alexine was perplexed, but felt she should remain quiet. Something personal, almost sacred filled the space between she and Annalynn. The older woman looked into Alexine's eyes and said two words, so softly Alexine had to concentrate to hear. "Read me."

Chapter Thirty-four
The Cultural Revolution

August 1966
Peking, China

Grasping hands, the room began spinning around the two women. From a blur, the scene abruptly changed and Alexine found herself in what appeared to be an apartment, although it was sparse.

"Come away from the window!" hissed a middle-aged woman who sat cowering in a worn chair in the corner of a small, dusky room. The sun was setting, withdrawing its warmth and light, and a muted blue hue settled over the room. It was, perhaps, early evening.

Raucous chanting outside readily penetrated the tiny dwelling and made Alexine nervous in its intensity and ferocity. Bouncing off walls, it seemed to surround them making escape impossible.

"Away from the window, now!"

A slender teenage girl who had been crouching below the window and sneaking peeks periodically by raising herself up slightly so that only the top of her head was exposed to the outside, reluctantly obeyed, mesmerized by what was occurring in the street.

"Yes mama," she replied morosely.

The woman in the corner scowled and shook her head. The pulsing fear emanating from the woman made Alexine nervous and jittery. Both women jumped when someone hammered on their door. "BAM! BAM! BAM!" The demanding pounding was followed by a harsh command. It was a man's voice, hoarse and gruff.

"Open the door now!"

Shaking, the older woman approached the entry and turned the knob slowly.

Suddenly the room was full of screaming people; they appeared to be teenagers, or perhaps in their very early twenties. Older boys and girls dressed in official-looking dark green pants and jackets, with white cloth hiding the lower parts of their faces and a red armband which contrasted sharply with the forest colored coat. Wide, leather belts cinched their jackets at the waist completing the imposing picture. Mother and daughter were shoved violently to the floor, forced into a kneeling position.

"Search for contraband!" barked a angry-looking young man who seemed to be the ring leader.

Trying to follow the intruders into adjacent rooms, Alexine felt herself tethered to the original space; held prisoner by an unseen cord that impeded her ability to wander too far.

"Intellectual scum!" the leader screamed at the older woman at his feet.

Excited whoops sounded from other rooms in the house. Alexine's heart sank. Obviously these thugs found what they were searching for, she thought, fearful for the women huddled like animals. A pock-marked boy marched into the room, dropping an armful of books, pictures and articles of clothing haphazardly on the floor next to the kneeling woman.

"Well, well…" The leader searched through the confiscated items, tossing them into a pile. Books of poetry, paintings, photographs, pottery, and articles of clothing were being mounded on the floor by various intruders parading in and out of the room. Alexine was surprised and perplexed by what these terrorists considered "contraband."

The search lasted at least thirty minutes. Sounds of furniture being over-turned, cloth being ripped and drawers being rummaged filled the living quarters as the helpless victims whimpered and shook. The time it took to search the house surprised Alexine; the home in which she found herself was quite small. Guards kept entering the room, dropping items at their leader's feet, then disappearing again to continue the pillage. Finally all was quiet and everyone had assembled back in the living room.

"Liu Jian-Ping!" the young commander screamed.

The older woman cowering on the floor raised her head only slightly and whispered a petrified and tiny, "yes?"

"We have come to help you tonight!" He laughed as he spoke and his comrades snickered in reply. "You have lost your way. We have come this evening to encourage you to reform yourself! Do you understand?" The words tumbled out methodically, as if spoken many times, to many people, in similar circumstances. They were harsh, angry criticisms, full of audacity and egotism. Alexine found herself becoming more and more angry at this injustice and insensitivity.

"yes," squeaked the terrified woman.

"What we have done here is a good thing; good for you, good for your country, good for this *daughter* to see."

The word "daughter" drolled out, insolent and obscene, and the older woman's eyes widened in fear. Alexine's skin crawled, as Liu Jian-Ping held her gaze steady, affixing her stare on the floor below where she huddled. Out of fear and horror, Alexine inadvertently followed suit, watching the boy now from the corner of her eye. The leader approached the younger girl and stroked her head. She shrunk down even further, recoiling from his touch. Her reaction clearly irritated him and he retaliated by grabbing a fist-full of dark, shiny hair. Pulling downward he forced her to look up at him. She diverted her eyes, and he laughed again, releasing her.

"It is time to purge our country of devils; feudalists, revisionists, capitalists. You agree?"

"yes."

The leader placed a foot on the table next to him and kicked it over. "It is time to purge our country of the old! Yes?"

"yes."

"It is time for change!"

"yes."

The boy seemed to be running out of things to say, as if his part in this travesty had been scripted and his lines were drawing to a close.

"Let's go!" he yelled to his cohorts. Several of them gathered the confiscated items and shoved them into large cloth bags. They disappeared as quickly as they had arrived, leaving the door ajar behind them. As their riotous laughter filled the street below, then slowly faded as they marched away, Alexine thought she might be sick.

She watched the young girl crawl to her mother, sobbing. Liu Jian-Ping seemed rooted to the spot, not sure if it was safe to move or even glance around. When her daughter's hand met her knee, she jumped then savagely grabbed the child and held her close, both women weeping and shaking in fear. Alexine found her arms wrapped around herself, protecting an unseen person in a fierce embrace.

"BAM! BAM! BAM!"

Alexine turned toward the door, aghast regarding what might enter the little room next. She scowled, something was wrong. The door was still partly open, and the two women continued to cling to each other in terror. They seemed not to have noticed the knock.

"BAM! BAM! BAM!"

Glancing around, she searched for the source of the intrusive noise. The women on the floor were still undaunted by the forceful rapping.

"BAM! BAM! BAM!"

The room spun quickly and Alexine splayed her legs to prevent herself from falling out of her chair. "What was that?" asked Alexine, confused and astonished. The brightness of her surroundings contrasted markedly with the darkened room she had just occupied, causing her to shield her eyes.

Annalynn whipped around and drew her index finger to her pursed lips in a shushing gesture. The same annoying "BAM... BAM...BAM..." filled the room. Someone was beating on the office door.

"Yes Devin?" Annalynn said evenly, cracking the door only several inches.

"I need to see you in the hall," he responded, just as detached. When the woman gave him an irritated glance, he smirked. "Wouldn't want your amazing student in there to hear something she would be better off not knowing."

Annalynn opened the door reluctantly and stepped over the threshold. The door clicked shut softly behind her.

"Just wanted to let you know," Devin began, obviously annoyed at her disrespect, "that Nautas will be here soon. No one is to know," he said swiftly, shooting a look toward Annalynn's office door and the girl seated just inside. The jocular man gave her a fiendish grin, "and he said you had better be prepared."

"Since when does Nautas send messages through you, Devin?" Annalynn questioned coolly.

The grin spread more fully across the large man's face. He shrugged non-committally and turned to leave. "*Very* soon Anna," he tossed back over his shoulder. "I would make sure my allegiance was set in stone by the time he returns."

Her allegiance? Her allegiance was being called into question? Annalynn closed the door reflectively. There were two people who knew about her change of heart. The young girl sitting several feet away, and Bethia. One of them had betrayed her. The third scenario: Bethia was on Nautas's payroll.

"What's going on?" asked Alexine.

"Nothing," answered Annalynn smiling. She tossed a annoyed look toward the door. "You know Devin." The older woman sighed. "Now...where were we?"

Devin's interruption had forced the recent vision out of Alexine's mind momentarily. At once, it sprang back, begging to be examined and discussed.

"Oh yea!" So keen was her interest in the scene Annalynn had just shared, all thought of Devin fled. It's pull pale in comparison to what she had just witnessed. "What the heck was that?"

"My mother," replied Annalynn softly. "The young girl was my mother, Zi-Hong. The other was my grandmother, her name was Liu Jian-Ping."

A little crease formed between Alexine's eyes. It deepened as Alexine fought to make sense of what her instructor had just said. "Your mother…and grandmother?" she repeated slowly, her mind spinning with the implications of this experience.

"It was anamnesis," Annalynn remarked thoughtfully. "A way of remembering."

"A-nam-ne-sis?" Alexine replied, trying the word out for size. "A-nam-ne-sis."

Annalynn chuckled, "yes. You see, I have descended from a long line of readers." Annalynn paused to see if Alexine wanted to ask a question. The young lady stared at her steadily, so she continued. "It is tradition in my family for each daughter who is born a reader to read her mother." Again, the older woman paused, again her invitation was met by silence. "This is a way of remembering. As each daughter reads their mother, they are able to witness seminal events in the lives of each reader in our family line. Because my mother read my grandmother, and my grandmother read my great-grandmother, and…"

"You have experienced what generations of your ancestors lived through." It was said with a tone of wonder and amazement. "Through your maternal line," she added analytically after a moment.

"Well, yes and no." Annalynn rolled her eyes upward, staring at the ceiling as if searching for words. Her gaze fell back on Alexine. "When you read someone, you can, of course, see what that person saw, you can witness the event."

Alexine nodded somberly. She was all too aware of that fact. The angry-red, scared face of the man in the market flashed before her, unannounced and uninvited. She shuttered. Would she ever be able to control its appearance? It interrupted her thoughts periodically, with no invitation, no warning.

"But, if I were to feel or actually experience what, potentially, hundreds of woman felt throughout their lives…"

"You would loose your mind," finished Alexine when Annalynn paused to allow the younger woman time to complete the thought.

The reading instructor nodded somberly, raising her eyebrows and pursing her lips slightly. "It is actually difficult to 'experience' a read. When you are first learning, you simply 'witness' what occurred. Only later are you able to 'experience,' to an extent. And then, you must be very careful to protect yourself from emotional overload. You must control how far you allow yourself to go into the read. You must be able to pull back from the vision." The older woman glanced to her right as if, again, searching for words. "This is especially useful in cases where you are reading someone who possesses thoughts and emotions you do not want carved forever in your mind."

Lost deep in thought, Alexine replied, "mmm," almost automatically. What Annalynn was telling her illuminated a dark room in which she had hidden fears regarding her reading ability. After the marketplace fiasco, she had been petrified to read another person. The pain of the injury, the overwhelming sorrow when his daughter had been ripped from his grip, the betrayal of his wife, the society that shunned him; it was almost too much for one man to endure. Even a taste of those experiences was overwhelming to a tender young woman, inexperienced in such agony. Was it possible to witness something too deeply? It was a question she asked herself ever since that experience, so she posed it now. "Could I 'witness' something too much? I mean, without actually 'experiencing' it?"

Her instructor smiled. "Sure. There are nuances to every read, and differences exist from one reader to the next. You take yourself into every read."

"I would hope so," replied Alexine, grinning at the obvious statement.

"What I mean is, all of us are different. All of us are shaped by three things: our heredity, our experience, and our choices. What we *take into* each read affects how we *perceive* each read. The person we are shapes how we think, feel, and react to each read."

Alexine pulled a perplexed face.

"Okay," Annalynn tried again, "you are an understanding, sympathetic person who has been taught to care about others. So, when you go into a heart-wrenching read, you feel sad. Right?"

"Definitely," came the quick answer.

"Well," continued the instructor, "some people are not sympathetic. Some people glory in other's suffering. So, the same read would have no effect on them at all. In fact, they might enjoy it."

"Ohhhhh," replied the girl, scrunching her face as if she had just smelled something rotten.

"When you go into a read, you can not change the experience at all; it's in the past. But, what you come away with varies incredibly from person to person. This reaction is always different. And so, in a way, each read is fluid. *It* doesn't change, but how it *affects* others, and thus how it *affects* the *future*, varies incredibly. These experiences, Alexine, echo through time, rippling into our reality through us. Through readers."

The young lady paused, trying to take in the ramifications of this information.

Pleased Alexine seemed to be considering this matter carefully, Annalynn waited for the girl to process and ask more questions.

"So," asked the young reader slowly, "when does 'witnessing' turn into 'experiencing'"?

Her teacher smiled, "when it does."

Although the answer seemed ludicrous, Alexine was already nodding her head and smiling knowingly. "Yea. True. You just eventually get there."

"Exactly."

"Annalynn?"

"Yes?"

"If I was a person who didn't care about anyone, if I was a person who enjoyed seeing other people suffer, could I 'experience' things all the time? It wouldn't affect me at all, would it? I wouldn't have to 'witness' anything, I could just jump right in every time, right?"

The smile faded from Annalynn's face as Nautas swept into her thoughts. As far as she knew, he 'experienced' every read which was shared with him, or, every read he stole. And, although he could sense dread, fear, torment and anguish, she was unsure he even processed these emotions anymore. Did he just ignore them? Or did he actually enjoy them now? "Yes, Alexine," she finally replied. "Someone like that could jump in with both feet and it wouldn't affect them at all."

"I have one more question then," the girl said.

Annalynn raised her eyebrows, reluctantly inviting Alexine to continue.

"Do you know anyone like that?"

Taking in an uncomfortable breath, Annalynn replied, "I hope not...so...anyway...what did you think of my grandmother's experience? My anamnesis?" she asked, not wishing to dwell on the man or his methods any longer.

Annalynn's discomfort was contagious, and Alexine pushed her question away, now sorry she had brought it up. "Wow," was all she could think to say. It was as if she had just watched a very compelling movie; her emotions still ran high from the experience.

"Yes...wow," mimicked Annalynn, pleased Alexine appreciated how important this was to her, how personal. Annalynn became somber as she pondered upon several of the situations she had witnessed during her anamnesis. "The experiences all these woman have..." she searched for the word. Endured? Yes. Suffered? Yes. The horrors, hardships and difficulties many of them had not survived; it was all a part of who she was, bound inexorably to the sordid history of her country. It would help Alexine understand the reasons why Annalynn had made certain decisions. Annalynn ached for Alexine to comprehend this, to truly know her, to bare record. Jerked back to the present, the older woman was startled to note her eyes filling with tears. She shook her head and laughed lightly. "I'm afraid many of the memories are not happy ones."

"What happened next? In the a-nam-ne-sis." Alexine said the word awkwardly, still attempting to master its pronunciation. "What happened after those people left?"

Lost in her own recollections, Annalynn spent several seconds digesting Alexine's question. As realization dawned on the older woman, she nodded her head slowly and smiled sadly. "My grandmother was sent away to reform herself soon after, and my mother was banished to the countryside, to make her understand hardship and work. To make her appreciate what the peasants endured."

Alexine moaned dejectedly, picturing the poor, terrified girl abandoned, and alone.

"But that is another, very involved story which will have to wait until tomorrow."

"Why did those people do that?" Alexine demanded, suddenly angry. "Why would they act like that?"

"The Cultural Revolution was a difficult time in China." Annalynn's response was measured and thoughtful.

"What did *that* have to do with *culture*?"

Annalynn blinked. The inconsistency of the term had never hit her so forcefully. What did that have to do with culture? "Nothing at all. That is merely what they called the movement...the Cultural Revolution."

Alexine's irritated look, in response to the illogical use of the word "culture" gradually melted into sorrow. "I felt so bad for the girl and the woman."

"I know," replied Annalynn softly. "I know."

"There was nothing we could do, right?"

The instructor flashed the younger girl a puzzled look. "Of course not," she replied, concerned. "You can't change a read, it happened in the past Alexine, many years ago, it's over."

"I feel guilty anyway," whispered Alexine, diverting her eyes as if trying to hide a dirty secret. "You know, for sitting there and not doing anything."

Annalynn frowned. Impossible. Alexine couldn't have "experienced" the vision, she was untrained in such things. "Still," thought Annalynn, "better play it safe."

"Alexine, where were you during the anamnesis?" Although the two women had been in the room together, Annalynn often became so enthralled with what her ancestors endured, she was only vaguely aware of her surroundings.

Alexine thought for a moment. "I was in the room, with you," she answered slowly, narrowing her eyes in thought. "I tried to leave once, to follow those people, but I couldn't move away from the room."

"Yes," replied Annalynn, not surprised. "But you were just standing in the room the whole time?"

"Uh huh," answered Alexine tentatively, confused by this line of questioning.

"You never got near the woman or the girl?"

"No."

"You're sure?"

"Anna, you were in the room with me." Alexine replied, slightly exasperated and surprised by the questions.

Annalynn smiled. "Sometimes I don't pay much attention, and sometimes sensing another reader can be challenging."

"I was standing next to you the whole time," answered Alexine firmly.

"I want you to stay away from the people in the anamnesis, you understand?"

"Why?"

"We talked about 'witnessing' and 'experiencing.'"

Alexine nodded her head quickly, wanting this lesson to draw to a close so that, perhaps, she could see more of these life stories.

"The way readers experience, instead of witness, is by actually allowing themselves to become part of the individual who originally shared the anamnesis. Does that make sense?"

"Kind of."

"I don't want you to get too close to the person who recorded any experience yet. Let's just keep you clear of them. If you inadvertently slipped into an 'experience'..." Annalynn didn't want to finish her thought. She had seen people go mad dealing with emotions surrounding certain histories. "You're young, and unversed in tragedy. We don't want you going into overload. Do you see why feeling too much of what they felt could be very bad?"

Still struggling to deal with the strong emotions of the anamnesis, Alexine answered quickly, "yes, yes I do." Alexine was so afraid, and yet so angry about the encounter, she was not sure quite where to put her feelings. She did not even want to *imagine* experiencing even more of what that poor girl or her mother went through.

Annalynn seemed satisfied. "Good. So, we're going to..."

"... stay away from the main character," finished Alexine, succinctly. "But I thought you said 'experiencing' took practice."

"So does reading. Yet, as soon as I gave you a mere overview of reading, you did it by accident." Annalynn smiled sardonically.

"Okay, just in case, steer clear of people in the anamnesis," her head bounced once for effect. "So…" Alexine implored, "can I see more?"

Annalynn smiled. "How about tomorrow?"

A pouty frown stole across the young girl's face.

"Tomorrow Alexine."

"But…"

"Tomorrow."

Chapter Thirty-five
Making the Decision

Devin left Annalynn's office and set his course for the gymnasium. Pushing open the double doors, he waved the instructor, Elizabeth, over.

"I need to talk to Callan," he said shortly. When the older woman hesitated, he added an irritated, "now."

Elizabeth crossed the floor and approached the young girl with blond streaks running through her red hair. She whispered something and Callan glanced around. Catching Devin's eye, she bounded over, breathless.

"Yes sir?" she asked respectfully, pulling up quickly in front of him.

Her wide stance, and the way she grasped her hands behind her back, made her look like a miniscule soldier; his soldier. He liked that: a student who knew their place. His decision was sound, Callan would make a fine addition to his army. Young? Yes. But strong, sure and devoted to him. Devin smirked, inwardly congratulating himself on his keen sense of instinct. He knew the girl was promising from the moment he laid eyes on her.

"Come," he said officially, leading the way out of the large room. The pair ascended the steps and turned right. Once seated in his office, Devin came to the point quickly. "You and Alexine are slated to leave in two days."

As her sister's name was mentioned, Devin glanced sideways, his eyebrows raising abruptly. He said "Alexine" as if she were a joke; something almost too unimportant to mention. The slight irritated Callan, but dismissing Devin's insults had become almost instinctual over the last month.

The little girl seated in front of him nodded slowly, her look unreadable. "You are aware of my interest in you, as a shifter."

Callan tried to suppress a grin, but found herself unable to do so. "Have I been training well?" She could think of nothing better to say.

"I think you already know the answer to that question little one." The large man flashed her an impatient yet playful look.

Callan smiled self-consciously and shifted uncomfortably in her chair at the obvious compliment.

"Have you thought about postponing your departure and making a serious commitment to the academy?" Devin gave her a knowing smile. "Full access, me as your mentor." The room turned uncomfortably silent, which surprised Devin. Where was the self-assured child he had been keeping a steady eye on over the past weeks?

When the question was posed, Callan's eye twitched in surprise. Surely not! She was too young to be given this opportunity. Although Elizabeth and the other group of shifters with whom she spent most of her time often discussed the implications of "making the decision" Callan had always assumed that honor was reserved for older shifters; shifters with more experience, surely not someone so young! The expectant look on Devin's face told Callan otherwise. The longer she remained quiet, the more uncomfortable Devin became. It was definitely time to move forward, time for her to make the decision. It was what they had been waiting for! But explaining this to Alexine was not going to be easy. After what seemed like an eternity of quiet, Callan smiled. "I would be honored, sir."

The tomb-like stillness that gripped the room flashed away as Devin brought his right hand down hard on his desk. SMACK! "I knew it!" he said, emphasizing the word "knew" with enthusiasm.

It was almost as if her hesitation had frightened him, and the ensuing relief, when she accepted, erupted uncontrollably. Callan flinched at the outburst. This was Devin; roller-coaster emotions and outbursts.

"The first time I saw you...I just knew," he said intensely, pointing at her with a jerk of his hand as if to emphasize his amazing foresight. The large man squinted at her, examining Callan closely, seeing through to the innermost workings of her mind. "I just knew," he whispered.

Five minutes later, when she re-entered the gymnasium, her heart still threatened to beat out of her chest. She was to meet Devin after lunch.

"So?" questioned Elizabeth when they entered the instructor's office during a break from training. John and several of the others had joined them to catch up on the latest news.

Callan waited, looking like the cat that swallowed the canary. She allowed the suspense to build until everyone was seated either on chairs, Elizabeth's desk, or the floor.

Finally John gave her an annoyed look and a jab in the ribs. "Spill it fireball," he threatened, playfully grinning.

"He..." she began, looking slowly around the room.

A collective groan ensued when she paused, toying with them.

"Callan," corrected Elizabeth sternly, "let's hear it."

"Sorry," the little girl said sheepishly, "it's kind of a habit." She made the announcement with no fanfare. "He asked me to join; full access."

You could have heard a pin drop, as if the lack of lead-up to those seven words threw the group off balance. Smiles and expectant looks disappeared in an instant, replaced by shock, concern and fear. Several people whispered quietly to their neighbor.

"What did she say?"

"Did you hear her?"

"Join?"

Elizabeth was silent and still, her expression un-readable. "It couldn't be true," she thought to herself. "Even Devin's not that that irresponsible." One look into Callan's eyes told her differently. And somewhere inside, she admitted, the truth was she *hoped* he wasn't that irresponsible. "He would do it," she relented. Elizabeth began connecting pieces of evidence, putting them into place to interpret the bigger picture.

Annalynn would never have allowed such an invitation to be extended, which indicated Devin was now operating alone. What would Nautas think of that? Annalynn must not know yet. There would be heck to pay when she made this discovery. Annalynn would have a raging fit! More concerning: devoid of Annalynn's steadying hand, what other impulsive decisions would Devin make? Nautas would not let things get too out of hand, would he? Elizabeth didn't know what to say. It was what they had all discussed, what they were hoping for: one of their number to be invited. But Callan? The infelicitous invitation Devin extended was an affront to Elizabeth's sense of propriety. She was torn now. The little shifter was just a baby.

Lost in her thoughts, the shifting teacher abruptly realized Callan was staring at her, looking to her for approval and support. Surrounded by the older teenagers and young adults in the room, the little girl seemed even tinier, her slight build emphasized by their size and maturity. Elizabeth sunk her nails into her arms in an effort to control the tears about to betray her misgivings. So young. So innocent. Forcing a smile, she nodded her head at Callan. The concern that had crept into the little girl's face melted away. As Elizabeth crossed the room, and wrapped Callan in a hug, whispering, "congratulations," into her ear, the rest of the crowd mobbed in around them.

Recalcitrance was swept away as the mood lifted. Elizabeth thought it was alright, her friends supported her, things would be okay. She would still have to deal with Alexine, but she would think about that later.

Laughing and shouting, some eyes sparkled as many high-fived Callan, shook her shoulders in support, or slapped each other on the backs. The room filled with revelry; one of their number had finally penetrated the inner core of the academy. Although many people supported Nautas and his goals, few were invited to join this exclusive group. Full access to the academy; it was a day to celebrate.

* * *

"You WHAT?" demanded Alexine incredulously. She grabbed her little sister's hand and turned it over. There is was; a pinprick like hole, red and angry. The tiny piece of evidence; proof of Callan's betrayal. Alexine sucked in breath and stumbled backward, astonished. "No…no…no…no…no!"

Callan wasn't surprised. She had braced herself for this reaction, expected it. Alexine didn't understand anything. But the young girl was tired, and impatient. The second half of her day had been spent touring the entire academy, even the places of which few people were aware; the basement levels. The technology, the control, it was staggering and completely overwhelming. Although she knew parts of it would be unpleasant, she had not completely prepared herself for the cells. Perhaps she had hoped Devin would hold something back, would wait for her to digest the impressive facets of the organization prior to exposing her to the questionable. But he had not. The prison that held those who dared betray the cause. Their faces haunted her.

The last thing she wanted to do now was argue. "I want to go to sleep," she said steadily, hoping her older sister would save this confrontation for tomorrow. The bewildered look on Alexine's face told her otherwise. She glanced at the bed longingly.

Taking a deep breath, Alexine fought to control her emotions. This was simply not an option, it was not happening. First thing tomorrow, she would go to Devin's office and explain that Callan had changed her mind, simple as that. They were a team, and the two of them were leaving, together. That was the end of it.

And what was *he* thinking? Asking a child to make a monumental decision such as this. Devin would release Callan from this commitment and remove the miniscule chip of metal now invading her little sister's body. The tiny chip betraying Callan's true allegiance; to her family, to Alexine.

As she panicked, distinction between logic and absurdity blurred, making her plans seem sensible. It comforted her. The situation was still fluid, Alexine was still able to alter it. "I am not going to let this happen," Alexine said evenly, working desperately to control her fears, the nightmarish possibilities now twisting and swirling around the two girls ominously.

"*You're* not going to let his happen?" Callan repeated with surprise, then stated simply, "but it's not *your* decision." It was abrupt, final and the little girl walked to her bed. Fetching pajamas, she retraced her steps and entered the bathroom, leaving the door ajar.

"It's really not a big deal." The younger girl's disembodied voice floated out from the adjoining room. "Just some additional training, that's all," she continued, as if discussing something completely innocent, like an innocuous summer camp.

Alexine scowled in disbelief and irritation. This wasn't happening. "And the chip?" she retorted, using all her energy to mimic Callan's calm demeanor.

"Oh, yea, it's dust soo dat I cun..." Callan's mouth filled with suds as she brushed her teeth. Spitting into the sink, she continued, "so that I can get into the building alone. You know, everyone who stays for advanced training has access to the building."

The younger girl failed to mention her particular chip also granted her admittance to the basement levels. Callan was sure Alexine was not privy to any information regarding the bowels of the academy; floor after floor of buried secrets, armies, weapons, plans, and prisoners. Best her older sister remain woefully ignorant of the many facts entrusted to Callan that evening, it was for Alexine's own safety. The depth of this plan, the astounding scope of it, the little girl was still reeling from the sensitive information Devin had so willingly divulged.

Standing up straight, she looked into the mirror and appraised herself for a moment. Was she doing the right thing? "It's a little late for doubts now," she whispered to her reflection. Her twin in the mirror immediately stuck her tongue out in defiance. Bracing herself for the argument she was sure would continue, Callan stepped into the hallway and walked to her bed. Alexine was sitting on the edge of it, transfixed. "Alexine?" Callan waved a hand in front of her older sister's face. "Are you there?"

The older girl smiled sadly. What more could she have done to prevent this? Her mother's words resonated in her mind: "You have to take Callan to China." You. You are in charge. You must protect her. "How could you do this?" Alexine asked softly, "without even talking to me about it?"

These quiet comments unnerved the little girl. She had prepared for a knock-down, drag-out war of words. Not this. Not guilt. She was much more versed at emotionally charged confrontations. Guilt had always been her Achilles heel. "It's nothing personal," she said lightly, climbing into bed. "I just want to stay a bit longer. I'm still coming home."

"When?" asked Alexine in despair. It was more than a question, it was entreaty.

Callan knew deceit was her only chance at pacifying her sister and getting any sleep tonight. "Thirty days," she said smoothly. "Devin and I agreed on thirty days." A bold-faced lie, that was what she had just told, and a whopper at that. Callan's pledge to the triangulum had been life-long. Devin's words rang through her memory.

"This is nothing to be taken lightly...A life long commitment...No way out."

Was that why she had been shown the prison? To impress upon her the dangers of daring to betray Devin? Daring to betray the cause?

The large man's comments regarding Alexine had been ominous also, but not unexpected.

"Not to leave us Callan...She must stay also...You will find out why soon."

The thought of being partner to Alexine's forced imprisonment at the academy made Callan's insides squirm uncomfortably. Signing herself up was one thing, but... She hoped one day Alexine would understand, would forgive her.

"Listen Doones," Callan said, giggling at the nickname Alexine had garnered when she was just a toddler. "I'm so tired. Can we please talk more tomorrow?" When Alexine remained silent, Callan added a retracted and innocent, "pleeaassee?"

"Yea... alright," agreed Alexine, too surprised and exhausted herself to argue, much less think. Sleep would be good, clear both their minds. Tomorrow Alexine would talk Callan out of this madness, and get rid of that chip. What that vile thing was transmitting and receiving, Alexine shuttered to consider.

Chapter Thirty-six
Betrayal

Entering Annalynn's office the next morning, Alexine shuffled to the couch and plopped down awkwardly. She had awoken to find Callan's bed empty.

"Ahhh, yes, leetle one, school, beddy early," the man at the front desk had informed her in heavily accented English, smiling broadly and jerking his head forward repeatedly in a semi-bow. Returning the gesture, she had thanked him and waited on the couch while the bellhop summoned a taxi.

"She did what?!" Annalynn yelled, outraged. "When?" the reading instructor demanded angrily. Without waiting for an answer she hissed, "how much did he tell her?"

"Uhh, yesterday," Alexine answered wide-eyed, surprised by the outburst. "I don't know what he told her, she didn't say anything about that." Alexine stumbled, "uh…just that she was staying for thirty more days to train."

Annalynn walked swiftly to the door, threw it open, and stomped down the hall, her heavy foot falls echoing conspicuously down the empty corridor. Alexine heard her pound furiously on Devin's office door, then gain entry. She suddenly felt wary, surrounded only by lonely silence.

Glancing at the clock, Alexine noted that thirty-three minutes had passed since she was abruptly abandoned by her instructor. Each minute that ticked by increased her concern exponentially. As quickly as haunting images invaded her mind, she willed them away by humming familiar tunes, or readjusting herself on the couch. Forty-two minutes. Forty-eight. Just as she felt inclined to wander down the hall and knock on Devin's door, just as she came up with some silly excuse to interrupt their meeting, Alexine heard Annalynn's heeled boots clicking on the tile in the hall. The clip-clip, clip-clip, clip-clip grew louder and louder as the older woman approached. Alexine sat on the edge of the couch, expectantly.

"He is a certifiable idiot," Annalynn began, slamming the door to the office behind her. "So intent on playing the pet! He's mad!" The instructor paced the floor; so irritated, remaining still was not an option. "He'll be sorry for taking such a foolish chance," she snorted ominously. "How could he possibly think that Nau…" She stopped mid-rant, catching sight of Alexine fretting on the couch.

"We have to get him to take that thing out of her," Alexine said. Catching scent of Annalynn's furor had sparked the younger girl's own sense of urgency. "As soon as possible!"

Annalynn shook her head slowly, refusing to meet Alexine's pleading gaze. She knew her own fear, sorrow and helplessness would be all to apparent if their eyes met. The girl was looking to her for hope that did not exist. "It's too late," Annalynn said quietly. "It's done."

"It's never too late," Alexine countered, standing to emphasize her point, yet feeling that familiar panic that always seemed to concern Callan. "Never."

"Alexine," Annalynn said seriously, "Callan has pledged her life. She's joined the….It's too late."

"No." Alexine shook her head, glancing around at unseen objects floating in the air, as if something would materialize and make all of this a bad dream., or a solution would mysteriously appear and she could grab it, hold it, force it to rectify the situation. "No, it's only thirty more days. You don't understand Annalynn. It's only a little more training. She promised me."

The night before, Alexine had sensed her sister's betrayal, had somehow known she was lying. But the enormity of that deceit was too much to process. She swept away her mistrust, Callan's inveracity, pushing it under the carpet like a pile of dirt and clutter. She hid it where no one could see, where she, herself, would not have to deal with it.

"Anyway…we're going home, we've already got the tickets, we're almost through here. I'll talk to her. She'll change her mind." She knew she was raving, but didn't care. Annalynn failed to understand. They were leaving this place. They were flying home tomorrow, together. "You changed your mind! Callan can change hers too!"

The older woman's face fell. How could she tell Alexine she doubted Nautas would allow her to live once he learned of her betrayal? That she did not plan on leaving the academy at all, but being carried from it? How could she tell her that Callan had crossed a similar line? That she was now in the same boat? That she would not be allowed to leave…unless…

"If you want to go home with your sister tomorrow," said Annalynn, her mind working furiously to form a plan, "you need to talk her out of staying. *If* you can convince her to go," she continued, "we *might* be able to get you both out before he arrives, before he finds out what Devin has done." She left her last thought unspoken: "but it's a long shot."

Nodding her head somberly, Alexine wondered what she could say, how she could convince Callan of the danger surrounding her decision.

* * *

Several hours later, down in the lunchroom, Alexine approached the familiar knot of students who occupied all of her little sister's time these days.

"Hey!" said John jovially, lazily chewing on his straw. "Join us!"

Alexine blushed, surprised the young man was happy to see her considering she stood him up not too long ago. He noticed the scarlet color blotching her cheeks and winked at her flirtingly.

"No hard feelings," he whispered as she pulled up a chair beside his. Alexine smiled guiltily, grateful for his chivalry.

Sitting at the end of the table, Callan watched suspiciously as Alexine approached and took a seat. She knew. Alexine had been given additional information. "Probably by Annalynn," thought Callan resentfully. That woman was always throwing a wrench in the works.

Each time Alexine tried to catch Callan's eye, the little girl diverted her gaze intentionally. Although Alexine would have loved to throw herself into any one of the conversations occurring around the table, she had to talk to Callan as soon as possible. Just when she thought she might miss her chance, when the students began dispersing for their classes, the fiery little girl approached *her*.

"Sorry for leaving this morning," she said, looking at the floor. "I don't want to argue."

"Neither do I," replied Alexine factually. She wasn't going to argue. She had made up her mind. She was going to talk sense into Callan, or else she was going to simply pick her up and force her onto the plane. Alexine had already figured out how to do it. It was an underhanded plan she had formulated easily, and that unnerved her, but only a bit.

Callan had lied to her. LIED! Out-and-out, bold-faced, complete lie! That wasn't done in their family. Lies were not tolerated. The answer was simple. Callan was prone to motion sickness. Their mother had sent medication to help Callan with the incredibly long plane ride. The medication made Callan very, very sleepy. The idea had sprung to mind as Alexine began packing her things. Dramamine: the perfect solution. The little girl would be out like a light.

Taken aback, Callan continued suspiciously, "I thought we could spend the day together tomorrow."

Alexine raised her eyebrows a notch, pursed her lips, and nodded as if to say "not a bad idea."

"You don't leave until late," the younger girl continued hopefully, "so we could see a lot of stuff before your departure time."

Outwardly agreeable, but inwardly conniving, Alexine vehemently, but silently corrected the statements in her own mind. "*WE* don't leave until late. *OUR* departure time."

"So it's a date?" Callan said hopefully.

"Definitely," replied Alexine. "Let's start early. I've read that everything begins before dawn in China. I should see authentic China before I leave." She strained to say "I" instead of "we." Her little sister seemed pleased, but wary. "Smart," thought Alexine. "She's right to mistrust me." Callan had lied to her. The rules had been thrown out the window. Fine. Two could play this game.

* * *

"It's set," Alexine told Annalynn thirty minutes later. "We're going to spend tomorrow together, sightseeing."

Her instructor looked surprised and doubtful. "It was that easy? You talked her out of it that quickly?"

"I'll talk her out of it if I can." Alexine set a hard look on her face. "And if not, I'm going to give her the motion sickness medication she takes and drag her on the plane with me."

Annalynn was perplexed, and her expression reflected her confusion.

"It makes her tired," Alexine explained, "very tired. She'll do anything if she takes it."

Following several moments of processing this plan, Annalynn shook her head and let out a procession of insincere chuckles. "You are a naughty little girl," she wagged an index finger at Alexine, then nodded in concurrence. "But I like it. Difficult times call for difficult measures." It was something Nautas might say; the ends justify the means, but at this point, it didn't matter. "It's a good idea," she finished resolutely, seeing no other way to wrench both Alexine and Callan from the dark man's grasp. "Keep her busy all day. I'm going to follow you. Give her the medication at dinner and I'll take it from there. We'll get you to the airport for your flight."

As long as she could keep Devin busy, which should be an easy task, the two girls could be airborne and on their way before anyone knew what was happening. She would need to alert Branch, so the two could be protected after arriving home. But once Alexine and Callan were clear of the country, once they left the academy, Annalynn could take chances, could contact Branch directly. She would pay for her part in the plan, of course, but what did it matter?

Although Annalynn knew Branch could protect the girls, she held little hope for herself. This wasn't about retaining a talented reader, not in her case. This was personal and Nautas would not take kindly to being betrayed by one of his generals, especially one in whom he had an emotional investment. Annalynn snorted. Well, as much as he was capable of having an "emotional investment" anyway. She cleared these thoughts from her mind. She needed to do as much good as she could, before the end.

"I'm glad that's taken care of because I would like to show you a few more things today," the older woman said. "I mean… if you're interested."

Annalynn's wistful tone surprised Alexine. Coming up with a plan to get Callan home had occupied Alexine's every thought since last night. She had pushed what Annalynn had shown her yesterday to the back burner. Her stomach dropped as she realized her teacher was offering to allow her back into the past, back into her memories. The younger woman's mind quickly jumped to the possibility of viewing more of the visions. She felt that, since experiencing the emotions entangled in the episode, she needed to see more, required closure.

"Come," invited Annalynn, motioning her to take a seat. "We have some time left. This will be our last training session together."

Alexine started. That fact, too, had escaped her. Departing China also meant leaving Annalynn behind. Suddenly her heart ached.

"Let's get started," the older woman said, interrupting Alexine's train of thought, as though able to see the separation approaching and unwilling to acknowledge it yet. It was going to be painful.

As they grasped hands, tears sprung to the instructor's eyes. Looking up, the emotion on Alexine's face mirrored her own. The two of them began spinning slowly, not dropping their gaze, each wanting to commit the other's features to memory. It was a melancholy dance, the last hours they would share together.

Chapter Thirty-seven
A Muddy Grave

The little home had changed. Several items were missing, but that was not what caught Alexine's attention. The room had been filled with fear yesterday, when she and Annalynn visited. Terror. Now it seemed permeated by sadness. A hunched old woman entered the room, her tiny feet scuffing as they dragged quickly across the floor in very short steps. The young girl whom Alexine now knew was Annalynn's mother, Zi-Hong, was sitting in the corner. Alexine examined the girl, trying to interpret what she was thinking, what she was feeling. Her look was indecipherable.

"There, there," the old woman consoled, approaching the young girl. "Courage."

Zi-Hong tilted her face up to meet her grandmother's gaze. "My father is gone, my mother is gone, and now I go. What will become of you?"

The old woman slowly dropped to the floor beside the girl and smiled softly, her eyes crinkled with sadness. "Me? Since when has anyone had to take care of me? Anyway, your mother will be home soon. I visited the reform center yesterday. She will be liberated shortly, I know it."

"How can you be sure?" The question hung in the air, awkward and unanswered as the girl dropped her gaze to the floor in understanding. "Nothing is sure," she whispered. "One day I think I understand what my country expects of me," the girl shook her head, her eyes squinting their confusion, "but it seems that what is good and right changes. How can that be? Good does not change, right does not change, yet, all around me, these concepts vary. What will 'correct thought' be tomorrow? Surely it will be different than it is today." The girl heaved a defeated sigh. "It seems what is deemed right changes too quickly."

"Shhh," grandmother hushed, glancing around nervously. "You must promise me child," she began worriedly, "that you will not speak like this when you arrive in the country. Promise me."

Betrayal flitted across the girl's features.

"I would never tell you to stop thinking," the old woman corrected soothingly. "Thought and reason are always good, never believe them if they tell you differently." Concern crossed grandmother's face. "But that does not mean you have to voice those opinions right now. It is not safe to speak, and you need to live. You need to witness and bear record."

The implications of this plea flew through the Zi-Hong's mind and she nodded understandingly. "To witness and bear record."

"Your sacrifices will not be in vain," the old woman promised knowingly. "And you are stronger than you know. Come now. I want to share something."

Grandmother grasped the young girl's hands and looked deeply into her eyes. "I'm going to show you, before you leave."

The young girl jumped, reclaimed her hands, then shook her head emphatically. "No, mama will do it."

"My dear," grandmother said solemnly, "when you two are together again, perhaps she will share more. But I am an old woman, and everything is so unpredictable." She did not want to say the words, did not want to give the possibilities any more power than they already possessed. I may be dead. Your

- 183 -

mother may be sent away; taken from this city and forced to perform hard labor in the countryside. You, yourself may never return from the countryside. These eventualities, though unspoken, were none the less understood.

Zi-Hong considered the offer for a few moments, mulling over the implications of her decision. Taking the old woman up on her suggestion would, in a way, be admitting the worst could happen. She pushed that thought from her mind. She was leaving, nothing was certain anymore, and she needed to begin making choices as an adult. Her childhood had been swept away during the last few years, one of many casualties in a social movement gone horribly wrong.

"Yes," she said decidedly. "Yes, you are right." If the time came that she could learn more from her mother, it would be welcome. But preserving what she could of her family's lengthy history, despite the anguish it entailed, was paramount. She was the last in a long line of gifted readers. Losing all of those experiences, simply because she was too childish to accept reality, would truly be selfish. "Yes, of course grandmother," she answered firmly. "I would be honored to see everything."

Alexine was caught up as the room began slowly circling, like a circus ride they had all paid money to experience. Both thrilling and nauseating, edifying and terrifying, compelling, it called to them, beckoning them to witness its intricacies and gauge its importance.

Alexine glanced around quickly as scenes flashed around her. This was very different than the other visions she had witnessed. Jumbled and confused, people and places appeared and were gone in an instant as if someone were fast-forwarding a long and complicated movie. Alexine reached forward, moving toward the scenes materializing, then disappearing, before her eyes; lost unless she was somehow able to grasp and hold them, make them her own. She yearned to witness these people's lives, the essence of who they were and would become. A strong hand snatched at the back of her shirt. Grasping hold it pulled her back sharply.

"What happened?" asked Alexine, stung with disappointment. "Why didn't we go back with them?" As soon as the words left her mouth, she blushed, surprised at their veracity.

"Today we see my grand-mother's life, Liu Jian-Ping." The instructor's eyes again filled with a wistfulness that saddened Alexine. "We can not traipse through hundreds of experiences." Her words, though smoothly spoken, threatened to crack with emotion. "Know this; my mother was shown our family history that day. Everything, everyone, back hundreds and hundreds of years." Annalynn's words did not calm the younger girl. Quite the opposite, they seemed to make her more pensive. "It is a tribute to my mother's strength; seeing so much at one time. Considering her own frame of mind, it should have been overwhelming."

Alexine's disappointed expectancy deepened with each word Annalynn spoke. Hundreds and hundreds of years of memories. Part of who Annalynn was and is. It must have been quite apparent that she longed to view these recollections because Annalynn's next comment was tentative and apologetic.

"I'm sorry. Perhaps another day we will delve further into those experiences."

Alexine lowered her eyes to the floor. After tomorrow, would she ever see Annalynn again? She wanted to understand her instructor, wanted to be a part of Annalynn's life by experiencing her past, wanted to finish what she had begun.

It felt as though she were sitting at the piano and her parents had told her to get ready for bed. She had to finish the song she was playing. It didn't matter how fast and how poor the performance became. Just finishing it, that brought an end, and getting to that end was important. She had no idea why, but her brain took over and screamed at her, demanding her to complete the task. That unfulfilled feeling, that sense of not wrapping up something she had begun, filled her mind now.

"Come now," Annalynn said encouragingly, taking particular note of how much stopping mid-vision upset her young pupil. Alexine was a worker, she needed to tie up loose ends. Interesting. For all the time they had spent together, Annalynn noted she had not been recording details regarding the young lady's traits and tendencies; information which would give others valuable insight regarding how Alexine was to be used in Nautas's bid for power, how to control and manipulate her. Annalynn smiled rebelliously, no report on this girl. Alexine would be gone and safe when the master of the academy returned.

"If we don't get started," the instructor began, glancing at her watch, "we won't be able to get through another portion of my grandmother's anamnesis." Annalynn knew it was not the vision which would take time, indeed, it would occur in seconds. Milliseconds. But internalizing the emotions, the feelings each vision generated, especially *this* vision, would be difficult and she did not wish to rush.

Alexine heard herself repeating familiar words. "Yes, you're right." She smiled guiltily at the congruity.

"What I am going to show you tonight is something that happened prior to the vision you have already seen."

Alexine nodded her head in acknowledgement.

"Come."

Once again, Annalynn and Alexine locked eyes, joined hands, and the room began whirling around them.

At the moment Alexine thought she would be sick from the prolonged spinning, a flash of light released her from the grip of movement, and the scene stopped abruptly. The breath Liu Jian-Ping sucked into her lungs became Alexine's breath and the two women stumbled out of the dirty hovel, its thatched roof heavy with damp mildew and moss.

"Cai-fa?" she mumbled hoarsely. "Cai-fa?" Alexine's brain was fuzzy and slow. Her stomach cramped uncomfortably, each step a new experience in pain. Trying to pull back, the young girl found the attempt hampered by an overwhelming feeling of exhaustion. All hope, all happiness had been sucked from the earth, leaving her wallowing in a vacuum whose only other occupant was misery.

She stumbled through the courtyard, the cobblestone walls separating her living area from the others was crumbling. They had built it together; stacked and mudded rock after rock. It symbolized their lives, their hopes, for themselves, for their country. It was disintegrating before her eyes. Her tired, bare feet met hard, packed dirt as she moved. One more step, just one more step.

Leaning heavily on the wall to catch her breath, she raised her gaze painfully. The men and women returning from the fields swarmed lethargically into the village. Following a crooked path, like worker ants, they mindlessly followed the person in front of them. No one looked in her direction. Living skeletons, they shuffled forward, only able to focus on the next step, and the next, slowly dragging to their homes prior to collapsing. A man stumbled. Losing his footing, he hit the ground clumsily; a jumble of skinny limbs, protruding elbows and knees, and worn, ripped clothing. His breath came in short, shallow gulps. No one broke stride. No one turned back to help. There was nothing they could do. Alexine and Liu Jian-Ping dropped to their knees, approaching the man at a crawl.

"Cai-fa?" she whispered upon reaching him. The man was still and silent; Gone; released from the torturous life which had been forced upon him. Alexine and grandmother envied him in a way, wanted to lie down and join him, tired of fighting, tired of suffering, tired.

"Cai-fa."

Lacking the strength and ability to do more, the women crawled down the path the production team had just traveled. Dust filled their eyes and mouth and the women blinked rapidly, too exhausted to wave the haze away. Rocks cut small slices into their legs and hands and pebbles clung to their flesh, yet they kept moving, kept moving.

After what seemed like a lifetime of groveling on all fours, Alexine and Jian-Ping found themselves back in the fields. They scanned the land searching for Cai-fa. Spotting a heap of dark clothing several hundred yards away, grandmother and Alexine rose. Managing unsteady footing, they slopped through the flooded field toward what they hoped was not Cai-fa.

The person was face down, partially submerged in the water trickling into the field. Despair griped the women as they tried to pull the mound into an upright position. Failing miserably, all three fell haphazardly into the water. The man's head lolled to the side, then came to rest against his shoulder. His sunburned, blank face looked through them, unseeing.

"Not Cai-fa," they whispered. Relief washed over them, renewing a fraction of their strength. "It's not my husband," they sobbed together.

Alexine's mouth was moving, and the words were emanating not only from the emaciated woman, but from her own lips. A bizarre duet, sung in panting sing-song Mandarin, yet completely comprehendible. The man they pulled from the water now faced upward, but began sinking slowly down into the flooded field once again, his gaze transfixed, gone. So tired.

Rising again, the women looked over the field and realized for the first time there were many piles of clothing scattered over the acreage. Bundled tombstones demarking the final resting place of the unfortunate. So many lost; there was no hope left in this place, it had abandoned them long ago.

A low, droning moan to their left sounded from a hundred yards away as a blur of blue came to life, flailing in its attempt to stand. The two women approached, staggering.

"Cai-fa?" Not a question, a plea, they could not survive alone. They needed him. The man turned toward them deliberately.

"Cai-fa!" A sense of euphoria filled the women as they whispered hoarsely, moving forward, their feet sticking in thick mud. He was alive! Joy replaced despair as they threw themselves into his arms and ended up, once again, wallowing in mire. "You're alive. alive." Together, they made their way slowly out of the shallow muck and onto the path leading home. For the moment, all was well; they had lived through another day. They were together, that was the only thing that mattered.

Cai-fa stopped moving, then teetered on calloused feet. His breath came irregularly, as trembling, forced bursts. In the quiet of the stifling summer evening, his gasps of air rattled alarmingly.

"Come," the women coaxed, pulling Cai-fa forward gently. The thin man returned to the ground, slowly sinking to a crouched position as his head dropped and chin met chest.

"No," the women begged, frantically pulling at what was left of his dirty, tattered shirt. "No! We are alive. Get up…please." Hopelessness crept into the exchange, placing a strangle hold on the spark of joy which was now quietly fading. "Please. You can not give up. You can not…"

Cai-fa lowered himself painfully into a resting position, on his side, then smiled up serenely at them. The effect was almost too much to bear. Alexine and grandmother joined him on the ground, kneeling beside him as if tending a wounded creature. "We must go home," the women rambled, half out of their mind. Their face still covered with dust, tears cut clean lines down their cheeks, then splattered on Cai-fa's shirt, speckling him with their sadness. "I will care for you," the women pleaded, tenderly smoothing back his hair, now wet with perspiration. They would not forsake him; as his wife, his lover, and his friend, they had vowed to care for him, to protect him. They could not fail, could not let him die.

"You are strong," the two women began. "They will allow us to return to the city. You will write for the paper again. We will visit friends and walk our daughter to school…together. We will grow old, care for our grand-children."

"Wife," the rasping man interrupted in a whisper. "Take care of Zi-Hong… she must live."

As this pleading last request filled their ears, the women shook their head viciously. "No!" they demanded. "You must not leave me. We will raise our daughter together. You will see…you will see." Tears continued to spill down Alexine and Grandmother's cheeks as their eyes met their husbands. Intense and sure, his gaze said more than words could convey. He needed them to be strong. This was not his doing, not his fault. He wanted to stay, wished to remain, but couldn't…couldn't. He was broken.

Jian-Ping forced herself to concentrate. A wild desire to read her husband filled her. Perhaps that would bring him back. Perhaps her strength could become his. Together they could push back their surroundings, force them away, escape. They could, once more, share thoughts and feelings, hopes and dreams, completely sheltered and protected from this world, from anyone and everything. No one could take that away from them. No one…

But they *could* take that away. They *had* taken that, and so much more. Strangled slowly over the hours, days and months she and Cai-fa had been forced to labor in the fields. They had taken everything; the city in which she was born, her family home, her job, her dreams, and now…her love; her precious husband.

This world had won its battle. She was too exhausted, too beaten, too full of despair to call upon her abilities. When had it happened? When had she lost herself? When had that part of her died?

In anguish, Jian-Ping and Alexine mournfully relented, accepting the horrendous truth. They had lost, had failed. Cai-fa was leaving them, he could not remain. They were going to be completely alone, left to endure a miserable existence with no hope of support, with no one on which to lean, on which to depend. In a few minutes, perhaps even seconds, he would be gone…forever. The women nodded somberly at their husband's final desire; take care of Zi-Hong, raise their daughter, she must live.

Cai-fa's soft smile rubbed salt in their wounded emotions. This would be the last discussion they would have on earth. A sick feeling filled Alexine as she realized that she and Grandmother were leaning forward to embrace Cai-fa for the final time. The young girl's eyes flew open in shock and dread as she shrunk back at the thought of intruding on this deeply personal moment. She closed her eyes in concentration and pulled back hard imagining Annalynn's strong hand at the nape of her neck.

With a soft popping sound, the two women separated and Alexine tipped her head sadly, tears streaming, as she watched grandmother's lips press hard against her husbands. She could not divert her gaze. It was a beautiful, tragic moment whose power seemed to halt time and repel the filth, horror and death surrounding them. For a moment, all was perfect.

They parted and he was gone. Something had left him; an aura of power, thought dim, was now missing. His eyes closed, and his face slackened, relaxing completely. She had never seen it so devoid of tension. so absent. He didn't even look like himself anymore; this was merely a shell.

It was unfair and unholy. Alexine screamed out in retribution, cursing whatever had caused this pain. Grandmother, several years younger and much less burdened and aged than Alexine remembered, lie down next to her husband. Pulling his arm around her, she closed her eyes. She could not forsake him. She would not leave him.

Glancing around Alexine saw Annalynn staring at her steadily, concern written on her features.

"How long have you been experiencing?" the older woman demanded seriously.

Looking around guiltily, Alexine stammered. "I… I don't know."

The brilliant setting sun lent a red tinge to Annalynn, its color emphasizing the older woman's mood. Alexine's attention was beckoned back to the couple laying silent on the ground. The light bathed the lovers in a warm glow, as if to seal them together for one last moment.

Turning her head slightly and squinting her eyes, Alexine realized Annalynn's look required a more specific answer. She thought back quickly. Had any of this vision been viewed from the outside? "I think," she replied tentatively, "from the very beginning."

Chapter Thirty-eight
The Deadly Duty

Grasping Alexine abruptly by the arm, Annalynn and Alexine left the muddy scene quickly, spinning to a stop in Annalynn's office. The older woman stood, shaking her head. "I'm sorry," she said solemnly. "I should have noticed."

Alexine jumped to her feet beside her instructor. "No, it was my fault, I did it...I think...I mean...I must have...right?" Even while these words spilled haphazardly from her lips, Alexine felt strangely detached from the conversationm there were more important things. All of a sudden Alexine felt as if many things she used to find so vital, or so disturbing, had been swept away to make place for things and experiences truly life altering, majestically profound.

Turning on her student, Annalynn whispered seriously, "I told you not to get pulled too far into the visions. I warned you... I warned you..." Her words trailed off.

"I know," answered Alexine, confused at her instructor's intensity. "I know...I just...when we first arrived...I was already... and then..." Alexine took a deep breath and exhaled defeatedly. "I just had to know more." She hung her head, overcome by the strange sensation of immeasurable loss. Something was gone that no one could return, and she was alone. This conversation really did not matter.

"Knowing more is not always a positive thing Alexine!" fired Annalynn sternly. "Don't you understand?"

"No," replied the younger woman softly. "No, I don't understand." A tear trickled down her cheek. "What happened to them? Why did he die? Why didn't anyone help?"

Annalynn approached Alexine and hugged her. As they connected, both teacher and student shook with silent sobs. They stayed that way for a long time, each consoling the other. The affection that had grown between them seemed to enlarge and entangle around them, sheltering the scene from anything which might take thought to intrude. When they parted, they were both wearing the same soft, understanding smile.

"I need to know what happened," said Alexine. Her desire to understand the scene from which they had just returned overwhelmed the sanctity of the moment. She had to speak.

"History, Alexine, is seldom an enjoyable tale. China's past, as with many other countries, is fraught with cruelty, evil, ignorance, fear, intolerance, addiction, confusion, stupidity."

"I think I get the picture," interrupted the younger girl, nodding her head.

"Yes...well...the times my grandmother lived through were no exception. Do you know anything about Chinese history?"

Alexine shook her head. "Very little, I'm afraid." She wiped her eyes on the back of her sleeve.

"It's a shame really," responded Annalynn, expecting to receive that very answer, "few people do." She raised her eyebrows to accentuate her point. "We could avoid so many mistakes, if only we could learn from the past. Why don't we sit down, and I'll give you a short lesson."

The two women moved to the couch. Alexine thought back to the first time she had entered Annalynn's office. It seemed like so long ago.

"China was under imperial rule for thousands of years." The older woman reminded herself she needed to keep things direct and to the point. "You know, run by emperors."

Alexine nodded her head quickly, sniffing. "The Forbidden City, The Temple of Heaven."

"Sure." The older woman pulled a playfully impatient face, causing her eyes to crinkle, and Alexine thought she looked beautiful; like an angel. "Most people know a bit about the emperors. But what do you know about Mao Zedong?"

"Um...there are t-shirts with his face on them in the market." Alexine smiled hopefully. "He's dead now," she finished nodding her head once as if to punctuate that last bit of knowledge.

"Yea," replied the older woman sarcastically, shooting Alexine a bemused look. "The events that lead up to Mao taking control of the country are important, but let's just talk about him today. When Mao and the communists took over, people were generally excited about the change. Things had been difficult for a long time, and perhaps the shift in control gave them hope. The impoverished peasants, I believe, were especially pleased. Freedom and fairness, that is what people were hoping for, although they may not have realized it."

"My mother, Liu Zi-Hong, was born on November 1st, 1949, exactly one month after Mao took over. Her name, Zi-Hong, means 'red from birth.' Many children born in 1949 found themselves in possession of names that reflected the politics of the time."

Alexine nodded in understanding, prompting Annalynn to continue.

"The first year went well. The new government was smart enough to realize they needed popular support to retain power. No one in the countryside, and few even in the cities, understood what exactly was happening. The rural areas of China contain many segments that are quite remote. News traveled slowly and was passed from person to person to person.

"As the years wore on, the Maoists demanded more and more of the people. Freedoms were trampled upon. Individuality, family loyalty, everything was to come second to the communist party. They used deceitful tactics to weed out any opposition. What they wanted, needed, to survive, was mindless rabble. It was a confusing time of fluid loyalties. At many points, a person could be brought under suspicion for nothing at all, nothing.

"It was also as if, the leaders wanted something done, mandated changes in law and procedure, but failed to provide precise limitations regarding how to carry out these orders. By the time commands trickled down to the cities, and eventually the countryside, lower level enforcers took liberties with how they believed their orders should be put into action. The results were extremely arbitrary and depended completely upon the individuals in charge. Many went too far, perhaps simply to prove their loyalty to the party, perhaps for promotions, power, and pettiness. They were often brutal and fanatical, blindly following orders which many times made no sense what-so-ever. And the leaders didn't even attempt to stem the violence. Many times, it was encouraged. Fear can force loyalty, force independent thought from a person's mind, from a society's conscience. It is a powerful tool, and complete subjugation was what the Maoists were looking for; nothing less.

"Coupled with these situations were various power struggles which sprang up periodically. These ended up becoming quite ugly and those engaging in bids for power cared very little about who was harmed and who perished as a result of their clamor to the top."

Annalynn's brows were so furrowed, they almost met in the middle. Anger; Alexine had only seen this woman display the emotion on several occasions, but felt she should remain very still so as not to disturb the passion Annalynn was more than capable of expressing.

"Many people were tortured and killed. Many people lived in terror. And some people…" Annalynn lifted her head quickly and stared at Alexine as if to intimate these next words were very important, "…were sent away to the countryside for hard labor because *someone*," the word "someone" was spat with more than a taste of contempt, "higher up decided they needed to be reformed, and that working as a peasant would teach them their place, perhaps give them a more acceptable outlook."

"Your grandmother, Jian-Ping, she was one of them…sent to the countryside…with her husband…with…Cai-fa." Alexine couldn't continue. The heart-wrenching memory was, once again, painted vividly before her eyes. The last kiss they would share, gone.

"My grandfather died in the countryside. That is why he was not there, when the guards raided the house years later. It was only grandmother, Liu Jian-Ping, and my mother, Liu Zi-Hong."

"Your grandfather had already died."

"Yes. Many people died at that time…of starvation."

"Starvation?" repeated Alexine, framing it as a question. Of course he had died of starvation; she had just seen it, had just watched the life ebb out of his body. But, it had not quite sunk in. "People died of starvation?" It struck the younger girl as ironic that, in the United States, just the opposite held true. People were dying of eating too much, not too little. In Alexine's sheltered world, no one died of starvation. They died of drunk driving, cancer, heart attacks; things they could, to a large extent, control. Starvation?

"Millions of them Alexine."

Millions? That could not be correct. Millions of people dying of starvation, only fifty years ago? Impossible. Why didn't someone help?

"Yes…tens of millions, in fact. Government policy, if it is misguided enough, can be a recipe for horror." Annalynn flashed Alexine a wry smile. "Don't look so disgusted," she said matter-of-factly. "European history is just as unflattering."

The younger woman did not know what to say. Powerful emotions swirling inside her bumped and mixed. She felt guilty, ignorant, sad, and sick. An overwhelming sense that something was missing, not able to be replaced, weighed heavily on her mind.

"I don't want to see anymore," Alexine whispered, shaking her head, somehow aware these scenes would forever be a part of her. That, even if she didn't see, hear or learn anything else, it was too late. A portion of her canvas of innocence had been ripped from its place. She was no longer a child. The scales had just tipped, and she had witnessed too much.

Annalynn pursed her lips, studying the young lady. She should have paid more attention. Her grandmothers anamnesis had always been compelling; Annalynn could easily loose herself in it, blocking out everything and everyone else. But she should have been more careful. And she should have suspected that Alexine would be able to readily experience a vision.

It took most readers time to master the complexities of experiencing, but this young woman! Before even being taught exactly how to delve deep enough to experience, she was adept at the formidable task, did it by accident! Anna had wondered if *that* was what happened in the alley, with Zeke. Alexine was so upset about reading the burnt man. Had that, too, been experienced instead of witnessed? She felt like kicking herself. This girl had to be watched closely. Reading came too naturally. It was as if her very existence had been planned, and she had been born for something, something coming up quickly, something vitally important.

"So, your grandmother Liu Jian-Ping was sent to the country with her husband, Liu Cai-fa."

"And their ten year old daughter, Liu Zi-Hong."

"And then?" She did not want to see more, but had to know more. Had to know what happened next.

"After her husband died, she and Liu Zi-Hong, my mother, made it back to the city. It was a miracle, really. Very few people were allowed to move from the country to the city."

"Mmmm."

"She was an educated woman, my grandmother, so she began working as a writer. They were stable for awhile, but when the Cultural Revolution took place…."

"They took her away."

Annalynn nodded, watching Alexine intently. "And sent my mother, by that time a teenager, to work with the peasants." The corner of the older woman's mouth twitched. "Back to the countryside, very near the place where she was born. Very near the place where her father had died."

"Anna?"

"Yes?"

"Were you born there, in the countryside?"

Annalynn was quiet for some time and Alexine wondered where her thoughts had taken her.

"Yes, Alexine, I was."

"What was your mother like?"

The question caught the older woman by surprise. It was an odd question. Of all the information Annalynn was willing to give the young girl, she was unprepared for a very personal query. Where were you born. Were you poor. What work did your parents do. All of these questions she could have answered quickly, without even thinking. The instructor bit the corner of her lip absentmindedly.

"She died before I turned one." Annalynn was not ready to speak of her mother, having never shared that portion of her life. The people to whom she had been given, as an infant, by her distraught father knew. But they had guarded the information closely.

"I'm sorry." Alexine felt overwhelmed, and it was all she could muster. "I think I should go find Callan," she murmured, gathering her things and walking toward the door in a daze.

"Alexine."

The young girl didn't turn around, but stopped, her hand on the doorknob. "Yes?"

"You experienced grandmother's life."

"I know."

"That is going to affect you in powerful ways."

The young girl was silent; it already had.

"You'll have to deal with the emotions and get past the experience, just as grandmother had to go on living."

That was easy to say, but difficult to wrap her mind around. How was she supposed to get past it? Nothing had really happened to her, personally, but Alexine felt as though she had lost the person she cherished most in the world. She felt abandoned, alone.

Annalynn didn't know what else to say. "Do you want to talk about it?" seemed appropriate. There was a pregnant pause.

"No."

"Okayyy," Annalynn drew out. People dealt with sorrow in different ways; some needed to discuss, some needed to forget. "Well, if you ever want to talk," began Annalynn, stopping mid-sentence because the rest of the statement would have truthfully been "it will have to be with someone else because you are leaving tomorrow and we may never see each other again." That was something she did not want to say.

"Yea." Alexine turned the doorknob.

* * *

In another office at the academy, a very different scene was unfolding.

"So you two are going sight-seeing tomorrow?" Elizabeth asked Callan.

The little girl nodded.

"Good, good, everything is coming along well."

The shifting instructor seemed pleased, but Callan was just plain tired. "I'm going to head back to the room for some sleep."

"Good, good," repeated Elizabeth absently. She had gone over the plan hundreds of times, sealing up every hole and tying up every loose end, it was as foolproof as possible. "Oh, but we'll need to go downstairs for just a second."

"Why?" demanded Callan, irritated. The thought of staying in the building even a few minutes more aggravated her. It was as if the academy were involved in some conspiracy to trap her within its walls and hold her hostage. Captive faces flashed before her eyes.

Elizabeth moved close and whispered in her ear. "We need to double check that chip sweetie."

She had completely forgotten. A malfunctioning chip would certainly pose problems. It rarely occurred, but the things Callan had been working on, mastering in fact, were not commonly done. How her various shifting experiences would affect the technology embedded in her hand was a huge unknown, which posed great risks.

Down in the round room, the little shifter's temper flared. "You know," she snarled, "I'm really tired, so let's get this over with."

"Uh, sure…" replied the tall, gangly man, stopping in the middle of a meandering thought.

He had been explaining the fascinating technology being perfected in the lower levels, using technical terms neither Callan nor Elizabeth understood. The hovering problem had been remedied; something about unsteady aerodynamic forces, airflow, amplitude, bumblebee studies and wing joints. The video was perfect. Audio was satisfactory. Power supply was the sole remaining obstacle. The little girl was in no mood to humor him tonight. Tiny, flying robots, honestly.

"Okay," he said awkwardly. Running a small device over her hand, a sensor flashed. "Yep. I think you're good."

The little red-head stalked from the room, pausing in the corridor to wait for Elizabeth.

After Callan unceremoniously left the room, Elizabeth turned inquisitively toward Milton. "All set then?" she whispered. Several seconds later, a computer screen appeared on the far wall in response to her query. The rounded walls caused the picture to bend toward them, and Elizabeth felt as though she were standing in some form of half-planetarium. Hundreds of light specks flashed on the screen, underwritten by a map of the city. Milton's fingers tapped a few buttons on his keyboard and one of the specks glowed red and steady.

"There she is," he said, satisfied, "it's working." He spoke in monotone, still eyeing the red dot, transfixed by it's progression and the deathly silence that filled the room.

"It's your duty to protect her," said Elizabeth in a low tone. Her voice suddenly choked with emotion, she bit back tears. "You know what that means." She would have traded places with the man in an instant, would have put her own life on the line if it meant protecting the little girl now waiting just around the corner.

His eyes never left the screen. "I know what that means."

Chapter Thirty-nine
Plans Gone Awry

"Good morning!" beamed Callan cheerily. "Up you go sleepy-head!"

"Ugh." Alexine was becoming increasingly disgusted by her sister's new-found knack for being way too up-beat in the morning. Thinking back, the older girl could not remember when that began. At home, Callan had always been difficult in the mornings.

Backwards, everything here was backwards. Alexine winced, realizing that without even being aware of it, she had learned not to trust anything, not even her closest sister's decision making abilities, not even her closest sister's loyalty.

"Come on," Callan cajoled, pulling Alexine's covers slowly off the bed. Her older sister moaned in retaliation. "You said you wanted to see China first thing in the morning." The little girl crossed her arms impatiently. "We're already late!"

"Alright, alright," Alexine relented. Rolling out of bed, she received her customary injury from the bed stand and rubbed the sore spot. That was one thing she would not miss. The annoying piece of furniture had inflicted its last blow.

The sun was just rising as the girls hurried down the steps separating the front foyer area of their temporary home and the hotel courtyard. Strangely, Alexine noted the courtyard always smelled tolerable. Not good, mind you, but alright. As soon as they left the courtyard however, the stench of Shanghai hit and she involuntarily began her customary shallow breathing.

"Okay, that is one smell I won't miss," she said in a low voice to Callan. Common in the city, the putrid odor, sharp and pungent, had an underlying hint of rancid oil. Whatever was cooking caused Alexine's stomach to tighten each time she was unfortunate enough to encounter it. As the little girl by her side smiled and nodded in agreement, Alexine wondered why she was whispering. It was doubtful any of the people surrounding them spoke English. A pair of women passed, their conversation, though quiet, was animated. How she missed hearing her native language!

"Can we stop?" Alexine asked absently, entering a small fruit and vegetable stand on their right. In the outskirts of the marketplace lay that section of old Shanghai untouched by the mechanism of development. Having wandered through the area several times, Alexine was now fond of it. It seemed like real China to her, a part that would soon be gone. She laughed at her own fickleness, recalling the first time she laid eyes on these enclaves. She had hated them.

The stand had caught her attention several times but, too intimidated to enter, she had stridden past. It seemed like a shop for Chinese, not American tourists. But it was her last day, her final opportunity to look around. She had been in China long enough to take chances. Two men were arranging items in the shop; one older and one younger. The shopkeepers noted her arrival and she could tell immediately the younger would be waiting on her. She was American, and would be treated to the more slick of the two men. Choosing a fruit, she picked it up and looked it over, having no idea what it was. It resembled an overgrown grapefruit that was not round, but oblong. The skin seemed to be very thick, but it was definitely something citrusy. The young man spoke in broken English.

"Hyes, hyes, beddy good."

"How much?"

He smiled, and she sighed. Although she knew it was part of every-day shopping, Alexine had grown weary of the bargaining process. She longed to see something with a price tag; its cost set. Something she could pick up, decide upon, and purchase or leave. Something she could count on., trust.

The clerk turned and took several steps toward the cash register. Returning with a calculator, he typed one number then presented the device to Alexine. 5 Yuan. She was sure no Asian customer would pay it, but she nodded in agreement. It would be a bargain in the U.S. Alexine walked deeper into the shop and picked up a gorgeous pink apple. She had never seen anything like it.

"Ahhh, hyess, beeedddy nice."

She smiled at him and he typed two numbers into the calculator, turning it toward her. 10 Yuan; over a dollar. For one apple? She raised her eyebrows and laughed. Shaking her head, she put it back. It was only a dollar, but she just couldn't justify it. A dollar for an apple? The young man picked it back up and followed her to the stand with it.

"Beeedddy nice," he tempted, turning it over for her to study.

"Yes, it is very nice," Alexine responded slowly. "But not 10 Yuan...no."

She expected the price to be reduced and was surprised when he returned the apple to the shelf and shrugged. She paid for her huge grapefruit-like object and walked back into the overcast alley. Ahh well, no pink apple.

The two girls continued east, pausing here and there, but the market had lost much of its luster. Visiting a few times had been enough for Alexine, especially smack in the middle of the National Holiday. Although relatively docile now, a couple of weeks previous the market was teeming with activity, a complete madhouse. Groups of teenagers, families on holiday, and older people shuffling slowly past the shops created a nearly impenetrable mass of humanity. The teenagers had been the most interesting; snapping pictures of foreigners on their cell phones. Some of them attempted to be discreet, many did not seem to care. Alexine wondered how many times her photo had been taken, and how many times her face had been posted on a website or sent to friends via email or cell phone. She smiled.

They turned left into the heart of the market. A stall set up in the middle of a street caught Callan's attention. Its operator, a girl who appeared quite young, but was probably in her twenties, held the cross shaped control of a puppet in her hand. The attached dragon dangling underneath by thin strings pranced with each flick of her wrist, obeying its master with exactness.

"Nice," the girl said, smiling at Callan. "They made good."

"Yes, they are made good," repeated Callan, noting the improper use of the word "good" but already feeling guilty for correcting the girl by adding the word "are." "How much?" the small girl asked.

"100 Yuan," responded the saleswoman quickly. "Good price...made good."

Callan smiled and began walking away.

"They made good!" the saleswoman repeated more loudly.

"Tie guay la. Tie guay la."

The woman started, as if surprised to hear her native tongue spoken by a foreigner. Then she furrowed her brow as if slightly offended. "No...made good."

As the girls walked away, Alexine shot her little sister a puzzled look. "Tie guay la?" she repeated, raising her eyebrows. "What does that mean?"

"Too expensive," the little red-head answered dismissively, "oh look!" Walking briskly to a nearby stall, Callan picked up a clay wind instrument which resembled a chubby pear. She blew over the top hole tentatively, readjusting her positioning as she exhaled. The object moaned a sorrowful, hollow note and the little girl grinned. "We have to get one for Mrs. Smyth!"

Mrs. Smyth, a woman who taught piano in Marcellus, had been Alexine's instructor since first grade. Although, in the beginning, Callan longed to take lessons too, her time learning the instrument lasted less than two years. Piano just didn't seem to be Callan's "thing." Mrs. Smyth had politely invited her not to return after spending a trying forty-five minutes with the little girl one Monday afternoon.

Callan began her lesson by playing a required piece hap-hazardly, banging her head against an imaginary wall in front of her, and repeating the mantra: "I.....hate.....piano....and....the....only....reason....I'm....here....is....because....my ... mother...makes...me... come." Each word coordinated perfectly with a bang of the head. Each bang of the head matched an ill-played note on the teacher's very expensive piano. Callan smiled remembering that day and her mother joking she had been "kicked out" of piano class. Home seemed so far away.

"I think she'd like it," threw in Alexine, observing the little girl's vacant expression with interest.

Callan emerged from her thoughts. She had made a commitment, no sense in thinking about home right now. "How much?" she asked the man sitting behind the table, afraid of his answer.

"60 Yuan," he responded quickly.

About $7 thought Callan. Because of her straight-forward personality, she detested the intricacies of bargaining and never did it. "I'll take one," she said, smiling, nodding, and holding up an index finger. The man wrapped the instrument in several pieces of Chinese newspaper then pushed it into a box. Accepting the item, Callan placed it in Alexine's shopping bag. "Make sure you tell her *I* picked it," said the little girl authoritatively.

Alexine winced. "Why don't you tell her yourself?" She faced the little shifter, fixing such a piercing stare at her, the girl's full attention was claimed. Before Callan could argue, Alexine launched into her well rehearsed logic, working fervently to keep her voice steady and imploring, with no traces of anger or dominion. "I can't go home without you. What would mom and dad say? They sent me here to watch over you. We're a team...a team. Callan, I don't know what happened, and I don't understand why you made this decision, but please, please just come home with me. Please.... I love you."

Uninvited tears sprang to Alexine's eyes, distorting her vision. She resisted biting them back; perhaps they would help her convince the stubborn red-head to think of something more than herself. She blinked and they rolled down her face. "I won't go without you," she whispered. "I can't leave you."

Callan's expression was unreadable. It was as if the little girl had taken an eraser and wiped all emotion from her face, leaving a blank slate staring up at Alexine.

"There's no reason for us to talk about this anymore," Callan answered methodically. Turning, she continued down the road, deeper into the maze-like market.

* * *

"You want to go in?" Callan asked over her shoulder, gesturing toward a ticket booth outside the Yu Gardens.

"Yea, sure," Alexine answered back. Her tears dried and her mind set, she fingered the small canister of Dramamine in her pocket. Talking sense hadn't worked, anger hadn't worked, an emotional plea was likewise fruitless, and patience failed miserably. Callan's stubbornness justified what Alexine knew she must do. The older girl paid for two tickets at the booth and the girls entered the garden to their right. Just inside the entryway an older Asian gentleman greeted them.

"Have you been to the gardens before?" he inquired, smiling.

Alexine was instantly suspicious. How much money did he want? "No, we haven't," she returned the greeting. The man seemed warm, congenial, and spoke English very clearly.

"Well, you'll need a guide then." It was not a question, but a statement, as if the decision had just been made and he was ready to go. "I charge 50 Yuan."

"No thank you." Alexine glanced nervously to her left. Callan had not stopped to acknowledge the man. Annoyingly aware of her sister's penance to wander ahead of groups, Alexine fought an intense urge to call after the little girl now crossing the bridge. Of all days, she could not loose the little girl now!

"But the gardens are large," the man cocked his head a bit, staring intently at Alexine as if to emphasize his point. "You will miss many areas if you do not have a guide, where are you from?"

The older girl had grown accustom to this question, often spoken quickly, and abruptly stuck at the end of another sentence. "Where are you from?" No segue. As if the person speaking the words was afraid that, if they failed to ask something compelling, something that pulled her personally into the conversation, they would loose an opportunity, typically a financial one. She sighed.

"America."

"My daughter lives in America," he replied knowingly.

Alexine paused, wondering if it was true. Actually, this man was not as pushy as most salespeople. He seemed less compelled to sell his services, more soft spoken, and his English was impeccable.

"I have visited. New Jersey."

She smiled guiltily at him again. "I really have to go. My sister..." Callan had already disappeared from sight.

"Yes, yes."

He seemed disappointed, but Alexine was fairly sure he would not grab her arm and attempt to drag her back in a bid to win the job, would not follow her into the garden offering to lead them through for less screaming "good price" all the while. "Thank you," she said graciously, and half bowed several times while backing away. "Thank you."

"Could you please wait for me?" The words came out sharp, but Alexine commended herself, having considered her scolding carefully and re-phrased it into a question. "You need to wait for me" was what she truly wanted to say; a command. And she wanted to not only say it sharply, but loudly.

"I thought you wanted to see a lot today. If you stop and talk to everyone, we'll end up missing a bunch."

"Talk to everyone?" Alexine thought angrily. The man had engaged *her* in conversation. *She* had not stopped to shoot the breeze. But she knew this explanation would fall on deaf ears. Callan would tell her she just needed to ignore them. The older girl had a very difficult time doing so, it was rude. Each time she walked past someone who was speaking, waving them off, she felt guilty.

Guilty. Guilty. Guilty. It seemed that particular emotion had been dominating her life for weeks. Sometimes she even felt guilty for feeling so guilty. She took a breath, no arguing today. "Sorry," she answered. "I'll keep up with you."

Callan eyed her warily. Suspicious, that's what this day had become. Alexine was trying way too hard, being way too patient, something was up. Not one to beat around the bush, Callan challenged her. "What's going on?" The innocent look her sister conjured up spoke volumes.

"Nothing."

Expecting that answer, her retort came quickly. "Why are you being so nice?"

"I want you to come home."

"No."

"Please."

"We're not talking about it anymore." Anger. She needed to be angry. If Alexine thought she might change her mind, this game would be all the more difficult. "Don't bring it up again," Callan growled.

The garden area was beautiful, but Alexine barely noticed her surroundings.

* * *

By the time the sisters reached the restaurant Annalynn had taken Alexine to several weeks previous, both girls were famished.

"Get the salad," Alexine said, smiling. "You'll love it."

"Yea, okay, order for me, will you?" Callan stood and walked toward the restrooms. "Oh, and a chocolate malt too."

Alexine's grin faded as the small girl disappeared down the hallway.

Crushing the Dramamine did not take as long as she anticipated and it dissolved readily into the thick malt sitting across the table. Their food arrived just as Callan returned from her lengthy visit to the lavatory.

"Thought you fell in," chided Alexine.

Callan smiled. The delay had been intentional. She wasn't about to spend ten minutes waiting for food while being bombarded with reasons why she should leave the academy. "Food looks good!"

"Told ya. It's the best regular food I've had in China." Alexine watched as Callan gulped down her malt, and then ordered another. "Perfect," she thought.

Twenty minutes later, the girls paid their bill and entered the elevator which would return them to ground level.

"Thanks for coming out with me today." Callan's sincerity took Alexine by surprise. "And thanks for letting the argument go, for trusting me. You don't know how much it means."

The girls stepped off the lift, crossed the foyer, and exited the building. Approaching the busy street, Alexine looked left. Callan's gait was hesitant, languid.

"I'm tired all of a sudden," the little girl droned dreamily, rubbing her face.

Alexine smiled. "It's been a long day."

"No," began Callan again, confused. "I mean… really tired. Like I can't walk another step." The little shifter stumbled, then swayed. She felt Alexine grasp her by the upper arm. As realization dawned, she turned slowly toward her older sister, horrified. "What have you done?" she breathed, in a forceful whisper.

"I don't know what you…" But those were the only words which managed to work their way out of Alexine's mouth.

Callan bolted toward the road. "We have to go…now…don't ask questions."

Alexine followed behind Callan, grabbing her sister's arm, steering her. "Okay, we're going." This was strange. Callan never reacted like this to Dramamine. It must be the stress.

"Where is it? Where is it?" After they reached the opposite sidewalk, the little red-head began babbling under her breath. "Where is it?"

"Where is what?" Alexine asked, confused.

"We have to get there. I think its one more block." Callan squeezed her eyes shut, then opened them wide again, attempting to clear her head, all the while pushing ahead.

"Where are we going?" Alexine asked again, in a whisper, as a sickening feeling crept over her. The little girl's accusation replayed in her mind: "What have you done?"

"One more block. One more block." It was as if the words she spoke drove her forward, enabled her to stay on her feet, compelled her to move on. They had to get there, one more block.

When they stopped at the intersection, Alexine peered across the street, it was mobbed with people. "Odd," thought Alexine. Glancing behind, and across the street, the crowds were thinner. What was happening ahead?

"Yes… the next block. Almost there." Callan shook her head slightly, again trying to clear it.

Alexine stole a glance in her little sister's direction, worried. "What's going on?" she hissed without looking at Callan. The growing feeling that something was amiss, that she had been deliberately excluded from vital information, and that, perhaps, they were being followed by someone other than Annalynn hit Alexine like a hammer. Her heart pounded in her throat but she forced herself to concentrate… hard. Danger, they were in danger.

"The next block," Callan murmured. "Just get us to the next block."

"Almost there," replied Alexine seriously, realizing they were now a team. All day long she had felt they were engaged in a tug-of-war, each sister intent on winning. But now, things had abruptly changed somehow.

They crossed the road together as the mass of people swarmed around them. Ahead, Alexine noted four doors, adjacent to each other, swing out simultaneously. Each door was open by a man who remained at the entrance, as if protecting it. Things began happening in slow motion. Several people glanced at the two girls. How many of them were involved? Were they here to help? Focusing on a small woman who had paused, only briefly, to look at the girls, Alexine entered her mind with force. No time to ask permission, o time to think.

"Are you here to help?"

The woman fell back a step. "Yes…the second door…duck down before you enter…hurry."

The woman was warm, and strong. Alexine followed the instructions precisely, pulling Callan forward as they passed the first door. The man who stood guard next to it flicked a glimpse at them, winking only slightly, then smiled at the passers-by, speaking quickly in Mandarin. He sounded like all of the other salesmen lining the many streets of Shanghai.

Leaving the first shop behind, Alexine bent at the knees, reducing her stature by over a foot. Fortunately, Callan's diminutive height made her shorter than the crowd and she did not need to further compromise her ability to walk. They moved quickly through the second door and it swung shut behind them. As it did, Alexine heard adjacent doors slamming. The muffled thunks, and tinkling entrance bells signaled all four doors had simultaneously closed out the bustle of the street outside.

"Come." A small woman grasped her forearm leading her toward the back of the shop. Alexine supported Callan who was now half falling, half walking forward. Stepping through a narrow doorway, the older girl pulled up in surprise.

"Elizabeth?"

Chapter Forty
Shifters are for Soldiering

"What's wrong with her?" Elizabeth demanded, moving quickly to Callan. The little girl fell, semi-conscious, into her arms. "What happened?"

Alexine was shocked. "What's going on?" she demanded angrily. "Why are you here?"

Elizabeth turned to the small Asian woman who had ushered the girls into the room. She spoke quickly in Chinese. The little woman nodded then began retrieving items out of a nearby box. Shoving them into Alexine's arms, she pushed the older girl toward the far side of the room, swatting at her impatiently.

"Take off everything you're wearing," commanded Elizabeth harshly as she sat on the ground, cradling the top half of Callan's body in her lap. "Everything! Put on what Zhang gave you." Looking up, Elizabeth barked, "what are you waiting for? Quickly!"

As Alexine peeled off clothing, Elizabeth spoke. "What's wrong with her?"

"Dramamine."

An awkward silence spilled into the room as the shifting instructor looked up in surprise, her expression moving from blank stare, to confusion, and then, sharply, to anger. "WHAT?"

"Dramamine," repeated Alexine quietly. "It makes her tired."

"You drugged her?" Elizabeth asked, incredulous.

"Yes."

Elizabeth heaved an angry sigh. "Oh, well, this is going to make things a lot more fun, isn't it?" The comment dripped sarcasm and animosity. Glaring at Alexine, she again yelled, "quickly!"

Alexine was pulling the black pants over her legs when Elizabeth sputtered, "everything, Alexine, take off everything, do you understand? Do you know what everything means?!"

Standing barefoot in the empty room, wearing nothing but her bra and underwear, the older girl hesitated, shooting the shifting instructor a scandalous look. Her shoulders hunched, partly bent over in an attempt to maintain some level of modesty, Alexine was mortified.

Elizabeth softened, trying to be patient. "You are carrying a tracking device. I have no idea where it is, but it's in your clothing, or in your hair, or in your bag, somewhere. We need to separate you from the device. Everything has to come off."

The older woman's attention returned to Callan. The little shifter's mouth was parted slightly, her tongue rested against her front teeth, and red-blond hair cascaded over Elizabeth's lap and onto the dirty floor. The shifting teacher sat puzzling for several protracted seconds, smoothing back the unconscious girl's hair, then made up her mind quickly. "Zhang! Call the others, we need to add a child. And I'll have to pull out too. It's the only way now." She had been prepared for the eventuality anyway. Now she could see no other avenue.

Zhang stood plastered to the floor. Alexine wasn't sure if the weathered woman failed to understand the command, or did not agree with it. Alexine was certainly confused by Elizabeth's cryptic statement.

"Callan has to leave too, it's our only option now."

The small woman finally nodded her head and disappeared.

"Are you ready?" Elizabeth asked as Alexine pulled on the new shoes that had been provided.

"Um…yea…I think so."

"Good," Elizabeth said, "because I'll need your help."

"Okay," Alexine replied cautiously.

Elizabeth rolled Callan carefully to the floor and left the room. She returned with a black bag dangling from her arm. Placing a white towel under Callan's hand, the shifting instructor ripped open a small white alcohol swap and rubbed it over the little shifter's newly acquired injury; that blasted microchip.

"Stop it!" Alexine yelled when Elizabeth took out a scalpel and sat down next to the semi-conscious little girl. "You'll hurt her!"

Elizabeth snorted and shot Alexine a condemning look. "You drugged her!" She turned back to her work. "We've got to get that chip out, they can't be allowed to follow either of you."

When Elizabeth made the small incision, Callan scrunched up her face. Her eyes fluttered open and she moaned sleepily.

"It's okay," the instructor soothed. Removing a pair of hemostats, it took Elizabeth only a moment to find the tiny piece of technology. Carefully, she picked it up and dropped it into a paper towel lined vial. "Zhang!" she yelled again, so her voice would carry into the next room. "I'll need your help."

* * *

"Ready?" Elizabeth asked a man who was standing in the front room when they entered. Alexine was unsure how or when he had arrived. The man nodded solemnly. He was definitely Asian, but was taller than Alexine and well built.

Elizabeth and Alexine stood at the door, supporting Callan who now resembled a Chinese boy. Sporting dark pants, a plain shirt, and a short black wig over which a tan baseball cap had been snuggly pulled, Callan would blend into the crowd. Alexine's hair had been searched for a tracking device, then quickly swept up under a very tight plastic cap that stretched her face upward uncomfortably. Her own wig was sweeping and black, with similarly long bangs. The entire effect camouflaged her features quite well. Although she and Elizabeth had attempted to bind her torso tightly, the only evidence she was not Asian, upon quick glance, was her size and curvature. To an extent, there was no hiding that.

"Listen carefully," Elizabeth addressed Alexine quickly. "You are to go with James, support Callan between you." The shifting instructor grabbed James's hand and pulled him into position. Squeezing Callan between them, Alexine and the well-built man grasped the little girl firmly. "Yes, yes, that's good."

Elizabeth turned her attention to the man named James. "The car will be waiting at the corner, do it fast." The young man again nodded seriously. "Annalynn is out there, avoid her." Another order, another nod.

"No! She's on our side!" Still a bit confused regarding what exactly *our side* meant, Alexine's voice was desperate and pleading. "She changed her mind!"

"We've heard." Elizabeth and James exchanged meaningful looks Alexine had difficulty interpreting. But she felt, and was not sure why, these people knew Annalynn and cared about her. Confused, Alexine did not have time to gather her thoughts before the older woman broke the silence.

"But *if* Annalynn has changed her mind, and anyone believes she is involved in your escape, she will be in even more trouble, especially now that *both* of you are disappearing. Does that make sense?"

"No *ifs*, Elizabeth. I'm telling you she definitely changed her mind."

"Which is why we need to avoid her – to protect her." The older woman nodded to pacify Alexine, then returned to the task at hand and rattled, "okay, we can talk about it later, you need to leave. Do not look around, do not make eye contact with anyone, keep your gaze down and let James lead you, understand?"

Alexine glanced up at the large man and he smiled reassuringly. She again nodded to Elizabeth who turned toward Zhang at the back of the room, then jerked her head. On queue, the old woman picked up what appeared to be a walkie-talkie and spoke one word.

Alexine heard door chimes tinkling in the adjoining shops. At the same moment, Elizabeth pushed the door open directly in front of them. Again, four doors, four shops, four possibilities. When James ushered the group quickly over the threshold and onto the sidewalk, she noticed others had similarly walked through the adjacent shop doors. Three people; one man, one woman, one child, at each door.

The group to their immediate right and left both turned right. Alexine, James and Callan, heading left, brushed past the group that had exited to their left. Alexine noted the furthest group, the fourth door's occupants, had mimicked their course and were now crossing the intersection just ahead, dodging traffic and moving quickly. She, James and Callan walked more slowly, keeping time with the crowds surrounding them, becoming one with a mass of people who moved and swelled around them casually.

Alexine followed Elizabeth's instructions succinctly: head down, no eye contact, let James lead you. She concentrated on squishing Callan between she and the young man. What was happening? Vying to keep the little girl on her feet until they reached the corner, Alexine redoubled her grip on Callan's arm. Just get to the corner, just get to the corner.

As they approached the intersection, a taxi lurched to a stop in front of them and James opened the back door. Pushing Callan in first, Alexine crammed in after her and shut the door. There would be time to adjust seating once they were moving. As soon as their door slammed, James flipped the passenger door handle and climbed in. The taxi entered traffic inconspicuously and headed north.

At the same time the little group exited the building by the *front* door, a young, wiry man was bolting from the *back* of the shop. He carried a backpack stuffed with clothing that best suited a fifteen year old girl, and a little plastic canister. A small object in the vial rattled quietly.

The man sprinted down the alleyway and jumped into the driver's seat of a running taxi. Jerking on a baseball cap, then twisting it backward, he pulled quickly into traffic and sped south of the city, flooring the gas peddle whenever the smallest space opened in front of him. Once across the Nanpu Bridge, the highway opened up and the kamikaze taxi raced down the road. 130, 140, 150, 160 kilometers per hour. He loved driving fast; the specialty that made him popular with people who wanted to get somewhere quick. And to think, his mother had always reprimanded him for the tendency! "Biao che!" she would scream at him, typically from the back seat while hanging on for dear life. Literally the words meant "whirlwind car" but were understood to mean "speeder!" Dodging around slower moving vehicles, the young man smiled.

* * *

"They're flying!" blurted Milton in the control room at the academy.

Devin scowled. What was happening? "Both of them?" he asked angrily.

"Yep." The dots whisked on the board, making quick turns here and there, edging toward the Huangpu River. "Must be in a car."

"What the...?" There was no way Callan had changed her mind, no way! Something had gone wrong, terribly wrong. Devin began sweating as the seriousness of these events unfolded in his mind. He had trusted Callan with everything, everything! There would be a monstrous price to pay. What could he do now? They were too far ahead of him. Even if he shifted, he could never overtake them.

The two men watched the flashes of light for several minutes. Just enough time to doom any attempts of catching up with Alexine and Callan.

"Looks like they're headed to the airport... Pudong."

"To the airport?" repeated Devin, dazed. Impossible; they couldn't leave. *She* couldn't leave. She had committed to the cause. She worshipped him! Something had happened to her. Something.... He was grasping at straws, searching for a way out. But he knew it was futile. He had failed.

"Man, they're moving!" Milton laughed nervously, not well versed regarding appropriate social skills. It was one of the disadvantages of dealing with technology more often than people. He cowered in the shadow of Devin's ensuing glare.

* * *

"There!" The woman with white-blond hair yelled at Annalynn, pointing to a group of three people who emerged from one of the four doors that had opened in unison. "Grab them!" The woman pushed her way through the crowd toward another group that had exited at the same time. "I'll check these."

"Do you see them?" the irritated woman hissed as Annalynn approached her quickly. Both women had returned to the area in front of the four doors as the crowd thinned.

"No," she breathed. "It wasn't them...just a couple with their kid. What about yours?"

"Where did they go?!" The overbearing woman was livid, obviously her targets were not their quarry either.

"I don't know," replied Annalynn evenly.

When the four doors opened, Annalynn knew they'd been had. Her mind tumbled over the possibilities. Was this good, or bad? She needed more information and wished she alone had been sent to tail the pair.

Having gotten wind of Alexine and Callan's excursion, Devin had insisted on another reader accompanying her, despite Annalynn's assurance she had the situation covered. Honestly! Interestingly enough, Ginna arrived at the academy thirty minutes later unannounced and volunteered to "help".

For hours now, Annalynn had been grappling with plans to get both girls to the airport. How could she do it with this woman watching her every move? It had seemed all was lost, but now, now! Perhaps Ginna's presence at this fiasco would buy her time. It was not solely Annalynn's fault the girls had been lost, her angry companion had to take a portion of the blame also. She quickly punched a number into her phone.

The vibration in the round room startled both men who were intently gazing at the large map. The flashes of light, Alexine and Callan leaving the academy, meant certain death for one of them, unless he fled.

"Do you have them?" Annalynn whispered when Devin answered his phone.

"Yes, they're moving fast on Longyang, toward Pudong."

"I see," she said calmly. "Do you know what this means?" A part of her felt sorry for Devin, but another part was glad she would probably never see him again, never again have to deal with his incompetence. She doubted Devin would plead his case to Nautas, knowing he would only die in the attempt. He was probably formulating his escape plan at that moment. She could stop worrying about what he might do next.

"I know what this means," he repeated, robotically.

"Good-bye Devin."

"They're headed to the airport," she reported when the white-haired woman raised her eyebrows impatiently.

"Let's go then!" Ginna barked, hailing a taxi.

"We'll never make it," Annalynn countered. "They have a head start and they're moving too fast."

"Are you going to tell Nautas we didn't even try?" the over-bearing woman hissed through clenched teeth. "That we stood here arguing about what to do?"

A taxi pulled over and Ginna flung open the front passenger door. Annalynn opened the back and sat down heavily, eyeing her partner blackly. She truly detested this woman.

"Pudong," Ginna said harshly to the driver. He nodded and pulled into traffic.

Several minutes later, Annalynn smirked in the back seat. This was the slowest taxi in the entire city of Shanghai, perhaps in all of China. And she had made up her mind, it was a very good thing, whatever "it" was, whatever was happening. And it *had* to be of Callan's doing. How had she missed it? Pride, that is how she missed it. Pride.

Shifters weren't good for anything but soldiering. They didn't think, they followed. They didn't plan, they carried out missions. The smirk changed to a smile, obviously both she and Alexine had underestimated the little girl.

So, what was Callan up to? Was it simply a bid to get she and Alexine away from the clutches of the academy, or was there more involved? How much did Callan know? Who was helping her on the inside? Was Branch involved? As he entered her mind, that kind strong face, her emotions sank. Her betrayal clenched a merciless fist around her heart and her breath caught, why had she stayed at the academy?

Meanwhile, in the front seat, the white-haired woman was growing more and more impatient. In a few minutes, Annalynn would fear for the driver's life. What could she do to help? "Stop the car," she said quietly, touching the man's shoulder. He seemed hesitant to do so, and glanced at her in the rearview mirror. The ranting woman in the front seat tossed her head to glare out the window and Annalynn shot the man a knowing look. Still, he seemed unsure. "We need to go back to the academy," Annalynn said definitively. "Turn around please."

The white haired woman spun and gaped at her.

"We won't catch up…we need to consult Nautas. Is he coming to the academy? Is he coming today?"

An evil smile twisted Ginna's face, and she nodded.

Annalynn tingled with fear and adrenelin. He was already at the academy, she knew it. Nautas was waiting.

"Back to the academy," Ginna agreed. No calling her master on the cell phone. They would do this in person. The little upstart Chinese girl had been a participant in this escape, and she would pay for her mistakes today.

Chapter Forty-one
Power is my Specialty

"Devin's office," the startled security guard stammered when Annalynn and the white-haired woman barked one word in unison: "Nautas." They raced up the stairs to the second level. The room was a mess. Papers were strewn about the floor. The garbage can had been hurled at the wall and lay dented and disregarded in the far corner. Both chairs were overturned. In the midst of chaos, Nautas sat calmly behind the large desk that now bore scars of anger across its top, as if someone had run a smoldering piece of metal over the flawless surface. He did not move when they entered, did not even acknowledge their presence, but sat staring out the large window over the busy concrete lot below. The eye of the storm, completely out of place in the wreck which used to be Devin's office.

"They're gone," Ginna reported with no emotion. "Pudong airport." She stole an angry glance at Annalynn.

"They're not there yet," Nautas countered in monotone. "Come."

He lead them to the elevator, then down into the deep of the academy. In the oval room, Milton stood to the side of the monitor, unwilling to do so much as blink without being explicitly instructed to do so. The space throbbed with tension and anger, both emotions emanating from the dark man looming over the other occupants; his captives.

"Don't do anything until he asks," the lanky computer engineer repeated in his mind. "Don't think, don't suppose, don't do anything until he asks."

"Show usss," Nautas whispered menacingly, teeth clenched. Milton punched several buttons on his keyboard and the map sprang up before them, spanning the arcing wall, as lights flashed to life. White blips, scattered incongruently across Shanghai, displayed the location of each micro-chipped member of Nautas's triangulum. "And Callan?" Nautas breathed quietly. Again, clicks on the keyboard, one of the lights flashed red. "Alexine?" Nautas muttered. Click, click, click, another light altered crimson. The dots of blood moved quickly down Longyang. "Now, take me to the flies."

Milton jumped. "Don't volunteer information," he reminded himself, although every fiber of his being begged him to do so. Just do what he asks. Just do what he asks. But the flies weren't ready! Just do what he asks. Don't speak.

The man walked jerkily across the room and Nautas glared at him in disgust. This man was annoying, but necessary. Yes, necessary. Like an intricate toy with so many buttons and options, so much information crammed into so little space, it was maddening to deal with. He loathed being in Milton's presence. Ignorance and fear, that is what flowed through this worm. Especially fear.

The group left the round room and walked down the hallway passing several doors in the process. They turned right, entering a workshop of sorts. Their leader eyed the intricate pieces of metal laying prostrate on the desk. They resembled perfectly aligned objects of art on display in a museum dedicated to the modern.

"And," asked Nautas quietly, "why don't they work?" Of course, he could have ripped every answer from this man in a matter of seconds. Entered his mind with such ferocity the engineer would spend the rest of his life babbling in a corner.

Pollution, that is what filled this man's head, pollution and filth. Better to not expose himself to feelings and emotions so noxious.

A drop of sweat trickled uncomfortably down the back of Milton's neck. It joined the others that now soaked the collar of his shirt. Succinct answers, just answer his question. "The batteries." It came out fearful and hollow.

Looking down at the impotent metal insects laying helpless on the counter top, Nautas froze. He closed his eyes, then paused. The tension in the room throbbed as seconds ticked by. Nautas's eyes snapped open so abruptly, everyone in the room jumped. His body remained perfectly still, but his eyes fixed on Milton, who now stood trembling slightly.

The deceit, the betrayal, the plan so carefully laid, it was pulsing just feet away from the dark man, just under the surface of Milton's veneer-thin façade, waiting to be uncovered. Milton knew Nautas could snatch it away from him, and be privy to *everything*, *EVERYTHING*, in a second. Perhaps intruding on his thoughts just wasn't worth the effort. Perhaps Elizabeth had been right; Nautas would avoid reading him. Trust her, trust her, he silently hoped this was the case. Whatever the reason, the awkward man was grateful the moment passed.

"What's wrong with the batteries?"

"If they are powerful enough to move the flies, they are too big, too heavy, for the flies to get off the ground."

"Power?"

Milton nodded, not daring to look at the current master of the academy again. "Keep calm," he repeated the mantra to himself. "You're doing fine…you're doing fine…keep calm." Nautas smiled slightly; it was an ugly thing full of distain, egotism, and condescension.

"Power," he croaked, "is my specialty." Waving his hand over the tiny, metal insects, the miniscule robots buzzed to life. "It amazes me," Nautas began as if teaching a class, "that science can be so close minded, so clouded with what they *know*, they fail to see what is right in front of their faces. Power is generated by everything. It sits, watching and waiting. So simple."

Milton gasped when the bugs jumped and began hovering above their home on the steel table. "But…" He clamped his mouth shut. Don't talk unless he asks something, only do what he tells you to do, stay alive. Fortunately, the low hum of the now serviceable robots masked his outburst.

"Send them." It was a command, and it also meant "now." Nautas turned and his cloak flew out around him. He left the room followed closely by the two women.

Milton walked to a panel across the room and logged into his mobile control system. Making up his mind quickly, he moved back to the metal desk and, glancing around to ensure he was alone, snatched one of the robots out of mid-air. Snapping the wings off, he quickly jammed the injured fly in his pocket. How had Nautas fixed them? Punching coordinates into the control system, the flies immediately jumped forward, swarmed through the door, and began splitting up to locate avenues out of the building. The mission that would cause their inevitable demise: locate the two beacons headed to Pudong airport, report back.

Chapter Forty-two
The Plan Revealed

"Where are we going?" asked Alexine when the taxi had traveled several blocks. "Where are you taking us?"

"To a safe place," came the reassuring answer spoken in perfect English. It was the first time she had heard his voice, deep and soft, but she wasn't surprised. Her first impression had been similar; large but gentle.

"A safe place?"

"Yes."

"What is going on?" she asked, not sure what question to pose next, at least a hundred filled her head.

"Please, your questions will be answered when we arrive."

"Arrive where?!"

"Please," he said kindly, "let's just get there."

* * *

"So, Callan planned this whole thing?" Sitting in the safe house fifteen minutes later, Alexine was astounded. The little red-head lay snoring on a nearby couch, her gauze-wrapped hand tucked snuggly under her chin.

"No, she did not formulate the plan, she just agreed to become a part of it."

They were sitting in a sparse, but pristine, room. One of the few clean places Alexine had occupied during her stay in China. It felt strange to have her shoes off, and to relax realizing she herself was probably the filthiest thing in the building. The light from the window gleamed off a perfectly polished wood floor. She adjusted herself on the overstuffed couch.

"How many people are involved in this plan?"

"Many."

The young man who had facilitated their escape was being very patient, but seemed unwilling to volunteer information. Succinct answers, that's what she was getting. She could ask questions, but James was not going to give away anything unless it was specifically requested.

"How long has Callan known about this plan?"

"She was brought in the day after your arrival. Elizabeth recruited her."

Alexine let out a sigh and threw a nasty look in her sister's direction. Callan was still sleeping soundly, oblivious. "And why didn't she tell me?"

The question was clipped at the end, and James knew he was steering into dangerous waters. Nervous for the first time, he answered flatly, "she couldn't tell you."

"Couldn't?" Alexine's temper ignited. All the worry, all the sleepless nights and tears, and for what? Because Callan couldn't trust her with this plan?! "Or wouldn't?"

"Couldn't."

"And why not?" It wasn't a question, it was a demand.

"Because you're a reader."

Anger morphed quickly into near hysteria. There it was again: keep Alexine in the dark, for her own good, because she was a reader. She focused to calm down.

James's expression was multi-layered and Alexine tried to pick it apart. Exasperation? Yes, a bit of that, she couldn't blame him. She was being quite annoying and sharp. Surprise? Yes, that too, tinged with a bit of humor, as if he couldn't quite believe Alexine was not figuring all this out on her own. Concern. For who? She and Callan were safely away from the academy, the plan had been successful.

"Alexine," James began, in an almost condescending tone. "You're a reader. So we knew, from the very beginning, once that fact was discovered, and perhaps made public knowledge, you would be watched closely."

"So?"

"So, there existed the probability that, eventually, you would be read by someone who was," James paused as if searching for a delicate way to frame something slightly offensive, "perhaps not sympathetic to our cause."

The same argument, and she understood it, it made sense. But it was still maddening to be kept in the dark all this time. Locked in a closet while everyone else roamed the house. Ignorant and useless while Callan was wrapped in a clandestine bid to right a wrong.

"Annalynn!" she exclaimed out of the blue.

"What about her?"

"She's on our side!"

James had heard the assertion the week previous, but was not sure he completely believed it. Alexine could tell. He diverted his gaze and shook his head slowly. Sorrow filled the room followed by pain and betrayal. They were oppressive feelings and Alexine wanted to banish them quickly, force them out before they had time to take root and fester.

"James," she said firmly, looking him in the eye, "she's helping us, she's on our side!" It sounded strange, since Alexine still had no idea who *us* was, exactly. "She was trying to get both of us out today – Callan *and* I!" Alexine nodded her head toward him with each word for emphasis. "You have to believe me." She was pleading Annalynn's case in her absence, defending her teacher, paying homage to her mentor.

James pressed his lips together, and Alexine wanted desperately to know what he was thinking. "Wait here," he finally said, sighing. The man who was an integral part of her escape from the academy walked out the door abruptly. It clicked shut quietly behind him.

When Branch entered the room, Alexine instinctively rose from the couch. He was their leader, she knew it. An air of authority and boldness emanated from every fiber of his being. Kindness, loyalty, dedication, understanding; every positive attribute she could fathom, they were embodied in this man.

"Hello Alexine."

The words caressed her ears. He understood her, felt her anguish, wanted to help.

"Hello," was all she could manage to say. It sounded wholly inadequate, ridiculous, but she could think of nothing else.

"James tells me you have information about Annalynn."

She nodded her head and heard the word, "yes," escape in a breath.

"Tell me everything you know, and believe, about Annalynn." He motioned for her to join him on the couch and the two of them sat, angled to face each other.

Afternoon sun streamed from the large window, falling on Alexine and warming her face. She glanced around the room. James stood, observing, in the far corner of the room by where Callan slept. A guard protecting his charge.

As soon as she looked into Branch's eyes, it was as if someone had thrown open a floodgate. Between tears and sobs, Alexine related the events of the previous month. Her feelings of abandonment and betrayal centered around Callan, laid out shamelessly for these two strangers to see. Things she had not voiced as of yet, highly personal observations, tossed like a communal scrap of information for anyone to claim. The visions Annalynn shared with her and her reactions to them. The abilities Alexine possessed which shocked her instructor. The respect and love she possessed for Annalynn, her confidant, her friend. She held nothing back, and was surprised at herself for being so open. When the last of her words tumbled out, it felt as if the entire conversation had circled around and become a well articulated defense of the only person in the world who had understood her during her stay at the academy, the only person in the world who had cared.

Branch's gaze slid to James. "And we're sure Ginna was present at the exchange? She accompanied Anna?"

James nodded his head solemnly. "She was there."

Thoughtful for a moment, Branch announced, "Bethia was right, we have to go."

"Bethia?" When the name was spoken, it startled Alexine. These people knew Bethia too? But no one acknowledged her outburst, and no one answered her question.

Before Branch's sentence was fully formed, James took several steps forward. "As far as I know, Elizabeth is still there. She is preparing to leave. We took Callan out and that forced her hand."

"Contact her immediately," Branch said quickly. "Tell her we're on our way, to stay put if she can. We'll need her."

The well built Asian man left the room briskly, leaving the door to creak closed of its own volition.

"Where are you going?" Alexine asked, confused and afraid she was about to be left behind.

Branch turned slowly back toward her. "To the academy."

"Why?" Hadn't they just escaped from that awful place?

"If what you have told me is accurate, Annalynn is now in grave danger." Concern etched itself deeply into Branch's features. He seemed bowed under its weight.

Alexine jumped. "Annalynn in danger?" The thought seemed strange. Annalynn, along with Devin, was in charge at the academy. Why would she be in danger? "Before he arrives," she whispered suddenly, recalling that conversation with Annalynn which seemed to happen so long ago. The urgency of the situation swept over Alexine like a blast of hot, putrid air. She inhaled loudly. "Branch!"

"There is something else?"

"A few days ago, we were talking. Annalynn said something about getting Callan and I out 'before he arrives'. It was important we left today, because he's coming. I don't know when exactly, but she was concerned about us still being at the academy. I could feel her fear. I think she was talking about…Nautas."

"Nautas." As Alexine revealed the name, Branch whispered it simultaneously. Then, after thinking a moment and connecting circumstances, he added, "today." A small wrinkle formed between his brows and he started for the door. That was why Ginna was present at the exchange. Nautas was returning today, ahead of schedule. "James! We move now!"

"I need to go too," Alexine pleaded, following after him. "Please."

Branch paused, as if analyzing the situation and weighing options. "Yes," was his one word answer. "Lin!" Branch yelled as they headed toward the door that lead outside. "We're leaving Callan with you!"

"Yes, yes, okay." An Asian woman's voice emanated from a room at the back of the building.

Still speaking to Lin, Branch continued, "the children will be picked up in," he glanced at his wristwatch, "seventeen minutes. Their escort will know the sign."

Lin emerged from a doorway at the end of the hallway looking frightened. She was petite, with cropped dark hair and a bulging midsection; she was very pregnant. In the split second Lin met Branch's gaze, Alexine knew they were reading each other and couldn't bear not knowing what was happening. What children? What escort? What sign? What was going on?

"I should just release them to whoever shows up at the door in seventeen minutes Branch?" Lin thought incredulously. *"Just because they are aware of the sign? Nautas may have the signs. If he gets a hold of these kids..."* The woman's thought shrunk to nothing, as if she were unwilling to entertain the possibility.

"They will be alright. You, the escort, and I are the only people on earth who have been given that sign. There is no way..."

"You can't be sure of that. We do not know who to trust, that has been made painfully clear." Lin's sorrow and feelings of betrayal were palpable.

"Trust Lin, and faith, we can not afford to relinquish either. The children will be fine."

"Can you tell me where they are going?" Lin asked abruptly. *"And who will be taking care of them?"*

"Away, they're going away. They will be well tended, I promise. And by the way, Alexine?" Branch directed his attention to the young girl butting in on this very personal exchange, *"never do this again. If we had wanted to include you in this conversation, you would have been invited."*

Lin searched uncomfortably, sweeping the area for Alexine. Finally sensing her, Lin's eyes narrowed in anger as the girl, now mortified, retreated from the exchange.

Back in the hallway, Branch shot Alexine an irritated look as James rejoined them and Lin disappeared back through the doorway at the end of the hall.

* * *

James slid into the driver's seat of the small, black car as Branch jogged around the front of the vehicle and opened the passenger's door. Alexine hopped in the back as the car rumbled to life and began moving. Both men sat in silent contemplation. Several minutes passed and their tag-along couldn't keep quiet any longer, despite her recent humiliation in the hallway. She had to know more. "Why was *Callan* trusted with this plan?"

The question surprised the men, as if she had broken their concentration at an inappropriate moment. "I'm sorry," she said quickly, still embarrassed about being caught sneaking into Branch and Lin's read.

"Not at all," Branch answered quietly. "Callan is a shifter, we knew she would be underestimated."

"By whom?"

The sadness which took possession of Branch, upon hearing this question, startled Alexine. "By the only person at the academy who was a threat to both you and Callan's safety."

Alexine puzzled. Devin? Zeke? Nautas? One of the many other staff or students residing in the building?

When the answer came, it was quiet and subdued. "Annalynn."

* * *

The mechanical flies were fast, but not fast enough. Several of them petered out on the trip to the airport. Some reached their destination, but they were no match for the ridiculous speeds with which the taxi driver was comfortable. By the time they arrived at Pudong, flight 537, a direct flight from Shanghai to Chicago, Illinois had departed. An orphaned bag of belongings, taken aboard by a sympathetic flight attendant, was making its way back to the United States. Inside two beacons continued transmitting their signal, although they could no longer be tracked. They were safely away.

Milton watched the flies' progression, alone in the oval room. Astounded at their abilities, he couldn't help but make animated comments to no one.

"Wow! One group is swarming! The swarm programming worked. Huh, imagine that. I can't believe it. Great depth of field! These pictures are amazing! Their responses are incredible! I have to call Bob, his neural systems are right on the mark, instinctual even. And the gyroscopes, yea, another surprise. Horizon detection, perfect." He was like a kid in a candy store, absently fingering the robot lying safely in his pocket. Its little joints still struggling in their futile attempt to catch up with its cohorts.

Chapter Forty-three
Alexine's Realm

"And when did you begin to make such important decisions on your own?" The anger seethed from Nautas, dripping off his words, clinging like coagulating blood, then smattering on the floor around him.

"I was only doing what I thought was *right*," she answered. It was the truth, and she knew Nautas would pick up on that ironic fact immediately. The diabolic laugh he screeched was like fingernails on a chalkboard.

"Right?" he said, disgustedly. "Right? Since when do you do what is right?"

Annalynn had been sitting on a short stool in the hallway since the inquisition began. Nautas paced back and forth, seething with hostility. Staring at the floor in front of her, she had not so much as glanced up when answering his questions, remaining silent and still as his accusations filled the air around her.

The vision residing in her mind came screaming into focus. Zao Lin, her grandmother, rendered helpless by fear. Kneeling in her small home at the feet of a cruel foe absent a conscience, a teenage boy swept up by the promise of power, a willing participant in the Cultural Revolution.

She would not repeat history. *She* would not grovel on the floor in front of her accusers. *She* would not bow to this man. Annalynn raised only her eyes in an intent, steadfast stare. "Since I changed my mind," she hissed threateningly, then stood contumaciously.

"No," he began smugly, not impressed. Wagging his eyebrows once, he smirked, "since you changed your mind... *again*." Moving forward, he circled her, not quite ready to pounce on his prey, but nearing that juncture quickly. "Since you changed your mind... *again*," he leaned forward whispering the last sarcastic word in her ear. She jerked away from him. "It seems you have a knack for abandoning men at critical junctures Anna."

Turning her head violently from him in anger and resentment, Annalynn clamped her mouth shut.

"Zeke!" Nautas roared, straightening quickly. The young man took several bold steps forward. "Devin has left us." Rage. "Annalynn has..." he paused to look at the defiant woman for only a moment, as if she didn't deserve even that split second of attention, "...changed her mind...*again*." Distain. "That would place you firmly in command of the academy."

The young man grew several inches as he swelled at the promotion. "I won't disappoint you master."

"See you don't," Nautas threatened, as he again leaned toward Annalynn, his breath hot and menacing. "See you don't."

* * *

As Branch, Michael and Alexine pulled up to the academy, Alexine shuttered. She and Annalynn had spent so much time devising a plan that would help her escape this place. Returning seemed wrong at a fundamental level.

"Alexine," said Branch, "find Elizabeth and help her."

"Okay," Alexine answered quickly as several security personal from the parking lot approached the car. She had seen it before. Not just anyone was allowed to park next to the academy. Taxis rolling in and out were acceptable, but very few cars obtained permission to remain. The guards who patrolled the area were typically very short and to-the-point with trespassers. Upon seeing Branch the men dressed in blue uniforms registered looks of surprise, and then… relief? Alexine sprinted away.

Bracing herself for the inevitable run-in with the guards who blocked the entrance, Alexine bolted through the doors. The space was empty, which she found very strange. Not wanting to yell for fear of alerting the wrong people to her presence, she turned right, jogging quietly down the hallway in her search for Elizabeth.

Several minutes later, she had not come across one solitary person, panic set in. Where was everyone? Throwing caution to the wind, Alexine raced up a flight of stairs and began pounding down the second level hall.

Suddenly, she burst upon a horrific scene that threw her stomach into a lurch. A large, dark man thrust a foot into the side of his victim, lying defenseless on the floor. Curled into the fetal position, the person was in terrible agony, silently writhing in pain. Inexplicably, Alexine flashed back to an afternoon, years previous.

Returning from a trip to the zoo with their mother, the family auto crested a hill near their home as a red truck sped by in the opposite direction. Dangerous for someone to be driving so fast. At once, each of the passengers in the car spotted it: the small, black family dog lying in the middle of the opposite lane. Her mother gasped and slowed the car, opening the door and jumping out even before they stopped moving. Mickey, their cuddly beagle mix was in the throes of death, writhing and jerking involuntarily.

The feelings of helplessness and dread were familiar. That sickening sorrow wrenched Alexine's soul. She had never been able to endure watching another living thing suffer. Never been able to stand by and witness such torment absent a cure.

She wanted to run away from the scene, but was compelled to remain, petting the small creature gently so he knew she loved him. So his final moments were filled with that assurance; she cared and remained despite her anguish.

The man laughed, and as he did so, threw back his head in tenebrous triumph. It was a wicked sound that grated on Alexine, irritated her, called her attention back to the person responsible for this heinous misdeed. Somewhere from the bottom of her soul a creature burst forth, dreadful in its fury, determined to rob evil of its prey, snatch the spoil away from this monster and secret it to safety. She would not allow this to end badly.

A woman with long, almost white hair snorted in derision, yet the man's attention remained on the person lying at his feet. Running long fingers over the shoulders of the dark man, the white-haired woman grasped his upper arm firmly, pulling herself toward him. Only then did he turn to her, a carnal grimace creeping onto his features.

"Yes Nautas," she said wantonly, "it's *me* you need... *me*."

Leering, he grasped her hand roughly and pulled her along behind him down the hallway, away from the horrific scene. Like a pathetic pet who adored its owner, no matter the mistreatment it knew was inevitable, she followed obediently. "Zeke!" he bellowed, not turning back. "Bring her!"

"Yes," replied the muscular younger man, a taint of resentment in his voice. Leaning down over the person now deathly still, he seized a handful of clothing and began dragging the lifeless body roughly down the hallway.

As Zeke re-doubled his hold, his prisoner's head rolled toward Alexine. It was only then she was able to identify the victim trailing behind Zeke. That beautiful, flawless face associated with so much complexity; her teacher, her friend, Annalynn. The older woman's eyes flickered open, her gaze finding Alexine in the semi-darkness.

The dark man and woman disappeared quietly, swallowed by blackness, as they retreated down the long hollow hallway. As they vanished, the long-haired woman cast an admiring look at Nautas. It was sickening.

"Noooo...!" screamed Alexine, forcing herself into her classroom, her "safe-place," in abject panic. What was she supposed to do?

She was alone in the well-lit room. The desks, blackboard, floors, walls; all the same. Each time her warning image appeared in her mind, it was identical; stable, pleasantly redundant, safe.

Stumbling to her feet, she sprinted toward the door and, flinging it open, raced down the hallway. Where the corridor lead, she could not imagine, having never left the confines of the room before. Run. She needed to run, to find Annalynn, to save her, NOW! Rounding a corner, Alexine pulled up in surprise.

The scene lay slightly below her, like a dream; wispy images of the very place so recently abandoned. She was still in her body, but somehow, at the same time, floating a fraction of an inch above it. Zeke pulled the battered pile of a person down the hallway. He whipped around in response to Alexine's cry, but his movements seemed hampered, slow.

"...ooooo!" The scream was still escaping her lips. Dropping Annalynn, Zeke stepped over the woman then ran for Alexine, outstretched fingers hungry for her flesh. Seizing the opportunity, she wrapped deft hands around his arms as he lunged. Her fingernails sinking in to retain a solid grip, Alexine pulled back with all the force she could muster.

Zeke fell to the floor, disoriented and confused. "What the...?" He glanced around quickly sensing things were different... somehow, but unable to quite place the sensation. The new commander of the academy shook off a feeling of foreboding warning him to escape. Leaping back to his feet, he turned on her and stalked forward, fists clenching in rhythm with each step. The little girl standing between him and his master's orders would pay for her interference.

Alexine rushed him with all the energy she could mobilize. The power built and pulsed as it pushed harder, faster. The speed was frightening, took her breath away, but focusing on the woman now sprawled below them both, she whipped it into a frenzy. Don't think!

Everything happened simultaneously. Zeke braced himself, legs wide in a solid stance, arms slightly outstretched as if about to catch something. "BAM!" The expressions in motion on Zeke's face as they collided were etched indelibly into Alexine's memory. They moved, transformed, as she approached; anger, distain, confusion, surprise...then fear. Thrown violently down the hallway, Zeke disappeared into the shrouded darkness of the landing, then hit the opposite wall with a sickening *thump*. Alexine knew he was unconscious, knew no one could withstand the blow just inflicted. Concentrating on the floor, then willing herself to draw close, she joined it, landing lightly in a crouched position, hands spread in front of her, still on guard and ready to pounce.

Annalynn watched the events unfold in bewilderment, Alexine's scream echoed in her head. "Nooooo!" The look on Zeke's face as he rounded on the young girl unnerved Annalynn, like a leopard spotting an unsuspecting gazelle. Tingling fear swept over the older woman lying helpless on the floor. Alexine was no match for Zeke. Devin's favorite henchman had been ruthlessly trained at the foot of Nautas. The powerful man moved toward Alexine, eager to attack even as his foe crouched down in response, as if ready and willing to engage him. Did she honestly think she could overpower Zeke?!

Overwhelmed with dread, the instructor knew Alexine was no match, had no chance. Would he spare her life? As Zeke approached, the two lunged at each other. Alexine grasped Zeke's arms. What was she doing? When they connected, Zeke diminished, somehow, as if someone had turned down the volume on his being. Thrown forward, he sprawled awkwardly onto the floor. What had happened?

Zeke regained his composure with lightening speed and was back on his feet, anger pulsing from him like the savage movements of a poplar whipping back and forth in a violent storm. Walking toward Alexine with purpose and heated conviction, the young man's hands contracted and released.

Annalynn opened her mouth. She wanted to tell Alexine to run, needed to tell her to save herself, but no words came. Speaking required the use of muscles already screaming in agony, spasming until she stopped commanding them to work. She ached horribly, as if every cell in her body had been thrown into confusion; turned against itself in a world gone completely wrong. Her eyes rolled back and she concentrated with all her might to remain present. As if her consciousness would help the young girl fighting for her life. As if she could will Alexine to defeat the demon now approaching.

Alexine sized Zeke up for a split second then disappeared in a streak of color and movement. A deafening "BAM" resonated through the empty hall as the young man hurtled through the air, twenty or thirty feet, disappearing into darkness. A muffled thump.

Realization spilled over the older woman like a golden, glorious sunrise. It warmed her and eased her pain, if only for a moment. A weary smile stole across her lips. Alexine had learned to pull people into her realm, and obviously, the young lady was a force to be reckoned with. Had she overpowered Zeke simply because he was caught off guard, or because Alexine was truly stronger than the well-versed mercenary?

Somehow Annalynn doubted she would live to discover the truth. Pain racked every fiber of her being, harrowing her into semi-consciousness. But she hoped, how she hoped the hours and days spent training Alexine proved valuable to the young lady. Annalynn yearned for evidence that her last few weeks on earth had been well lived. That even though she had faltered, she had made a difference in the end. She had returned. As eyes fluttered closed, she relented to the darkness, welcoming its ability to provide escape from the agony.

Alexine heard voices approaching from downstairs. The clamor of the fight between her and Zeke had caught the attention of someone.

"What was that?" a man's voice asked.

"Don't know," came the reply from someone unseen.

"Upstairs," answered a concerned women.

Although the hallway below had been empty just minutes prior, Alexine could tell it was now filling with people. Where had they come from? Glancing toward the spot where Annalynn lay, she watched the sad smile fade from her instructor's face. Annalynn lay motionless.

Not wanting to attract negative attention, Alexine thought, "HELP!" with as much emotion as she could garner. It seemed wholly inadequate, but her only option for sounding the alert. Annalynn was dying…or dead. "HELP ME!"

Chapter Forty-four
Borrowed Time

Figures materialized silently in the hall. Jumping back, startled and ready to attack, a huge man ran toward her. She dove to her left and rolled into a crouching position. The man completely ignored her and, not breaking stride, sprinted directly at the pile that was Annalynn; her teacher, her friend.

"Stay away!" Alexine screeched angrily. "Leave her alone!"

"Someone's up there," a high female voice yelled from below, "they just screamed!"

"Come on!" came the resounding answer.

They were ascending the stairs.

Branch was riveted to the spot. His eyes darted between Michael, racing toward the injured woman, and the stairs, soon to be a source of opposition.

"*ALEXINE!*" The thought slammed into her like an unanticipated blow. Overwhelmed, her breath caught. The person now reading her so forcefully stood behind her. How did she know that?

She wheeled around, filled with hostility at whatever reader had so abruptly stolen into her mind. She had to get to Annalynn, to protect her. "Branch!"

"It's alright. Michael is on our side." He flicked a glimpse at the man bearing down on Annalynn. "We're here now." Branch's gaze returned to the woman lying helpless on the floor prompting Alexine to spin again toward her injured instructor.

Still running, Michael scooped Annalynn into his massive arms in one easy movement. Her limbs hung rag-doll limp as she was lifted from the ground. The large man gathered her together, clutching her to his chest. Her breathing was shallow and labored. Almost imperceptibly she stirred. The woman whom Alexine had grown to admire and love was alive! She felt a wave of relief rush over her like a warm wind. Anna was alive, things could be fixed, and it could still be alright. Annalynn's eyes fluttered opened. She gazed into the face of her protector, blinking to focus on the man cradling her.

"Michael?" she whispered hoarsely, lifting a tremulous hand to his face. A guilty tear rolled down her cheek. Could it truly be? Was she still here? In the hall? "Michael," she gasped, both in relief and horror. Her head rolled uncontrollably, coming to rest against his heaving chest.

She was a betrayer, having chosen Nautas. She had earned her demise; the death of a traitor. "Leave me," she whispered, wincing in pain. She did not deserve to be rescued, did not deserve their help, did not deserve...Branch.

Tears bathed her face, wetting Michael's broad chest. It did not matter that she had been working against the evil that had a vise-grip on the academy now, did not matter she had changed her mind, it was too late. Too late to undo her treachery, too late to go back and change her mind.

"Just leave me," she screamed, pleading, but it came out as a whisper. Stolen away by the misery threatening to overwhelm her, hidden in a dark place where no one would ever hear. A part of Annalynn wished they had never come, had left her to die, saving her the humiliation of being reminded she did not truly belong, not anymore. Saving her this agony, the pain that racked every part of her being. Permitting her to surrender control to the darkness, it offered escape.

Crouching down to protect his charge, Michael smoothed back her hair with a strong hand. He smiled down at her, but his face, full of concern, betrayed his words. "It's alright Lynnie," he said in a low voice, tears filling his eyes. "We're here now…it's alright." When Annalynn's eyes rolled back involuntarily, Michael's smile relinquished its authority, fading to alarm. Something was wrong, very wrong. "Lynnie?"

Annalynn shook. Too good; they were too good for her. For a moment she fought to remain conscious, but failed in her endeavor. She felt drained, sapped, robbed of anything honorable clinging to life in her. And the pain; it washed over her, engulfed her, slamming her body stubbornly against an unforgiving wall. She wanted to leave, to forget, to stop these throes of agony, to die. The room went black.

Michael jumped to his feet and whirled around to find his leader. Several students had bolted up the stairs and attacked Branch simultaneously. Branch's right hand flashed through the air, throwing the oncoming hoard back down the steps they had just cleared.

"Branch!" Michael yelled, locking eyes with his leader. Glancing down at the woman in his arms in question and concern, Michael shook his head.

How many times had Michael been there for him? The two men practically functioned as one. Branch immediately sensed the urgency of Annalynn's situation, felt Michael's hope fading. She needed help now. They were working on borrowed time. He could feel it, had seen it before. If something, someone, didn't intervene soon… they would loose her.

Although it took only seconds, it seemed to happen in slow motion. Michael watched Branch register concern. Winced as his leader's eyes fell in despair on the limp woman. Understood as Branch made the decision. He wanted to stay, wanted to defend his leader, wanted to fight for the cause he knew was true, the cause that blazed in his soul. But he knew what the order would be before it was placed in his mind.

"Take her! To Bethia, now!"

Michael didn't hesitate. The decision had been made, and he followed. Michael and Annalynn disappeared in an instant.

It felt as though his heart had been torn from his chest. Deserted and beating helplessly on the floor, it lay faltering where the dying woman had fallen. Alone and exposed to any who happened by. "Anna," Branch groaned as they left, a tortured whisper grasping for hope. "Anna." Pulling himself back, Branch focused on their immediate circumstance. They needed to secure the academy quickly, before either side suffered more causalities.

Things were happening so fast, Alexine had little time to think, much less react to the confusing situation in which she found herself immersed. How many of these people knew Anna? Where had Michael come from? Where were Michael and Anna now?

As crowds gathered below them, their voices pulsed and ebbed, traveling up the stairway to the spot occupied by Branch and Alexine.

"We have to get into the basement levels, free the prisoners." Branch glanced toward the landing. People were coming.

"I didn't even know there was a basement here!" Alexine interjected nervously, her eyes similarly darting to the stairway. She could hear tentative footsteps and muffled breathing.

Throwing a last look behind him, Branch grasped Alexine's hand and together they melted into the surroundings.

* * *

Devin's office was a disaster.

Alexine walked across the floor, kicking papers out of her way as she went, like a child blazing a trail through fresh snow. Her thoughts turned back to the day she had spent with the man. The look of horror on his face as she played the part of a rambling teenager popped into focus and she snickered inadvertently. She absently righted a dented metal garbage can resting in a corner. The loud clatter in the quiet of the room startled her and she grit her teeth in a bid to silence the clamor. Unwanted noise would attract unwanted attention. How could she be so stupid?

Branch had stopped in the middle of the room, his head tilted upward slightly as if examining the white drop ceiling tiles. Unfazed by the loud noise, a sad smile gradually fell upon him, and he nodded his head almost imperceptivity.

"You can come out now."

Alexine's face scrunched in question. "I'm right here," she whispered.

Branch flicked a glance at her then repeated softly, "you can come out now...Devin."

Chapter Forty-five
An Unlikely Ally

"I had nowhere to go, no one to turn to. I gave up everything, everyone. This place is my life. My life…."

Windswept and rough, Devin teetered on the brink of despair. Hair tangled, he appeared disheveled, as if accosted on the street during his brief absence from the only place he could call home. Pallid faced and wild eyed, Devin's focus darted confusedly around the room as if trying to make sense of a situation that had no viable answer, no way out. Always too confident, too sure, even egomaniacal, Devin was now sobbing. All pride and self respect sacrificed on the alter of dread and regret.

Alexine never imagined, in a million years, she would actually feel pity for the large man. She knew him well enough to realize this was no act, and the sight of him suffering now made her uneasy. As if she was eavesdropping on something highly personal, sacrosanct. Branch sat across from the distraught man. Reaching out, he laid a hand on Devin's shoulder and squeezed reassuringly.

"I ran…fled…knew he was going to kill me if he found me…but then…I came back. No where… No one…"

"I understand," came the velvet reply, smooth and soothing.

Devin slowly raised his face to parallel Branch, but his eyes remained downcast, ashamed. He shook his head slightly. "You can't understand…what I've done…what I've become.

"It's not too late Devin. We're here, and we need you." The reproach was absent animosity or anger. It was a sagacious invitation spoken with an understanding that transcended the immediate circumstance.

Devin's eyes found Branch; pleading and confused. "I'm sorry," he whispered hoarsely. "I'm so sorry." The men regarded each other and a fervid understanding filled the space between them, more powerful than any words they could have spoken.

"It's never too late Devin. Never."

Tears welled up in his eyes as Devin clung to those words. It's never too late. Never. Syllables of redemption and forgiveness. They pierced him, made him feel inadequate and undeserving. And yet they also embodied hope. Flickering feebly, his chance to begin to right his wrongs. He could never go back and undo them, could never return all of the things he had taken. But perhaps, perhaps he could turn around. Leave the path he had so recently decided upon, and find his way back, back to his original course, the road they had begun together, back to her. Perhaps he could accept this man as his leader. Patience and understanding replacing retribution and intolerance.

Devin pressed his lips together firmly to keep from breaking down again. It seemed so far away, and the effort would entail great changes on his part, but he had seen enough over the course of the last few weeks to realize the road he had chosen was wrong. And he now stood on the precipice of accepting another route, the noble path, or continuing to stumble in darkness. He diverted his eyes, thinking. When he met Branch's gaze again he wore a look of determination, thoughtful and intense. "You need to get to the basement."

"Yes."

"I can do that," Devin nodded.

"You're the only one who can get us down there quickly."

* * *

The elevator descended smoothly. As it slowed, the men on either side of her tensed, anticipating what might await them when the hallway revealed itself. As one, they stepped forward and moved together. A living blockade shielding Alexine from whatever lay in wait on the other side of the partitions. The doors slid open and only silence met them.

"This way," whispered Devin, gesturing down the dimly hit corridor. He exited the elevator in a crouch and turned left. Moving quickly down the hall in a half bow, he was followed closely by Alexine, then Branch. Resting his hand on a door to their right, Devin looked back at Branch and mouthed the words, "holding cells." The man bringing up the rear nodded in understanding. Reaching past Alexine, Branch pushed her first left, then back so she now stood behind him, the last in line.

Alexine tilted herself to look around Branch. Devin extended a thick index finger, signaling their attack. One. He put up the next finger and Alexine's stomach dove downward. Two. She silently took a deep breath, preparing to bolt through the door after the two men. Devin nodded, mouthed the word, "three," and turned the handle.

* * *

"Eewww," Alexine whispered through clenched teeth, shuttering as they passed a large Plexiglas case the size of a small room. There were actually two transparent boxes, one inside the other, separated by several inches of space. The see-through room came complete with a door, designed in the same fashion. It was what writhed, scuttled and squirmed between the two panes of glass that made Alexine's skin crawl.

Bugs, worms, centipedes, cockroaches of enormous proportions. Small lizards, snakes, mice. Every creepy crawling thing one could imagine moved in the space, supported by intricate tiny floors of Plexiglas which tilted up and down in a complex labyrinth designed to allow the creatures to crawl, slither or scamper around the entire perimeter of the miniature room. Top, sides, floor and door, all squirming in a dizzying race to move forward, find new passages, or snack on another occupant of the crammed habitat.

Speaking out of the corner of her mouth, Alexine breathed, "what in the?" She pulled her arms tightly into her body and, clenching her fists, drew a disgusted breath. Flashes of the bugs all inadvertently spilling out of their prison sprang to mind as she took a cautious step backward.

Devin snorted derisively. "It's for shifters, phase two."

"What?"

"It's for phase two shifters," he shot, glancing at her slantwise. "To keep them in."

Not know what on earth Devin was talking about, Alexine turned her attention to the rest of the cavernous room. They had met no resistance upon entering the prison, and immediately released the people being held there. Branch had gathered the liberated around him and was giving rushed instructions regarding a plan of attack.

Many eyes focused on Devin when they entered the area. As keys slid into locks and doors were thrown open, shock registered on some faces, wariness and confusion. But more often anger and resentment shone forth. Devin was not popular with this particular group of people.

When everyone had been freed, he sloped to the back of the queue. Alexine was sure Devin hoped to diminish the attention he was receiving. It worked fairly well, although some people stole glances at the cowed man. She could tell he was more at ease when engaged in conversation with her. It lessened the discomfort of being the center of extremely negative attention. Wanting to help, she groped for something, anything to talk about. Scanning the room did not help matters. There was nothing but jail cells.

"So…um…what's that?" Alexine whispered being careful not to interrupt Branch's organizational efforts. She gestured toward a smaller enclosure. It stood barely six feet tall and was a bit wider than it was high. Gleaming burnt orange, the sides and roof were metal mesh but the floor was solid concrete. Light spilling from overhead reflected off the cage caressing it in a hazy glow.

Devin's eyes slid to the small box then left it abruptly, as if even viewing the object caused him discomfort.

Alexine stared at him steadily, waiting.

He turned toward her and paused as if chewing on words. In the silence, the murmurings of the group around Branch grew more pronounced. "That is a holding cell for phase three shifters."

Alexine shook her head, bemused. "What's a phase three shifter?"

Devin's face was blank, then slowly his brows furrowed in disbelief. "What have you been doing with Anna? Didn't she teach you about shifters?"

Alexine suddenly did not feel like continuing this conversation. It had turned into a fault-finding activity centered on Annalynn. "Well, of course, we just…" Alexine stammered, not sure how to defend the fact she knew very little about anything having to do with the academy. And not wanting to explain her ignorance was intended.

Anna. Her thoughts turned to the woman lying somewhere. Was she alright? Were they helping her? Or…

When Devin spoke again the hairs on Alexine's neck stood on end. "This cell is for shifters who can move through any object, inanimate or animate. This cell, Alexine, is for Callan."

As those final words spilled from the large man's lips, Branch stood to his full height and made his way through the throng of people surrounding him. He gestured for Devin and Alexine to follow, but Devin hung back, recalcitrant.

The others following closely behind their leader were now passing Alexine and Devin. Myriad looks of animosity were hurled at the man now slouching next to her and Alexine's first reaction was one of defense. It was Devin who had made possible their release. It was he who had enabled them to descend into the depths of the academy so quickly. Couldn't one of them, just one, display a bit of mercy?

As the question flashed in her mind, a woman caught Alexine's eye. Standing on the far side of the crowd now moving toward the door, she paused tentatively. Averting her eyes as if contemplating her next move, the woman remained still until everyone had passed. Alexine followed her movements in confusion.

Devin lurched forward as if to follow the crowd out the door but Alexine grasped his arm. The woman was taking tentative steps toward them as if drawn inexorably closer.

Devin's gaze remained with the group following Branch. He sensed the woman's presence, Alexine was sure of it, but intentionally diverted his attention, not wanting to lay eyes on her. Alexine was caught in the middle of this strange interaction, one hand grasping Devin's muscular bicep, the other reaching out to take the woman's hand. The stranger's tremulous fingers stretched toward them, as if she wanted to initiate contact with Devin, but at the same time, needed something between them, a buffer: Alexine. Her hand closed around Alexine's as they stared into each other's faces. The woman brimmed with fear, confusion and sorrow.

She was lovely. Her pale blue eyes pierced Alexine. She wanted to shrink back. On trial for she knew not what, the younger girl longed to escape the torment and questions that held her transfixed.

Devin stood rigid as the woman moved first to Alexine. Releasing her grip, she ran delicate fingers up Alexine's arm, slowly crossed her body, and then traveled down the opposite arm as if feeling her way to the large man. Never diverting her gaze from him, those blue eyes wide and wistful. As she spoke, her fingers brushed Devin's hand. The powerful man relaxed at her touch, surrendering.

"Devin?" Soft and melodic, it left her in a whisper.

The trance broken, Devin blinked as if being awaken, then spun so quickly Alexine stumbled backward. He caught the woman up in a fierce embrace, burying his face in the woman's neck, her hair obscuring them, as he swayed with her.

"Susan, I…"

"You're here. It's alright."

"No, it's not, I…"

She pulled back and placed a tender hand on his cheek. He pushed his face toward her touch, solidifying the connection, then shut his eyes wistfully.

"I know baby brother, I know."

Chapter Forty-six
Level Seven

"Elizabeth is working her way down. We need to start at the bottom and meet her in the middle." Branch directed the comment to Devin who had joined him at the front of the group after being authoritatively waved forward by their leader. It was clear several people following considered trusting Devin injudicious.

"We'll need you to run the elevator. Secure the opposition."

Devin's right hand flexed involuntarily as Branch spoke the words, the small scar standing out, as skin stretched taunt. His chip lent him access to the lift; the only way in or out of the basement. "I understand."

Devin, Branch and many others squeezed into the confines of the elevator as the parted doors began to join each other. Seconds before the hallway disappeared, Devin's eyes found Susan, still standing next to Alexine, and his lip twitched upward. He and his sister were united in purpose once again. Inhaling, the large man allowed himself to be engulfed by the image.

The group which remained stood in anxious silence, seconds lolling by maddeningly. When the doors split, Devin alone appeared. The people standing in front needed no prompting. They joined the large man spontaneously and disappeared once again. Over and over, until all but a handful of people remained behind, the elevator consumed then disgorged the fighters like an insatiable creature. Alexine and Susan stood with the final group, eager to descend.

"He didn't understand what he was doing." Pensive, Susan's eyes darted, then fixed on Alexine, pleading.

The younger woman appraised the older. Others surrounding the two stood in rapt attention, although attempting to appear oblivious.

"Devin. He's always been easily influenced." Susan shook her head thoughtfully. "He didn't understand."

Alexine nodded, unsure how to react, how to respond. She thought back to her experience with the large shifter and winced. She had loathed the man, and, standing next to this woman who obviously loved him very much, regretted her previous assumptions. Her thoughts turned to the events of just an hour previous, his regret and anguish.

"He brought us to you. He liberated these people." Alexine gestured around the group, wanting to not only assuage Susan but make it crystal clear Devin alone facilitated their release. "He understands now, and he's back. That should be good enough for everyone."

* * *

Alexine and Susan ascended to level seven, and began moving down the hallway crouched and on alert. Their group was to enter this area, sweeping the corridors and rooms for any of Nautas's followers. A man ahead of them whipped around silently. Gesturing to a door, he pointed into the room beyond, shaking his finger twice. They were going to enter this area next, re-taking the academy one person, one room and one floor at a time.

Alexine wondered how the other groups were faring, if everyone was safe, if John was alright. Concentration was of paramount importance just now, no time to indulge in pondering situations over which she could have no influence. Anna's lifeless body being dragged down the hallway by Zeke. Shuffling noises around the corner pulled her back to task, and Alexine braced herself for confrontation.

Nine of them bolted into the room catching the people working off guard. Gathered around large crates, they appeared to have just secured the boxes. The two groups were evenly matched, Alexine was relieved to note. But when every member of the opposition vanished, she was at a loss. Shifters. All of them.

Half the people standing shoulder to shoulder with Alexine and Susan disappeared also, following, and the young girl was unsure which way to move, what to do. Two of their number spun, so they were standing back to back, a united force unable to be separated. Fluid and graceful, the movement seemed like a dance, practiced and perfected.

She was fighting something invisible: air. It could materialize before her, morph into human shape instantaneously, like some bizarre hologram. Or, perhaps more deadly, behind her, in milli-seconds. Standing back to back suddenly seemed very smart indeed. No sooner had the danger inherent in the situation registered, than arms encircled her chest like an iron band. Painfully hauled upward, feet met floor a violent second later. Stumbling, she crashed to her knees.

Pain jolted through her legs. Pushing it away, Alexine rolled onto her back and extended her legs to meet the man now bearing down. He leered and melted into the surroundings once again; gone. Next second, the ogreish man lay sprawled on top of her. Straddling her, he grabbed her arms and forced them upward, rendering her powerless. When he drew back his right fist, Alexine knew she had moments to retaliate. Her right arm pinioned to the floor, the left was her only hope. She thrust upward unbalancing her attacker.

Again she was in her calm classroom. The disparity between her current situation and her warning image seemed ludicrous. incongruent. Opening the door, she hurtled down the hallway, pulling up upon her arrival at the exact spot she had vacated milli-seconds before. She needed to loosen those ties which made this man her superior. She needed to separate him, to a small degree, from his physical presence. Left hand flashing through the air, she grasped the front of his shirt, pulling him viciously forward.

He hadn't expected it. She was supposed to be trying to escape, to get away, to maintain the distance between them, increase it. Alarms rang in his head. He knew something was wrong and stood. Turning to shift, he found the path impenetrable, as if an invisible barricade had sprung up around him, trapping him, rendering him helpless, unable to alter. What was happening?

Devoid of his ability, the man panicked and in that moment, that fraction of a second, she gained the upper-hand. Alexine drew back her legs and pushed. Adrenaline and survival instinct screamed at her to use every once of energy, but she resisted the urge. When her feet collided with the man's chest, he hurtled upward and crunched into the drop ceiling, eyes wide in surprise as he was launched skyward. She rolled left to avoid being struck by his descent. Falling to the floor, the man landed with a muffled thump. An exaggerated breath told Alexine that, upon meeting the concrete, the man had the air knocked out of him.

He outsized her. Alexine knew she could not move her attacker to the elevator where Devin waited to transport prisoners to the holding cells. And it had to be done quickly, before he gathered himself and was able to shift, before he had to be defeated all over again. She glanced around, searching.

Susan faced a woman who vanished and reappeared repeatedly. Popping in and out of view like a slowly run, old, clunky picture show. Glimpses of movement frozen in each absurd appearance. She was taunting Susan.

"Suzy!" she drolled sarcastically. "Where's your little brother?" She threw back her head and laughed viciously.

It was the pause Susan had been anticipating. Her right hand shot forward and a white orb materialized just in front of the woman's face. Finding its mark with a sickening crack, Susan's opponent crumpled, her nose streaming blood. The softball clunked to the floor and vanished.

"Why you little!" The injured woman breathed through clenched teeth, her hand flying to her face.

At the same moment Alexine whispered, "a changer?" Speaking loudly to be heard above the crashes and tumult of battle, she yelled, "Susan! You're a changer!?"

The woman ignored the question. "Marcas! Get her to Devin, now!"

The man whom Susan addressed rushed forward and grabbed the bleeding woman, dragging her from the room quickly. She thrashed and beat at the hands now gripping her from behind, but she was no match. Unable to focus, a direct result of her injuries, she could no longer call upon her shifting ability and could not free herself from the man now hauling her from the room.

"Susan, this one!" Alexine pointed at her opponent, still groaning beside her.

"We'll take him together."

They looped hands under each of the man's armpits, Susan taking the right side and Alexine the left. Shuffling backward through skirmishes, they dodged two men grappling with each other.

Susan released their quarry. The two men were extremely close, she had to be careful to disable the correct person. Searching the space surrounding the men, her arm moved in a circle through the air. Bookshelves teetered next to the two men, then began falling slowly. The man facing away from the descending mountain of wood, cardboard, cloth and paper and had no idea what was about to hit him.

A man Alexine recognized as one of the people recently released from the prison took several steps backward to be clear of the falling books. He cocked his head, observing the full scene as it unfolded, his opponent oblivious to the descending mountain rocking in the background. Too late, the doomed man turned and shielded his head in a vain attempt to protect himself from the collapsing rampart.

Susan and Alexine resumed pulling their charge, still incoherent, through the doorway and down the hall. his head falling back and forth like a bobble-headed doll.

"It's alright, he's not going anywhere," Susan smiled, appraising the man through wide eyes. "What the heck did you do to him?"

Alexine smiled guiltily. "Just caught him off guard."

"Yea."

"Special delivery for you brother." When the elevator doors parted, Devin was standing in the midst of several bodies lying bloody or groaning on the floor around him. He smiled wide at Susan and readily lifted their prisoner into the elevator, adding the man to the growing heap of humanity. "Back in a second," he breathed quickly, then added, "wait here for me."

Susan turned to Alexine when the doors slid shut and frowned. "Wait here?"

"Aren't we supposed to keep moving down the hall?"

Susan's gaze shifted back and forth as the women listened to the ensuing fight being waged down the hallway. It seemed to be under control. "Why would he want us to wait?"

Alexine shrugged.

Their question was answered several minutes later when Devin arrived and leapt from the elevator. Another man had joined him and Devin turned now to address the sole occupant of the lift. "Most of them can go into the cells. You know who needs to be put in the bug cage. *Don't* turn on the copper room. Dimitri will wait in the prison to help you unload."

"Devin!" Susan reprimanded. "You're the only one who can operate the elevator!"

"Not anymore," he snapped playfully, his lips twisting into a sardonic smile. Her eyes fell to his right hand now wrapped in gauze. A single drop of blood escaped the bandage, traversed the back of his hand, and ran steadily down his finger. Finally collecting on a fingertip, it cascaded to the floor, smattering on tile with a small splish.

"Let me see that!" she demanded, grabbing his hand and tentatively unwrapping the make-shift dressing. She gasped when the gaping slash revealed itself. Glaring at him reprovingly she spat, "that's going to get infected!"

Devin laughed uproariously, looking around the hallway. "Infected, yea!" He re-wound the gauze tightly and, grabbing her hand, thundered down the hallway, Alexine giggling hot on their heels.

Taking the seventh floor took less than fifteen minutes. Circling around the corridor, and finding themselves back at the elevator, they waited. Several times the doors parted, but the space was so full of half-conscious bodies, the defeated opposition being transported to holding, they had to wait. When the doors parted once again several minutes later, Branch and several others appeared, bent double. Heaving labored breaths, they were obviously recovering from their conflicts on the lower levels.

"How are things downstairs?" Devin's question was one everyone waiting to board the elevator wanted answered.

"Level twelve cleared," Branch reported quickly, gesturing them all into the lift as he struggled to master his breathing. "Ten, nine and eight have almost been taken. But eleven…we need help."

Feeling completely overwhelmed and out of her element, Alexine stuck close to Branch as he fought his way down the hallway of basement level eleven. The first indication things weren't going well on this floor was the chaotic clamor which reached them even prior to the elevator doors opening. Sounds of battle raged in the areas just beyond the safety of the lift, and a rippling tension swept over the occupants in the crammed space as the elevator slowed, then stopped.

They seemed to come from nowhere, and everywhere; Nautas supporters left behind to defend their stronghold. Branch had not over-exaggerated when he told them the fighters on level eleven needed help. From the looks of things, Alexine was under the impression they needed more than "help." They needed a miracle.

For some mysterious reason, the young lady found herself unable to leave the confines of her classroom. Having attempted it several times, Alexine was baffled. The room was the same, but the door wouldn't budge. It was maddening, and she analyzed the possibilities, reasons regarding why she had been suddenly rendered inept, as she followed in Branch's wake.

When she had pulled Zeke in, Annalynn was in trouble. Panicked and longing to defend her tortured mentor, the event had drawn itself out with ease, without her even knowing what she was doing.

And on basement level seven, the man had attacked her from behind, completely caught her off guard. Recalling the event, she realized at the onset of the attack, she had not immediately responded by pulling the man in. It was only when there was no way out, no other option available, that was when that facet of her abilities kicked in.

Moving down the hallway, no one attacked her, no one challenged her or placed her in danger. Surrounded by skirmishes, it seemed ludicrous no one even noticed the young lady.

Shifters popped in and out of view; running and following, running and following. Susan overtook a man to Alexine's left with an impressively accurate baseball the second he materialized two feet in front of her. Alexine couldn't help but wonder if baseballs were Susan's specialty. Then suddenly, Michael was there, running toward Branch at full speed.

"Bethia wants you on the roof," he barked to be heard about the clashes of battle.

"Why?"

Michael paused as if pained to provide an answer to Branch's single word question. "Anna."

Chapter Forty-seven
The Destroyer

Branch dashed toward Alexine. Grasping her upper arm, he caught her at a full run. Sprinting to the elevator, Branch slammed a fist onto the call button and the doors parted immediately as if unwilling to disobey such a powerful command.

Punching the "1" button, the lift raced upward, out of the depths of the academy. Upon breaching the basement levels, Branched wasted no time and wrapped decisive fingers around Alexine's upper arm.

She had the strange sensation she was moving through partly congealed Jell-O. Although their movements felt laggard and slow, the hallway was whizzing past at a dizzying rate. Alexine squeezed her eyes shut and swallowed hard to keep from being sick.

Moving upward, being tugged ahead by the man who had a firm grip on her, Alexine found herself melting through the ceiling. Heating pipes, insulation, tiles. They moved from top to bottom, scrolling past her field of vision, like a roll of pictures being drawn downward by an invisible hand. She reached out, and her arm appeared to travel through the objects barring her vision. But no, not through, they became part of the objects, became one with them. The spaces occupied by nothing but air still held her, still contained parts of her arms, legs, torso. But the other things, the pvc, metal and concrete, she mixed with them. They were part of her as she passed.

She and Branch breached the shingling and found themselves melding upward, emerging from the imprisonment of the building below. The force of their motion propelled them several feet above the roof decking. As quickly as the odd, Jell-O-like feeling had begun, it vanished. The man dropped her arm, landed resolutely, ran forward, and threw himself into a crouch. Alexine fell with a thud onto the roof. Toppling onto her backside, head swimming, she looked from side to side in a daze, trying in vain to gain her bearings.

"How is she?" she heard Branch say through the haze, his voice full of concern.

"Who did this Branch?" the woman demanded angrily. "WHO?"

Branch shook his head slowly, concentrating on an unseen object just below his line of vision. "Nautas," he whispered hauntingly. "My brother."

There was a pregnant pause. The woman demanding answers glanced to her right, seeing Alexine for the first time. Her expression did not change one iota.

"Bethia?" whispered Alexine. "What's going on?"

The healer ignored the question. Leaning toward Branch, she breathed quietly, "he's a destroyer." Only Branch heard the assertion.

Tears sprang to his eyes. He raised his head and met Bethia's gaze, his face imploring, as if begging her to recant the statement. Although Branch already knew the line had been drawn, already felt the plan had been set in stone. Now that the proof Nautas had truly made this horrific choice lay before him, it was almost overwhelming.

Bethia reached out and placed her hand over Branch's. "I've done all I can," she said with such compassion and understanding Branch took a deep breath to maintain self control. He focused on the victim curled motionless between them.

"*She's* got to do the rest," continued Bethia thoughtfully, "and I'm not sure she's willing to fight."

Branch kneeled and leaned low, brushing Annalynn's forehead with his lips. "Anna?" he said softly in her ear, "please."

Alexine jumped when a young man materialized next to her, landing with a thud. She saw only the back of him, but recognition was instantaneous. "John!"

He turned his head and flashed her a quick, tired smile. Pointing at her authoritatively, he spoke over his shoulder while still walking forward. "For the record...I wanted to tell you everything from the beginning." The young man strode toward the cluster of people gathered around Anna.

"When you guys showed up," John began, "Elizabeth had a group hiding in the first level of the basement, ready to fight." John paused. "Branch?" he continued, furtively, "I don't know how but, Nautas knew you were coming."

Branch's brow furrowed in concern.

"Anyway, only levels three and four still aren't secure. Three is going to be especially tough. I'm not sure about four. What should we do sir?"

Branch looked at Michael, who had materialized moments after John appeared. Panting, Michael nodded once each time John completed a sentence, as if to collaborate the young shifter's report. The large man's jaw tightened when he glanced down at Annalynn.

"We are in the right," Branch nodded in Michael's direction. "We end this."

Michael breathed deeply, then bowed his head.

* * *

"Have you seen anyone?" Branch asked as he and Elizabeth moved down the hallway in the third basement floor. They were partly crouched and whispering.

"No one on this floor yet. But that's just it, they're here...somewhere." Elizabeth threw Branch a warm smile, grateful to see his face again.

He returned the gesture, glad to be back, but troubled by the lack of contest. "Strange," he thought. It wasn't like Nautas to run from a fight, to miss the opportunity to inflict injury, to encourage bloodshed. The answer came quickly.

"BROTHER!" a gruff voice thundered. It reverberated off walls and surrounded them.

Branch straightened and stood.

"Do not think I will remain here and waste my time," Nautas boomed. "My soldiers will annihilate yours and defend this institution without my aid."

"Then where are they?"

Nautas's chuckle rang rancorous. "You should not have relinquished your foothold here. It was a mistake, a grave error."

"No, it wasn't," Branch said quietly.

"IT WAS!" Nautas countered, irritated. "You should have pressed your advantage. You should have driven us out!"

"No," Branch answered back calmly.

"YES!" screamed Nautas. "And now," he continued, "you will loose them all...as I foresaw."

Silence. Nautas had left. "No," replied Branch to the emptiness, "I won't. Elizabeth!"

The woman looked up and saw the blow approaching. She ducked and her attacker missed his mark. Spinning into a squatting position as she descended, the shifting instructor extended her leg and swept the man's feet out from underneath him. He fell to the floor with a crash. "Not bad for an old lady, hey?" She winked at Branch.

Reinforcements arrived behind them, just as the enemy appeared in front. All around, skirmishes were born as more people entered the level; screams, thuds, moaning. Shifters faded, then reappeared feet away. Those following struggled to keep up and resume battle.

Alexine raced toward John who was attempting to engage two men. She recognized them as fellow shifters.

"So Little John," one taunted as he lunged playfully. "None of your buddies here to help you now, hey?"

"Forget about me boys?" Alexine said, swaggering up in her best imitation of Callan. John looked at her, and smiled broadly.

Their opponents turned to each other and laughed. "Bryan," one said to the other, "you ever seen this little lady before?"

"Yep," answered Bryan, "Larry, I sure have."

"She's kind of a pretty little filly," Bryan said in a mock-southern drawl. "What say we corral her, brand her, and keep her for ourselves?"

John's smile faded like the brilliant colors of a sunset at dusk, his expression becoming dark, stormy and disturbed. He tensed beside Alexine. Her fingers found his, and she shook her head in warning. John's attention dropped to their intertwined hands and he squeezed.

Alexine was standing on an expanse of lush, green, perfectly manicured lawn. The temperature was perfect; not too hot, not too cold. White, billowing clouds graced the magnificent blue sky. She breathed deeply; fresh cut grass, and burning leaves in the distance. Where was she?

"It's a rugby field," John answered her unspoken question. Bounding toward her, he smiled self-consciously, then shrugged, "my warning image."

"Your what? Wait…you're a…?"

"Yea, a reader."

"But you're a…" Alexine was bewildered.

"A shifter too, yea, multi-talented. Pretty good shifter, not a great reader. As you can see, my 'safe place' is fairly accessible." He glanced around the deep green field.

Upon facing her again, John's smile had fallen. "I want you to get behind me." He clenched his jaw and took a wide stance in front of her, as if standing at attention, preventing something from reaching the girl, a human barricade designed to shield, protect. John's eyes narrowed, and his intense gaze caused Alexine to redden noticeably.

Something else was hidden in those eyes. It developed so abruptly, Alexine was caught off guard. The longing wariness made the young man appear slightly vulnerable. "I would never let them hurt you. You know that, right?" He again took her by the hand. "I would never let anyone hurt you."

Alexine smiled softly at him, taken aback, and nodded. They were still at the academy, facing two people about whom Alexine knew very little. Were they strong shifters? Surely not as daunting as Zeke. But they would attack, of that the young girl was sure. Would she be able to pull them in?

"Yea, John," Larry spat, "listen to your girly-friend. No-no."

The larger of the two, Bryan, launched himself at Alexine like a bull elephant. Before she had time to react, John plowed into him from the side, burying a rock solid fist into Bryan's side. The pair grappled each other to the floor as Bryan's partner, Larry, grinned and joined the fray.

Whisking into the classroom, Alexine did not have time to open the door before a curtain of black was wrapped around her.

Chapter Forty-eight
I didn't protect you

"Michael," Branch said warningly, his chest heaving. The large man swung his head around slowly, eyeing up his opponents as he struggled for breath. Five at once, too many, too many; they were desperately outmatched. Where was everyone?

Branch, Michael and seven opponents stood in a large room located on the fourth basement level. Under the impression level three was minutes from being taken, Michael and Branch had moved ahead to level four with the assurance others would follow quickly. Now backed into a corner, Branch faced two attackers, but stood his ground, the wall behind him serving as a partial shield. His eyes flitted from one man, to the other, and back.

Michael was twenty feet away, to Branch's right. His five opponents circled him. Moving steadily back and forth in a five foot perimeter, like hyenas taunting their prey, the men kept just out of the large man's grasp. Michael's head rotated fluidly from side to side in an attempt to keep everyone in view; a longhorn surrounded by bullfighters. Having endured at least twenty minutes of shifting, reappearing and vanishing again, only to be met by several opponents at once, both Branch and Michael were exhausted.

"Michael, Michael, Michael," an older man taunted. "Now, what is happening here?"

"Lotus," Michael said, inclining his head, and straining to speak through panting breaths. "Didn't ever think you and I would be in this position."

"You were wrong, my friend, dead wrong."

"No," countered Michael authoritatively. "I am *right*, my friend. *You*...are wrong."

Instead of lunging forward as Michael had anticipated, Lotus drew back, pulling a pistol slowly from his pocket. The firearm was small, but deadly; an unanticipated situation. "You're kidding me," Michael snapped, "a gun?"

Lotus smiled, cocking the hammer. "No joke."

Michael glanced at Branch and they both disappeared simultaneously. The competition followed suit and several seconds later, appeared near the door next to the two men. Once again, Michael and Branch's attempts to reach the exit were blocked. Again they vanished, popping into view standing back to back. Their opponents materialized, forming a barricade around the two men.

"You're sure we can't get out?" Branch whispered.

"Whole rooms electrified," came the bitter answer as Michael shook his head. "Can't get to the door, no way out."

"We can't do this much longer." Branch's shoulders drooped as he uttered the words, his stamina flagging.

"I know."

* * *

When Alexine regained consciousness, her head ached so badly she thought it might split open. Large hands restrained her when she attempted to sit up.

"Uh-uh. You stay right there."

John's distorted image rippled unsteadily a foot away when she opened her eyes. He was kneeling beside her, holding an intense conversation with someone else in the small room they now occupied. She squint her eyes shut as blurred images of their surroundings swam in her head.

"I'll figure it out eventually," John snapped.

"John, I don't think that's a good idea. I mean, vengeance? Retribution? That won't un-do…"

"I didn't ask your opinion."

The cool retort was so unlike John, Alexine's eyes fluttered open again and she winced in pain. "What happened to me?" she croaked. The voice, gravely and rough, did not sound like her own. She swallowed, her eyes flitting shut involuntarily in an attempt to quell her pounding headache.

"We don't know." It was spoken in the John-voice to which she was accustom; gentle and concerned.

"What's wrong?"

"Just relax, how's your head feeling?"

Before she had a chance to answer, John snapped, "where is she? Go get her yourself Shulin, will you?"

The ensuing silence indicated Shulin's reluctance to perform this task. To "get her."

"You sure I should leave you guys?" Shulin asked warily.

"We'll be okay, just hurry."

All was quiet and Alexine knew the other man had gone. "John?" She could feel the warmth of his body and knew he had leaned in close. Her eyes still clamped shut in a bid to hold the pain throbbing in her head at bay, she laid a hand on his chest.

"Yea?"

"What happened?"

The uncomfortable pause frightened the young girl and she raised a hand to her eyes, pushing on them in hopes the pressure would enable her to focus on John for a moment, read his expression. When she opened them, what stared back surprised her. Guilt? Why would John feel guilty?

"I'm sorry."

Alexine breathed deeply, allowing her eyelids to sink shut again. "Why? Did you hit me?" She let out a pained chuckle. "Keep this up and I'm going to have to report you to the proper authorities."

John squeezed her hand, but said nothing, forcing Alexine to open her eyes again to gauge his reaction. He turned away as her gaze fell upon him.

"John?"

"I didn't protect you." It was spoken softly and bitterly as if the words left an undesirable taste in his mouth.

"Well, you were kind of busy as I recall. Bryan and Larry…where…?"

"In holding. Someone attacked you when they jumped me. I don't know who, I couldn't see. According to Shulin it was a shifter. Whoever it was wasn't too bright. They tried to shift with you in tow, so that narrows the possibilities." He paused as if rifling through a list of "not-to-bright" shifters in his mind. "What moron would attempt that?" he snickered, obviously disgusted.

Hesitating to ask the question, Alexine's curiosity overcame her sense of pride. "Why couldn't he shift with me?"

John froze as if the question caught him completely off guard, then sized Alexine up questioningly. "Because you were unwilling, of course."

"How could I be unwilling if I was unconscious?"

"Alexine," it was spoken as if she were a child who should already understand this concept, "unless you're dead, your will is still in operation. A part of you always knows what is happening, despite your physical condition. Didn't Annalynn…"

He was cowered into silence by the glare Alexine shot as him.

"Okayyy…obviously not."

When Bethia and Shulin popped into view, John jumped to his feet in surprise, his face a mask of determination.

"Easy boy," Shulin smiled a bit nervously. It's just us."

"Sorry. Still a little jumpy."

Bethia sank to Alexine's side, quickly placing a confident hand on her head. "Kind of a habit with you, isn't it? Geez Alexine, should we get you a helmet?"

Alexine let out an involuntary snort of laughter that caused her head to throb even more. She winced, then moaned.

Bethia's hand felt warm and comforting as if generating its own heat. Once again that sensation of time being stretched swept over her. When she opened her eyes, the room blurred, sprang into focus, then blurred again. Voices echoed around her, floating about the room as if bounding off the sides of a large barrel surrounding them. Concentrating hard, Alexine pulled the room into focus. Realizing John, Shulin and Bethia were all studying her intently, Alexine stood, self-conscious. Never had she been so grateful to not be in pain.

John smirked when Alexine piped up, "well, what are we waiting for?"

* * *

Alexine and John burst into the room precisely at the moment Branch and Michael were contemplating their next move, exhausted. The doors banged, remaining open to the hallway and Michael's heart slammed in his chest. An escape route!

Alexine and John both pulled up short as the scene met their eyes. John was suddenly torn regarding his next move. Should he remain by Alexine's side, or throw his lot in with Branch and Michael, currently painfully outnumbered?

Lotus glanced at them, flashed a wicked smile and grasped the firearm firmly, wrapping his long fingers around the butt of the gun, his index finger sliding onto the trigger. Leveling the gun directly at Michael's chest, just seven feet away, he paused.

Lotus's comrades darted and weaved around Branch, holding the man's attention to such an extent that he failed to catch the conversation unfolding between Lotus and Michael.

"Ahh, Michael, now here is an interesting situation," Lotus seethed, just loud enough for only Michael to hear. The gun wielding man gestured to the two young sillemlem who had just entered the gymnasium. "I'll make you an offer: it's you…or them,"

Michael clenched his jaw and took in a protracted breath. It exited as a half-sigh, half-growl, as the large man's eyes narrowed in contempt. He pressed his lips together, then gave Lotus a curt but surrendering nod. He would not shift.

"I thought so," Lotus flashed the trapped man a bored look of disinterest. "Good-bye then."

Branch screamed, "no!" as the realization of what was playing out behind him overshadowed his circling opponents.

Whisking into the classroom, then barreling out the door, Alexine once again found herself observing the scene. A part of it still, but somehow, above it. She threw herself at the man brandishing the gun. It fired, and at the same instant Lotus was flung roughly sideways, Michael roared in pain. His scream filled the auditorium with a sickening cacophony of anguish.

Too late, she had attacked Lotus just a second too late. Standing that close to Michael, even the most amateur of marksmen would hit their target. And Alexine had the undeniable feeling this gun-wielding man was no novice. In her haze of disappointment she willed herself to rejoin the floor and turned to look at what used to be Michael. She had failed.

"You know!" Michael screamed deeply. "It really hurts when you do that Callan!"

The scene that met her eyes sent waves of shock through her. Alexine stumbled backward in surprise, falling to the cement. It's rough surface dug into the skin of her hands, tiny bubbles of blood appearing along the angry scrapes. She ignored the searing pain, too confused by what she was witnessing.

Branch scooped the gun up from the floor and yelled something incoherent. Startled, the eight opponents, minus Lotus who was laying on the cement, quite still, turned toward the now open doors then disappeared in an instant.

"John!" Branch bellowed. "Follow!"

John shot forward after the men, melting into the surroundings.

"Callan?" was all Alexine could manage to utter. "What?"

Michael was still bellowing in agony, thrashing his head from side to side, but trying to remain still. In a bid to claw himself away from the pain, the agonized man's hands attempted to dig into the concrete floor. Scraping and scratching, he exerted such force that within moments his fingers were covered in scarlet scratches. The blood seeping from his injured hands painted swaths of color onto the unforgiving concrete, like a child's coarse painting project.

"Just a minute you big baby," snapped Callan, her right fist buried deep in Michael's chest; it was as if they were conjoined. Alexine shook her head. Surely she wasn't seeing this. There was Callan's face, her arm, her wrist, and then...Michael's chest. Callan's hand had become part of Michael's body, and it was obviously causing the muscular man an incredible amount of pain.

"Hurry...up...please!" he punctuated each word, gritting his teeth, and continuing to squirm uncontrollably.

Callan's hand began slowly emerging from Michael's chest, clutched in a fist.

Branch bolted toward the two people sprawled on the ground. Sliding to Michael's side, he placed a hand on the injured man's shoulder. "Hang in there buddy, almost done."

"Luckily the gun wasn't very powerful," Callan grunted, concentrating as she withdrew her limb. The hand emerged and Michael's chest looked horribly bruised and battered where it had been penetrated. The large man's shirt had been ripped partially open where the bullet had entered, and Alexine could see a small hole which seeped blood, but the wound didn't appear serious. In addition, Callan had created another bullet-sized hole in Michael's side when she removed the deadly piece of metal. Two tiny crimson stains now stood out against Michael's white shirt.

The little shifter fell backward onto her seat and dropped a flattened slug to the floor. It chinked on the cement, and Michael threw himself onto his belly, gulping encumbered lungfuls of air. Each breath whistled ominously as air escaped through the hole created by Lotus's well-aimed round.

"You're telling me!" Callan commented knowingly. "It's no picnic on this end either!" She studied the palm of her right hand for a moment, now speckled with blood which had clung to the bullet. Breathing deeply, the small shifter suddenly jerked her head up. "Especially when you've been drugged!" she yelled in Alexine's direction.

The older girl blushed guiltily as Callan's gaze fell on Lotus who lay several hundred yards to her right, facing away from the group gathered around Michael. Her expression hardened. "Get Bethia," the little red-head barked through clenched teeth. "She needs to fix the holes in his left lung...fast."

Lotus lay very still, his eyes darting, frantically filing away the facts he had just uncovered. Callan Kovar, the little shifter Devin had clumsily recruited, was not only in league with Branch. She was a phase four shifter.

Chapter Forty-nine
Liberated

"What do *you* think we should do then?"

"Keep him!" Callan replied angrily. "He tried to kill Michael!"

Branch shook his head sadly. "Where would we keep him?"

"Let's see," she glanced flippantly to the side as if searching for an answer she already possessed, then shot, "there's a basement full of cells down there. I'm sure we have plenty of room. It will be a fitting twist of fate; being locked in the prison he helped build!"

"Callan," Branch began in a reprimanding tone, "Nautas imprisons people indefinitely. Do you truly think we should follow his lead?"

"We're not talking about locking him up because he disagrees with us. We're talking about a murderer here, that's a lot different." The little girl placed hands on hips defiantly, challenging Branch to disagree.

"Yes it is, but even if we were to keep him here, we won't stay here forever. What would we do with him then? As we dismantle parts of this building, make it safe to occupy, the cells downstairs will not hold him anymore. It would be reckless for us to keep him so close. If we call the police, turn him over to them, we have done our part."

Callan snorted derisively. "Nautas has too many connections. He'll be out by tomorrow. You might as well just set Lotus free."

Branch sighed. "Michael?" He turned toward the hulking man standing a few feet from the fuming little red-head. Michael met Branch's gaze in retort. "What should we do with Lotus?" The large man's hand found the partly-healed wound on his chest. He touched it absently.

Callan's blood was still boiling, and now she focused that frustration on Michael, angry he was even thinking about the question. "Keep him," she said under her breath. Michael heard her and turned to look at the little shifter, then smiled softly. "Make the call."

The little girl stamped her foot and yelled, "no!"

Michael moved close to Callan and placed a powerful hand on her shoulder. She looked up at him, tears sparkling in her eyes. "He tried to kill you," she whispered, "and he'll do it again."

"Maybe."

"Then why?"

Michael exhaled a weary burst of breath. "Lotus was my teacher, my mentor, my friend."

Callan cringed, then uttered bitterly, "well, he's not anymore."

The comment caused Michael to wince. "I know that if we turn him over to the police, it will be a waste of time, I'm no fool Callan." He smiled down at the little girl and she dropped her head sheepishly. "I also know we can't imprison him; logistically, it's impossible. The academy is in disarray. Housing a bunch of prisoners would be a monumental task. Our only options are to kill him, or turn him over to the authorities.

Michael fixed Callan with an intense stare, searching for signs of recalcitrance which never came. The petite red-head held his gaze, frozen, not blinking, not even breathing, to prove her point. "Be careful little one," the large man said seriously. "Making a life or death judgment should not come so easily."

Callan dropped her head, the implications of their predicament sinking in. "Maybe it will help Lotus."

Michael's disappointed and wistful comment stung Callan. "I still think it's a mistake," she breathed.

"It may be," replied Branch. The sides of his mouth curled upward, yet no humor presented itself. "But I think we should allow Michael to make the decision, don't you?"

Callan considered the question for several moments. No, she didn't think they should let Michael decide because Michael was going to let Lotus go. Michael was going to do something Callan didn't want him to do. But she had argued and disagreed to no avail. The decision had been made, and she needed to accept it. "Yea," she said unconvincingly, then shot an angry glance at Michael, who shook his head in return.

"Yes," Branch smiled for the first time, raising his eyebrows. "Forcing Michael to bend his will to yours is tempting isn't it? Parts of Nautas's methods are compelling.

Callan threw him an irritated look.

* * *

After the fighting had subsided and the situation settled, Lotus was removed from his holding cell then escorted to an adjacent room. He knew there was no use trying to escape. The ceilings of each floor in the basement levels were still alive with power. Metal bars hidden overhead were set up in a parallel circuit with a fifty-thousand volt power supply, courtesy of step-up transformers installed on each floor. In addition, many of the walls and doors were similarly fashioned. No way out except the elevator, which held its own secrets. He was sure the elevator would be heavily guarded anyway. The lower levels of the building had been designed with one purpose in mind: keep shifters in if necessary, confine them. He chided himself for coming up with that idea, never imagining his own brainstorm would work against him one day.

Heated debate had actually surrounded the small shifter on whom Devin had focused his attentions; Callan. Could she squeeze through, if necessary? The bars were situated eight inches apart, too small for adults to shift through, but the girl? She was so tiny.

Lotus's meandering was interrupted when Michael entered. Wary at first, it soon became apparent Michael was not going to retaliate for the earlier attempt on his life and Lotus sat, perplexed.

"That's it? You're calling the authorities?" Lotus couldn't believe what he was hearing.

"Yea."

"What's the catch?" The tall, thin man was still sitting. Right leg crossed over left, he rotated his foot nervously. They had to want something. They had to know Nautas would eventually arrange for his release from the authorities. Was he to deliver a message to Nautas? Were they going to follow him, try to gather information?

"The catch, Lotus, is that you agree to stop fighting against us."

The seated man snickered in response. "You know I can't do that."

Michael rounded on the man, fury in his eyes. "Then you will not leave this building alive." A vein in the large man's neck pounded as anger seethed through his powerful body. Michael's fists were clenched, his knuckles blanched white in response to the pressure.

"Uh huh," replied Lotus slowly, attempting to sound confident. But weakness and fear hung around the man, betraying his misgivings.

"Your answer then?" Michael demanded.

"Fine," Lotus shot too quickly, shrugging his shoulders. "No more fighting against you. Done." The older man attempted to grin agreeably.

"I thought so," replied Michael, disgust heavy in his voice. "I see your loyalty is not the only thing for sale Lotus. Your integrity is on the auction block also."

"Your condition was that I agree not to fight, and I agree." Lotus held up his hands in surrender.

"You're a liar Lotus." Michael studied the man intently. Anger slowly shrinking to disappointment, the large man turned to leave, his hand resting on the door handle.

"Wait."

Michael paused but did not turn back to face his old instructor.

"Do you have a message for Nautas? Should I tell him anything?" There had to be a catch, had to be something going on here. Michael knew he was lying, knew he would return to fight again. Why would they just allow him to slip through their fingers? Perhaps if he kept Michael in the room, kept him talking, he could weasel out some information of his own.

"Yea, tell him he's wrong." Michael turned the door handle and walked sadly from the room.

"He's wrong," repeated Lotus, a tinge of regret in his voice. Michael had always been his favorite student. It was too bad really, they were now turned against each other. If only Michael had seen reason. The older man's eyes were glued to the door long after his former student had left him there, alone.

* * *

"I don't know," said Elizabeth calmly. "It's as if many of them just abandoned the facility."

Branch nodded solemnly. Taking back the academy had not been extremely difficult, all things considered. Although the prison held about ninety members of the opposition when the battle ended, the rest of the facility was empty, deserted. He could not believe so many of Nautas's soldiers would turn tail and run.

"We know there were about 500 people here prior to our arrival." Too many; there was no way Nautas or anyone else would have ordered most of their fighters to just leave, abandon their posts. "This will not fare well for those who left before they were told to, I'm afraid," Branch said quietly. "He will make them pay dearly."

Those in attendance at the meeting nodded their heads, some of them exchanging quiet comments.

"But there were some who left purposefully, their mission was to remove the things we were hoping to acquire, and to relocate a portion of the people we were hoping to set free."

Michael averted his gaze, his disappointment evident.

- 243 -

"James?" said Branch quietly. "How many were we able to release?"

The large Asian man half-smiled hopefully. "Probably half." James looked around the room, as if providing the answers to the group and not one individual person. "According to them, there were one hundred and thirty-two dissenters being held. We have seventy-one upstairs."

There were several sad smiles. Seventy-one was good, it was a start.

A gentle knock caused everyone to glance at the door. "Come in!" called Branch, but no one entered. The rightful leader of the academy strode across the room and attempted to admit the person on the other side. But apparently the person knocking had a firm hold on the handle which prevented Branch from opening the door completely. All Alexine heard Branch say was, "what?" and then he stepped over the threshold, into the hall, the door clicking shut behind him.

The other occupants in the room stared at the entryway in confusion, but no one got up, they just waited. Five long minutes ticked by, which seemed more like thirty. Just when Alexine was inclined to whisper a question regarding how long they were going to sit there in silence, the door re-opened and Branch took his place at the desk once again.

"Where were we?" he asked politely, as if he had simply lost track of the conversation.

Alexine tried to exercise patience, but during the period of quiet, she had found more and more questions elbowing their way into her mind. What was happening? Who were all these people? She couldn't wait a moment more. Obviously there was nothing imperative happening, so she stood to pose her questions. "I'm sorry," she began, shaking her head, "but I am still a little lost." Branch nodded, encouraging her to continue. "Can someone please tell me what just happened?"

John stood quickly. "May I?" He looked hopefully toward Branch.

Bethia's smart retort, flung out before Branch had a chance to speak, stung the young man. "Go ahead, you've been dying to tell her everything since the beginning!"

When Branch raised his eyebrows at Bethia, she looked kow-towed and turned her head. "If it's okay with you boss," she threw in, humbled but still a bit flippant.

Branch laughed. Part of what made this healer so endearing was her sassiness. "Bethia," he began and she braced herself, "you are a breath of fresh air."

The healer smiled gratefully while others in the room grinned, rolled their eyes to the ceiling, or shook with silent laughter.

"Okay," began John, not able to wait another minute, "you kind of messed things up today Alexine."

A collective groan emanated from the group, followed by several reprimands.

"Perhaps I should fill her in John," said Elizabeth, rescuing the young man. "From the beginning."

Chapter Fifty
The Gathering

"Michael, may I talk to you for a moment?" Branch asked as the meeting broke up.

"Sure." The large man sank back onto the couch as the last of the leaders left the room.

"Actually, let's go outside," Branch said, in a low voice.

Once they reached the parking lot, Branch and Michael turned left and walked slowly down the sidewalk. Michael's right hand found his chest injury and he broke stride.

"Still hurting?" asked Branch.

"Some," replied Michael dismissively.

"Why don't you go see Bethia again? It's been a few hours since she took care of that lung. I'm sure she could get rid of some of the bruising now."

"Bethia's done enough," answered Michael shortly. "The poor girl is exhausted."

Branch studied his companion for a moment and decided against arguing the point. "Charlie is here," Branch whispered.

"What?! He's supposed to be in the United States," Michael hissed. "Who's going to protect the…"

"He brought them with him." Branch answered the question before it was completely finished.

"All of them?" Michael asked, dubiously.

Nodding his head, Branch ran a hand through his ruffled hair. "All of them. The Denique weren't safe."

"Weren't safe? Why not? Where are they now?" Michael shot questions quickly, his face a mask of incredulity. "I mean, there must be at least fifty."

"Fifty-seven, to be exact. But he only brought thirteen with him."

"Thirteen? Where are the rest of them? How the heck did he manage that? Transporting thirteen kids half way around the world without being detected?" Michael again spewed questions before even one could be considered.

Branch barked a laugh. "This is Charlie we're talking about, remember?"

"Yea, but…that's a stretch, even for him."

"None-the-less, they are all here now."

"*All* here now? I thought you said he only brought thirteen?

"For months I have felt it was time to call everyone in. Several weeks ago we began gathering the Denique. I was afraid that Nautas would search for them, so we have been bringing them here slowly. They needed a secluded spot to hide, to wait, until we were ready to join them. According to Charlie, my fears were confirmed. Nautas set hunters on them."

Michael pulled to a stop when the word "hunters" was uttered, a look of dark panic creeping into his features.

"Yes," Branch raised his eyebrows. "Two days ago. Charlie tells me that our seekers were able to avert many tragedies, to collect the Denique for which they were responsible, before the hunters arrived. None were lost. Charlie arrived with the remainder of them yesterday."

"Where has he hidden them?"

The leader of the academy shook his head seriously, "he wouldn't tell me. They're safe though."

"Wouldn't tell *you?*" Michael snapped, slightly exasperated.

"He's being cautious. We *are* still in this building, who knows what Nautas set up in our absence. So, we cannot be completely sure who is listening. To tell you the truth, I'm surprised he even showed up to tell me."

"Showed up? In the building? When?"

"When I left the meeting."

"The person who knocked on the door? It was Charlie?"

Branch laughed out loud. "Yes, dressed as an old woman."

The look on Michael's face was a mix of shock, disbelief and hilarity. "Why would he risk coming to the building? Why wouldn't he just call?"

Branch raised his eyebrows, as if trying to decide whether the explanation he was about to reveal was viable. "Charlie doesn't trust the phones. Says Nautas may be able to tap into the cellular frequency."

"Charlie's not going nutty on us, is he?" Michael laughed.

"Charlie's always been a bit nutty, that's why he's so good at what he does."

* * *

It seemed strange to still be in China. Alexine had not anticipated spending another night in the country. They were supposed to be in the air at this very moment, heading home. Instead, she and Callan lay on make-shift beds in the auditorium at the academy, exhausted.

It had been decided that all students and teachers should remain in the building for safety's sake. Where each of them had been staying was known to Nautas and his followers. Separating would be folly, placing each of them in danger. There was unarguably safety in numbers.

"So you knew from the very beginning," Alexine said, for the sixth time. Callan had known everything; about Branch, and the plan to take back the academy. About who supported the cause, and who opposed it. About Nautas's supporters and many of the plans they had formulated.

Callan flipped onto her side to look at Alexine, and adjusted her pillow. "Yea."

"And you couldn't tell me because you thought that someone might read me? That I might be a weak link that could give away the entire operation?"

"Yes," answered Callan, impatiently, "we've been over this."

"I'm sorry," shot Alexine. "You've been living this reality for a month now, but it's only a few hours old to me!"

Callan smiled. If she were completely honest, she would admit that, in the beginning, the thought of keeping secrets from Alexine was fun. But she soon grew weary of having to play the game and was glad it had ended. "They weren't sure exactly what was going on in the basement levels," Callan said, providing Alexine with new information.

Several hours earlier, Elizabeth had given her a rough outline of how the academy had been divided, with part of the participants siding with Nautas, and the larger portion remaining faithful to Branch. But there had not been time for specifics. Although Alexine wasn't exactly sure what needed to be done now, she sensed there were loose ends to tie up. The group had dispersed quickly, the students taking up residence in the auditorium, and the leaders organizing meetings to make decisions.

"They knew people would be changing their minds, wanting to abandon Nautas's cause, but it seemed like anyone who wavered disappeared." Callan frowned. "It surprised people, when the split happened, that so many sided with Nautas. Some of the people you met today, on our side, had brothers…sisters…friends…fiancés." The little girl shook her head.

It felt good to hear Callan say "our side". "Our side" was now, not only Callan's team, but Alexine's as well. Grateful for the reunion, she grinned.

Callan eyed Alexine, who was still smiling. The little girl seemed confused. "What's funny about that?"

"Oh." Alexine was both surprised and embarrassed. "Nothing's funny. I was just thinking that…our side." The older girl beamed. "It feels good to be back on your side. I've missed you."

Callan gave her a disbelieving, and slightly embarrassed look.

"Listen," said Alexine playfully, "you've been on the 'team' since you arrived. I've been an outsider. You have no idea what that feels like."

Callan's expression softened. "Actually, I do." The little red-head had lived her entire life, up until this point, feeling like an outsider. Someone whom people might like, but could never understand. No one she had ever met, before arriving at the academy, could relate to her experience. "Sorry," she said sheepishly. "I didn't even think about it." She laid back, gazing at the ceiling. "We've been working so hard, that it's all gone by so fast."

"Well, it's gone by really slowly for me." The older girl tried to block out several memories acquired during the previous few weeks; arguments with Callan, the market with Zeke, screaming at Annalynn. Annalynn. "But tell me more," she said, swallowing down the knot in her throat which sprang up each time she thought about her instructor.

"Kay." Callan sat up. This would surprise Alexine. "Annalynn was engaged to Branch."

Shocked, Alexine sucked in a breath. "No!"

But the little red-head was already nodding. "Yes, and she opted to stay with Nautas."

"I gathered that much."

"We weren't sure where she stood." Callan looked up at the corner of the room, as if seeing another time and place. "Some said she was loyal to Nautas, others thought she might be playing the double-agent, a few insisted she had changed her mind and wanted to return to Branch."

"She did."

"I know now," said Callan, fully expecting Alexine to defend the woman. "Bethia told us when you confided in her, but we had to be careful about who we trusted, and she was a question mark."

Alexine sighed. "She feels really bad about the whole thing. She cries about it sometimes."

Callan's eyes narrowed, doubtful. She cocked her head to the side, as if just given a confusing fact that would be more understandable if viewed from a different perspective. "Asian people don't cry about stuff like that."

The older girl looked scandalized. "Yes they do!" she hissed. "What? You think they don't have feelings?"

The little shifter shook her head, calmly. "You don't understand. It's a different culture. They're very stoic."

"Stoic?" repeated Alexine, contemptuously. "I didn't think you knew words like *stoic*."

"Ha ha," Callan forced out. "Anyway, it's not an insult. I think it's a good quality. They're tough, emotionally." She paused. "Although…"

"Although what?"

"Although, Annalynn was raised by members of the academy, so I guess it's not too surprising. She's not completely Chinese."

Again, the older girl looked incredulous. "What does 'completely Chinese' mean?!"

"Oh my goodness," replied the littler shifter impatiently. "Stop being so politically correct."

"And how do you know so much about Annalynn?" demanded Alexine. In a way, it hurt. *She* was supposed to be Annalynn's friend. *She* was supposed to know more about the woman. Callan knew about the plan, but Alexine knew Anna.

"You know, Alexine," Callan retorted shortly, "I'm tired." The small shifter snuggled into her bedding. "So, why don't you ask questions and I'll give answers. It requires less thinking on my part."

"Good idea," Alexine half-snapped. Realizing Callan would soon be too tired to talk, she mentally prioritized her questions. "What did John mean when he said I really messed things up."

The little girl lying on the floor next to her laughed quietly. "John was never good at keeping his mouth shut," she said. "You were supposed to leave today…alone." Callan pushed deeper into her pillow. "I had an all-access chip, which are hard to come by, compliments of Devin."

Alexine shuttered as her mind flipped back to Elizabeth cutting the chip out of Callan's hand.

"That is something no one on our side had. So, we were trying to keep things quiet for a few days. That would give me some time to poke around; find people who were being held, figure out what Nautas has been working on in the basement, you know, important stuff."

"Oh," was all Alexine could think to say. She was beginning to feel more and more guilty about making a mess of things.

"So, we were sending you away, because when I started investigating, things were going to get complicated. It was hard for me to lie to you constantly, it took a toll on my focus. You were the weak link, constantly in danger of being read."

"Okay, okay, I get it."

Callan smiled, realizing she was teasing. "But you threw a bit of a wrench in the works when you DRUGGED me." The little girl sat up quickly and paused to glare at Alexine. "We'll talk about that later though," she continued and again fell back against the pillow. "In our original plan we would get you out of the academy without *anyone* being brought under suspicion. We were going to make sure Annalynn saw several known Branch supporters after you left with James. We knew she would be following. I was supposed to run around, find her and tell her that you were taken by someone. They would assume it was Branch. Tah-dah. Branch is blamed for everything. You're out of the picture. But…" the young girl paused.

"But what?"

"We were counting on Annalynn remaining loyal to Nautas. Once the possibility of her abandoning his cause came to light, it changed things. Devin was suspicious of her. If he shared his thoughts with Nautas... Well, Nautas knows her, and he's very paranoid. Anything she said, or did, would be called into question. So, without Annalynn - as a staunch supporter of Nautas - collaborating my story about your disappearance, *I* would be under suspicion, and, of course, so would she."

"Oh..."

"So, we came up with a solution. If Annalynn pursued us alone, Elizabeth would have to disappear. If she disappeared, they would suspect Elizabeth as having a hand in your kidnapping. The heat would be transferred from Annalynn and I to Elizabeth. But if Annalynn pursued with someone else, someone whom Devin and Nautas trusted completely, we could stick with our original plan. Elizabeth could remain because the story I told would be witnessed by two people, at least one of whom Devin and Nautas trusted. When we saw that Annalynn had Ginna with her, we decided to go with the original plan; everyone stays. Make sense?"

"I guess."

"Things went well, except I had to be yanked out too because I was OUT COLD."

Alexine's face fell.

"So, Elizabeth decided to pull out of the academy in an attempt to divert attention away from Annalynn, maybe keep her a little safer than she would have been otherwise. Elizabeth became our scapegoat."

Alexine nodded absently, trying to sort out all of the scenarios and reasoning behind the responses. "But, what if Nautas read *you* and found out *you* were in league with Branch?"

"Well," Callan had a far-away look in her eye. "I was supposed to be gone by the time he arrived. But, to tell you the truth, I was worried about that too. Everyone seemed fairly confident that, if I were ever to meet Nautas, he wouldn't read me; a little girl, and a shifter to boot. I get the feeling shifters aren't read often. We're not thinkers, you know," she threw in sarcastically. "We're soldiers." She peeled down her covers and climbed under, creating a tiny bump on the small patch of floor. "I trust Branch. He knows Nautas best."

"So, why was everyone worried I would be read?"

Callan looked exasperated. "You're a reader Alexine! Don't you get any of this?"

"Yea, Callan," she snapped. "I get that I'm a reader. What I don't get is why readers are read more often than anyone else."

Callan took a deep breath as if preparing a lengthy monologue. "Readers can have more than their own experiences stored in their memory banks. So, reading a reader is like hitting the jackpot. But, Nautas is kind of selective I guess; doesn't want to pollute himself with too many memories from people he considers inferior." The little girl shrugged her shoulders absently and several minutes stretched by. The silence was broken by Callan's next stuttering comment. "So...Branch and John...they act like reading people...is hard. Like it...changes you somehow...when you do it."

It was phrased as a statement, but Alexine understood it to be a question. Slowly, as if searching for a way to describe the experience, she began stumbling over her words. "It is difficult. To see what other people saw. If what they saw was sad or scary. When you read someone. You never know. How they reacted. How you will react."

Realizing she sounded fractured and childish, Alexine collected her thoughts and tried again. "When you feel the pain and anguish, the fear and frenzy of difficult experiences, it can be overwhelming. Other people's thoughts and feelings can be hard to process."

The dazzling sunset, and their last kiss on earth. Would she ever forget that?

"You have to be strong to handle it. And, I guess you should be cautious regarding who you read, or you take that part of their life into your own memory, and you can't get rid of it."

The two women fiercely embracing on the apartment floor after the Red Guards left.

"At least, I don't think you can get rid of it."

The burnt man; his sorrow and despair.

Alexine took a deep breath and readjusted herself on the bed to clear away those thoughts. They screeched to the front of her mind unannounced at the most inopportune times, would it ever stop?

Callan watched her sister carefully. "Hmmm… And you've…done this?"

Alexine sighed. "Yea, but let's talk about that later, okay?" She did not wait for Callan to answer. "Anyway…a liability…that's what I was…a liability."

"No," corrected Callan, breathing deeply, "honestly, Alexine, you were a threat."

Alexine looked up quickly in surprise. "How?"

"Word is, you're a pretty powerful reader," Callan said smugly. "Don't deny it, we all know." The older girl blushed furiously. Callan had always found it interesting Alexine's cheeks could be so purple, and yet that little dot of tan remained in the middle. Alexine hated it, but Callan thought it made her look healthy or something. "We didn't want you to side with Nautas, but we couldn't tell you about the group working against Nautas."

"Because I'm an inexperienced reader who can be easily read."

"Yea."

"So you had to remove me from the picture."

"Yes," said Callan, glad Alexine understood. "If you choose to join Nautas, we would have to fight you. If you choose not to join Nautas, were the option presented, you would have disappeared, been imprisoned, like the others."

"I'm kind of surprised," Alexine remarked sadly.

"By what?" Her little sister looked completely puzzled.

"That you would think I would side with Nautas. I mean…do you really think I would go along with that stuff?"

Callan studied Alexine thoughtfully. "Annalynn did," she commented in a subdued voice, "and she's a very intelligent woman who has seen a lot. Honestly, Alexine, I get the feeling that, when decisions are made, many people believe and do things that are shocking."

Alexine sighed, that seemed to be true. And somehow, it made her feel better. She flicked a weary smile at Callan, then poured over their conversation in her mind, searching for glitches. "Wait a minute. Why couldn't Elizabeth poke around the academy? She has a chip. Lots of people have chips."

"Everyone has limited-access chips," Callan looked disgusted. "Devin never trusted anyone."

"But Devin knew *you* were close to Elizabeth."

"Noooo," Callan drawled, "*you* knew I was close to Elizabeth because *you're* my sister. We kept our relationship very hush-hush." The little girl smiled. "You see? You knew things that put us in jeopardy. We had to get rid of you." Of course, she could have said "remove you" or "protect you" but "get rid of you" was much more fun.

Alexine threw her a disgusted look in retaliation. She sat and thought about all of this new information, and things began falling together. "So, what you're telling me, is that *I'm* the reason we didn't rescue all of the people being held today. It was *my* fault."

"In a way," said Callan carefully, "but honestly, we have no idea how things would have played out had the plan come off without a hitch. They may not have believed Branch took you. And with Nautas returning today, ahead of schedule," she shook her head, "that was an unexpected twist. I would have been returning to an academy with *him* on site. All of our plans had focused on keeping Devin in the dark and holding Zeke at bay, but Nautas himself? Now if *he* had decided I was a threat, and wanted to reclaim my chip, I bet he wouldn't have been too gentle about it." She looked down at her bandaged hand, it still stung. "All-in-all, I think everyone is relieved things turned out this well." She was quiet for a moment, then shrugged. "Maybe you helped."

The older girl considered this. Maybe she had helped. For several minutes, she couldn't think of anything else to ask or say. She was tired, her mind was blank, and her bedding felt so soft and inviting.

"I know! What in the heck was that you did to that big guy…Michael?"

The little shifter laughed silently, her shoulders shaking. "Some shifters can learn to alter themselves, once they've mastered passing through certain materials. Steel seems to be one of my specialties."

"Steel?"

"Yea," she continued, as if discussing the weather. "I knew I had arrived just a second too late, but…" Callan paused, then squinted in concentration, "the bullet seemed to have gone in at an angle. I don't know," the little shifters shook her head, "maybe Michael tried to turn at the last second or something. The slug had made it completely through part of his lung, and was headed toward his heart." Her sister's features relaxed a bit, "It felt like it was between the parietal pleura and the pericardium. I don't know for sure though, so that's a guess." Callan laughed at Alexine's stunned expression. "What?"

"Partial-what?"

"Parietal pleura," the little red-head giggled again. "You know, the lining surrounding the lungs," she answered matter-of-factly.

"Where in the heck did you learn that?!" replied her shocked sister.

"I've been working on this stuff, remember?"

"Yea…well…working on shifting…maybe…but…biology?" Alexine stuttered almost incoherently.

Callan laughed lightly. The stuff I've been working on required that I know a lot about the human body. Can you understand why?"

Alexine paused. "Yea. I guess it would be important to know what you're doing if you're reaching inside people. Aren't you nervous when you do it though? I mean, you could hurt someone, couldn't you?"

"Definitely. We've been working the ability very slowly. I had never actually altered inside a person before, just a dog," Callan attempted to stifle her giggle.

"A what?!"

"A dog, but I'll tell you about that in a second. I knew that Michael was a goner if I didn't at least try. If that bullet hadn't been stopped…had reached Michael's heart...well, lungs, although delicate, are repairable. But once a person dies," the red-head's eyes opened wide, her face becoming more serious, "there is no going back."

A dark quiet surrounded the girls as they contemplated the loss of Michael. Although Alexine had only just met the man, it was apparent her baby sister was quite attached to him. Callan's gaze was unfocused and far-away, as if she were contemplating a worst case scenario.

"Anyway," the little red-head continued slowly, snapping out of her trance. "I stuck my hand in. That, by the way, is not what hurts so badly."

"Good to know," said Alexine, slightly sarcastic.

Callan heaved a breath. "The problem is, once I'm inside, I have to stop the bullet. My flesh is just as vulnerable as his, so I have to alter and become something stronger than the bullet."

"Steel."

"Yes, and that really stings, steel expanding in your chest cavity. You have to be really careful not to fish around too much," Callan instructed, "or you can do more harm than good. Stop the bullet, change back quick. Once the bullet was stopped, I had to get it out. That part isn't a lot of fun either."

"It didn't appear to be," remarked Alexine, remembering the anguish Michael went through. She had the feeling the man was no wimp, that must have been some serious pain.

"And it has to be done carefully, to minimize damage. Luckily I was able to keep hold of the bullet with my bare hand, which was also Michael's own chest, and there was a clear pathway out of his body. When I alter inside someone, we kind of become one, does that make sense?

Alexine nodded, but her look indicated the opposite answer. "Sure," she said, throwing up her hands.

"So, I perfected the technique on a dog," remarked Callan, as an aside.

"This I have to hear."

"Someone's dog had a piece of metal stuck in its foot, only, I couldn't keep hold of it with my fingers. Steel pinchers. I pulled it loose with steel pinchers." She tapped her thumb and forefinger together, making a quiet tapping sound. "Once it was loose, I altered back and pulled it out."

"Interesting."

"That dog still won't come near me," Callan said, bemused. "But that is when I really got the technique down."

Alexine bowed her head. Shaking it, she covered her eyes with her hand. "So, all shifters can do that?"

"No," replied the little girl, surprised. "Annalynn didn't teach you about shifters?"

When Alexine shook her head yet again in answer to this oft posed question, Callan frowned. "That's strange. Well, shifters are divided into five categories. All shifters can mimic air as they move through it. They are just referred to as 'shifters.' Some can mimic inanimate, natural objects, like plants, trees, and water. They are called phase one shifters. The next level can copy man-made objects, plastics, and stuff like that; phase two. Next come the ones who can move through animate objects, animals. We refer to them as phase three shifters. But all of these abilities hinge on moving through these objects, the objects already have to be there. Very few can mimic the molecular structure of substances they've experienced before, even if the substance is not around. Instead of shifting through these substances, they kind of, recreate them at a molecular level. Shifters who are at this level are called phase-four. The only thing they are not able to duplicate is people." The little girl's eyebrows knit together. "It's pretty high-tech, I don't get a lot of it."

"Why not people?" asked Alexine.

"Huh?"

"Why not people? Why can't you duplicate people?" The older girl repeated the question doggedly.

"Oh, because they're too complex. They're of a 'higher order', duh," the red-head finished, bobbling her head, and sporting a condescending sneer.

Alexine frowned, not so much at Callan's snide behavior, but at the entire conversation itself. "You know," she began dryly, "all of this is impossible."

"What?"

"You 'shifting,' me 'reading.' It's all impossible."

"And yet," said Callan, vanishing into thin air. The lump of blankets slipped quietly down, as if deflating when the small girl disappeared. She reappeared seconds later, in the exact same spot, only on top of the covers, "here we are."

Pondering the implications of shifting, Alexine shook her head in confusion. "When Susan and I were in the basement, there was a shifter giving Susan a really hard time."

Callan nodded, indicating she was following the story.

"Susan hit her, square in the face, with a baseball. It was pretty nasty. Anyway, someone else dragged the woman from the room to the elevator."

"Right," the little red-head answered back impatiently, not catching the question at all.

"Well, why didn't she just shift again, to get away?"

Callan smiled, then answered matter-of-factly, "she was hurt."

"Yea, I told you that, hit in the face with the baseball."

"That's why she didn't shift. Shifting isn't something that is really easy to do. It's hard, believe me, and dangerous."

"Dangerous?" Alexine asked, surprised.

"If you loose your concentration, in the middle of a shift, things can get really messy. Imagine being stuck inside of another object. Shifting can kill you, Alexine. It's nothing to mess with."

The older girl's eyes flew open in shock as she exhaled loudly. "I guess I never really thought about that. Yikes."

A somber silence filled the room for several minutes as these latest facts settled into Alexine's memory banks. Upon coming to terms with the idea that her baby sister had been engaging in potentially lethal behavior for the past month, her mind flew into over-drive, and another pressing question presented itself. "Okay," she finally piped up.

"Yea?"

"How on earth can someone shift into another object, and have that object stay the same size? I mean, if you add yourself to an object, wouldn't that object become bigger?"

Callan's gaze slid to the right. "Good question. We actually talked about this in shifter training one day. Trust me, I don't know everything yet, but there are infinitesimal spaces between everything which exists; between atoms, between molecules, between cells. Shifters are able to move into those spaces, to occupy them. And space, as I understand it, can hold a amazing amount of 'stuff' even if it appears to be very small."

"So," reasoned Alexine slowly, "shifters…kind of…concentrate an object, instead of adding to it?"

Callan laughed once. "I guess. I've never really thought too hard about it. In fact, I'm surprised I remember that lesson."

"A phase four shifter, hey?" Taking a deep breath, a half grin lifted Alexine's features. "No wonder everyone thinks you're so cool."

Callan shrugged.

"One more question," said Alexine.

"Shoot."

"Why did Devin trust you?"

The little girl smiled. "I, as you know, am a great actress." She sat up, pulled her feet under her body, then rose, sauntering several steps as if walking a red carpet, before returning to her pile of blankets.

Alexine gave her a wry smile.

"I made him feel good about himself," Callan said seriously. "He's really kind of sad." The little girl flashed back to when she and Devin first met. "He needed people to look up to him, he needed acceptance and respect. He just didn't know how to get it, or give it for that matter." Her face fell. "And now, he's in a great deal of danger. Nautas will hunt he and Annalynn. Nautas will not let this go."

Chapter Fifty-one
Finding Anna

The next day, the girls awoke early. It seemed like they were students in a new academy; the building was now clean and bright, somehow. The same guards stood in the foyer, but the computer was gone and they did not look angry when the girls passed by. Instead, they greeted them with a clipped and heavily accented, "hi."

The girls replied, "hello!" then Alexine added a, "shay-shay" for good measure.

When they rounded the corner, Callan repeated mockingly, "hello, thank you?"

"Hey, I'm using my Chinese!"

Both girls laughed.

Not able to resist the urge, Alexine lead Callan to Annalynn's office. It felt right to go there, so familiar, like home. She knocked, sure the room was empty, but wanting to be respectful. Alexine was surprised to hear a voice reply, "come in." She opened the door slowly.

Many people were seated inside the room. The quiet which met the girls when they entered indicated the occupants had been discussing something important. Callan imagined there had to be many things to do now. Reorganize the academy, begin teaching again, contact all potential students, not to mention the work that needed to be done in the basement. It would take months!

"Sorry," said Callan quickly, "we didn't know…"

"Nonsense," replied Elizabeth, walking to them and taking the little girl by her left hand. The older woman glanced at the Callan's right hand, still bandaged from the chip removal. "You two have earned the right to participate in this little talk." Others in the room nodded their assent.

There were no seats left, so the girls joined leaders already on the floor.

"We have much to do." Branch's comment was directed at the two sisters, bringing them up to speed. "We're compiling a list." He smiled down at the two new comers. "Perhaps you have some items to add?"

Callan laughed lightly. "I'm sure you know much more than we do," she answered respectfully, hoping Branch took note of her humility. Callan felt guilty about her tirade regarding Lotus the previous afternoon. When she looked hopefully up at their leader, he smiled at her benevolently and Callan broke into a grin. "We're honored to simply be allowed in this room."

The gentle man's eyes softened.

A deep voice from the corner rumbled, "we know what Callan can do." Michael absently placed a hand over his chest and winced when they met. The little red-head smirked. "What are you capable of young one?" The question was directed to Alexine.

She froze. "Honestly, I don't…"

"Don't be shy," piped up John. "I've already told them about you being able to pull people in."

"Is it true?" Michael said quickly. His head cocked to the side, looking wary. "It's very hard to master."

She wasn't sure what to say, but the longer she remained quiet, the more difficult it was to speak.

"That means she can," said Callan dryly, "right?" The little shifter looked impatiently at her sister.

"Yea," admitted the older girl sheepishly. "But I can't control it, and can't even do it sometimes."

Several people exhaled loudly, some raised eyebrows, other nodded their heads in acknowledgement. But Branch's eyes narrowed slightly in concern. It was dangerous, especially for one so inexperienced.

"And you've already read people?" asked a dark, petite woman. She did not wait for an answer, as if already privy to the knowledge. "Is it true you can *experience* visions?"

The room grew quiet. Just as Callan was about to answer for her, Alexine replied, "yes...well...by accident. I didn't mean to..."

"Amazing," the woman breathed, studying Alexine intently.

The two sisters looked at each other, and Callan smiled. As small conversations broke out around them, the girls picked up bits and pieces.

"Rarely happens...."

"Must be genetic...."

"Less than 1 percent...."

"My great-grandmother...."

The little red-head reached out and squeezed her sister's hand. "Welcome to the club."

When the room had quieted again, Branch suggested everyone adjourn to the cafeteria. As people filed out of the room, he found Alexine and Callan and invited them up to visit Annalynn after breakfast.

It was the best meal they had shared in a long time. The mood was light and jovial. Those who had been released from their jail below joined friends and family. Tears were shed, hugs shared, and there was an aura of relief that permeated everything and everyone.

Callan couldn't help but grin. By the end of breakfast, her cheeks hurt. Glancing over at Alexine, she smiled and said, "ready to find Branch?"

"Sure," replied Alexine. "Hey Cal?" Callan glanced at her expectantly. "I love you sis."

"Yea," Callan laughed. "Love ya too."

They stood, deposited their trays, and moved into the hallway. It was filled with laughter. The girls took a deep breath, it felt good. As they headed up the nearest stairwell to the 2nd level, Bethia approached.

"Going down to breakfast?" Alexine asked.

"Yes," she sighed, the girl looked very tired. "Where are you two off to?"

Callan spoke first. "To see Annalynn."

The healer's face fell. "They're in Mr. Rush's old classroom."

"Are things bad? Maybe we shouldn't interrupt," said Callan quietly.

"Actually," replied Bethia her look of concern deepening, "maybe you can help." She bit her lip absently, as if debating whether or not to say more. Then, without another word, passed and descended the stairs.

The classroom was bright; the curtains had been taken down allowing the light to flood in. Annalynn lay on a make-shift bed at the far end of the room, Branch huddled beside her on the floor. As they approached, he lifted his head and smiled wearily. The man looked strained.

"She's hurt," Alexine stated.

"No," croaked Branch, shaking his head sadly. "We found her in time. Nautas hasn't completely…" he broke off. "Anyway, she's healed." He looked tense for a moment, then averted his gaze. "This is of her own doing. She's punishing herself for staying at the academy."

"But she changed her mind!" said Alexine defensively.

"You don't have to prove her case to me," Branch said. It was not stern, but *was* absolute. "I forgave her long ago. But it seems she will not forgive herself." He looked down at the woman laying prone under the soft blanket.

"But you can make her," Callan shot. "Read her."

"She won't let me in," Branch said softly, eyes intense.

"Then force her!" Callan's face was livid and impassioned. "It's ridiculous!"

The look Branch gave the little girl caused her to recoil. "Is that what you've been fighting for?" he asked softly. "Coercion?"

The little shifter's face fell.

"You'll learn," Branch replied, as if reading her mind. "You're young and full of energy." He turned back to the woman lying unconscious next to him. Caressing her face, he leaned down and whispered something inaudible, then stood. "You try," he motioned to Alexine, "try anything to bring her back."

Alexine knelt by Annalynn. "Hi," she began awkwardly. Racking her brain for what to say, she blurted, "what are you doing? You *are* being ridiculous!" The older woman remained so very still.

An answer came slowly. At first, she discounted it; Anna had denied Branch access, why should she be different? But the more she thought about it, the more right it felt. Grasping her instructor by the hands, the room spun around them. Gathering momentum, the scene burst open. She was at Annalynn's door…and Alexine was surprised to find it opened, wide opened. The older woman stood awkwardly, just inside the house, her head hung, her gaze diverted. Alexine reached for her mentor. As they touched, the two women were swept to a glorious day. Fluffy white clouds meandering across an endlessly blue sky. Long, lush and green, the grass frolicked in the breeze. Annalynn sat uncomfortably in the midst of this scene. She seemed so out of place; a smear of darkness on an otherwise perfect picture.

The meadow hid them from everything and everyone. And they talked.

Chapter Fifty-two
The Seer

"Elizabeth," Callan called down the hallway happily, "can you round everyone up and meet us in Annalynn's office?" The older woman looked puzzled, then nodded her head. "Thanks!" The little red-head raced upstairs.

It took only minutes for everyone to gather. Callan thought it was amazing; everyone cooperating, no secrets, no missions, no plans, just openness and acceptance. This was so different than the past four weeks! She glanced around and took a mental roll-call, no one was missing, no one except Branch.

"Okay," she stood and announced, "be right back," then ran from the room.

Although she entered with her head down, leaning heavily on Branch, it did not remain that way for long. After several seconds of shock, Annalynn was being supported and passed from person to person; smiles, hugs, more smiles, tears, more hugs. It lasted for at least ten minutes. She ended up back with Branch as if passed around like an interesting new gift for all to admire, and then return. Michael gave them his spot on the couch, and the couple sat down together.

"I wanted to get everyone together one last time today," began Branch. "Before tomorrow hits and we start re-organizing, some situations must be discussed."

Those in attendance listened attentively, silent now as Branch spanned the crowd then began. "Nautas is a destroyer."

Although most people in the room looked confused, and whispered questions could be heard, several wore looks of shock. One woman said, "no!" in a horrified whisper.

"Yes," replied Branch. "Yes. This information is not to be repeated, even between ourselves. Dwelling on the subject would not be...well..." he stopped as if unsure what to say. "But you all need to know, as the new leaders of the academy, that my brother poses a very real threat to everything and everyone on earth."

Callan jerked her head in surprise. *Everyone on earth?*

An older woman in the corner nodded knowingly. The movement caught Alexine's attention and, once she studied the woman, Alexine found herself captivated by her. Although she failed to come up with any solid reason regarding why, she found herself unable to look away. *Who was she?* The woman seemed a bit older than Branch. Tall, thin and graceful, her fine features were silhouetted by a veil partially covering her face. It took concerted effort for Alexine to force her attention back to the conversation.

It seemed many people in the room were surprised by Branch's comment, so he reiterated, "everyone on earth."

"Why?"

She wasn't sure who posed the question, but Alexine was sure many people wanted to ask.

Branch let out a long, tired sigh, then weighed his words meticulously. "A destroyer is the opposite of a creator, the antithesis of a creator. A destroyer's main objective is to destroy creation, period." The man with kind eyes looked over at the older woman in the corner. She shook her head, ever so slightly, and he gave her a knowing small smile. They held each other's gaze, then the moment passed. "That is all we should say for now," he finished. When several people looked distraught, he added, "we have a long time to learn, and a long time to teach."

* * *

By 10:00pm, most others had left. Only Branch, Michael, Annalynn, Alexine and Callan remained in the office. Callan and Michael were caught up in a playful conversation on the couch. Alexine couldn't help but laugh at the dichotomy. A tiny, petite, red-headed girl engaged in an engrossing discussion with a huge, muscular, dark-haired man. She wished she had a camera.

Alexine, Branch and Annalynn were seated around the desk. Branch and Annalynn occupied two chairs behind the desk, and Alexine leaned forward from the opposite side, resting her elbows on its surface. She smiled softly at her mentor.

"You look tired," Alexine said, a bit of concern in her voice.

"Yes," Annalynn replied, "I am." She turned her head to gaze at Branch. The love between then was evident. "But I need to tell you something."

Alexine opened her eyes a bit wider and leaned in.

"We need to talk about what happened here a few months ago." The reader paused, as if she didn't know what to say, where to start. How could she explain this? Michael and Callan had heard Annalynn, and were now listening intently. "I have seen what force brings," she began, wavering. That was all she could voice.

Branch pulled her in close, then took over. "What most people fail to realize, especially my brother, is that freedom is more than an abstract concept. It's more than a movement, or a state of being. Freedom isn't a political party. It's an irrevocable law; a vibrating living force. And, in the end, it is going to win, because it is right. The choice we must make is whether or not we accept it, support it, embrace it, fight for it. Whether or not we watch, and are aware of decisions or situations which attempt to stamp it out of existence. And then, we are faced with another decision: are we willing to sacrifice so others may attain it. Is it *that* important to us?"

Michael was nodding his support, and rumbled into speech when it became apparent that Branch was finished. "Freedom will emerge victorious, of that we can be certain. But in the interim, it will be attacked, spat upon, and ridiculed. Many battles have and will continue to be waged against it, cloaked in an array of smoke screens. Some will use violence and terror, some fear, some anger and resentment, and some apathy.

"All around us forces fight against the rights of individuals to make basic choices regarding their lives. Where to live, what job they will be engaged in, how much schooling is available to them, who they marry, how many children they will have, what they can read, how much information they have regarding the world at large, who and how they worship, and the list goes on and on. All of these things, which you two probably take for granted, are denied to many.

"The problem is, if people are denied basic rights regarding how they will live their lives, they cannot progress as human beings. If they cannot make decisions for themselves, their level of culpability is diminished. This is wrong, and it thwarts the very purpose for us being here.

"When all of these battles are brought to an end, there will be three groups of people; those who fought for freedom, those who stood idly by, and those who rebelled against it. Our decisions each day lead us to one group, or another.

"Although it is quite popular today to blur lines between right and wrong, in doing so, we only fool ourselves. This universe is governed by laws, period. Just because we choose to turn our backs on them, does not will them out of existence. That attempt is egotism beyond comprehension."

Callan and Alexine sat in rapt attention. A feeling had come over the five people deep in conversation. Warm and comforting, it impressed upon both girls the truth of Branch and Michael's statements, although the girls were not able to completely understand the intricacies of the concepts presented.

A tear trickled slowly down Annalynn's cheek. She buried her face in Branch's shoulder and he ran his hand through her hair. Raising his attention to the other occupants of the room, Branch replied, "well said my friend, well said. And on that note, we have many days of learning ahead of us. It's time to turn in."

* * *

Later that evening, the girls lay awake in bed.

"Who was that older woman in the corner tonight?" Alexine had been dying to ask her sister about the stranger. "She seemed so familiar, it was like...I don't know."

"It was like you were drawn to her."

"Yea."

"Me too, and it seemed like everyone really respected her. But I have no idea, I've never seen her before today." Callan pulled her bedding up tight under her chin.

"She and Branch were talking." When Callan furrowed her brow in confusion, Alexine finished, "in their heads, to each other, you know."

"Ohhh."

"So, she must be a reader."

"What did they say?"

Alexine made a face. "I'm not sure. I didn't listen to their conversation."

"Why not?"

The older girl looked sheepish, recalling Branch's stern reprimand when she had eavesdropped on the discussion between him and Lin at the safe house. "Well, it's rude. And, they might sense that I was there."

"Oh." Callan shrugged. "I don't know how any of your stuff works."

"And you were making fun of me for not knowing about shifters?!"

Callan laughed. It was quiet for a few minutes until the younger girl broke the silence. "I've been thinking about what Branch said."

"Yea, me too. Have you ever heard of a 'destroyer?'"

"Nope," answered the little red-head succinctly. "I get the feeling I don't want to hear about them." Her eyes widened in apprehension. "What was your take on the freedom speeches?"

Alexine looked thoughtful. "I didn't understand a lot of what they were saying. But I do know something; I've taken a lot of things for granted. You know? We live in a time and place where we can, basically, do what we want."

"I never realized many people in the world can't."

"Me either," whispered Alexine. "I've been thinking, that being able to make day to day decisions about our lives is something we need to consider precious. We need to protect that ability. I don't know, it seems like we need to hold onto it, because it could slip away."

The little red-head nodded thoughtfully, then rolled onto her side. "I think it's good we came," her eyebrows raised a notch, and she pressed her lips together in determination. "After everything that has happened…I think it's been a good thing."

"Me too," replied Alexine. "Me too."

* * *

Across town, Branch and Michael stood on the elevated cement walk-way surrounding the academy. Buildings glowed neon and cars whizzed past on the street below, oblivious to the battle which occurred the previous day. Their honking, a symphony of the city, ebbed and flowed up to the two men. People walked into the supermarket located on the bottom floor of their building, exiting with arms full of bags loaded with groceries, or huge bottles of oil for deep frying. They loaded their purchases onto sturdy bicycles or set off for home on foot. Dumplings were being cooked across the road at the little stand. All was as it should be.

"What is most important now?" Michael rumbled into speech, his body drained of energy from the day's events.

"Dismantling this facility, making it safe again. And then, we'll leave. Regroup."

"Leave Shanghai?"

Branch nodded slowly, eyes blank. "To Xian, but that is to remain between you and I.

"Xian? What is in Xian?"

Branch's sardonic smile surprised Michael, and he furrowed his brow. When his leader's grin deepened, Michael couldn't help but follow suit. "What?" he half-laughed. "What's funny about Xian?"

"John is there."

Michael's smile vanished in an instant, his forehead wrinkling in disbelief. "John? How the heck did you find *him*?"

Branch shook his head, suddenly serious too. "He found me. He knew we needed him, knew what to do, and was anxious to return to Xian."

Michael nodded thoughtfully. "I've missed him. It will be good to see him again. So, John's been preparing for us, I'll assume."

Branch said nothing, but flicked a knowing glance at Michael."

"I thought so," the large man answered, "his forte." Michael added in a whisper, "I'll assume the Denique have been gathering there."

Again the leader of the academy eyed Michael knowingly.

"A good place for them. John will defend them to the death."

Silence enveloped the two men again for several stretched minutes. Branch finally broke the quiet. "Nautas searches for the Book of Kaish."

"No!"

"Yes," the leader nodded. "It is not the book that holds power, per se. It is the person who is willing to engage in the book's instructions. I am confident my brother will be willing to…."

"It seems as though we are beginning all over again," Michel interrupted, in exasperation. "As if we've fought this fight before, won this battle before. And now we are, once again, starting over." He was tired, and it was incredible how badly his chest ached.

"We must find the book before he does."

Michael nodded, focused once again.

"And we must gather the records. We will need them."

Again Michael agreed. Then thoughtfully posed the question he had been wanting to voice for some time. "Will this ever end?"

Branch wished he could supply the answer Michael yearned to hear: yes, it will be over soon, just hold on, we're almost there. "No. This fight never ends. Never."

Michael dropped his chin and sighed. "I didn't think so."

Branch shook his head. He thought about all of the people who had stood up, supported him, and he smiled. "But our roles are changing. These young ones, they are strong."

"Yes," the powerful man sighed, "but are they good? Because that is more important."

Branch turned to face his friend. At one time they had both been so young. Now their faces were etched with the fine lines of toil, worry, and age. Michael's eyes narrowed in concentration, and the wrinkles developing at the corners of those eyes became more pronounced. Diverting his gaze, Branch stared at nothing in particular, as if checking on the answer. "Some…some of them are good."

Michael contemplated those words for several seconds, then stood to his full height. "And others will follow."

Branch nodded. "And others *must* follow, my friend… They must."

Coming up in Book Two

Alexine watched, transfixed, as the women formed a tight circle in the intruding darkness. Placing right hands gently on their neighbor's shoulders, a grim but determined silence filled the space between them as their eyes slid over each other's faces.

She knew the moment it began, the second the anamnesis whisked the women to distant places and times past. In part because the seers swayed unsteadily, as if the force of the vision surprised even them. But perhaps she felt it.

The courtyard was engulfed in profound sorrow, the weight of a years worth of torrid world history compressed into those few moments and that small space. A tear slid down Alexine's cheek as she mourned the seers, regretted they had to witness and record so much hatred and cruelty.

"They volunteered, Alexine." Branch's explanation rang in her mind. "They wanted to serve. Were strong enough to do it. Were willing to sacrifice."

She knew it was true, and the importance and necessity of this event burned in her. But that knowledge and surety didn't extinguish the anguish that threatened to become unbearable. It failed to make witnessing the event any less heartbreaking.

The huddled women faltered, sinking to their knees and Alexine started forward, wanting to help. She felt a strong, restraining hand grasp her shoulder firmly, and spun around in surprise.

John shook his head "no" his gaze affixed on the seers overcome by their experience. "We can't get near them, it's too dangerous." His eyes groped for hers as if he too found it painful not to buoy them up, offer a modicum of relief.

She wanted to throw herself into his arms, hold him, comfort and be comforted. She wanted someone, anyone, to assuage the grief now palpable in the courtyard.

"Look," the young man whispered reassuringly.

From various points around the yard, people moved toward the women now prone and heaving desperate breaths on the hard, dry earth. The seers remained together, clutching each other's shoulders through wave after wave of experience. Still fulfilling the duty to which they had dedicated their lives. But now, now they were being lifted gently back to their feet by strong arms, young hands. By…shifters.

Alexine cried out when she spotted Callan in the midst of the rescuers, helping to brace up the staggering women. The seers seemed to summoned strength from those now encircling them.

"Shifters?" She turned her head and looked over her shoulder to take in John, who, she just realized, had his arms around her waist and stood so close she could feel the heat from his chest, and the pounding of his heart, on her back.

"It's safest for them. Readers wouldn't stand a chance. Can you imagine?" His face filled with terrified wonder. "Experiencing even a second of what they're seeing? I wouldn't wish that on my worst enemy."

Publications I found insightful and invaluable while writing this volume:

Discover Magazine.
Journey Into China. National Geographic. 1982
Life and Death in Shanghai. Neien Cheng. Grove Press. 1987.
Oracle Bones, A journey between China's Past and Present. Peter Hessler.
HarperCollins Publishers. 2006
Son of the Revolution. Liang Heng & Judith Shapiro. Vintage Books. 1984.
Spectrum Magazine.
The Bible.
The Book of Mormon.
Walk Without Notice. Karin Mei Li Inouye. Palmyra Press. 2006.
Wild Swans, Three Daughters of China. Jung Chang. Simon & Schuster. 1991.

There are several people I would like to thank in connection with this work.

My husband, the first person who read my final manuscript, and admitted ruefully to our daughter that he, "hated to admit it, but Mom's book is pretty good." He has taught me more about myself than anyone on earth. He continually challenges me to reach. He loves me and is my biggest supporter. He is perfect – for me.

My children. In reality, I am not creative. Had I not been able to use my children's lives as a basis for writing, this book would never have been completed. It turns out that, in order for me to compose anything, I have to experience it first. Like I said, just not that creative. In addition, my children inspire me each day. They have taught me more about others than any college course, self improvement book, or individual I have had the pleasure of meeting. Children are truly life's best instructors.

My mother, who is quite deluded and believes me to be capable of anything. When you have someone like that behind you, how can you fail? The woman is a saint.

My sister, Tara, who painstakingly edited my final manuscript over the course of several long months...and subsequently tore it apart, pointing out each incongruity, suggesting plot alterations, encouraging thoughtful analysis, and mandating verbiage change. The book improved so dramatically under her tutelage that I should have probably included her as "co-author."

The Chinese people, who are truly a testament to the strength of the human spirit.